HOW TO COOK

FROM FIRST BASICS TO KITCHEN MASTER

HOW TO COOK

FROM FIRST BASICS TO KITCHEN MASTER

The cook's guide to baking, poaching, casseroling, steaming and roasting more than 140 tasty recipes

BRIDGET JONES

LORENZ BOOKS

This edition is published by Lorenz Books, an imprint of Anness Publishing Ltd
www.lorenzbooks.com; www.annesspublishing.com
info@anness.com; twitter: @AnnessLorenzBks

If you like the images in this book and would like to investigate using them for publishing, promotions or advertising, please visit our website www.practicalpictures.com for more information.

Publisher: Joanna Lorenz
Editorial director: Helen Sudell
Editor: Simona Hill
Designer: Ian Sandom
Cover design: Adelle Mahoney
Production controller: Ben Worley

With thanks to the recipe contributors and photographers.

NOTES
Bracketed terms are intended for American readers.
For all recipes, quantities are given in both metric and imperial measures and, where appropriate, in standard cups and spoons. Follow one set of measures, but not a mixture, because they are not interchangeable.
Standard spoon and cup measures are level. 1 tsp = 5ml, 1 tbsp = 15ml, 1 cup = 250ml/8fl oz.
Australian standard tablespoons are 20ml. Australian readers should use 3 tsp in place of 1 tbsp for measuring small quantities.
American pints are 16fl oz/2 cups. American readers should use 20fl oz/2.5 cups in place of 1 pint when measuring liquids.
Electric oven temperatures in this book are for conventional ovens. When using a fan oven, the temperature will probably need to be reduced by about 10–20°C/20–40°F. Since ovens vary, you should check with your manufacturer's instruction book for guidance. The nutritional analysis given for each recipe is calculated per portion (i.e. serving or item), unless otherwise stated. If the recipe gives a range, such as Serves 4–6, then the nutritional analysis will be for the smaller portion size, i.e. 6 servings. Measurements for sodium do not include salt added to taste. Medium (US large) eggs are used unless otherwise stated.

Contents

Introduction

Everyone needs to eat, and learning to make food that we want to eat is a skill that we all can master. Dishes that feed our hunger and provide our bodies with essential nutrients should also be visually appealing, smell tempting and taste delicious. Unlike many domestic chores, however, cooking is a skill that many people enjoy, and most people can learn to cook the foods that they like to eat.

Cooking for yourself, friends and family should be fun, rewarding and stress-free. If you have success cooking simple dishes, you will be encouraged to develop your skills and experiment further.

This book aims to help you create something good to eat in an organized and easy way, beginning with deciding what to eat, making a shopping list, choosing the ingredients and developing a range of cooking skills. Making nutritious everyday meals that fill the kitchen with wonderfully promising aromas will become routine, rather than a chore to be dreaded or a frustrating and unfulfilled dream.

Above: Scrambled eggs with smoked salmon are quick to make and provide an indulgent brunch or light lunch dish.

WHY COOK?

There are many different motivating factors for people to ditch the ready meals and don an apron. Living alone for the first time and having to cater for yourself, setting up home with a partner, expecting a baby, or wanting to encourage toddlers to eat healthily are all life-changing experiences. Alternatively, suddenly facing an illness or wanting to follow a specific diet may force you to start cooking from scratch to include or exclude certain ingredients. Maybe you're trying to cut down on food bills or have simply realized that the colourful fresh ingredients available look far more appealing than plastic-wrapped pre-cooked meals. Whatever it is that has precipitated your desire to cook, this book will nurture your skills and develop your undiscovered talents.

Above: Hot and spicy foods are a taste that many people enjoy.

Cooking can be a great hobby, an opportunity to take time out alone or to plan and create fabulous food to share later with a friend or partner. Most people like being involved with cooking as a sociable activity, either as chief cook, helper or observer, stirring, sampling and seasoning. Being able to make brilliant scrambled eggs (with smoked salmon on the side, perhaps), the best-tasting Bolognese sauce (that classic that everyone loves) or super-crunchy baked potato wedges (irresistible with soured cream, salami and a bowl of rocket) are all good reasons for sharing meals. For cooks who have mastered the basics, combining different tastes and textures as well as styles of cooking can be a creative experience. For others, feeding family and friends is both a sociable and nurturing activity. Home-made usually tastes better than ready-made and will satisfy your hunger for longer, too. Added to that, when you know exactly which ingredients have gone into each meal that you prepare, then cooking for yourself becomes much more appealing.

Above: Often simple ingredient combinations work well together and deliver on taste and visual appeal.

SIMPLE FIRST STEPS

Learning to shop successfully means buying only the ingredients that are needed, ensuring that they are of a quality suitable for the dishes that you wish to cook, and at a price that you can afford (cooking can be as economical or as expensive as you wish it to be).

Being a good cook does not mean having to master a whole host of savoury and sweet recipes. Start by making the foods that appeal to you, such as a hot snack of cheese on toast. Move on to learn to make a cheese omelette and then macaroni cheese. One of the most rewarding ways to learn to cook is to make a favourite all-in-one dish that always tastes better home-made, such as fish pie or pasta with creamy eggs and bacon (carbonara style). Becoming expert at one recipe is the best encouragement for trying something new.

Above: Combinations of cold ingredients are a good way to start experimenting with food.

EXTENDING THE REPERTOIRE

A little knowledge goes a long way and it is easy to enjoy experimenting with inexpensive ingredients. Modern eating is eclectic and international, not necessarily governed by main dishes and accompaniments or matching courses. It is exciting and flexible. Eating and cooking are about enjoying variety and knowing how to combine basics rather than working through traditional stages of complex cuisines.

Vegetables are often the focus for modern meals. Baked potatoes are a great starting point for adding lots of different fillings that involve little more than grating cheese, or chopping and mixing a few salad ingredients. Roasting vegetables is easy and they can be served in a wide variety of ways. Stirring up a savoury sauce is not difficult and is perfect for combining with pasta or vegetables to make successful meals.

To progress you don't have to master new methods: simply adapt existing skills and try them out with new ingredients. In this way you will learn how to combine flavours and textures. One-pot meals and big bowls of mixed hot-cold salads, such as a Niçoise with warm potatoes and green beans, are excellent for inexperienced cooks because they do not demand critical timing.

Above: Chicken is quick to cook and can be flavoured with many ingredients.

USING THIS BOOK

This book is not a rigid cooking course, so there is no need to start at the beginning and work through to the end. The information is presented in such a way that you can dip into it and mix and match recipes that appeal to your taste buds, and in making them, you will be adding to your repertoire of skills. The cooking methods used are thoroughly practical and acknowledge that there is often limited time available, so unnecessarily complicated processes are avoided. The book adopts a sensible attitude to ready-made products, with guidance on the types of food to make or buy, as well as having a store of canned and frozen foods that can be turned into high-quality meals in minutes.

The introduction will help you learn to plan weekly menus to cater for different lifestyles in the household, as well as achieve a nutritional balance. It shows you how to shop for and store different foods, and plan and organize kitchen cupboards, refrigerator and freezer space to work efficiently for you. Helpful information is provided on choosing useful and essential equipment, such as the pots and pans, as well as selecting utensils for cutting, peeling and shredding. All the cooking terminology that is included in each of the recipes is clearly explained.

The recipe chapters are organized according to ingredient, such as eggs, meat, poultry, fish and shellfish, vegetables, pasta, rice, beans and grains, and pastry, as well as chapters on sauces and desserts. Each provides an overview of the main ingredients and the ways in which they can be cooked. A selection of recipes includes classic dishes, each made with minimal ingredients. The recipes offer a variety of different cooking styles, as well as meals for different occasions, such as snacks, light lunches, main course meals and quick supper dishes, so you need never be short of inspiration or a meal to savour.

Above: A favourite home-cooked dish, such as cottage pie topped with creamy mashed potato, is satisfying to make.

First steps

Whether you've dabbled in the kitchen a little bit before or never dared to boil an egg, it's essential to get to grips with a few cooking methods and to understand a little about nutrition and food hygiene at the start of your journey to successful cooking. This chapter will give you all the guidance you need on planning meals, shopping for ingredients, storing food, cooking equipment and the all-important basic techniques.

A balanced diet

The starting point for any cook is selecting what dish to cook and choosing the ingredients that go in it. On a day-to-day level this means that you should try to prepare food that is nutritionally balanced, so that on the whole you eat a varied, healthy diet. The occasional treat is by no means banned. It is good for the soul, if not for the body!

Eating three well-balanced meals a day can create a strong basis for great health and loads of energy. For most people, time constraints mean that during the week two of those meals are usually simple affairs of cereal or toast for breakfast and a sandwich or a salad for lunch. However, at the weekend there may be time to experiment a little in this area and add some new dishes to your repertoire. You'll find plenty of inspiration in the pages that follow.

The majority of people learning to cook focus their attention on one main meal a day. Plenty of ideas for simple workday meals are included, as well as recipes for those occasions when you may have more time to spare.

Good eating is about enjoying a balanced diet that contains a wide variety of foods and the chapters that follow show just how easy it is to do.

ESSENTIAL NUTRIENTS

All activity (simply living and breathing) involves some cellular breakdown in our bodies, which is replenished with nutrients from the food that we eat. The body needs all the following nutrients in the right proportion: carbohydrates, protein, fats, vitamins and minerals as well as fibre and water. Individual foods contain a variety of nutrients in different mixes and proportions. Including a wide variety of foods in your diet increases the amount of nutrients you eat.

Carbohydrates This food group can roughly be split into two categories: simple carbohydrates and complex carbohydrates. They offer our bodies the main source of energy. Simple carbohydrate is the term for sugars, including those used in cooking or for sweetening. Fruit contains natural sugars that are simple carbohydrates, as do some vegetables, and milk contains lactose, which is also a simple carbohydrate. On their own, sugars are digested and absorbed quickly.

Starches are complex carbohydrates that are not digested as quickly as sugars. This group includes refined flour, rice and grains. Wholegrain carbohydrates, with a higher percentage of fibre, are digested more slowly. Complex carbohydrates are found in foods such as wholegrain bread, potatoes, brown rice and wholemeal (whole-wheat) pasta.

Above: Complex unprocessed carbohydrates contribute essential fibre to a healthy diet.

Protein This is required for building and repairing the body. Main sources of protein include fish, poultry, meat, eggs, milk, cheese, beans and legumes, grains, nuts and seeds.

Fats A little fat is essential in the diet but only in small quantities; saturated fats especially should be minimized as they have been linked to coronary heart disease.There are different types of fat in different foods: animal fats and vegetable fats. Fish, poultry, meat, dairy foods, nuts and seeds all contain fats.

Vitamins These play a wide variety of essential roles, facilitating many functions in the body. They come from eating a wide range of foods.

Plant chemicals As well as vitamins and minerals, a huge number of compounds are obtained from plant foods. Their discovery and function is relatively new to nutrition; they possibly have valuable protective roles.

Left: Adding fresh fruit to your daily diet will add vital nutrients and fibre.

Right: Children develop a taste for food from first experiences, so encourage them to enjoy a wide range of food and help with food preparation.

Minerals These are essential for a variety of different purposes to keep the body functioning well. They are available in a wide range of foods.
Fibre This is the indigestible part of some foods. There are soluble and insoluble types of fibre found in some complex carbohydrates, fruit and vegetables. Fibre helps to slow down digestion and the absorption of nutrients, thereby helping to regulate blood sugar levels, which is the body's main source of natural energy. Fibre also helps to regulate cholesterol levels, important for reducing the risk of heart disease. Insoluble fibre absorbs water and is passed out of the body, along with other waste products to promote a healthy gut and prevent constipation.
Water This is not a nutrient, but is essential for health. Foods, such as fruit, milk and yogurt, provide water, as do all dishes with a high liquid content (such as soups, sauces and jellies) as well as drinks consumed over the course of the day.

NUTRITIOUS UNREFINED FOOD

Unrefined ingredients and foods that are not highly processed are the vital foundation for a good diet. They are satisfying and helpful for controlling the amount of food you eat, and they contribute fibre and retain nutrients, which would otherwise be lost in processing. Fresh fruit and vegetables are good examples of unrefined foods that are easy to include in your daily diet. Highly processed foods and products have lost a lot of their natural fibre; the fibre is broken down, making the product easier to eat and digest, so the energy content is more quickly absorbed. These highly processed foods are intended to be 'moreish': intensely flavoured, with a high fat, salt and/or sugar content, and ideal for over-indulgence, but without satisfying hunger or offering nutritional value.

Below: Meat, fish and dairy products (eggs, milk and cheese) provide protein.

Below: Fresh vegetables provide many of the essential vitamins and minerals.

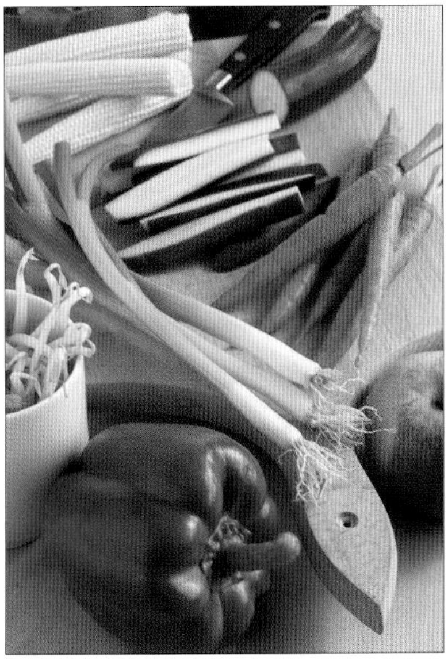

Below: Legumes, nuts and tofu provide valuable vegetable-based protein.

Planning meals

Deciding what to eat and writing a shopping list is the key to successful cooking. Planning a menu for an entire week may seem like a huge task, but it will help you to shop sensibly, buying just what you need to make up each recipe. It will remove daily decision-making about what to eat, and cut down on food costs by stopping random impulse purchases. You can plan one or two more adventurous meals at the weekend, or when you have more time. Then, gradually, with practice and experience, preparing everyday meals can become less daunting and very enjoyable.

A MENU PLAN

Begin to think about main meals for one week at a time. Start by choosing simple recipes that you like to eat, so that cooking doesn't become a chore. Avoid any with a long list of ingredients or that take time to prepare. Once you have learnt a few basic techniques, meal planning and cooking will soon become a pleasure.

Having a standard repertoire of dishes that you enjoy eating and that you can cook with confidence is the aim, and you can gradually build on this. Think about your weekly schedule. A typical week may involve providing staggered food for different family members on some evenings or late snack suppers. Consider the time that you have available for shopping, preparing, cooking and clearing up on specific days and plan your menu around this.

Weekends may allow you time for experimenting with new ingredients or methods, or for making a big batch of a favourite home-made dish that can be chilled or frozen and then reheated for a mid-week meal when time is short. Some weekends may be particularly busy, when whizzing up a simple one-pot meal is best.

COOKING FOR ONE, TWO OR MORE

Meal plans and menus that work well for someone living alone will not necessarily be suitable for a couple with children, or a group of friends sharing a house; however, the basic approach to planning and shopping is the same. Answering a few basic questions about who expects to eat what and when will help fit menu ideas to a lifestyle.

- Which meals will be eaten each day at home and when?
- How many will each meal cater for?
- How much time is there likely to be for cooking and eating?
- Will everyone eat the same food?
- Will people eat together (at the same time) or at different times?

Below: Make Bolognese sauce in large quantities and freeze it in portions for a really quick supper.

Above: Recipes with few ingredients may be easier to prepare.

In a shared house, where three or four people may eat a main meal at different times on some days, a one-dish meal, such as soup, stew, pasta or salad, can be cooked and divided into portions ready for serving or reheating later. This is also ideal for families where one adult may eat with the children if the other is late home from work, or where different family members have evening activities.

COOKING FOR DIFFERENT DIETS

If someone follows a specific diet, it is best to plan everyday dishes to suit them, which everyone else can enjoy. For example, sugar-free cooking for diabetics should not affect the majority of everyday main meals. Vegetarian meals have a valuable place in a well-balanced diet but on some days when fish, poultry or meat are the main course, a vegetable-based side dish could be planned that is also suitable for a vegetarian main course.

ONE-DISH MEALS

Focusing on making one main course dish is sensible for beginners. These dishes may be served on their own, or

Right: Weekday dinners need to be quick to cook if time is limited.

perhaps with an accompanying salad or some warm crusty bread. They are often the best dishes to serve when time is limited. The advantages of making a one-pot meal is that it can be cooked ahead and reheated, is quick and easy for hectic schedules, and is good for using stored ingredients.

There are endless options for one-pot dishes. Pasta in a sauce or simple dressing is popular with nearly everyone. It can be made with store-cupboard (pantry) ingredients, such as pesto, or with a cheese, tomato, vegetable or meat sauce made previously. Asian-style noodle dishes can be quickly stir-fried for a super-fast supper. Risotto is an excellent choice if you want to minimize the washing up. A wide variety of different vegetables can be added to it, as well as fish or poultry. Hearty soups served with bread are easy to reheat and handy to keep on the stove if people are eating at different times. Savoury crumbles and potato-topped bakes can be made in advance and reheated. Crunchy salads are an excellent no-cook option.

SUPPER DISHES

Served late in the day, supper dishes are often lighter, less robust meals than those served in the early evening. Recipes such as omelettes or salads make perfectly good supper dishes, served with other filling accompaniments. Generally they are quick and easy to prepare, appealing to all ages and tastes, and easily adapted to suit whatever food is available.

Other good light meals include macaroni with a gratin topping and a cheese sauce served with vegetables, baked potatoes with hot or cold fillings; grills (broiled dishes, fishcakes with salad or steamed vegetables and new potatoes, and toast toppers, such as Welsh rarebit or grilled mushrooms.

MAIN DISH AND ACCOMPANIMENTS

These are dishes to serve when time is not so precious, and depend on the occasion and time available. Take into consideration that some dishes can be cooked ahead, may need two or more pans or bowls for mixing and preparing, or may need last-minute attention, even if the main dish is cooked ahead.

The main dish may be a meat, fish or vegetarian recipe with side dishes of vegetables or a salad and some filling accompaniment, such as rice or potato. Ideas include a traditional roast or meat pie served with potatoes and steamed vegetables; grilled or fried meat, poultry or fish served with couscous and roasted vegetables; braised beans or legumes made into patties; home-made beef burgers with chips; or chicken fajitas with accompanying dip; meat sauce with pasta and salad and vegetable chilli with rice and salad.

Left: If you have a sweet tooth, baking your own cakes and cookies is a good way to learn basic cooking techniques.

SNACKABILITY

Everyone loves snacks, so plan to include them as part of your eating agenda. Home-baked cakes, teabreads and flapjacks freeze well for months. Individual buns or slices take seconds to defrost in the microwave or 15 minutes in a warm place. They are also fun to make, taste terrific and are less expensive than bought equivalents, so set aside a morning to fill the freezer with your favourite goodies.

WEEKEND CHANGES

The weekend may offer an opportunity to vary breakfast and lunch when there is more time in the morning or, possibly, less space for lunch. The main meal can be more complicated than usual, when time is not so short. Sunday lunches are perfect for relaxing with friends. Weekends are good for sharing the cooking, baking, making a treat or involving children.

A meat-free balanced diet

Meals based on mainly vegetables, without fish, meat or poultry, should feature regularly in every well-balanced diet and not only as part of a vegetarian foodplan. The idea that vegetarian main meals always have to include beans or legumes, tofu, nuts, eggs or cheese is out-dated and the more important point about eating a healthy diet is including lots of variety and balance.

PROTEIN BALANCE

The body needs protein every day and, just as for other nutrients, this comes from many food sources. Many Western diets include more protein (and fat) than is essential, with far too few vegetables and fruit for good balance. In a traditional 'meat and two veg' diet, a large portion of protein (often more than the daily requirement) comes from a single portion of fish, poultry or meat in a main meal. In addition, eggs may be eaten for breakfast or a light meal; canned fish, cooked meat or cheese in sandwiches; milk at breakfast and throughout the day in drinks or desserts; yogurt; nuts and seeds in snacks; and, of course, rice, pasta and vegetables also contribute some protein.

Getting enough protein is not necessarily about having a large amount of one food type, but remembering that all foods provide some of the components (amino acids) that give the body all the protein it needs. While some proteins provide the full complement of amino acids needed in a diet, regularly eating a good variety of other foods will also provide the necessary nutrients. Animal protein, from fish, poultry, meat, eggs and cheese, provides the body with all the amino acids it needs. Soya beans, tofu and nuts also provide similarly 'high-quality' protein. Beans such as lentils, kidney beans and chickpeas, are valuable for supplying protein, and combining them with rice or other grains, such as wheat, ensures a supply of all the amino acids. When thinking about the combined nutrients throughout the day and week, having one main meal consisting mainly of vegetables, with a small quantity of nuts, seeds or grains (or a small amount of cheese, for example) will not lead to protein deficiency.

Below: These days there are many more people who have adopted a meat-free diet and innovative vegetarian options is a routine part of cafe life.

Right: A Greek salad with feta cheese, olives, salad leaves, tomatoes and onions is a flavourful vegetarian lunch.

COOKING FOR VEGETARIANS

The difference between vegetarian meals and vegetable main dishes is often subtle but vital to anyone following a vegetarian diet. For example, using chicken stock in a vegetable soup or vegetable and bean curry is not a problem for anyone who normally eats animal foods but this is unacceptable to a vegetarian. As well as stock, the other ingredients that can be overlooked when non-vegetarians cook for vegetarian friends include anchovies (so easy to forget that relatively small amount in a big salad or pasta mix), and even some sauces contain meat or fish – Worcestershire sauce, for example, includes anchovies.

Cooking vegetables alongside poultry or meat is also unacceptable, for example roast potatoes cooked around meat, or peppers (sweet bell peppers) barbecued beside sausages or fish. The fat and juices from the meat contaminates the vegetables.

When planning a meal for non-vegetarians and vegetarians, it is a mistake to make a big deal about what is and is not suitable for 'the

Right: Lasagne can be made with a wide variety of different vegetables, such as mushrooms and bell peppers.

vegetarian'. Having a big meaty main dish with a few miserable vegetables or a single, sad nut cutlet as an 'odd one out' meal is embarrassing and can be easily avoided.

MIXED-MENU TIPS

Instead of planning around one main dish, think about having two or three complementary dishes, with a salad or other accompaniment on the side. This makes a versatile arrangement to which additional dishes can be added, which can be useful when a meat dish is all that will do to satisfy some guests.

- Cauliflower cheese and roast peppers (sweet bell peppers) are delicious together, with salad and crusty bread or new potatoes; they are also good accompaniments for roasts or grilled (broiled) fish, meat or poultry.
- Roast mixed vegetables, such as carrots, mushrooms, peppers, garlic, courgettes (zucchini) and tomatoes, are excellent served with a mixture of lightly boiled broad (fava) beans and green beans drizzled with pesto. Couscous makes a filling addition. A poultry or meat casserole could also be served.
- Creamy mashed mixed swede (rutabaga), carrot and potatoes complement baked beetroot (beet) sprinkled with a little blue cheese, spring onions (scallions) and walnuts. For meat-eaters, these go with chicken.

USEFUL VEGETARIAN TOPPINGS

Boiled mixed vegetables (roots and beans), stir-fries, baked vegetables or salads can often be transformed into full-flavoured meals by adding a generous topping. Toasted or fried breadcrumbs, croûtons, tortilla chips (plain or with toasted cheese on top), chopped nuts, dried fruit (small whole or chopped) and fresh herbs are all excellent. Herb or nut pastes and tapenade (olive paste) and flavoured oils are also good.

The following are a few different ideas to add flavour, colour and food value to your meals.

- Chopped walnuts with grated orange rind, chopped fresh tarragon, sage, marjoram or rosemary (chop rosemary very finely as it is tough) and chopped spring onions.
- Pine kernels, sliced black or green olives and shredded fresh basil leaves.
- Diced fresh tomatoes with grated lemon rind, chopped garlic and lots of chopped parsley.
- Chopped hard-boiled eggs, drizzled with pesto.
- Greek (US strained plain) yogurt, crème fraîche, fromage frais or soured cream, with a mixture of grated carrot and cucumber, and snipped chives or chopped spring onions stirred in. Add a sprinkling of cashew nuts or pecans.
- Lightly toasted and diced naan or pitta bread tossed with a little olive oil and lots of chopped fresh mint and coriander leaves (cilantro).

Below: Roast vegetables, olives and a herby dressing work well together.

Below: Stuffed peppers can be served as a main or side dish.

Below: Taboulleh can be served as a main course or accompanying side dish.

Smart shopping

Fresh produce purchased in any food store has to adhere to a minimum standard of quality by legal requirement. This, together with freezing, refrigeration, and fast stock turnover means that today's shoppers can have confidence in the quality and the freshness of the produce they buy.

MAKING A LIST

For beginner cooks it makes sense to plan meals ahead and then make a list of the ingredients you will need for each so that you don't get side-tracked once in the supermarket. The list should include all the ingredients as well as the seasonings, if you don't have them in stock. Group them according to type on your list, so that all the vegetables are together, for example, to save time once in the shop.

A good list saves time and money, prevents waste and means that essential items are not forgotten. An 'active' list is most practical, so keep a pad and pencil in the kitchen and jot down items as they run out or as you remember them. Alternatively, keep a 'live' shopping list on the computer ready to print and go; or keep a list on your mobile phone and delete items from the list while shopping.

Organize the list by food type and position in the store you generally shop in: fruit and vegetables at the top, if they are near the store entrance; dairy, packed fresh meats and fish or deli items next; canned and packet items; and so on, with frozen foods at the end, so that they go in the trolley just before you reach the checkout.

Left: A good selection of dried legumes in your storecupboard will prove useful for many types of meals.

TROLLEY TIPS

Be sure to keep chilled, damp foods away from dry ingredients, for example, freshly wrapped fish separate from a bag of sugar or flour, and unwrapped items well away from raw poultry or meat. Put the heavy items at the bottom of the trolley or basket and delicate items on top to avoid crushing them. Unload everything on to the checkout belt in groups, and in order, and then pack them again in the same order. This also makes unpacking them at home so much quicker and easier.

COMPARE PRODUCTS

Check use-by dates before you put anything in your shopping trolley. It's no good buying meat that you want to use in five days time if the date runs out the next day and you don't have room in the freezer for it. Compare prices of different brands for standard quantities as well as various size packs of the same product. Larger sizes can be better value if the goods have a long life or are suitable for freezing in smaller batches, provided you have space to store them. Compare own-brand products with named brands – reading the ingredients list is a good way of assessing quality. Whizz over to the deli counter or in-store butcher or fishmonger to compare quality and prices with pre-packed products; and have a look in the freezer section too to see what's available.

Left: Plan a week's worth of menus and make a shopping list before you go to the supermarket.

BEST BARGAIN OR BAD DEAL?

Two-for-one, money back and bumper-size offers are excellent when they tie in with the shopping list or items that are used regularly and/or keep well or freeze successfully. However, products that are always available on some promotion or are seriously superfluous to requirements may be nice to have, but are not necessarily a good buy. Some deals simply mean eating more of a food that you might otherwise restrict to being an occasional treat, or spending money on food that is not needed, or more expensive but not better quality. Be selective.

Some bulk buys can be excellent value, however. Plan to make maximum use of cupboard or freezer storage space for bulk purchases. 'Family packs' can work out less expensive than individual-sized products, particularly of everyday items, such as breakfast cereals, long-life juice and canned vegetables. Share multi-packs with friends, and split the cost.

STORE-CUPBOARD ITEMS

Spread the cost of expensive store-cupboard items by alternating the weeks in which you buy them. Stock up on some before they run out to avoid having a large shopping bill when everything needs replacing at once.

Above: Wonderfully fresh fruit and vegetables, locally sourced, delivered to your door, are available through 'box schemes'.

DO SEASONS EXIST?

Larger supermarkets stock virtually all fresh foods year round, however they may have been transported for long distances and the inflated price may well reflect that fact. Locally grown items may cost less and taste better, but certain products may only be available when they are in season. Frozen fruit and some vegetables can be a worthwhile alternative, providing excellent flavour and good nutritional value for much less money.

BEYOND SUPERMARKETS

There are alternative one-stop shopping options: internet shopping, plus the popular organic box schemes. Internet shopping can be invaluable for people who work full-time or for harassed parents for whom a trip to the supermarket with children in tow is nightmareish. With on-line shopping you can do the shopping from the comfort of your home or office and have the goods delivered at a time to suit you.

Farmers' markets and other local markets offer more than just local produce. Such speciality markets can be expensive and, although some do offer fine foods, superior quality is not always guaranteed. Do not be fooled by fancy labels or twee packaging. Sample the produce before you buy it, if you are invited to. Local growers, producers and bakers often provide excellent quality for which it can be worth paying a premium.

PACK AND GO

Get food shopping home and unpacked promptly, storing chilled items in the refrigerator and frozen foods in the freezer before they have time to warm up. Insulated bags are useful for transporting food in a warm car and on hot days.

Tidy the contents of refrigerator and freezer before putting away new items. In cupboards, bring older items to the front for use first. If storage containers have a little food left in them (sugar or flour, for example) do not add a fresh batch to the leftovers. Use the remaining food first, then wash and dry the container before refilling it.

Below: Make use of market stalls that stock good-quality fruit and vegetables. The turnover should be fast, ensuring fresh produce.

QUANTITIES

Recipes usually state clearly how many portions the finished dish will divide into, making buying produce for the right number of portions easy. However, deciding what to cook as an accompaniment to the main recipe and how much of it to buy can be confusing. In supermarkets, all chilled foods contain advice on labels but for fresh fish or meat ask for guidance at the counter. Staff are usually well trained and very helpful. Frozen, canned and packed dry foods include a guide to portion sizes on the labels.

Vegetables and fruit can be selected by number – a couple of small carrots, per person, perhaps, or one large carrot for two; or a red (bell) pepper for two in a salad. Look at large vegetables in terms of cut-up pieces – imagine a wedge of cabbage or lettuce. Think of small cut-up items by the handful, such as a handful of green beans, little mushrooms or watercress as being a portion for one.

Finally, remember to be flexible when shopping. If a particular ingredient is not available, you may have to adapt a recipe to include a substitute. This may seem daunting at first, but will become much easier with experience.

Storing food items

The traditional concept of having a stock of foods for times when fresh alternatives are not available is as relevant to the way we live now as it was more than 50 years ago, but for different reasons. The emphasis has changed from one of preserving seasonal items to that of saving time, having food in store for when there is no time to shop and still being able to eat well. This is also a great way to save money instead of buying relatively expensive ready meals. The focus here is practical – what to store where and for how long, including what to store in the refrigerator and the freezer as well as in cupboards.

STORING FOOD IN CUPBOARDS

A food cupboard on an outside wall of the kitchen is ideal for storing food as it will be cool. A cupboard next to a radiator or cooker, or a freezer or refrigerator that is vented at the back and generates a lot of heat, will warm up in an undesirable way. Food cupboards should be cool and dry.

Store loose ingredients in their original containers if they are airtight (screw-top jars, lidded containers) or place open packets inside airtight containers. If ingredients are poured from a packet into a container, the label and use-by information should be taped to the outside of the container or transferred on to a sticky label. The following is a guide to the type of ingredients to store in cupboards and the approximate length of time they will remain fresh, but check the use-by date on each product. Unlike chilled foods and some perishable foods, the majority of ingredients that have a long shelf-life have a best-before date. This is the date until which the food will retain its optimum condition and the quality will be unimpaired.

Left: Decant foods in cardboard or paper packaging, if the packets do not reseal securely, in order to retain maximum freshness.

Left: Soft fruit should be eaten soon after purchase because it will not keep.

Dry ingredients These include cereals, flours, dried pasta, grains, dried beans and legumes. Depending on the type and the storage conditions, these foods will keep for anything from a few months to a couple of years.

Sugars and syrups These include treacle, honey and golden (light corn) syrup, but not lighter fruit or flavoured dessert toppings and syrups. All such items have a long shelf-life.

Dried fruit and nuts The majority of whole, ground or chopped nuts, dried fruit and desiccated (dry unseetened shredded) coconut all keep well for months, if not years. Some ready-to-eat types should be chilled once opened: check advice on the packet. Raisins, currants, sultanas (golden raisins) and mixed dried fruit keep for about a year. Because they have a high fat content, nuts become rancid in a warm place (especially in the light) or if they are stored for too long, but they still keep well for at least six months or more.

Canned foods These have a very long shelf-life, extending to years.

Bottled foods, sauces and condiments Unopened, these have a similar shelf-life to cans but once open, some foods have to be stored in the refrigerator and used quickly.

CUPBOARD HYGIENE

Have an annual cupboard clear-out. Sort cans and packets, bringing items to use up to the front. Wipe down shelves and let them dry before replacing the foods.

STORING FOOD IN THE REFRIGERATOR

The size of the refrigerator should be appropriate to the size and lifestyle of the household. There should be plenty of space for fresh ingredients, dairy foods and all perishable items as well as opened jars of preserves and condiments. Even though refrigerators and freezers are designed for heated kitchens, they are more efficient and economical to run when positioned away from cooking appliances and radiators.

All perishable foods and prepared ingredients or dishes that are sold from chiller cabinets have to be stored in the refrigerator, in their original packaging, and used by the date on the packet. Do not remove pre-packed items from their wrapping. Once opened, if the entire contents are not used at once, wrap leftovers in clear film (plastic wrap) or place in an airtight container and use within the recommended time on the packet. The point about storage times in the refrigerator is that they are not hard and fast rules. Food goes off more quickly if it is all crammed in. There must be air circulating. Plastic bags around carrots, (bell) peppers, tomatoes and other similar vegetables keep the content moist and this makes them deteriorate quicker. Fruit that is stacked or bundled (for example in citrus bags) does not keep as well as when it is laid out in a single layer in a plastic tray. Check items daily and use up ingredients in good time. Follow use-by dates.

Fresh meat, poultry and fish
Pre-packed items in this category should be left unopened in their packaging or stored according to instructions on the packet. Fish should be used within 24 hours; loose poultry and meat within 1–2 days.

Dairy produce Milk (except unopened long-life varieties, which can be stored in a cupboard), cream, yogurt, cheese and eggs should each be stored in their original packaging.

Spreads and cooking fats Butter, margarine, spreads and lard should all be refrigerated.

Vegetables The majority of green, soft-leafed vegetables and salad leaves are best left in their original packaging. Peppers, tomatoes, aubergines (eggplants) and cucumbers keep well loose, spread out in a single layer. Mushrooms are best in their open containers so that they do not sweat. Carrots keep best if stored upright in an open plastic container – as if they were still in a bunch – but they are not the greatest of keepers. Soft leafy vegetables do not keep long – a few days at the most. Firmer vegetables, such as white or red cabbage, keep for up to 2 weeks. Peppers and tomatoes keep for 2 weeks or more. Celery, fennel, celeriac, parsnip, turnip, and swede (rutabaga) keep well for at least a week; cauliflower, leeks and broccoli keep for several days.

Below: All home-made preserves need to be stored and sealed properly, otherwise they will go off quickly.

Above: Place cooked foods in covered containers. Cool, chill and use promptly.

Fruit Citrus fruit, soft fruit and stone (pit) fruit all keep well in the refrigerator, either in a single layer in trays or in their containers. Bananas must not be stored in the refrigerator, as they turn black when chilled, but should be kept in a cool room.

Cooked foods and leftovers
These should always be placed in suitable covered containers and used up promptly.

REFRIGERATOR HYGIENE
Cross contamination is what happens when potentially harmful bacteria from uncooked food get on to cooked food or other ingredients that are not going to be cooked. If the bacteria are not destroyed by cooking, they may cause food poisoning. Always keep fish, poultry and meat tightly wrapped or in suitable dishes and never let them drip. It is important to clean out the refrigerator regularly. Check the condition of food instead of leaving it to go off. Throw away anything that is no longer edible. Empty and wash compartments occasionally. Wipe down the shelves and inside of the refrigerator with hot soapy water, then dry it before putting everything back.

Above: It is always useful to keep a loaf in the freezer, whole or sliced.

Above: Large and small cuts of poultry and meat can be frozen.

Above: Cheeses, whole, grated, sliced and diced will freeze.

STORING FOOD IN THE FREEZER

The best place to site a freezer is in a cool utility area. In a busy lifestyle, a freezer offers essential storage for lots of ingredients that can be cooked quickly with minimum preparation, as well as for keeping treats and snacks. Follow packet instructions for storing frozen products if they are provided. Fresh produce may include freezing guidelines. Always pack foods in tightly closed or sealed containers to prevent flavours or odours escaping and to keep the food in good condition.

Below: Raspberries freeze well in a single layer and pre-frozen raspberries are excellent.

Freezer burn is the term for dry patches on food that has not been closely wrapped and sealed in freezer bags. All the storage times given are guidelines and it is always best not to take chances with food.

Fish and seafood There is an excellent range of ready-frozen fish and seafood products. Once the packets are opened, double wrap them in another freezer bag and tie to prevent fishy smells escaping and tainting other foods (particularly important with smoked fish). Fish that is bought ready frozen should be stored in the freezer as soon as possible after purchase and will keep for 3–6 months.

Poultry and meat Large and small items freeze well for 6 months or more and bought products have a long freezer life. Pieces that are small and separate (loose mince (ground meat), dice, thin strips and fine slices) can be cooked from frozen as they cook through quickly. Large items usually have to be thoroughly thawed before cooking or cooked slowly and for far longer until completely cooked through. Bacon and similar salted meats do not keep well. The high salt level may make the fat content turn rancid during freezing. About 3 weeks is long enough as they rapidly begin to develop 'off' flavours that get stronger as time goes on.

Vegetables The majority of vegetables keep for about a year in the freezer, if not more. Commercial products are free-flowing so that the required amount can be removed from the packet, and home-prepared vegetables can be frozen on trays before packing for the same result. Frozen vegetables provide as much goodness as fresh ones. They taste good, are inexpensive, and quick and easy to cook.

Fruit Commercial soft fruits and fruit mixes are economical and a great choice for making all sorts of desserts, or for perking up a plain fruit salad.

Below: Freeze fresh fish in adequate wrapping so it does not taint other food.

Right: Frozen fruit is useful to keep for baked puddings, crumbles and pies, when the original texture of the fresh fruit doesn't need to be retained.

Open-freeze fresh berries on a tray, prepare apples for cooking or cook them before freezing. Bananas do not freeze well as they go black. Soft and stone (pit) fruit may soften, but they still have excellent flavour and goodness, and are ideal for baked puddings. Fruits freeze for up to a year.

Dairy produce Cheese and butter both freeze well. Grate, slice or dice cheese so that it thaws rapidly and can be used quickly in cooking, salads or for snacks. Pack butter packets in a polythene bag or cut them into smaller portions if you want to take out individual amounts occasionally. Milk and plain yogurt are not typical freezer candidates but it is useful to know that they do freeze well. Egg whites also freeze well (useful to know when making mayonnaise with just the yolks) and are good for meringues. Beaten eggs can be frozen if they have a little salt or sugar added; similarly yolks can be frozen when beaten with a little sugar or salt and a spoonful of water.

Breads and baked goods Savoury, plain or sweet breads, rolls, buns, cakes (large or small, plain or filled) and pastries (pies, quiches, pasties, samosas or filo pastries) are good freezer candidates. Cut them into individual portions for removing small amounts as required. As well as cooked items, part-baked breads, raw croissants or risen rolls, and uncooked pastries freeze well. All types of pastry are sold prepared, chilled or frozen, ready for using as required. Most breads and baked goods keep well for 3–6 months in the freezer.

Below: Chorizo has a high fat content so can only be stored for up to one month in the freezer.

Cooked dishes Cooking more than you need and freezing portions for a later date saves time and often money. Casseroles and stews, soups, mashed potatoes (and/or carrots and swedes (rutabagas)), gratins, pies and pancakes are all good examples. Pack dishes in suitable rigid containers or wrapped as individual portions; always freeze in amounts that will be used in one go when thawed and reheated. Storage time depends on the shortest time for any of the ingredients in the dish. For example, a beef casserole dish that includes onions, mushrooms, carrots and bacon, will only keep for about one month because even though the beef and vegetables will keep for many months, the bacon will gradually develop rancid flavours.

Thawing and reheating depends on the type of ingredients in the dish. For food safety, it is vital that a frozen dish that is to be served hot is reheated right through to its original temperature before serving.

DEFROSTED FOOD

Once thawed, frozen food should be treated as fresh food with a very short use-by date. It should be chilled and used promptly, particularly if the item was placed in the freezer close to its original use-by date. Never refreeze frozen food unless it has been cooked since it was last removed from the freezer.

Everyday foods to keep in stock

There are certain basic foods that are always handy to keep in stock for everyday cooking. Below are some suggestions for the sort of ingredients that are useful for everyone to have in their kitchen, from someone who shares kitchen space, for example in a student house, to an avid cook who loves shopping for fresh food in their lunch break.

In the store cupboard (pantry) it's always useful to have cereal, rice, pasta, canned beans and legumes, chopped tomatoes, canned tuna, canned fruit, olive oil, vinegar, eggs, seasonings and sugar. In the refrigerator, stock up with milk, cheese, natural (plain) yogurt and fresh vegetables. In the freezer keep a good supply of frozen peas, beans and corn. Finally, keep bread, onions, fruit, eggs and potatoes in a cool place.

Once you become more experienced, you may find that there are more items that you would like to add. Below are the most likely ingredients you will need to keep on hand and how they might be used for day-to-day cooking.

DRY STORE-CUPBOARD FOODS

Cornflour (cornstarch) This can be used for thickening and keeps fresh longer than ordinary flour.

Below: Flour is essential for baking and making sauces.

Flour – plain (all-purpose) This is used for sauces and thickening stews, pastry and crumble toppings. **Self-raising (self-rising) flour** is the basis for baking cakes, American muffins and similar goodies. Alternatively, have baking powder to complement plain flour for baking.

Sugar This is used for sweetening and in baking and desserts. Caster (superfine) sugar is often suggested for baking as it dissolves quicker, giving better results, but granulated (white) is also fine. Icing (confectioners') sugar is used for cake fillings and toppings.

Dried fruit Sultanas (golden raisins), raisins, apricots, figs and dates are useful for baking, desserts, salads, stir-fries, casseroles and for snacks.

Plain unsalted nuts Almonds, walnuts, hazelnuts, Brazil nuts, pistachios, flaked (sliced) almonds and pine nuts are all handy for stir-fries, salads, gratin toppings, stuffings, casseroles, baking and desserts.

Rolled oats and breakfast cereals In addition to porridge and muesli, mixed with dried fruit and/or fresh fruit, oats make good savoury gratin or sweet crumble toppings and are good for thickening soups. Other breakfast cereals can also be crumbled to make sweet or savoury toppings.

Pasta, rice, noodles, and grains of all kinds These are all good to serve with a main dish, or with a sauce and salads.

Above: Canned fish keeps well and has a wide range of uses.

CANNED STORE-CUPBOARD FOOD

Canned fish Family favourites such as tuna, sardines and anchovies are excellent for salads (especially with canned legumes, pasta, rice, (bell) peppers or eggs); baked potatoes; and for making pâtés with soft cheese, toast toppers or sandwich fillings. Tuna is good in savoury white sauces, such as onion and/or egg sauce, with rice, couscous, pasta or baked potatoes.

Canned beans A range of red kidney, cannellini beans and chickpeas is useful for casseroles, soups, salads and stir-fries.

Canned vegetables The main ones here are tomatoes and corn, for use in casseroles, soups and sauces.

Canned fruit Peaches, mandarin oranges, pineapple and pears, in syrup or juice, all mix well with fresh fruit and dried fruit to make fruit salads. They are all good with natural yogurt for breakfast (add oats and some nuts), or with ice cream for a speedy dessert.

BOTTLED STORE-CUPBOARD ITEMS

Condiments, oils and vinegars Aside from the obvious – salt, black pepper, extra virgin olive oil – sunflower oil, cider vinegar, dried herbs and spices, mustard, honey and maple syrup are all

Left: Rice is a good food to keep in the store cupboard. It forms the basis of many dishes.

useful items. Olive oil and/or sunflower oil is used for cooking and in dressings. Cider vinegar is milder and more versatile than wine vinegars. Mustard is useful for dressings and sauces. Honey and maple syrup sweeten natural (plain) yogurt, pancakes and vanilla ice cream.

REFRIGERATED FOOD

Dairy Milk, butter, margarine or other spreads and natural yogurt are everyday necessities.They form the basics for simple meals. Natural yogurt is endlessly versatile and used for savoury dips or sweet desserts with fruit and/or syrup.

Vegetables Tomatoes, (bell) peppers, white/red/Chinese cabbage, celery, carrots, long-life vacuum-packed plain beetroot (beet) (without acid or vinegar) are all useful ingredients. They are versatile for cooked or uncooked dishes, sandwiches or salads.

Soft summer berries and grapes keep well in the refrigerator to use in desserts and salads.

Lemons These are useful for flavouring a variety of dishes.

Jars Peanut butter, marmalade and fruit preserves have multiple uses, but all need to be chilled once opened. Peanut butter is useful for dressings and stir-fries as well as for spreading.

Below: Lemons are good to keep handy for salad dressings, drinks, cakes, pasta sauces and for serving with fish.

Above: Peanut butter can be kept in a store cupboard until it is opened and should then be stored in the refrigerator.

Marmalade is versatile for use in savoury cooking as well as desserts and for spreading. Sweet fruit preserves are good in natural yogurt and for baking as well as for spreading.

FROZEN FOOD

Fish and seafood White fish fillets, salmon fillets, smoked haddock and peeled cooked prawns (shrimp) are all available frozen. Fish fillets cook quickly from frozen by baking, grilling (broiling) or poaching. Inexpensive peeled cooked prawns can be cooked again from frozen in sauces or stir-fries or used in bakes. Thawed and drained, they can be added to salads or combined with mayonnaise to make a filling for baked potatoes.

Poultry and meat Thin fillets of turkey breast or chicken, stir-fry strips or finely diced turkey or chicken, diced meat for casseroles and free-flow minced (ground) meat can all be cooked successfully from frozen. All of these can be used in a wide variety of dishes, from quick stir-fries or meaty sauces to slow-cooked casseroles.

Vegetables The popular freezer varieties are peas, broad (fava) beans, corn, mixed vegetables, chopped cooked spinach and sliced leeks. These versatile examples can be added to sauces, stews or casseroles, stir-fries, or just steamed alone to serve as an accompaniment to the main dish. All these vegetables cook quickly by various methods – steaming, boiling, frying – for serving hot or cold.

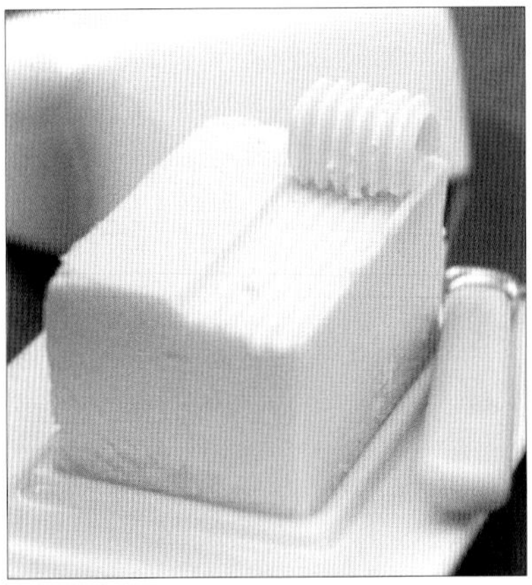

Above: Butter is used for spreading on sandwiches and toast, for baking and for frying food.

Fruit Mixed berries are versatile. Any fruit mixture is excellent for all kinds of desserts and smoothies and usually less expensive than fresh.

Breads French, pitta, naan, ciabatta and good-quality pizza bases are a few examples. Warm bread always makes a good accompaniment to a dish. Good-quality pizza bases can have excellent toppings added.

Butter and cheese Store these items whole, or diced and ready to use.

Below: Olive oil is used in many savoury dressings and sauces.

Seasoning food with herbs and spices

Simply adding seasonings can help to transform a handful of food ingredients into something delicious to eat. Salt and pepper are the basic seasonings and nearly everything you cook will benefit from a sprinkling of salt and a grinding of pepper. Government guidelines recommend that our daily intake of salt is not more than 6 grams per person and less for children.

Fresh, dried and frozen aromatics provide an amazing choice of seasonings from all over the world. As well as fresh or dried herbs and spices, seasoning mixes, marinades, powders, pastes and essences are available, ranging from classic combinations to celebrity chef creations. Buy dried herbs and spices in small quantities that will be used up quickly and store them in airtight containers in a cool, dark place. Begin by buying a few basics and add to them gradually over time.

SALT AND PEPPER

Salt There are various types of rock salt or salt crystals, but table salt is all you need to get started. Use sparingly.

Pepper Freshly ground black pepper contributes good flavour. It is worth investing in a sturdy pepper mill. Buy a mill with a strong metal grinding mechanism. Keep peppercorns in an airtight container ready to top up.

Below: A bouquet garni contains four or five different herbs tied together.

Above: Snipped chives, sprinkled over potato salad, give a flavour boost.

HERBS

Keep fresh herbs in their packaging (if any) in the refrigerator. Chopped fresh herbs freeze well and can be used straight from frozen. If you grow your own, use them to flavour oils and vinegars. You could also dry or freeze them for later use. Many dried herbs are useful to keep for an emergency. The following herbs are those you are most likely to come across.

Basil There are several types, all with slightly different flavours. Basil has a heady aroma popular in Italian cooking. It is excellent in salads and combines well with other herbs, such as fresh coriander (cilantro) or mint. Basil with garlic, pine nuts and olive oil, and usually Parmesan cheese, made into a paste forms a classic pesto (this freezes well). Basil leaves bruise easily and lose flavour dramatically when chopped. With the exception of pastes, basil should be lightly shredded with scissors straight over the dish, just before serving. Basil can be used to flavour olive oil. It can also be puréed with olive oil and frozen in ice-cube trays.

Bay leaves Fresh or dried, these are good in soups, sauces, casseroles and other cooked dishes. A bay leaf is also good in sweet rice pudding. Fresh leaves freeze well for years. Crumple a bay leaf before adding it to the food to help release the flavour. It is not over-powering, but provides a delicious background flavour for all sorts of savoury cooking.

Above: Coriander is used in Chinese and Asian cooking.

Bouquet garni Classically, this bunch of herbs contains a sprig each of thyme, parsley, chives and a bay leaf. A piece of celery may be added along with other herbs. The bunch is tied with string and added to soups, sauces and casseroles that are slow-cooked.

Chives Thin, long and green, these have a distinct onion flavour. Snip them with kitchen scissors. Use in cooking and/or add to raw dishes or sprinkle into cooked food just before serving.

Below: Basil is a delicate herb and must be handled carefully to retain its flavour.

They are good in dips, dressings, sandwich fillings, salads, in savoury butter, and to garnish soups.

Coriander (cilantro) leaves Fresh coriander leaves have a pungent, distinct flavour. They are versatile for salads and dips, for garnishing as well as cooking in food. Chopped fresh coriander freezes well.

Dill Feathery, fresh dill resembles fennel in appearance, but it is not similar in taste. It has a distinct but delicate flavour that is easily lost when cooked. Excellent with fish and vegetables, dill is good in salads, sauces and dressings. It is also used to flavour pickled cucumbers. Dill freezes well.

Fennel This feathery herb resembles dill but has a stronger, aniseed flavour. It is delicious with fish and seafood, poultry, ham and vegetables, and good in soups, sauces, dressings and salads. Avoid dried fennel as it is inferior. Chopped fennel freezes well. Do not confuse it with the vegetable fennel, which is a different plant.

Marjoram This has a strong flavour associated with Mediterranean cooking. It is good with fish, meat and vegetables, on pizza and with pasta, especially with tomatoes. The dried herb is useful, and stronger than fresh.

Mint Aromatic, with a distinctive, pronounced flavour, fresh mint is a classic accompaniment for lamb. It is also good with vegetables, grains, in dips and salads. Mint is also good in sweet dishes, such as fruit salads and drinks. Fresh mint freezes well or it can be used to flavour vinegar. Dried mint is best avoided as it is a poor substitute.

Oregano A type of wild marjoram, this is similar but with a stronger flavour. It is good fresh or dried, and is used to flavour meat or vegetables.

Parsley Flat-leaf or curly parsley are both fresh-flavoured herbs. Their flavours and textures differ subtly; although the general opinion is that flat leaf is stronger, this is not strictly true. It is useful raw or cooked, in salads, soups, sauces, casseroles and all types of savoury cooking. Chopped parsley freezes well. Dried parsley is best avoided as it has an unpleasant flavour.

Rosemary A powerful herb with small, tough spiky leaves. Rosemary is good with meat and poultry, especially lamb, and with vegetables. It is also delicious on Italian breads.

Sage A peppery herb with soft tender leaves. Fresh sage can be finely shredded or the leaves may be used whole. Good with poultry, meat and vegetables. Sage dries successfully and the leaves are rubbed to a fluffy powder. Dried sage is slightly more peppery than fresh but not as rounded in flavour.

Right: A set of measuring spoons is very useful for dried herbs and spices.

Tarragon A strong aniseed-flavoured herb that is excellent with fish, chicken or vegetables, especially carrots. French tarragon is the plant to buy when growing this herb as the alternative Russian tarragon plant has virtually no flavour. It is good in cooking or added at the end and excellent in salads. Dried tarragon is acceptable in cooking. Tarragon is an excellent herb for flavouring vinegar.

Thyme A strong but fresh-flavoured herb of which there are many types with subtly different flavours. It is good with fish, poultry, meat and vegetables. Fresh thyme freezes well on its stalks and the tiny leaves can be rubbed off in the bag when frozen. Dried thyme is an acceptable alternative, but it is more pungent than the fresh herb.

Below: Parsley stalks are good for flavouring soups and casseroles.

Below: Sage combined with onion flavours a traditional stuffing.

Below: Dill adds flavour to sauces or dressings and complements fish.

SPICES

With so many spices readily available in supermarkets and local stores, there is no excuse for bland cooking. Experimenting with the wonderful flavours and aromas is all part of the joy of learning to cook.

Allspice The whole spice consists of small dark berries about the size of peppercorns. Used in sweet dishes, they have a flavour that resembles a mixture of cinnamon, cloves and nutmeg.

Aniseed Tiny dark seeds with a strong flavour, these are used in baking and Chinese cooking. Star anise is a different spice with a similar flavour – the slightly larger shiny brown seeds are enclosed in a star-shaped seed pod.

Caraway Small, pale, slightly curved seeds with a dark stripe, these are used in sweet and savoury cooking, with pork or vegetables for example, and for flavouring breads and cakes.

Cardamom Green cardamoms are small, pale green-beige papery pods with tiny black (or brown-beige) seeds clustered inside. The seeds are fresh-tasting and aromatic with eucalyptus and citrus flavours. Black cardamoms are large, hairy brown-black pods with stronger tasting seeds. They are not as widely used.

Cayenne pepper A fiery red spice made from ground, dried, hot-tasting cayenne chillies. It is used in tiny amounts to season cheese dishes, sauces and other savoury cooking.

Below: Crush juniper berries to release their distinct aroma.

Above: Vanilla pods contain fine seeds, but it is the crystals that form inside the pod that produce the flavour.

Chilli Fresh, bottled or canned, dried whole, flaked (sliced), or powdered, there is a wide variety of chillies available. They range from mild to extremely hot. Flaked dried red chillies are useful as they keep well and a little can pep up all sorts of dishes, such as salads, salsas, stir-fries and casseroles. Added at the end of cooking or before serving, they spike the food with occasional bursts of heat; alternatively, if they cook in a dish or are allowed to stand in a mixture, they will make it uniformly hot.

Below: Saffron threads are expensive and are always sold in small quantities.

Above: Cardamoms are used in savoury and sweet cooking, especially in Indian dishes and many European cakes.

Cinnamon Whole sticks or ground to a powder, cinnamon is a sweet and distinctive spice. Used in savoury cooking as well as sweet dishes and baking, this is also one of the key spices in mulled wine.

Cloves These small, strongly flavoured buds are used in savoury and sweet cooking, especially with apples in pies or crumbles, in baking and pickling. Ground cloves are very strong and should be used sparingly.

Coriander Coriander seeds are about the size of small peppercorns and beige in colour. This spice is aromatic when ground and mild in flavour. Available whole or ground, it is used in a wide variety of dishes, including curries, Italian-style marinated vegetables, pickles and chutneys.

Cumin Black or pale beige, these small seeds have a mild, slightly earthy aroma and flavour. They are delicious with rice and used to flavour Indian breads.

Curry powder Curry powder is not an authentic ingredient in Indian cooking, where individual spices are combined to suit the particular dish or the cook's preferences. Inferior curry powder has a limited range of flavour but there are better-quality products that are mild, medium or hot and with the flavours of curry spices evident.

Fennel These are small, oval, pale green to beige seeds that reflect the flavour of the herb and vegetable, but with a stronger flavour. They are good with vegetables, fish or in a wide range of savoury cooking.
Fenugreek The seeds look like tiny, orange-brown stones and they are very hard and seldom used whole. Ground fenugreek is beige and the best description of its flavour is that it is distinctly 'curry' and mild, making it a key ingredient in curry powder.
Five-spice powder This Chinese spice mix includes cloves, star anise, peppercorns, cinnamon and fennel. It is very powerful and aromatic.
Garam masala An Indian mixture of roasted and ground spices, typically cardamom, coriander, cinnamon, cloves and cumin. Garam masala may be added during cooking or be sprinkled over a dish just before serving.
Ginger Fresh root ginger is knobbly and beige-coloured, smooth and fairly thin-skinned when fresh, with juicy flesh. Older roots look wrinkled, with coarse thick skin and slightly shrivelled ends – so should be avoided. Fresh root ginger is slightly hot and has a fresh flavour that is slightly citrus, with eucalyptus tones. It is also sold pickled, crystallized or candied, or preserved in syrup. Dried ground ginger is a beige powder that is hotter than the fresh spice and without the intense fresh flavours. It is widely used in savoury and sweet cooking. Store fresh root ginger in the refrigerator, unwrapped, where it will keep for a few weeks, depending on condition and the size (larger pieces keep reasonably well) when purchased. It also freezes well.
Ground mixed spice This spice mixture contains cinnamon, coriander seed, ginger, nutmeg and cloves, and is used in baking and desserts.
Juniper Small, dark brown-red berries, that are dried but not crisp or hard. Juniper is one of the flavourings in gin, which resembles it in flavour. They tend to be used with meat and game.
Mace The blade of mace is an orange-coloured net-like web that surrounds the nutmeg. This is sold in large pieces or ground. The strongly flavoured, aromatic spice is delicious in savoury or sweet cooking, including sauces, meat mixtures and baking.

Above: Caraway seeds have a hint of fennel or aniseed in their flavour.

Mustard There are many types, including black or yellow mustard seeds, and they produce a variety of different spices. Some are mild and used whole, for their crunchy texture, others are hotly flavoured. Bright yellow English mustard (powder or paste) is hot; wholegrain mustard is medium; pale Dijon mustard is mild.
Nutmeg It is slightly smaller than a walnut, hard, and sold whole or ground. Miniature graters are available for grating the whole spice. It is used in savoury and sweet dishes.

Below: Turmeric gives the characteristic yellow colour to curry powder.

Paprika Usually mild but there are hot versions of this red powder, which is ground from dried sweet red (bell) peppers. Used in Hungarian goulash and a wide variety of savoury dishes, paprika is also good for seasoning egg and cheese dishes.
Pepper Black or white peppercorns are sold whole or ground. Grinding them freshly in a mill is the way to get the best flavour. White pepper is best for mashed potatoes and savoury white milk sauces.
Saffron The stamens of a particular crocus variety, these are dried and sold, whole or ground, in tiny amounts. They impart a vibrant colour and distinctive but delicate flavour.
Turmeric Fresh turmeric resembles fresh root ginger, but with bright yellow flesh under the paper skin. Ground dried turmeric is most common – it has a warm, earthy flavour. It is used in savoury cooking, including curries.
Vanilla Whole pods (beans) can be simmered in liquids, drained, dried and used again. Vanilla extract is usually good quality, but avoid synthetic vanilla essence. Vanilla sugar can be made at home by infusing caster (superfine) sugar with a vanilla pod by storing them together in an airtight jar.

Below: Grated nutmeg is aromatic and delicious in milk puddings.

Cooking kit

Delicious meals can be stirred up in the simplest of pans but budget-busting cookware will not work magic on tasteless mixtures! Good-quality basics, such as pans and knives, will literally last a lifetime and need not cost a fortune. Kitting out a kitchen for the first time means choosing a few essential items, then adding to, or upgrading, these with an expanding cooking repertoire, or as finances and space allow.

STORAGE SPACE

Before putting together a list of basics that you need to purchase, check out the storage space that you have, especially in shared accommodation or a studio kitchen. The worktop space should be reserved for essential everyday items, starting with a kettle. The more cooking that happens in the kitchen, the more 'everyday' certain equipment becomes, such as weighing scales and a utensil pot. Heavy or awkward appliances (such as food processors) have to be out ready for use or within easy access, otherwise they become too much effort to move and are likely to stay in the cupboard.

Kitchen areas usually contain shelves, hanging space and drawers. Shelves need to be strong to cope with the weight imposed upon them by heavy cookware. Shelf space has to be reserved for mixing bowls, measuring jugs (cups) and baking tins (pans).

NON-STICK PANS

Cheap pans last a short while, more expensive, heavier pans last longer. Even the most expensive are not as resilient as stainless steel and they do not last as long. For durability, the manufacturer's instructions on the use of non-stick coatings have to be followed and this usually includes an instruction to avoid high heat, which can limit your cooking options.

Hanging hooks or racks can be useful for big items, such as pots colander and sieve (strainer), even pans, if they will be out of the way on a wall or stored above head height. If there is no drawer space for knives, spoons, spatulas and whisks, they can be stored in pots on the work surface.

CHINA AND CUTLERY

Crockery and cutlery for serving food are usually stored separate from utensils. When starting with nothing, a couple of sizes of plates, bowls for cereal, soup or dessert, and some cups or mugs are the basics. (One set for everyone including cutlery.) Big shallow bowls are practical for breakfast cereals, soup, pasta, rice, salads, hotpots or casseroles and desserts, and are an ideal choice, especially when storage space is limited.

POTS, PANS AND CASSEROLES

Available in an amazing array of shapes, sizes, finishes and prices, these are absolutely essential for home cooking. High-quality, heavy stainless steel pans will last a lifetime, withstanding high temperatures, minimum content, and minor cooking accidents, such as overbrowning or burning ingredients.

Pans Not all pans suit all types of hobs, so check the instructions before you buy. Establish your budget before comparing products. The material that the pan is made of is the main feature for comparing cost. It is worth paying for heavy stainless steel pans with aluminium or copper sandwich bases because they conduct the heat well. Smart, heavy enamel-coated pans are not cheap and they will not last as well as stainless steel. Inexpensive, lightweight, thin-base pans tend to buckle and burn easily, so if the budget is tight, go for the heaviest if not the most attractive.

Handle design is important. Large pans should have a small and large handle, both of which should be strong and well attached. They should be made of heatproof material or there should be an intermediary coating between the main part of the handle and the pan to reduce heat conduction along the metal.

Lids are essential. They should fit well and have strong, heatproof handles on them. Domed lids allow steam to condense and run back into the pan.

Depth of pan is another feature to compare. Some pans are wide but not deep. Deep pans provide maximum space for liquids to boil.

Once the basic features have been compared, think about the

Left: A set of good quality pans is essential. Clockwise from top left: two lidded pans, flameproof casserole, bain marie, omelette pan and cast iron frying pan, non-stick frying pans, sauté pan and copper pan.

sizes available. Small pans are good for boiling eggs, heating small portions of soup or cooking individual servings of rice, but they do not allow space for boiling pasta or simmering one-pot meals. Medium and large pans are more versatile than very small sizes.

Frying, omelette and sauté pans, skillets, griddles and woks These come in all sizes, varying in depths and are usually round, square or oblong with rounded corners. Uncoated cast iron pans have to be seasoned (heated with oil and salt) and kept oiled, otherwise they rust. Stainless steel pans vary in quality: non-stick finishes do not withstand high temperatures, but cheap and cheerful non-stick frying pans can be replaced relatively frequently.

Omelette pans are shallow with a well-curved lower rim and sloping sides for sliding out the omelettes. Pancake pans are smaller. Sauté pans are large, shallow and straight-sided, and intended for frying food quickly over high heat; skillets are deeper, straight-sided and with lids. Ridged or flat griddles are heavy, with no sides or a shallow rim. A high-quality large skillet with a slightly domed, close-fitting lid is versatile for stir-frying, braising, simmering and stewing. It can also be used for frying.

Below: The different surfaces on these graters are for grating and slicing to different sizes.

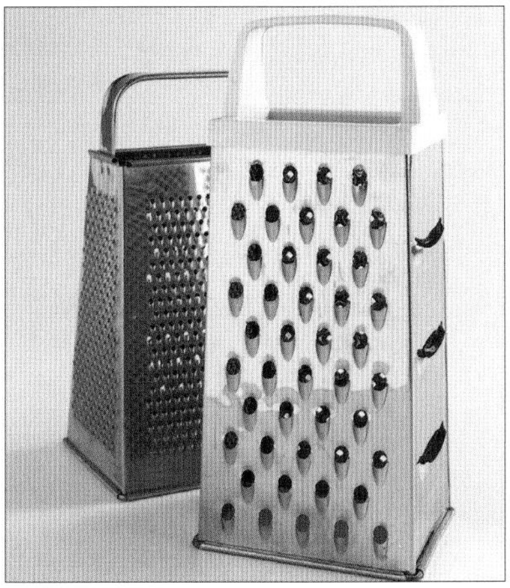

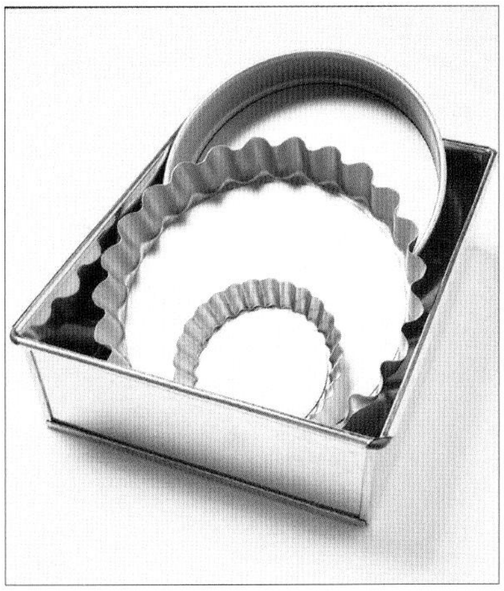

Woks vary from traditional, thin steel (the inexpensive carbon steel type is brilliant for high-heat stir-frying but they have to be wiped out and oiled after each use) to flat-bottomed non-stick varieties. They are useful for stir-frying, braising, steaming and simmering (when sold with lid and steaming rack). They can be used for 'deep-frying' small amounts of food with relatively little oil. A heavy pan doubles as a stove-top casserole for long, slow cooking (traditional meat stews, for example) but a wok is not ideal for this. For frequent use, a wok needs a hanging hook or shelf space that is readily accessible.

Casseroles and stewpots The best are those that can be used on the hob as well as in the oven, allowing foods to be fried in the pan before liquid is added. Heavy cast-iron casseroles are excellent for long slow simmering in the oven or on the hob. Look for tight-fitting lids and ovenproof handles on both pot and lid.

OVENPROOF DISHES

All sorts of colours, shapes and sizes, from little individual ramekins and shallow gratin dishes, to large, deep soufflé dishes and deep, straight-sided lasagne dishes are available. Buy them when and as you need them.

Ovenproof glass casseroles are inexpensive, versatile (they can be used in both the oven and the microwave) and durable. They will last a lifetime!

Left: A wide range of baking containers is available. A few basics are all you need.

Not pretty but practical, they make sensible serving dishes. They are also good for savoury and sweet cooking, including stews, bakes, gratins, pies and crumbles.

When selecting a lasagne dish, look for deep, straight sides. Dishes with shallow sloping sides do not allow sufficient room for sauces, which tend to bubble over during baking.

BAKING AND ROASTING CONTAINERS

Traditionally baking containers were always tins (pans), but now there are flexible silicone containers in fun colours for baking small or large cakes and quiches. Best advice: be practical and buy as you need, remembering that every item needs a storage space.

Roasting tins or pans should be suitable for using on top of the hob as well as in the oven. They should have handles or sides that can be gripped easily when wearing oven gloves and deep sides to hold lots of cooking juices and fat. Thin tins or cheap baking sheets will buckle and bend, so avoid them. Having a metal rack in a tin allows fat to drip away from meat or poultry during cooking.

Below: Baking sheets are useful for biscuits, scones, pizzas, free-form pies and to catch drips from casseroles.

Above: Measuring jugs and spoons are essential cooking kit. Use the same set of measurements when cooking.

Good-quality, deep roasting tins with dimpled lids can be used for braising, pot roasting and stewing as well as open roasting. A roasting tin doubles as a lasagne 'dish' or pizza pan.

SMALL UTENSIL CHOICES

Useful items to have are a long-handled slotted spoon, a ladle, a palette knife, tongs, a potato masher, a lemon squeezer, a timer, a long two-pronged fork, a rolling pin, a pastry brush and a can/bottle opener.

Vegetable peeler Select a swivel-bladed peeler (rather than one with a fixed blade) for removing a thin layer of peel.

Grater Look for a large box-type grater, with a comfortable handle and sloping sides, that includes several different types of cutting blade.

Citrus zester Not essential but fun – cheap and cheerful from the economy range in supermarkets will do! This can be used for removing citrus rind in shreds (fine or coarse according to the pressure applied) and it is easier than washing up a grater.

Sieves (strainers) and colanders There are many styles and grades of sieve – look for a fine stainless steel mesh with a strong rim without an overlap in which food can be trapped. A strong handle and hanging hook are essential. Colanders come in all shapes and sizes – match size to likely cooking quantities or buy bigger than needed.

Cutting boards Plastic boards are practical, inexpensive and hygienic. Buy big for plenty of cutting space. Expand the collection to include at least a couple for cutting different types of food when preparing a meal. These will need replacing every few years (depending on how much use they get).

KNIVES

Quality is vital when selecting knives, so this is an area where it is worth paying a bit more when equipping your kitchen. Cheap knives will not stay sharp, they are not well-balanced and often do not feel comfortable to hold. Stylish blocks that come complete with an array of cheap knives are not the best choice. Buy individual knives from a cook shop or reputable store. They should feel well-balanced with riveted handles that are washable and dishwasher safe (for the future if not immediately). Look for good-quality blades that will sharpen well. Make sure that the knife feels comfortable to hold.

A small to medium-sized vegetable knife is useful for cutting smaller items. A large cook's or chef's knife is versatile – it is just a matter of selecting one that is large enough to tackle big vegetables, but not too large to handle efficiently. If the knife is heavy, well-balanced and kept sharp, it can be used for fine cutting and for small to medium items as well as for larger foods. Practise cutting techniques for success.

A serrated knife is practical for tomatoes, fruit and hard-boiled eggs. Serrated knives are not sharpened on a stone and are not expensive, but a good one will last for ever. A large serrated knife is good for large loaves, French bread, slicing through rolls or cutting cakes and buns.

Left: If space is limited, consider equipment that has several uses. This steamer could also be used as a colander or for cooking pasta.

WEIGHING AND MEASURING

Adding the accurate amount of ingredients is essential when cooking recipes that are unfamiliar. You can start to experiment with quantities to adjust the flavourings with experience.

Scales Electronic scales are the most accurate, neat and easy to use. Any container can be used, the scales recalibrated and ingredients added. Standard scales do not need batteries.

Measuring jugs (pitchers) Look for clear glass or plastic, with well-marked levels, a stable base and a good pouring spout.

Measuring cups and spoons Suitable for dry or wet ingredients, these are standard in volume, have good handles and plain sides. Cups should be straight-sided. Stainless steel measures will last for ever.

MIXING BOWLS AND UTENSILS

Bowls for mixing are inexpensive and useful for different aspects of preparation, as well as for serving the cooked food.

Containers and bowls A large, medium and small bowl are useful for holding prepared ingredients, mixing batters and doughs, tossing salads or whipping up a quick dessert. Measuring jugs can double as containers, as can deep cereal or soup bowls when combining small quantities. Storage containers can be used for mixing and making: look out for bowls that are heatproof, ovenproof and come with airtight lids for storage when cold.

Spoons, slices and spatulas Wooden or heatproof plastic spoons with shallow bowls are used for stirring dry and liquid foods during cooking, as well as for mixing raw ingredients and creaming cake mixtures or beating batters. Pick the size that feels comfortable and matches the size of pans and bowls. These are inexpensive and long-wearing. Spoons with non-stick coatings are intended for non-stick pans but they are more expensive and unlikely to last well. A flat fish slice or spatula in heatproof plastic (useful for frying not only fish) will not scratch non-stick pans. Metal fish slices are good for uncoated pans. Check the shape and size of the flat blade and choose ones with plenty of flexibility as rigid ones will not slide under delicate foods. Match the size to the frying pan. Plastic spatulas clean out a bowl of cake or other mixture more efficiently than a spoon. Consider them essential if you bake a lot of cakes.

Whisks There are all sorts of whisks: select a basic, medium-sized wire balloon whisk with a strong handle that is securely attached. Useful for making smooth sauces, as well as for eggs and liquid mixtures. Different sizes have different uses.

ADD-ONS: WHAT'S USEFUL AND WHAT'S NOT?

Beginners need basics – save sophisticated equipment for later culinary adventures. Everyone finds a favourite knife, pan and other items that become the first choice for a variety of different tasks. It may be the size, shape or other features that make it practical, comfortable to use or easy to clean. Once certain features are identified, it is easy to buy additional equipment that shares the good design. On the other hand, every well-used kitchen has items that are never used – awkward to handle, too big or small, too fiddly and difficult to clean.

Right: A basic selection of good-quality kitchen equipment will last for years.

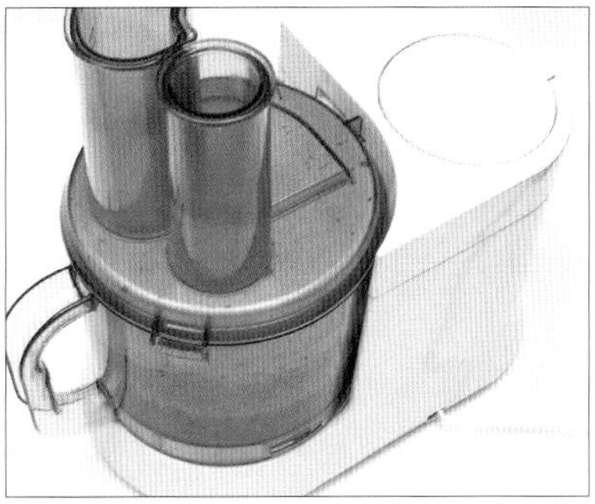

Above: A food processor is invaluable if you make lots of sauces and soups.

In terms of quality, as a general rule, for occasional baking or one-off dishes buy something cheap and cheerful, then upgrade to a better-quality product if you find the item becomes invaluable. This applies to all kitchen equipment.

SPECIALIST ITEMS

Steamer, stockpot, preserving pan, different-shaped baking tins (pans) and extra baking dishes These should be added as you gain experience. Some cooks simply never need them and many kitchens are not large enough to accommodate equipment that is likely to have only occasional use.

Electrical appliances Toaster, sandwich toaster, popcorn maker, coffee machine, food processor, blender, bread maker, rice cooker and so on…there is a huge variety of different appliances to fill every space on the work surface. No one has limitless worktop space, so it is important to select which of these, often bulky if time-saving, devices you will use regularly. A basic hand-held electric beater is useful for whipping cream, making batters and creaming cake mixtures A hand-held blender or stick blender with a whisk and beater attachment and mixing container can be used for whisking, whipping, creaming light mixtures, blending and puréeing. Food processors come in many sizes. They will chop, mince, mix, purée, grind and blend. The more powerful the motor, the tougher the machine and the more it will handle. A food processor does not purée thin liquids (such as soups) as successfully as a blender. Goblet blenders often come as individual appliances or alongside a food processor. They are better for making smooth thin purées but do not handle the quantity of dry ingredients a food processor will blend, and they are not as versatile.

EQUIPMENT IMPROVISATION

If the tools are not available, there are often alternatives that work very well. Try some of the following classic items of improvised equipment. When these are used frequently, it is time to invest in the correct tool.

- Snip the corner off a polythene food bag to make an impromptu funnel.
- Mix dry or semi-dry ingredients by shaking in a polythene food bag instead of a bowl, for example gratin toppings, crumble toppings, pastry mix or the mixture for meatloaf.

Starting to cook

A few simple food preparation techniques are used time and again in all sorts of cooking, from the simplest to the most sophisticated dishes. Preparation of the raw ingredients, especially meat and poultry, can take time and there are some basic guidelines to follow as you work.

Above: Thoroughly wash fruit and vegetables before cooking.

KITCHEN HYGIENE

Advice on food hygiene sounds either patronizing or scare-mongering, but it is important to avoid minor stomach upsets as well as major food poisoning. It is easy to let standards fall when sharing a house or flat or when life is so busy that leftovers are forgotten at the bottom of the refrigerator. Few people have time for frequent cupboard, refrigerator and freezer cleaning sessions. Adopting a few simple standards prevents minor hitches from building up into a big problem.

Clear kitchen It is vital to start off with a clear and clean food preparation area to avoid contamination.

• Keep clutter off work surfaces. Keep the sink and draining board clear so that they can be wiped down quickly and frequently. Thoroughly wash and rinse the sink area daily.

• Use a lidded bin in the kitchen lined with a removable bin bag or newspaper and empty it frequently. Keep the bin clean by washing and drying it regularly.

• Wash out packaging that contains meat and fish products to minimize unpleasant odours.

• Brush and wash the floor regularly. Clean up spills from surfaces, floor, refrigerator or cupboards immediately.

• Keep pets away from your food – do not let them put their heads in the refrigerator or leap on to work surfaces. Have separate feeding dishes for them, well away from food preparation areas.

• Rinse dishcloths in hot water after use, shake out and hang up to dry. Rinse and hang up washing-up brushes.

• Wash dish towels frequently. After use, open them out and hang them up to dry.

• Scrub cutting boards in hot soapy water after using them, especially after cutting fish, poultry or meat, and never reuse the same unwashed board for uncooked and cooked food.

• Wash up all equipment in hot soapy water immediately after preparing food. Wash up dishes after a meal or snack promptly, then rinse in hot water and allow them to drain or dry them with a clean dish towel – it is better to let them air dry, then put them away, than to use a damp, dirty cloth. Select a sufficiently high temperature if using a dishwasher.

• Properly wrap or cover food before putting it in the refrigerator.

• Do not leave food hanging around in a warm environment for long. Cover food to prevent flies from getting at it while it is standing or cooling.

• Allow food to go completely cold before putting it into the refrigerator or freezer.

Left: Store leftover food in the freezer in suitable containers and make a note of what is inside and the date.

PERSONAL HYGIENE

In additon to surfaces and utensils, it is vital to pay attention to personal hygiene when preparing food.

• Keep hair back out of the way and long sleeves rolled up before cooking.

• Sneezing, coughing and touching the face can transfer unwanted bacteria on to food, so use disposable handkerchiefs and wash hands.

• Always wash hands before, during and after preparing food and immediately after handling raw fish, poultry, meat, eggs and dairy produce.

• Wear an apron if you're a messy worker and launder it regularly.

Above: Greasing a baking sheet with oil or melted butter stops food sticking.

Above: Chopping thin julienne strips of vegetables can take time.

Above: Marinating fish in wine or oil-based dressings gives added flavour.

PREPARATION TECHNIQUES

Here is a quick guide to some of the techniques that you may need to use when preparing ingredients for the recipes featured in this book.

Chop To cut up finely into even pieces with a sharp knife, special chopping gadget or a curved chopper in a wooden bowl. Finely chopped means cut up very small; roughly or coarsely chopped means in slightly larger and not as even pieces.

Dice Cut into small even cubes.

Grate To shred, either coarsely or finely depending on the food item, against the abrasive surface of a grater.

Grease Brush or wipe with fat, usually oil or butter, to prevent food from sticking to the tray or tin (pan). Jacket potatoes are lightly greased before being baked in the oven. The butter makes the jacket crunchy.

Hull Remove the stalks and core from strawberries by twisting them out.

Infuse To flavour or scent a foodstuff, usually liquid, by steeping the aromatic ingredient in it.

Julienne Fine thin sticks of vegetables cut with a sharp vegetable knife.

Macerate Soak sweet ingredients,such as dried fruit, in a flavouring to soften it.

Marinate To soak ingredients such as meat, game or poultry in a marinade in order to tenderize and add flavour to them. A marinade is a mixture of seasonings, such as wine, fruit juice, vinegar or oil with herbs or spices. It is often discarded when cooking begins.

Melt To change the consistency of a solid to a liquid by heating, usually fat or chocolate.

Shred Cut into very fine short strips that are larger than grated pieces.

Strain To press a mixture through a sieve (strainer), rubbing it with the back of a mixing spoon. This removes lumps and any unwanted bits, such as seeds.

Below: Melt chocolate in a heatproof bowl over a pan of simmering water.

Below: Macerating a mixture of fruits for compotes and sauces.

Below: Pressing dense ingredients through a sieve removes lumps.

Above: A bain marie provides gentle heat for delicate foods.

Above: Deep-frying parsnips gives a crunchy texture and adds to the flavour.

Above: Grilling using a ridged griddle pan.

COOKING TECHNIQUES

Some foods can be cooked in a wide variety of ways, and some dishes can be cooked in the oven or on the hob and will achieve the same results.

Bain marie A container of water in which to stand a dish or tin (pan) of food during cooking, either in the oven or on the stove. The water should be hot but not boiling. The outer container, such as a roasting tin, should be deep enough to hold enough water to come half to three-quarters of the way up the outside of the dish of food. Dishes cooked by this method include custard, crème brûlée and other egg dishes.

Bake Cook in the oven, in a container, without additional liquid or fat.

Blanch A technique to prepare food, usually vegetables, often before freezing, by immersing them briefly in boiling water.

Boil Heat liquid until it is bubbling rapidly. The liquid may be boiling (soup, for example) or food may be boiled, which means cooking in water or other liquid that is bubbling away steadily.

Braise Similar to stewing, but using less liquid and usually for less time. This method is usually used for cheaper cuts of meat that are not quite tender enough for roasting.

Casserole To cook in the same way as to stew food although, strictly speaking, this is a dish with a lid used for cooking food this way.

Deep-fry Heat a large pan about a third full of fat (no fuller as it bubbles up when food is added) until very hot and then cook food in it. Electric deep-fryers are thermostatically controlled. The food may be cooked in a basket or a draining spoon is used to remove it.

Fry Cook in a little fat, which may be oil or melted solid fat (such as butter). Pan fry is the same. The amount of fat depends on the recipe, but this is shallow-frying for which the minimum amount of fat may be used or there may be enough to cover the bottom of the pan with a thin bubbling layer.

Griddle Cook on a ridged frying pan or on a heavy flat iron bake stone or

Below: Boiling fruits in a pan softens the fruit.

Below: Frying an escalope of meat in butter and oil is a quick-cook method.

Below: Poaching fish in water or milk produces a fine flavour.

Above: Sweating garlic and sage in a pan on a gentle heat.

Above: Steaming vegetables over a pan of boiling water.

Above: Blanching destroys the food enzyme that affects flavour and colour.

griddle (usually referring to pancakes).
Grill (broil) Cook under a grill (broiler), which is a source of direct heat. The American term for grilling is broiling.
Parboil This is to partially cook food by boiling, to continue cooking, possibly by a different method, later.
Poach To cook food in a pan covered with seasoned, barely simmering liquid such as milk or water. It can be done in an open pan, or a dish in the oven.
Pot roast Cook with a little liquid and fat, in a covered container, either in the oven or on top of the cooker. This is halfway between roasting and braising, with moisture from some liquid, which helps to tenderize foods that are too tough for roasting.
Roast Cook in additional fat in a tin (pan) (traditionally on a rack) in the oven, or on a spit, turning in the oven.
Sauté Fry in a small quantity of fat over high heat, stirring or turning the pieces of food all the time. It is the European equivalent of stir-frying but not quite as vigorous, and in a frying pan not a wok.
Simmer Bring liquid to the boil, then reduce the heat so that it bubbles gently and less frequently. It should not be completely still, but it should not bubble vigorously. Simmering steadily means it should simmer quite fast.
Steam Cook in a perforated container over boiling water. The water does not touch the perforated container. The water boils rapidly, producing lots of steam, which provides heat and moisture. A steamer set consists of a lidded perforated top over a pan.
Stew Cook slowly in lots of liquid, in a covered container either in the oven or on the hob. Comparatively long and slow, this moist cooking method tenderizes food and intensifies flavours.
Stir-fry Fry in a little fat over high heat, stirring and turning the food all the time. A wok is the traditional pan for this – it has a very hot area in the round base and the deep curved sides allow food to be tossed and turned rapidly.
Sweat A similar method to sautéing, but done at a lower temperature. The purpose is to soften foods without colouring and to release liquid.

Below: Sautéing potatoes in a large pan over a medium heat.

Below: Stir-frying in a wok is a fast cooking technique.

Below: Simmering vegetables in a pan over a gentle heat.

Above: Baking blind with ceramic beans part-cooks the pastry.

Above: Whisking adds air. Use an electric beater for speed.

Above: Glazing pastry with milk before baking helps to colour the pastry.

BAKING TECHNIQUES

Cooking and baking are not too different and many of the skills are the same, even if the ingredients are not.

Bake blind To partially cook pastry cases, so that the base is not soggy once the contents have cooked in the next stage. The pastry may be completely cooked (if it is to be filled with a cold filling). Line with baking parchment and weigh down with ceramic baking beans or dried beans and then bake.

Beat This is a vigorous mixing of ingredients around and backwards and forwards, using a wooden spoon.

Cream To beat butter or margarine until soft and pale. This usually refers to cake mixtures, when creaming butter with sugar. The mixture becomes very soft and light, but not quite fluffy.

Fold To mix ingredients into a light (often whisked) mixture. Instead of stirring around, a large metal spoon is used as it has fine edges, whereas a mixing spoon has thicker edges designed for beating not cutting through. Leading with the side, the spoon is cut across the middle of the bowl of mixture, then it is folded spoon up and turned over towards the back of the bowl. The spoon is cut through again in the same way but at an angle, working in a figure of eight movement. This is used for adding flour to a sponge cake mixture, especially whisked sponges.

Glaze To brush pastry or bread with beaten egg or milk before baking. Cooked foods or fruit can be glazed with a syrup to give them a glossy coating and improve their appearance.

Sift To shake dry ingredients through a sieve (strainer) by tapping the side, to remove lumps and incorporate air. Remaining bits are pressed through with a spoon.

Whisk To vigorously beat light ingredients, using a wire whisk, such as eggs or egg whites, or cream. This is lighter than beating and incorporates air. An electric beater has fewer and wider wire 'blades', whereas a whisk attachment has fine wire 'blades'.

Below: Beating butter with sugar produces the basis for cakes.

Below: Folding in whisked egg whites is done with a metal spoon.

Below: Sifting flour adds air to the ingredients and removes lumps.

Above: Baking a vegetable dish. Raw or cooked ingredients can be baked.

Above: Deglazing a roasting pan to make gravy.

Above: A gratin is a savoury topping for a dish, like a crumble for a dessert.

OTHER TECHNIQUES AND TERMS
General terms apply to both cooking and baking techniques.
Al dente This means to cook until tender but still firm, with a bit of bite or resistance (not soft or soggy). Used when cooking pasta.
Baste To spoon fat or juices over food during cooking, typically when roasting but also when grilling (broiling) or when frying an egg to cook the white lightly.
Blend To mix together well but not as vigorously as beating. It is also used for whizzing food in a blender or liquidizer.
Deglaze To remove sediment and juices from a pan after browning or cooking food in fat, for example when frying or roasting. A little liquid is added and brought to the boil, the sediment is then scraped off the pan and dissolved in the liquid, making a full-flavoured sauce. Wine is often used for deglazing.
Dissolve Changing a solid, such as sugar to liquid, usually by heating the ingredients in a pan with another liquid.
Drain Pour off liquid from solids, usually in a colander or sieve.
Escalope A thin slice, usually of poultry or meat, placed between sheets of baking parchment and beaten out thin with a rolling pin or meat mallet.
Garnish To add finishing touches, such as sprigs of parsley, to a savoury dish to make it look appealing. Sweet dishes are 'decorated' not 'garnished'.
Gratin A crisp and brown topping, for example breadcrumbs and cheese on top of cauliflower in a sauce. It has a crumbly consistency.
Melt Change from solid to liquid by heating in the oven, on the stove or in the microwave.
Purée Reduce food to a pulp, which may be coarse or smooth. Traditionally done by pressing food through a sieve, a food processor or blender is usually used. The purée may be pressed through a fine sieve to remove seeds to make it very fine or completely smooth.
Refresh Rinse under cold water. When vegetables are blanched, they are then refreshed to cool them rapidly and prevent them from cooking further.

Below: Basting fried eggs with hot oil helps to seal and cook the egg on top.

Below: Puréeing with a hand blender makes light work of making soups.

Below: Basting a roasting joint of meat with fat from the pan.

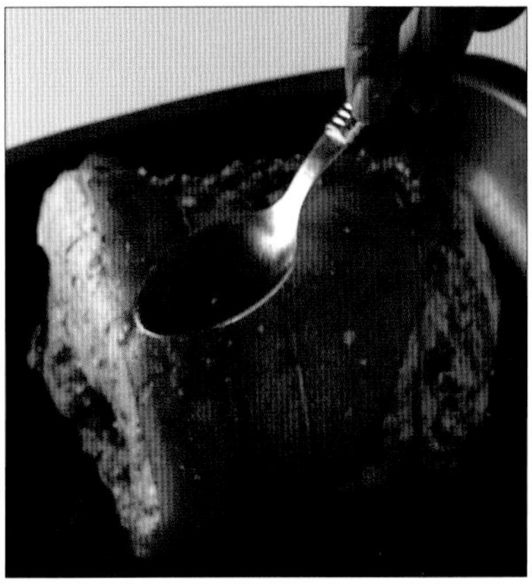

Preparing, planning and presentation

When you have built up your confidence in the kitchen, cooking for friends becomes a possibility. However, even if the kitchen is large enough to accommodate a crowd while pans are sizzling and salads tossing, few cooks and guests want to hang out in the kitchen for too long. This means that there has to be lots of 'behind the scenes' preparation. For most cooks, it is more practical to be organized, with minimal last-minute cooking, leaving you time to sip a cool drink and chat with friends. The trick is to plan ahead – after preparing a few meals, it is surprising how easy it seems to make a wide variety of recipes.

PLANNING AHEAD

Start by deciding on the menu. Read the recipes and check for the level of difficulty or familiarity, the equipment needed and whether there will be sufficient oven or hob space. Look at how much preparation is needed and whether you have the time to do it. At the same time check if anything can be cooked ahead or if the recipe calls for last-minute cooking. Work out how much marinating, setting, chilling or any other standing time is required, as well as how much final attention is needed.

Think about prepare-ahead options such as starters that are plated and ready to serve or require only a brief flash in the oven before serving. Many main dishes can be easily cooked without too much attention, or reheated successfully, or alternatively choose stylish cold main dishes to serve with hot accompaniments. Find a dessert that can be finished in advance, ready to take to the table.

Make a shopping list, noting what's already in the store cupboard and refrigerator/freezer, and what can be bought in advance. Are there any unusual or expensive foods that might take time to source? Are there any ingredients that have to be bought at the last minute?

Finally, have a simple list of what to do and tick off the items as they are done, such as what to prepare ahead and where to store the dish until it's needed. List each dish and when or where in the oven to cook it, and remember dressings or sauces. Don't forget to preheat the oven, and then work out when to put prepared dishes in to cook, as well as when to put vegetables and other accompaniments on to cook.

Below: This baked potato dish is perfect for serving at the table. This is comfort food at its best and smells fantastic.

PRESENTATION SKILLS

Serving irresistible-looking food is not about adding fussy garnishes or elaborate decoration. Good food presented simply is the key concept, although the aroma of food cooking is a significant part of the appeal. Think about the following when planning a special meal and you will not fail: Colour and texture are vital. Select vegetables and foods with contrasting and/or complementary flavours, textures and shapes.

If the food is hot, the plates and dishes should be warm. Ensure that you serve the food piping hot, unless it is designed to be served warm. Ingredients that taste best at room temperature should be removed from the refrigerator just in time, so that they are not too warm.

Above: Making food look good is a skill to be practised even when the simplest ingredients are cooked.

Serve cold salads in cold dishes or in a bowl and have cold plates on the table. Do not pile the food on to warm plates. Arrange a small amount of food neatly on the plate and take the rest to the table in serving dishes for guests to help themselves.

Avoid drowning food in sauce; instead add a modest amount and serve the rest in a jug (pitcher) or bowl with a ladle.

WILL IT WORK?

Review lists and ideas. If something that started out as a relatively straightforward informal three-course meal suddenly looks like an organizational nightmare, then think again! Check out the recipes and opt for easier dishes; think about the cooking plan and replace recipes if they look too complicated. You could always make the dishes and test them on friends first.

Clean the edges of all plates and dishes – a quick wipe with a paper towel does the trick. Splattered plates with food untidily presented never look very appealing, even if the food that they contain does.

Any savoury garnishes should be simple, edible and taste good with the main food. Herbs that wilt into hot sauce are irritating and a hindrance to the pleasure of eating a good sauce.

Citrus fruit that is served for its juice should be cut large enough to squeeze, in decent wedges. When serving lemon segments with plain grilled (broiled) or fried fish, provide thick pieces that can be squeezed easily without twisting and disintegrating.

Glorious, aromatic, long-cooked stews that taste infinitely better than they look are often best served from their cooking pots. Remove the lid at the table with a flourish and let everyone appreciate the aroma and richness as the food is ladled on to warm plates. This is particularly appealing when served with bright vegetables, handed around for everyone to tuck in. A sprinkling of finely chopped herbs adds colour and last-minute flavour to the stew.

Below: Getting all the food cooked and hot and on the table ready to eat at the same time takes careful planning.

PREPARING ROAST DINNERS

Everyone loves a traditional roast dinner, but it's not the easiest meal to prepare. There are often several different pans to attend to at once and a variety of dishes to serve and keep hot.

Weigh the meat (pre-packed meat will be labelled with weight) and add on the weight of any stuffing; work out the cooking time in advance and make a note of it. Prepare the vegetables in advance, ready to cook. and boil a kettle of water to use for vegetables instead of heating a pan of cold water.

Roast vegetables are convenient as they will cook in the oven at the same time as the meat. Quick-cook vegetables such as peas, carrots, broccoli or cauliflower can be boiled or steamed while the gravy is being prepared. Have a colander ready in the sink for draining vegetables, dishes ready to hold them and space nearby on which to rest the empty pan. Braised vegetables, such as red cabbage with apple, are a good cook-ahead choice. Bring drained boiled potatoes that are slightly cool back to temperature by putting them in a suitable dish in the microwave for 1–2 minutes.

Have all serving dishes ready and warm, including a jug (pitcher) for gravy. Warm a plate for the meat, tent it with foil (shiny side inwards) and let the meat rest while making gravy or a sauce from the juices in the pan. Carve in the kitchen and arrange slices on a warm serving platter.

MAKING FABULOUS DESSERTS

Appealing desserts, simply presented and decorated, are not difficult to make. Individual desserts are often easier to prepare, chill or cook and serve. Keep decorations simple, either on the dessert or on the plate. Baked desserts, such as tarts and cakes, should look mouth-watering as well as stylish. Caramel colours and crumbly crusts that look 'untidy' may promise melt-in-the-mouth or glorious gooey textures, as well as smell divine. It is easy to disguise baking dishes or tart

Above: Cheesecake can be prepared ahead of time.

tins that are sticky (where the content has overflowed), by wrapping a neatly folded white table napkin or dish towel around them.

Avoid over-whipping cream as it becomes buttery and curdled. Alternatively, swirly, thick fromage frais, crème fraîche or Greek (US strained plain) yogurt may be more manageable than whipped cream. You could also serve ice cream.

Pieces of fresh fruit are brilliant for finishing all sorts of desserts as long as they complement the flavours. Berries and soft fruit are extremely versatile; if they do not fit on the dessert itself, then add them as plate decorations. Make sure they are clean, and ready to eat.

Dusting a plate with icing (confectioners') sugar or cocoa works well with some desserts when the sweet flavour of the dusting complements the food. Use a tea strainer and keep your hand light.

Buy fine biscuits (cookies), petit fours or high-quality chocolate decorations for adding to soft-set desserts.

Good-quality confectionery can make clever decorations for cakes and desserts and to serve with tea or coffee after the meal.

Batch cooking

Cooking a large quantity of some dishes is no more trouble than making one or two portions. The extra quantity can be stored in a covered container in the refrigerator for up to 3 days or frozen for weeks or months, then thawed and reheated for an instant meal. There are a few basic ground rules to follow:

Be sure that there is refrigerator or freezer space for the food that you are cooking before you begin. Have suitable containers available for storing food. Cool, chill and freeze the food as quickly as possible. Freeze practical sized portions that can be thawed and used in one go. Always label and date food before freezing and include any notes, for example, whether extra liquid is needed. Thaw food at room temperature, or in the refrigerator or in the microwave. If serving food hot, always reheat foods thoroughly – right through and to the original cooking temperature.

Dishes that freeze particularly well include soups, stews, bakes, pies, pizzas, patties, burgers and fishcakes.

SOUPS

These can be thick or thin, smooth or chunky. Large yogurt pots with good lids make useful freezer containers. Remember to fill containers three-quarters full to allow space for expansion when freezing.

STEWS AND CASSEROLES

These include poultry and meat stews, as well as curry and chilli. Make sure there is plenty of liquid so that the pieces of meat are well covered. Meat sauces, such as Bolognese, also fall into this category.

BAKES

Vegetable bakes, such as sliced potato dishes and foods with similar mashed toppings freeze well. It is a good idea to make them in ovenproof dishes that are also suitable for freezing. Assemble cooked ingredients ready for final baking or three-quarter cook layered bakes such as lasagne. Large bakes can be cut into portions when cool, wrapped in clear film (plastic wrap) and frozen individually inside airtight bags.

PIZZAS, PIES AND PASTRIES

Home-made pizza can be made in large trays. When baking pizza for freezing, remove it when just cooked and not quite browned enough. Cool, cut into portions, pack and freeze.

Pastry pies can be frozen ready-baked, or, alternatively, just cook the filling, allow to cool and put into a suitable dish, then top with pastry and freeze. The pie is then ready to thaw and bake. Alternatively, make individual pies or cook, cool and freeze portions ready for reheating. Short pastries freeze well raw or cooked. Puff pastry also freezes well raw, but it is fragile once baked and easily damaged in the freezer. Part-baked pastry cases (for quiche or tarts) freeze well in suitable tins (pans) or dishes and can be filled and baked from frozen. When preparing a quiche with a beaten egg filling for freezing, add 5–10ml/1–2tsp cornflour (cornstarch) to the egg mixture to keep it firm once frozen.

Potato-topped pies (sliced or mashed) are great freezer candidates. They may be cooked completely, cooled and frozen ready for thawing and reheating in the oven. If they are in suitable containers, they can be thawed and reheated in the microwave.

Above: It is easy to make a big batch of fishcakes to freeze, ready to cook quickly when time is short.

PATTIES, CAKES AND BURGERS

It is so easy to make a big batch of fishcakes, burgers or patties, or simple rounds of mashed mixed vegetables. Shape and freeze them on trays, then pack in airtight bags and cook straight from frozen. They cook through quickly in the oven or under the grill (broiler).

SAUCES

Savoury white sauce, cheese sauce and onion sauce all freeze well. Savoury sauce is very useful because all sorts of ingredients can be added to make excellent pasta, rice or couscous toppings or fillings for baked potatoes. Just thaw, reheat, in a suitable jug (pitcher) or on the stove in a pan, and whisk until smooth, and add hard-boiled eggs, spring onions (scallions), mushrooms, canned tuna, or frozen prawns (shrimps). Finely chopped mushrooms can also be used to flavour sauces for freezing. There are lots of other sauces that freeze well, but these are the ones that save time when it comes to making instant meals.

Making the most of leftovers

When in doubt about how much to cook it makes sense to be generous rather than mean because leftovers rarely have to be wasted. There are, however, a few 'food safety' rules to follow when using leftover food and lots of ways to enjoy it.

Wasting food is a bad habit that can be avoided. Even if money is no object, wasting is bad for both the local and global environment. Stinking bags of food waste are expensive, anti-social and unnecessary, so only buy the quantity you need.

Keep tabs on ingredients in the refrigerator and on use-by dates on food in cupboards and in the freezer.

Depending on type, unopened chilled food that is just within its use-by date can be frozen, if necessary.

Get to know how much to cook for everyday foods, such as rice and pasta. Avoid serving up too much and having waste on plates. Make a habit of saving leftovers for another snack or meal. Sometimes the remains of a special meal can be transformed into a real treat! Here are some inspiring ideas to get you started.

USING UP LEFTOVER FISH

There may be times when a small piece of fillet remains uncooked or there are leftovers from a large fish, such as salmon. Cooked fish does not freeze well, but will keep chilled for one day.

• Add to salad, mix with mayonnaise (to fill baked potatoes), or toss with cooked pasta or rice and a dressing or sauce, such as an olive oil, garlic and herb dressing or tomato sauce.

• Mix with mashed potato to make fishcakes, which can be frozen for later use. Fishcakes do not have to be neat little breadcrumb-coated rounds, but can be one large round (without breadcrumbs), shaped in a quiche dish or on greased foil, sprinkled with cheese and grilled (broiled), then cut into wedges. Alternatively, just make some delicious mash, with butter, milk and parsley, then fork in the flaked cooked fish. Drizzle with olive oil, add some lemon rind, and have a salad, peas or even baked beans on the side.

Right: Mexican-style wraps are a good way to make use of cooked meats.

USING UP LEFTOVER POULTRY AND MEAT

This includes cooked chicken, turkey, duck, beef, lamb, pork or ham. Remove meat from the carcass or bones, discard skin and excess fat. Cut the meat into chunks or dice and serve in the following ways:

• Mixed with cooked pasta, rice or salad potatoes, or alternatively tossed in dressing and served with salad.

• With mayonnaise, fromage frais or salsa in baked potatoes or wraps.

• Diced, in plain white sauce, with mushrooms, spring onions (scallions) or leeks, to go with pasta, rice, in pies (potato-topped or with pastry), with a crispy breadcrumb topping, in pancakes or with Yorkshire puddings.

• Added to a sauce of onion, garlic, celery and canned tomatoes to serve with rice, pasta, in baked potatoes or on grilled sliced polenta.

• In a stir-fry with chillies, celery, spring onions and beansprouts and sprinkled with sesame oil and soy sauce.

Below: Leftover chicken from a roast dinner can be used to make soup.

USING UP LEFTOVER POTATOES

There are many ways to use cooked leftover potatoes:

• Slice or cut into chunks and fry in a little oil until crisp and golden, turning once or twice. Add chopped onion, garlic, dried chilli flakes and canned tomatoes for a main dish and serve sprinkled with Parmesan cheese or pesto – great with poached eggs.

• Slice and use in omelettes, with chopped spring onion and herbs.

• Toss with olive oil, crushed garlic and chopped fresh coriander (cilantro), then

COVER, COOL, CHILL

Three things to remember about perishable leftovers: cover, leave to cool and then chill them as soon as possible. Never leave leftovers hanging around, uncovered, at room temperature at the end of a meal. Try to use them up promptly – depending on the type of food, within a day or two. Some dishes may be suitable for freezing and reheating later. Good examples include lasagne, cottage pie, meat casseroles and soups. Pack or wrap the food in suitable portions or containers when cold, label with the date, quantity and any notes about the dish, then freeze at once.

layer on naan bread and sprinkle with a little cheese. Toast slowly under the grill (broiler).

• Make a salad with chopped hard-boiled egg and cherry tomatoes, peeled cooked prawns (shrimp) (thawed and drained if frozen) or canned tuna, and toss in dressing or mayonnaise.

• Mix with fresh mashed potato, herbs and grated cheese, then pat out into a large cake and grill (broil) until golden. Cut into wedges to serve.

USING UP LEFTOVER VEGETABLES

Leftover cooked root vegetables such as carrots, swedes (rutabaga), parsnips and beetroot (beet), leafy vegetables and peas or beans can all be used in a wide variety of dishes.

• Dice and mix with garlic, mint (or other herbs) and thick yogurt to make a dip, topping for baked potatoes or filling for wraps. Or serve as a raita with curry.

• Cut up and use in omelettes.

• Spread over ready-rolled puff pastry, sprinkle with garlic and olive oil and bake until the pastry is cooked. Good with cooked mushrooms, (bell) peppers, potatoes (add some chopped rosemary or sage), cauliflower (crumble on some blue cheese or goat's cheese), broccoli, asparagus, carrots (add fresh tarragon and dollops of ricotta cheese) or spinach (brilliant with cheese and nutmeg).

Below: Add a pastry top to a stew to make a different meal option.

• Stir-fry in olive oil with garlic and toss with pasta; top with grated Parmesan.

• Serve mounds of wonderful mixed-vegetable mash topped with Parmesan shavings – this is especially good with leftover roasted peppers, onions, and aubergines (eggplants), with poached eggs on top.

• Stir-fry with chickpeas, garlic and a little curry paste, sauce or powder, then serve with noodles or rice.

• Use as a pizza topping – great sprinkled with cooked ham and cheese.

• Spread plain pancakes or wraps with soft cheese, top with vegetables and roll up. Coat with chopped canned tomatoes, sprinkle with grated cheese and bake until bubbling.

• Coat with cheese sauce, sprinkle with breadcrumbs or crushed crackers and cheese and bake until golden.

• Use as a sandwich filling.

USING UP LEFTOVER RICE

Leftover rice can be reheated but only once: it must be thoroughly heated and not kept warm for a long time, otherwise bacteria may germinate and cause an upset stomach. Reheat rice in a covered dish in the microwave, over a pan of boiling water or in the oven. Serve with a sauce or toss in freshly cooked vegetables, canned or cooked fish, or cooked sausage, salami or ham.

• Add to soup, use in an omelette or as a topping for meat or vegetable sauces (instead of a layer of mashed potato or a gratin topping), then sprinkle with cheese and grill until golden and crisp.

Above: Leftover rice can be used to make fried rice for a quick supper.

• Mix with chopped spring onions (scallions) or chives, sliced or chopped olives, crushed garlic and beaten egg, then drop spoonfuls into a little olive oil in a frying pan. Fry until golden, then turn and press gently. Cook until golden. Serve with fried eggs and/ or tomatoes.

• Stir-fry until hot (add frozen or fresh stir-fry vegetables). Push the mixture to the sides of the pan and add beaten eggs and spring onions to the middle. Stir until just set, then mix the eggs and rice. Serve immediately, sprinkled with soy sauce and sesame oil.

• Stir-fry with leeks or spring onions, garlic, ginger and red kidney beans, borlotti beans or chickpeas. Serve with leafy salad, such as watercress, rocket, baby spinach and lamb's lettuce.

USING UP LEFTOVER PASTA

It's easy to over-estimate the amount of pasta you need. Never fear, with so many ways to use it you won't be stuck for ideas. Cool down excess pasta quickly and drizzle with oil to prevent it from sticking together.

• Add to soup, use in omelettes or mix into casseroles, stews or sauces just before serving.
• Toss with canned fish, canned beans, diced cooked meat or poultry (or spicy sausage) and serve as a salad. Excellent with tomatoes or a few cooked beans and an oil-based dressing, pepped up with chilli flakes.
• Use small pasta shapes as a filling for roast (bell) peppers. Toss with a little olive oil, garlic and black pepper. Spoon into the roast peppers and top with sliced mozzarella 5 minutes before the end of cooking. Serve with pesto.
• Toss with tzatziki to make a quick pasta salad. Serve with halved cherry tomatoes and shredded salami for a stylish starter.
• Add diced avocado, drizzle with basil oil and sprinkle with toasted nuts. Serve with lemon wedges and crusty bread.

USING UP LEFTOVER SOUPS

Most leftover soups freeze well and can be thawed and reheated from frozen in the microwave, or at room temperature, and then reheated in a pan. Soups with cream added (or thickened with egg) do not freeze. They will curdle.

• Use a small amount of soup as a light sauce for pasta. Reheat and toss with cooked pasta, adding fresh ingredients for flavour, such as chopped spring onions (scallions), canned beans, tuna or anchovies, or stir-fried vegetables to add bulk and flavour.

Above: Cooked potatoes mashed with cooked vegetables can be reheated.

• If there is not quite enough left for a sensible portion, make it go further by adding canned chopped tomatoes, some stock or a little milk. Alternatively, make it chunky and substantial by adding cooked diced root vegetables, then stir in some baby leaf spinach: good topped with poached or fried egg and drizzled with chilli oil.
• Turn a little soup into a tempting hot-pot by adding canned beans or pulses, diced smoked sausage and canned or frozen corn.

Below: Leftover cooked pasta can be dressed and added to salad dishes

USING UP LEFTOVER SAUCES

Any sauce thickened with flour will freeze successfully and just needs a good whisking during reheating. Sauces with eggs and cream will curdle. Freeze gravy, tomato sauces, white sauces (cheese, mushroom, onion and so on), remembering to label them with the number of portions.

• Use a small amount of cheese sauce or other savoury milk sauce as a filling for wraps or pancakes. Spread it on thickly, top with vegetables, cheese, cooked fish or meat and roll up. Spread with more sauce, if there is any, and/or sprinkle with cheese, then bake.
• Add stock and/or milk, canned tomatoes and vegetables to sauce or gravy to make a soup.
• Mix leftover traditional gravy or sauce with chopped cooked vegetables such as cabbage and potatoes to make bubble and squeak. Serve with any cooked vegetables. Heat a little oil in a pan, then turn the mixture into it and cook over medium heat until bubbling and hot. Brown under the grill (broiler).
• Tomato sauces can be used as a base for salsa or for topping pizza (try naan or pitta bread as a base).
• Milk sauces are a good base for soufflé. Add flavouring, such as grated cheese, and beat in a sprinkling of extra flour or a handful of fresh breadcrumbs without heating the sauce. Beat in egg yolks, then whisk the whites until stiff and fold them in. Turn into a soufflé dish or individual dishes and bake until risen, golden and set.

USING UP LEFTOVER SALAD

Leftover salad is not very versatile but this is a brilliant tip for everyone who hates wasting green leaves. Those fabulous salads that were tossed with dressing only to wilt by the end of the meal make magic soup! Really! Fry an onion, add some stock, and a diced potato and simmer until tender. Add some frozen petit pois (or peas) or spinach, bring to the boil, stir in the salad with its dressing and bring to the boil again. Whizz up in a blender until smooth. Season and serve.

Eggs

Eggs are so familiar it is easy to forget what an exciting ingredient they can be. They are brilliant for both savoury and sweet cooking, from making the simplest meals to the most stylish concoctions. Not only are they versatile, but they are also inexpensive, full of nutritional value, and quick and easy to cook. Eggs keep well and are an essential item to keep on hand in a cool store cupboard.

Egg basics

Made up of roughly one-third yolk and two-thirds white, eggs are primarily a protein food and the protein they provide contains all nine amino acids that are essential for growth and repair of cells in the body.

Egg yolk contains fat but eggs are not a high-fat food. A medium egg yolk contains about 1.6g fat, just over 50 per cent of which is unsaturated, with 29 per cent saturated fatty acids. Eggs contain vitamins D, A, E and many of the B vitamins. They are also a useful source of minerals, including phosphorous, iron and a small amount of calcium, and the essential trace elements zinc, iodine and selenium. The energy provided by an egg varies from 66kcals/276kJ for a small egg to 94kcals/394kJ for a very large egg.

BUYING EGGS

The majority of eggs are hens' eggs, with speciality eggs from certain breeds sold for particularly good flavour. Usually, the eggs are packed and priced according to the means by which the hens are farmed – check packs for details of housing conditions.

Organic eggs have a paler yolk than standard eggs. They are laid by hens that are able to roam outdoors, and are fed a purely organic grain diet. They are not given hormones, chemicals or antibiotics. Free-range eggs are laid by hens that are housed in barns, but have room to roam outdoors. Vegetarian eggs are produced by hens that are fed a purely vegetarian diet. Barn-laid eggs are eggs produced by hens that are kept inside in pens, but have room to move freely. Standard eggs are usually lower in price than other eggs. The hens that produce these eggs are reared in cages without room to behave in their natural way. They are fed a high-protein diet that may contain hormones, chemicals and antibiotics.

Right: Discard eggs with cracked shells. The egg inside will be rotten.

Duck eggs are larger than hens' eggs, with a firmer texture and richer flavour. They can be cooked in the same way as hens eggs and used in the same recipes. Being larger, they require slightly longer than small or medium eggs when boiling. An over-boiled duck egg will be unpleasant.

Quail's eggs are the smallest of all commercial eggs. The shelled eggs are served as garnishes and canapés.

STORING EGGS

Check the use-by date when selecting eggs and buy those that have a long life because they can be stored for several weeks in a cool place.

If you need only the yolk or the white for your dish, the remaining part of the egg can be kept in the refrigerator for 2–3 days until required. The yolk can be used to enrich sauces or pastry or to make mayonnaise. Leftover egg white can be used to make meringue. To store egg whites, put them in an airtight container or bowl and cover with clear film (plastic wrap).

A tough, thick skin forms on whole yolks when they are exposed to air – even the air inside a container is enough to do this. Put the yolks in the smallest container you can find, then pour in enough cold water to cover the yolks and cover the container. To use the yolks, carefully drain off the water.

Beat broken yolks with 15–30ml/1–2 tbsp cold water, put into a small container and cover tightly.

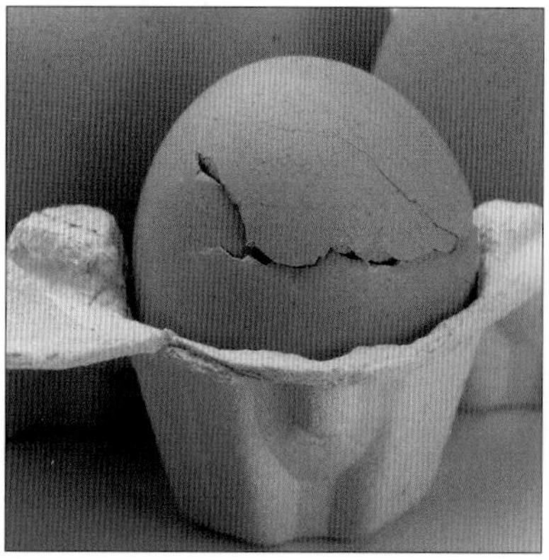

Above: Whole eggs can be stored in an airtight plastic container in the refrigerator.

Above: Covering the egg yolk with cold water will prevent it from hardening.

Above: Protect beaten eggs from drying out by covering with clear film.

Above: Egg whites can be frozen in a small airtight container.

CAUTION
Avoid giving raw eggs or foods containing partially cooked eggs to the elderly, children, pregnant women and anyone who is ill.

Right: Appearance varies according to the type of egg. Duck eggs are larger than hen's eggs; quail's eggs are very small. There is no difference in nutritional value between a white and a brown hen's egg.

YOLK COLOUR
The colour of the egg yolk depends purely on the diet of the laying hen. A diet rich in yellow corn will produce medium-yellow yolks. Natural food colours can be added to produce the popular rich yellow-orange colour. Yolks occasionally have blood spots on them and, although unsightly, are a sign of freshness and do not indicate that there is anything wrong with the egg.

FREEZING EGGS

Plain, cooked eggs do not freeze well. The whites of hard-boiled eggs become rubbery, seeping water, and the yolks become powdery in texture. Raw egg whites, on the other hand, freeze really well, which is great when you have mastered techniques for making mayonnaise and custard because there are leftover whites to use up another day. Simply put the whites in a small airtight container for freezing. Thaw them in the refrigerator.

Beaten egg can be frozen with a little salt or sugar added and yolks can be beaten with sugar or a little salt. Freezing yolks is not as successful as whites. The yolks will harden a little even with salt, sugar or water added.

HOW OLD IS TOO OLD?

As soon as the egg is laid, moisture begins to evaporate through the porous shell. Air enters the egg and starts the natural process of deterioration. The warmer the egg, the faster the rate of deterioration. As the egg ages, the membranes that separate the various elements of the egg begin to soften, causing the egg to become flabby.

Although freshness does not influence the nutritional value of eggs, it does affect their cooking quality.

Older eggs spread, looking flatter and flabbier when poached or fried, but they are easier to peel when hard-boiled.

It is also possible to check how fresh an egg is without breaking it. Put the egg in its shell in a glass of cold water. A very fresh egg will contain only a small air sac, so it will be heavier and should lie flat at the bottom of the glass. A very old egg will have a larger air sac, it will weigh less and be more buoyant at the blunt end of the egg that contains the air sac. An older egg will settle part way up the water or, if it is extremely old, it will float. If the egg floats it has probably gone bad and should be discarded. The recommendation for shops is to only sell eggs that are less than 21 days old. This recommendation is very safe. If eggs are stored under correct conditions, they can be safe for up to 28 days. If you have an egg that may be older than this, break it into a saucer to make sure it has not gone off. Bad eggs smell vile and must be thrown away. Slightly old eggs should be thoroughly cooked, for example in baking, or hard-boiled.

Below: A very fresh egg has a rounded plump yolk and two distinct layers of white. The inner is gelatinous and the outer more liquid white.

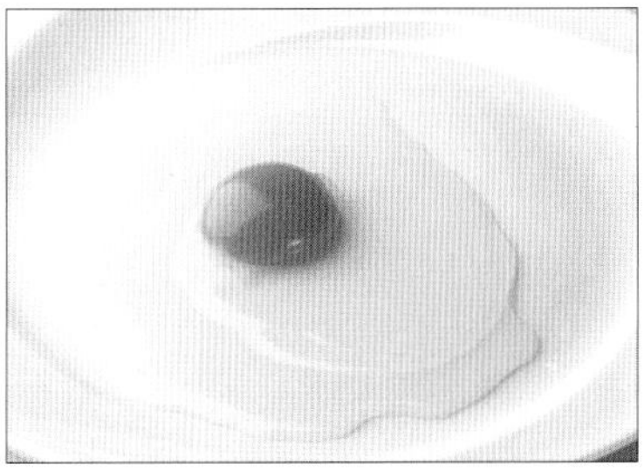

Below: A 12-day-old egg will spread more and have a flatter yolk.

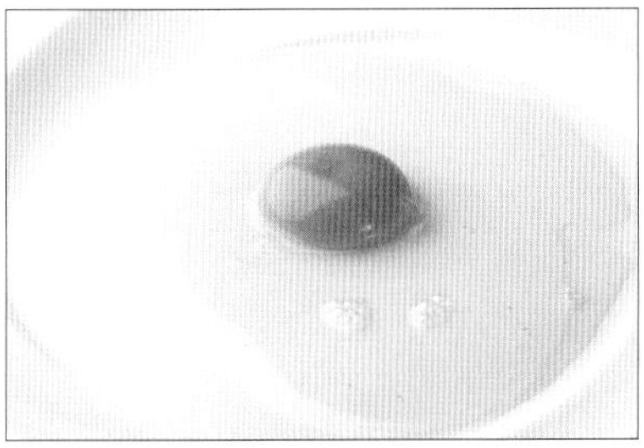

Below: A 21-day-old egg will lose the definition between the layers of white.

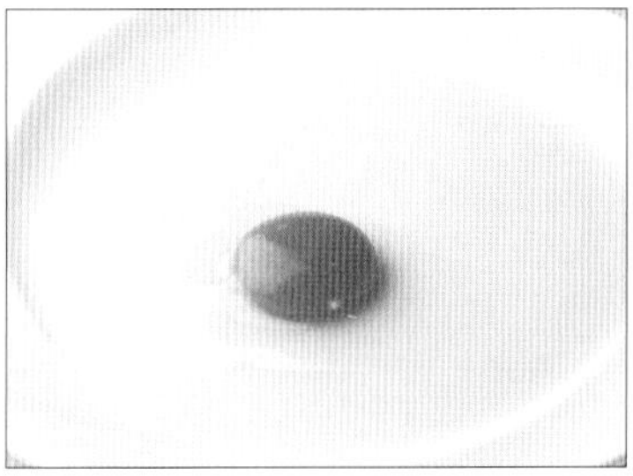

BEATING EGGS

The egg yolk and white are mixed together with a fork. Beaten eggs are used in scrambled eggs, an omelette or in baking.

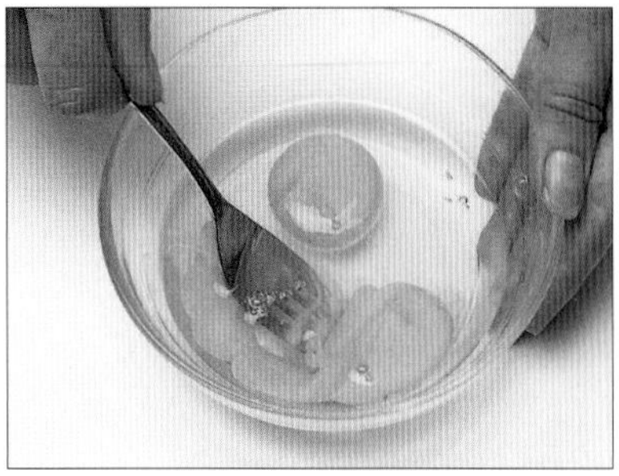

1 Beat the eggs together using a fork to incorporate air. A whisk will do the job more quickly.

BEATING EGGS WITH SUGAR

Sponge cake recipes were once made by whisking eggs and sugar together in a bowl set over a pan of hot water so that the eggs become thick and creamy with maximum volume. If the mixture wasn't thick enough, the sponge would fall flat when baked.

When beaten with sugar, whole eggs become thick and pale. An electric beater is far more efficient than a wire whisk for this and it does not take long on high speed.

1 Use an electric beater to beat the sugar and eggs together to get good thick results quickly. Eggs and sugar beaten over water may be slightly firmer, but as long as the mixture holds the trail of the whisk well, no one will notice how the sponge cake was started. This method can still be used.

SEPARATING YOLK AND WHITE

This is not difficult but it requires a steady hand.

1 Have two bowls and crack the egg around the middle, then separate the halves, holding them over one bowl. Keep the yolk in one shell half.

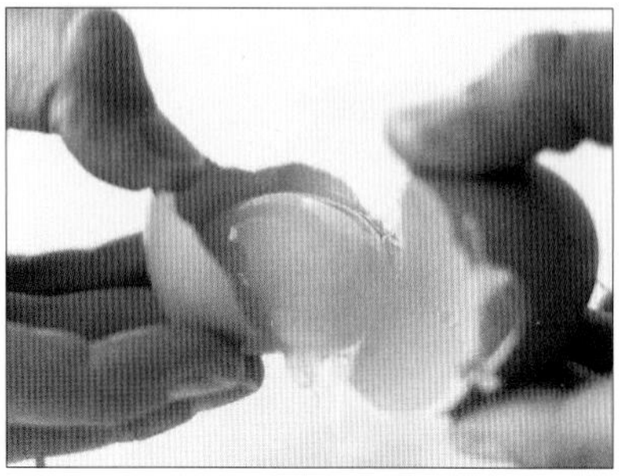

2 Pour the white from the other shell half into the bowl, then tip the yolk from one shell half to the other, allowing all the white to run into the bowl.

WHISKING WHITES

Whites whisk into a stiff foam that holds its shape. The slightest hint of fat, however, from a dot of egg yolk or if the bowl or whisk is greasy, will prevent the egg white from whisking until stiff. It is also important that there is no water in the bowl, and make sure that the bowl is cold, not warm.

1 Whisk the whites until they become stiff and hold their shape in peaks. They will still retain a slightly soft texture. With more whisking the whites become very stiff and dry and their texture is more crisp. At this stage, the bowl of whites can be inverted quickly and the whites will not drop out.

EGG SEPARATOR

This is a type of miniature strainer, large enough to hold the yolk and with slats through which the white can run. It is no fuss to separate eggs without one of these – its usefulness depends on cupboard space available and how often you separate eggs.

BEATING YOLKS

Yolks can be beaten with a little water and salt to make a glaze, for example to brush over pastry or breads before they are baked. This is usually used for savoury items. The eggs may be beaten before they are mixed with a little liquid from a soup or sauce to which they are then added to enrich the dish. Eggs can be whisked with sugar to make a light fat-free cake such as a Swiss roll (roulade).

1 Beat yolks with sugar until thick and creamy. The yolk and sugar mixture will become pale and will increase in volume and the sugar will lose its grittiness. For some recipes, such as sponge cakes or certain custards, a wire whisk or an electric beater is better. Electric beaters are efficient and convenient, since this is a slow manual technique.

Boiled eggs

Eggs should never be boiled rapidly as this is too fast and fierce, frequently causing the shells to crack, resulting in whites with a very rubbery texture. Timing is most accurate when eggs are added to water that is simmering steadily or boiling gently. Start timing the cooking when the water is bubbling gently again. This method is good for soft-boiled eggs, when timing is crucial if the white is to be just firm and the yolk runny. Serve with buttered toast cut into fingers.

1 If the eggs have been chilled put them in cold water. Heat the water until bubbling gently, then begin timing the egg.

2 If the eggs are at room temperature, lower them on a spoon into simmering water, taking care not to let them drop on to the base of the pan or they will crack.

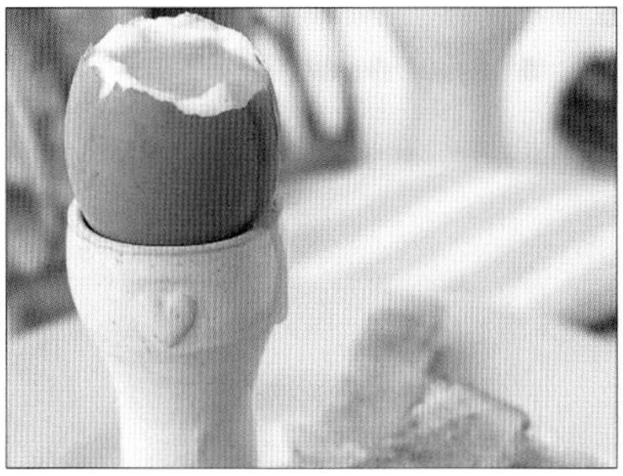

3 Cut off the top of the egg with a sharp knife.

COOKING TIMES

Start timing the cooking when the water boils gently. If you start off with hot water, reduce the cooking time by about 30 seconds. Allow an extra 30 seconds for really fresh eggs and more if they are very cold.

Cooking times in minutes

	small	medium	large
Soft	3	4	4½–5
Semi-firm	4	5–6	6–7
Hard	7	8–10	10–12

COOK'S TIPS

- When cooking hard-boiled eggs, cover them with cold water and bring to the boil.
- Timing hard-boiled eggs is not as critical as when cooking a perfect soft-boiled yolk with a white that is softly set. However, over-cooked hard-boiled eggs have rubbery whites and dry crumbly yolks.
- As soon as the water begins to boil, reduce the heat so that the eggs barely simmer. Cook the eggs gently for the recommended time and never leave them to boil for too long.
- As soon as hard-boiled eggs are cooked, drain and crack them, then place them in cold water. This prevents a black ring from forming around the yolk. Shell them when they are cool enough to handle, or to shell them while they are still hot, hold them under cold water to avoid burning your fingers.
- Finally, rinse off any bits of shell before using the eggs. Egg shell is hard and will spoil the dish.

Serving ideas

Egg and potato salad Mix cooked sliced salad potatoes, spring onions (scallions) and mayonnaise and then top with roughly chopped hard-boiled egg. Alternatively, toss halved cooked potatoes and spring onions with oil and vinegar dressing, then mix in the roughly chopped eggs. Chopped canned anchovies and drained capers are good with this salad.

Egg and cherry tomato salad Halved cherry tomatoes, spring onions, lots of chopped parsley and a drizzle of olive oil are fabulous with wedges of hard-boiled egg. Add some sliced black olives and basil for a stylish dish.

Egg and beetroot (beet) salad Cooked plain beetroot is excellent with eggs. Dice the beetroot, top with chopped hard-boiled egg and sprinkle with spring onions. Drizzle with olive oil and sprinkle with pine nuts for a great salad.

Eggs mornay Coat hard-boiled eggs with cheese sauce, sprinkle with grated cheese and grill (broil) until golden. Delicious on a layer of cooked spinach.

Egg curry Add hard-boiled eggs to curry sauce and heat gently. Serve with rice and a raita or spinach. For a dry or slightly moist egg curry, cook an onion in oil or butter, stir in curry or tandoori paste and cook for a few minutes. Add shelled, whole, freshly cooked hard-boiled eggs and stir to coat well. Remove from the heat and stir in a little cream or yogurt and chopped fresh coriander (cilantro). Halve the eggs and serve with rice or naan.

Energy per egg 94kcal/392kJ; Protein 8g; Carbohydrate 0g, of which sugars 0g; Fat 7.1g, of which saturates 2g; Cholesterol 244mg; Calcium 36mg; Fibre 0g; Sodium 90mg.

Fried eggs

Super-quick to make, fried eggs are perfect on toast, in a sandwich or served with fried bacon, mushrooms and tomatoes for a filling breakfast. The trick is to work quickly. The fat must be hot enough for the eggs to bubble and cook as soon as they are added to the pan, but not so hot that they break up. Keep watch on the eggs all the time or they will quickly burn.

COOK'S TIPS

- For fast-cooked, slightly crisp-edged fried eggs, a light vegetable oil and a pan that will not stick are essential.
- Olive oil is excellent for shallow frying eggs but at a lower temperature than vegetable oil. The eggs will not fry quite as fast and will produce an evenly set white that is not crispy around the edge. Use just enough to thinly coat the pan and season the eggs with pepper and a hint of salt just before serving.
- Butter is excellent for frying eggs, either alone or with some oil. Do not overheat the fat or it may burn. Do not use too much butter and oil or the eggs will be greasy.

Serves one

1 or 2 eggs
oil, for frying

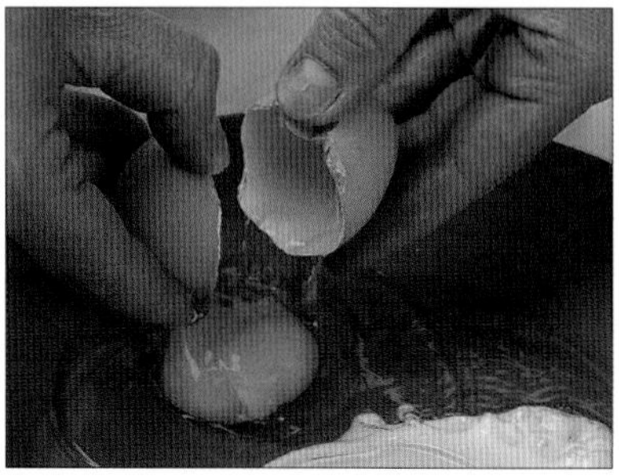

1 Heat 30–45ml/2–3 tbsp oil in a frying pan over medium heat. Crack the egg into the pan and allow it to settle and start bubbling gently around the edges before basting or adding another egg.

2 After about 1 minute, spoon a little hot oil over the white to cook the egg evenly and then over the yolk.

3 Cook until the white has become completely opaque and the edges are just turning bown. For a firmer yolk, cook the egg until the yolk is set, basting it with oil. Use a fish slice or metal spatula to lift the egg out of the pan, carefully allowing oil to drain off.

4 Or, for a firm white and soft yolk, flip the egg over, using a fish slice, as soon as the white has part-set and is firm enough to turn. Cook for 1 minute.

Serving idea

Halve and grill (broil) lots of ripe tomatoes. Sprinkle with a good handful of chopped fresh parsley Serve on toast for a quick supper. Top with eggs fried in olive oil.

Energy per egg 148kcal/613kJ; Protein 8g; Carbohydrate 0g, of which sugars 0g; Fat 13.1g, of which saturates 2.8g; Cholesterol 244mg; Calcium 36mg; Fibre 0g; Sodium 90mg.

Scrambled eggs

Scrambled eggs are a quick meal, served simply on toast, warm pitta, plain bagels, or naan bread. Scrambled eggs should be creamy and fluffy – lightly set or slightly thicker, but never firm. They are made by gently heating a mix of eggs and milk and stirring constantly to produce a scrambled effect. Use three eggs for a hearty appetite, less for a quick snack.

Serves one

3 eggs
salt and black pepper
15g/½oz/1 tbsp butter, for cooking

1 Beat the eggs well with a little seasoning until the white and yolk are thoroughly combined.

2 Heat the butter over low to medium heat to melt but do not let it get sizzling hot. Ensure the bottom and lower part of the pan sides are well coated wwith melted butter so that the egg does not stick.

3 Add the egg mixture to the pan and stir frequently over a medium heat for 1–2 minutes, until the eggs are lightly set but still very moist and creamy. Remove from the heat.

4 For more firmly set egg with a drier texture, cook for about 4 minutes.

COOK'S TIPS

- Getting the toast ready on time is vital: beat the eggs, melt the butter in the pan and set it aside, then toast the bread, butter it and place on a warmed plate (a cold plate makes toast soggy). Quickly scramble the eggs. Abandoning the eggs to toast the bread or butter the toast will mean they may overcook or set in a lump. There is a point early on in the setting when a few seconds of not stirring will not cause disaster. With practice, it is easier to toast the bread and butter it while cooking the eggs.
- Cook 1–4 beaten eggs in the microwave for 30 seconds at a time, whisking well each time, until barely set. Stand for 30 seconds.

Serving ideas

- Serve on split warmed croissants with smoked salmon.
- Try them in baked potatoes, sprinkled with cooked ham or peeled cooked prawns (shrimp).
- Stir in grated cheese and sliced spring onions (scallions), or diced ripe tomatoes, just before serving and serve with potato wedges.
- Serve in roasted (bell) peppers, and top with anchovy fillets.
- Stir-fry baby spinach in a little butter or olive oil and spread over soft wheat flour wraps, sprinkle with grated cheese and spring onions and keep warm under the grill (broiler) or in a warm oven on plates while scrambling eggs. Top with scrambled eggs, fold and serve.

Energy 390kcal/1617kJ; Protein 23.8g; Carbohydrate 0g, of which sugars 0g; Fat 33.3g, of which saturates 14g; Cholesterol 758mg; Calcium 111mg; Fibre 0g; Sodium 379mg.

Poached eggs

This simple, but delicate cooking method still provokes debate about whether to add vinegar, to make the water swirl causing the egg white to wrap itself around the yolk, or to add the egg and turn off the heat. All are successful in their own way. The most important thing is to use really fresh eggs, otherwise the whites spread into wisps. Serve on buttered toast or muffins.

Serves one

2 eggs
15ml/1 tbsp vinegar

1 Pour 2.5–4cm/1–1½in water into a frying pan. Add the vinegar and bring to the boil. Reduce the heat, if necessary, to keep the water bubbling gently.

2 Crack an egg into a cup, then tip it into the water, controlling where you put it in the pan. Add the second egg.

3 Cook the eggs very gently for 1–2 minutes undisturbed. Carefully spoon a little water over the centre of the eggs to cook the yolk.

4 The eggs are cooked when they can be loosened easily from the bottom of the pan. Use a skimmer, draining spoon, fish slice or metal spatula to lift the eggs from the water. Drain the eggs well and place them on a warmed plate. Snip off any scraps of untidy white with scissors before serving.

Serving ideas

Poached eggs are delicious on thick buttery toast, toasted English muffins or crumpets. They are also excellent with grilled (broiled) bacon, sausages, mushrooms and black pudding for a healthier (and less greasy) alternative to fried eggs for a traditional breakfast.

- Coat poached eggs on toast or muffins with a little cheese sauce or hollandaise sauce.
- Serve on poached smoked haddock, with lots of black pepper (cook in separate pans).
- Flavour mashed potatoes with crushed garlic and chopped black olives, adding olive oil instead of butter, and serve topped with a poached egg.
- Spinach and poached eggs are fabulous together – add shavings of Parmesan or finely crumbled feta or blue cheese.
- Serve in a bowl of soup – try spinach, broccoli or pea soup.
- Try poaching an egg in broth: thin broths with vegetables (especially seasoned with spices) are fabulous with egg.
- Serve on basmati rice cooked with peas and drizzle with a little chilli oil.
- Serve poached eggs on freshly cooked pasta shapes mixed with peas or asparagus, and sprinkle with shredded cooked ham and a little Parmesan cheese.
- Turkish-style poached eggs served in a puddle of plain, creamy yogurt are really good – especially sprinkled with herbs, such as chopped fresh coriander (cilantro), parsley and basil. Season with chilli oil and serve with warm bread.

Energy 188kcal/783kJ; Protein 16g; Carbohydrate 0g, of which sugars 0g; Fat 14.2g, of which saturates 4g; Cholesterol 487mg; Calcium 73mg; Fibre 0g; Sodium 179mg.

Pancakes

A batter is a mixture of flour and a liquid, such as milk and eggs. It can be used to make any number of wonderful dishes from thin French crêpes, large pancakes or small, thick drop scones (with a raising agent added) and baked specialities, such as Yorkshire pudding. Serve with either jam, sugar, golden syrup, lemon juice, currants, sultanas or raisins.

Serves four

225g/8oz/2 cups plain (all-purpose) flour
2 eggs, beaten
pinch of salt
300ml/½ pint/1¼ cups milk
butter for frying

1 Put half of the flour in a bowl with the beaten eggs and beat until the mixture is too thick to continue. There is no need to sift the flour.

2 Add a small quantity of milk to slacken the mixture and continue to beat.

3 Add the remaining flour and beat to a paste.

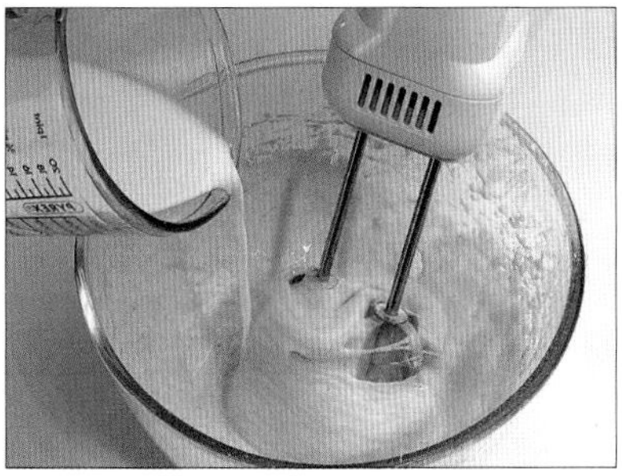

4 Gradually add the remaining milk and beat until smooth. Set aside to rest for 20 minutes. Stir well before using.

5 Preheat a pan over a medium heat.

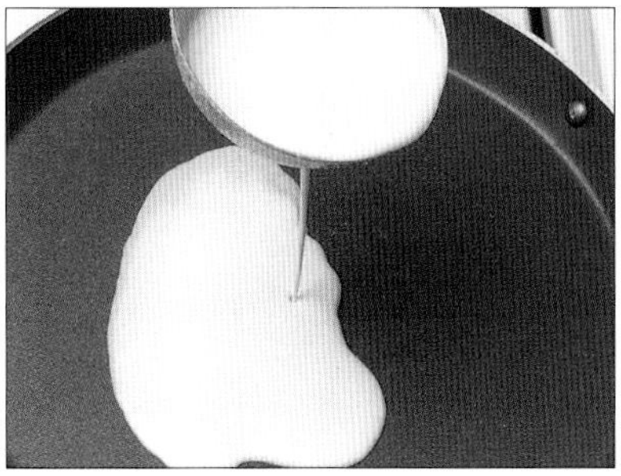

6 Melt a small knob of butter in the frying pan. Turn so the entire base of the pan is coated and sizzling gently. Add a small ladleful of batter.

7 Swirl the batter quickly around the pan to completely coat it. Cook for a minute or so until the underside is golden.

8 With a wide spatula, flip the pancake over and cook the other side for a minute until browned.

Serving idea
Serve pancakes with savoury fillings too – cheese or mushroom sauce work well.

Energy 84kcal/352kJ; Protein 2.8g; Carbohydrate 13g, of which sugars 0.8g; Fat 2.7g, of which saturates 1.3g; Cholesterol 32mg; Calcium 40mg; Fibre 0.5g; Sodium 26mg.

Omelettes

Perfect on its own for breakfast, lunch or supper; all sorts of seasonings, fillings or toppings can be added to make an omelette more substantial. Traditionally rolled, or folded to enclose a filling, an omelette can also be served flat and topped with any flavouring ingredients.

COOK'S TIPS

- Although special omelette pans are available, any non-stick frying pan will do.
- Prepare the flavourings and fillings first and have a warmed serving plate ready.
- Do not start cooking until you are ready to eat.

BASIC OMELETTE

There are several types of omelette: classic, set or soufflé. This classic omelette is set on the outside, but slightly runny in the middle, with a creamy texture. An omelette makes a quick lunch for a small appetite. Top with cheese, or fill with chopped mushrooms, for more flavour.

Serves one

2 eggs, seasoned with salt and pepper
chopped herbs, if liked
15g/½oz/1 tbsp butter

1 Beat the eggs with the herbs, if using. Heat the butter in a frying pan until very hot, but not smoking. Pour in the eggs, so that they cover the pan base.

2 Cook the eggs for a few seconds until the base has set, then use a fork to push in the sides so that the unset egg runs on to the hot pan. Cook until just beginning to set.

3 Tilt the pan and fold over a third of the omelette using a plastic spatula.

4 Still tilting the pan away from you, flip the omelette over again and slide it out of the pan on to a warmed plate, with the folded sides underneath. Alternatively, an omelette can be folded once, in half. Serve at once.

Energy 205kcal/854kJ; Protein 9.5g; Carbohydrate 11.9g, of which sugars 11.9g; Fat 13.8g, of which saturates 3g; Cholesterol 285mg; Calcium 49mg; Fibre 0g; Sodium 686mg.

SOUFFLÉ OMELETTE

When the yolks and whites are whisked separately, and the whites folded into the yolks, the result is a soufflé omelette.

Serves one

2 eggs, separated
15g/½oz/1 tbsp butter
chopped strawberries, to serve

1 Beat the yolks in a large bowl. Whisk the whites until stiff, then fold them into the yolks until evenly blended. Heat the grill (broiler) to the hottest setting.

2 Heat the butter in a frying pan, add the eggs and spread out. Cook for 2–3 minutes, until firm underneath. Place under the grill until set and browned on top. Spoon the strawberries over.

TORTILLA

Thick, set omelettes, such as Spanish tortilla or Italian frittata, can be served warm or cold; they can also be cut into small portions to serve as finger food. The mixture is cooked slowly until set.

Serves three

15g/½oz/1 tbsp butter
30ml/2 tbsp oil
1 small potato, thinly sliced
1 small onion, peeled and sliced
6 eggs, separated
salt and ground black pepper
1 garlic clove, crushed
15ml/1 tbsp parsley, chopped
small chunks of vegetable

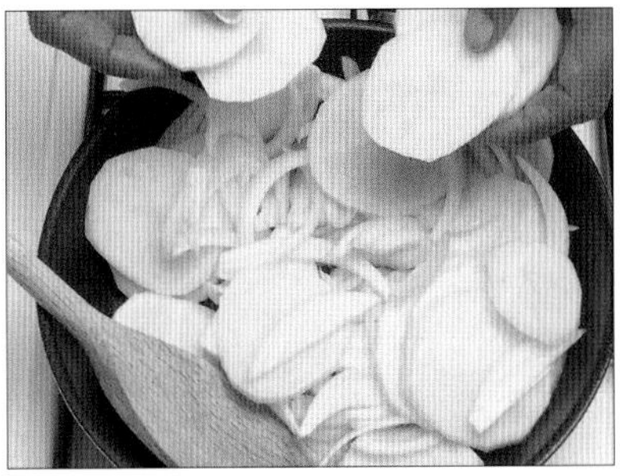

1 Heat a mixture of butter and oil in a large pan. Add the sliced potato and onion and cook gently for about 20 minutes, until tender.

2 Beat the eggs with the seasoning, crushed garlic and chopped parsley. Pour the eggs over the vegetables.

3 Cook gently until the egg has just set. This will take 30 minutes or more. Keep the heat low or the underneath will burn.

4 Place a plate over the pan. Put your hand firmly on the top, then quickly turn over both pan and plate together.

5 Lift off the pan and allow the omelette to slip out on to the plate. Slide the omelette back into the pan, cooked-side up, and continue cooking until set and golden underneath.

Serving ideas

- Grated cheese, finely chopped parsley and/or shredded basil and diced tomato.
- Sliced mushrooms – cook in a little butter or oil first, then remove from the pan while the omelette cooks. Alternatively, leave them in the pan and to set in the omelette.
- Herbs – chopped fresh parsley, dill and tarragon are excellent in omelette; add to the beaten egg. Alternatively, sprinkle shredded basil leaves over before folding, or add chopped coriander (cilantro) before the egg sets.
- Diced cooked ham or salami are good plain, with herbs or cheese.
- Canned tuna mixed with soft cheese and parsley are delicious in plain or soufflé omelettes. For a creamy version, make a little cheese sauce, add drained canned tuna, parsley and chives, then spoon this over the cooked omelette before serving.
- Top a thin, set omelette with shredded ham, chopped spring onions (scallions), tortilla chips and grated cheese. Sprinkle with dried chilli flakes, if liked, and grill (broil) until the cheese is bubbling.
- Sliced mixed red and green (bell) peppers are delicious with sliced olives and spring onions.
- Served with a side salad, an omelette can make a simple snack.
- Include lots of vegetables and serve the omelette with hot crusty bread, new potatoes, a spoonful of creamy mash or instant couscous for a substantial meal.

Soufflé omelette Energy 377kcal/1570kJ; Protein 19g; Carbohydrate 14.9g, of which sugars 14.8g; Fat 27g, of which saturates 9.2g; Cholesterol 405mg; Calcium 249mg; Fibre 0.3g; Sodium 648mg. Tortilla Energy 163kcal/682kJ; Protein 5.8g; Carbohydrate 14.7g, of which sugars 2.8g; Fat 9.5g, of which saturates 1.9g; Cholesterol 127mg; Calcium 32mg; Fibre 1.2g; Sodium 56mg.

Vegetables

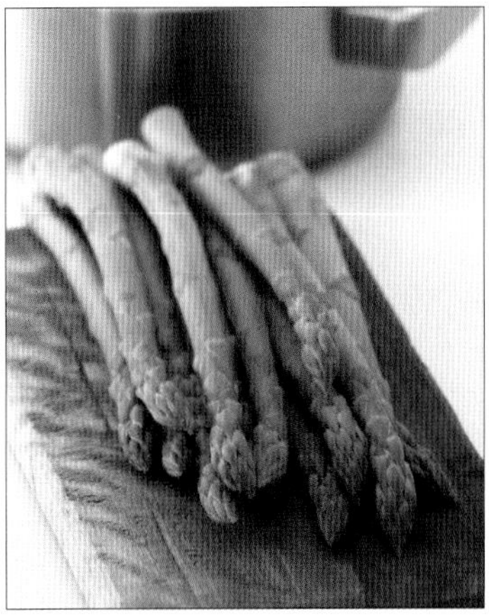

Vegetables are essential to our diet. They contribute colour and texture to our meals, making food visually appealing, even when cooked by the most basic of methods. They provide vital flavour to many savoury dishes as well as adding nutritional value. Imagine a casserole without an onion, even if only to flavour the stock or cooking liquid. Vegetables can be cooked by a whole host of methods, with each subtly affecting and adding to the taste of the dish.

Vegetable basics

Vegetables are the plants that we eat. They can be grouped by type. Root vegetables such as potatoes, carrots, turnips, swedes (rutabaga), beetroot (beet), sweet potatoes and celeriac all grow underground into bulbs and tubers. Leafy greens include cabbage, kale, spinach, broccoli, winter greens and Brussels sprouts. The onion family includes all edible plants in the *Allium* family such as onions, leeks and garlic. Vegetable fruits are botanically fruits, but are most often eaten as vegetables. They include cucumber, tomatoes, squash, aubergines (eggplants), pumpkins and bell peppers among others. Pods and seeds such as peas, beans, and corn are the final group.

Not only do vegetables make meals more interesting, they are also full of goodness. Vegetables are packed with essential nutrients, including vitamins and minerals, that are needed daily to keep the body functioning properly. Vegetables also contribute fibre, which is the indigestible part of food that helps to carry away waste products through the gut, keeping the system healthy and preventing constipation.

This general overview highlights just how good vegetables are – they are light, satisfying and bursting with lively flavours. They have an incredible 'feel-good' effect, allowing everyone to eat lots without feeling overfull and without consuming more calories than they may use up in regular activity. All ample reason for getting to know how to make the most of a wide variety of vegetables.

Above: Vegetables that are traditionally in season at the same time usually taste good together.

Below: Dark green leafy vegetables bring flavour, texture and essential food value to a meal so it makes sense to eat a good variety.

BUYING VEGETABLES

Follow these tips when buying vegetables. Avoid fresh vegetables that look limp, wrinkled, old, faded, discoloured, softened or spotted with signs of decay. This may seem like stating the obvious but inferior vegetables are not always that easily identified. Inspect loose vegetables by picking them up, turning them over and generally having a good look (without being rough). Look closely at prepacked vegetables for the same thing.

Onions should be dry and firm, with firm tip and root ends. Carrots, parsnips and other root vegetables should be dry and firm. Reject potatoes that show signs of sprouting or going green. Check pre-packed bags to make sure the contents are dry and not damaged. Gently feel along pre-packed cucumbers for any soft spots. Bell peppers, aubergines and tomatoes should be bright and firm. Broccoli and cauliflower should feel firm and have a good colour: yellowing broccoli is not worth having. Cauliflowers with little black spots should be rejected.

Cabbages, lettuces and any other leafy ingredients should be firm and/or crisp. Check the stalk ends.

Vegetables that are sold prepared – trimmed or washed and ready to eat – should look fresh. For example, slightly dry carrots or discoloured bean ends are not acceptable.

When buying from a market stall, make sure the produce you get is either from the display or equally as good (that is, not from a decaying box of vegetables at the back).

FROZEN VEGETABLES

Vegetables that have been frozen are just as good as fresh, if not better in terms of vitamin C content because they are frozen soon after harvesting when their vitamin content is at a peak. The nutrients are not destroyed by freezing. Plain frozen vegetables are easy to deal with, taste good and are perfect to store.

STORING VEGETABLES

The majority of vegetables should be stored in the refrigerator and the best way is to remove them from plastic bags and arrange them in plastic trays or baskets so that air can circulate. However, pre-packed sealed vegetables (especially those in rigid protective packs) and prepared vegetables should be left in their packet, for example asparagus, leeks celery, broccoli and cauliflower, salad leaves and chicory (Belgian endive).

Small packs of salad potatoes or baking potatoes, or small quantities of potatoes can be stored in an open container in the refrigerator for 1–2 weeks. If they are stored in plastic bags they quickly become sweaty, soft and bad. The best way to store maincrop potatoes is in a thick brown paper bag or small cardboard box in a cool, dark and dry place. They should not be in plastic or any other airtight container, or left in a warm light place where they will turn green and/or begin to sprout. Buy potatoes in quantities that will be used quickly – a large bag (multi-thick brown paper) is good for a family that uses potatoes every day (and when they have the right place to store them) but a waste for one or two people who use few potatoes only occasionally.

It is worth remembering that mashed potatoes freeze well for at least 6 months (and they can be thawed and reheated quickly in the microwave), so buying a large bag and having a cooking, mashing and freezing session can be practical and economical. Onions should be kept (unwrapped) in a dry, dark and cool place, such as a utility room or ventilated cupboard. However, if this is not an option, they can be unwrapped and kept in a container in the refrigerator for a week or two but they do not keep well as they tend to become wet and then begin to rot. Garlic is best in a ventilated clay pot in a dry cool place.

Bell peppers, aubergines (eggplants), tomatoes, courgettes (zucchini) and cucumber should all be unwrapped and are best if they are stored in a single layer. Leeks and spring onions (scallions) are best unwrapped and stored in a basket in the refrigerator. Brussels sprouts, cauliflower, greens, kale, cabbage, lettuces and salad leaves should be wrapped in plastic to prevent them from turning limp. Mushrooms sold loose and wrapped in a paper bag should be stored in the refrigerator for up to about 3 days, after which time they soon start to look past their best. Plastic containers of mushrooms should be left covered and used by the date on the pack. However, larger containers can be stored open in the refrigerator, where they will keep for up to 2 weeks.

PRESERVED VEGETABLES
Canned tomatoes, bell peppers and corn, tomato purées and pastes all make a useful, delicious and practical contribution to everyday meals.

Below: Cauliflower should be firm and creamy-white with fresh-looking leaves.

Below: Open-cap or closed, mushrooms should be firm and dry.

Below: Leeks should have bright green tops. Buy them in season.

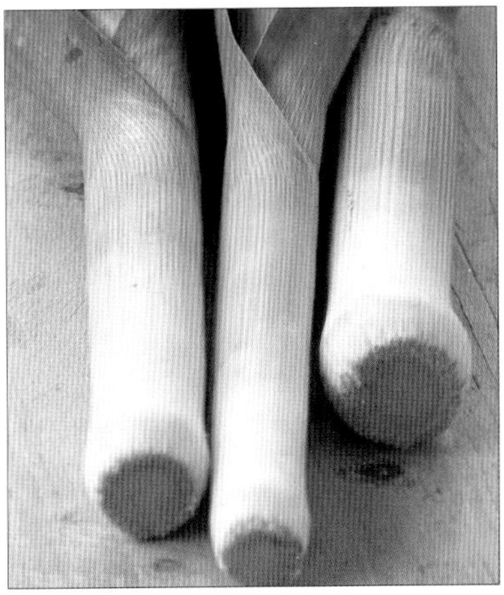

Preparing root vegetables

The most common root vegetables are potatoes, sweet potatoes, carrots, parsnips, beetroot (beet) and celeriac. Often associated with winter, although mostly available all year round, root vegetables are a staple part of many people's diet. Economical to buy and widely available, they add bulk to a dish, or when served as an accompaniment, and help to make us feel full for longer.

Root vegetables offer a wide range of flavours that can be enhanced by the cooking method. They are used to make or to thicken soups and stews. Served as a side dish, they can be cooked in a wide variety of ways such as boiled, steamed, stir-fried, fried, braised, mashed with other root vegetables, roasted and baked. In addition carrots and beetroot can be juiced and used in sweet dishes as well as savoury ones. Carrots can be grated for salads and eaten raw.

VEGETABLE PREPARATION

Root vegetables may be scrubbed, scraped or peeled according to type. Young, fine-skinned carrots, new or salad potatoes need no more than a good scrub to remove any dirt. Main crop or 'old' potatoes can also be cooked with their (cleaned) peel on, for example when baking or when cut into wedges and roasted. Many main crop potatoes have fairly fine skin, which also tastes perfectly good when boiled – to a large extent it is a matter of taste. Scraping is useful for potatoes with flaky peel, or for young carrots that are only slightly coarse outside. Parsnips are peeled because the skin can be quite tough. Beetroot is always cooked with its skin on, or the colour bleeds. Once cooked, the skin is removed. Swede (rutabaga), turnip and celeriac have thick skin that needs removing before cooking.

Once the vegetables are washed, scrubbed or peeled, the method of cooking will determine how each is chopped and to what size.

CLEANING ROOT VEGETABLES

Most vegetables bought loose or pre-packed from supermarkets are clean, so giving them a quick wash will be sufficient, if you are going to cook them with their skin on. Locally grown vegetables may still have some earth attached to them. Use a small brush with stiff bristles to scrub root vegetables. Remove any discoloured or green patches and cut out black eyes.

1 Brush off excess dirt with a dry brush before storing them. Before cooking, clean and remove any loose peel, using a small scrubbing brush or a scourer.

PEELING ROOT VEGETABLES

Much of the goodness and flavour of many vegetables is in the skin and just below it. Leave the skins on occasionally to give more taste and texture. It will also add a vital source of roughage and fibre to your diet.

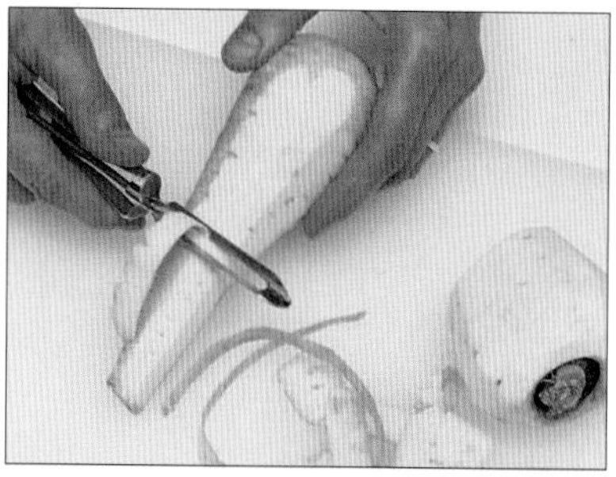

1 To peel vegetables use a potato peeler to remove the thinnest layer in long even strips. For long vegetables, such as carrots and parsnips, peel towards the wide end.

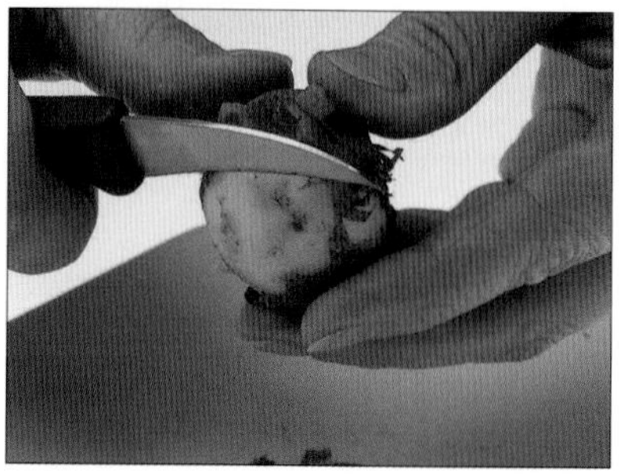

2 If the vegetables have very fine peel, use a small sharp knife to scrape away a thin layer of skin and rinse thoroughly under cold water. Once peeled, immediately place the vegetables in water so that they are just covered to prevent them from going black until ready to cook. Cook them immediately if you can to avoid any loss of vitamin C.

PEELING THICK-SKINNED ROOT VEGETABLES

Swede, turnip and celeriac have thick skin. A peeler is too fine for peeling these, so use a small sharp knife. This method of cutting off peel is also used for squash, pumpkin and marrow. When handling large vegetables, cut them in half first (down through the middle from stalk to root end), then place cut side down. Use a sharp, large knife for this task.

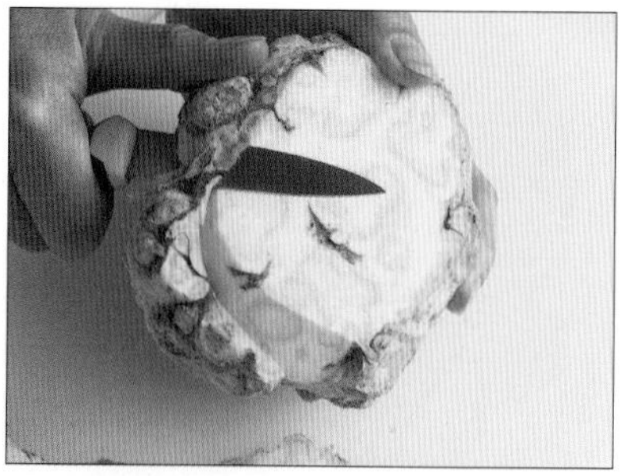

1 Trim off the top and bottom, then stand the vegetable on a board and cut off strips of peel from top to bottom. If the vegetable is tinged green, it has not been peeled thickly enough and will need another layer removing.

PREVENTING DISCOLORATION

Potatoes, parsnips and celeriac turn brown if exposed to air after peeling. Vegetables leech nutrients as soon as they are peeled, since many nutrients are contained in the skin or just under it, so peel vegetables as near to cooking them as possible.

1 Have a bowl or pan of cold water ready. To keep celeriac particularly white (for example, if it is to be used raw), add a good squeeze of lemon juice to make acidulated water.

CHOPPING CHUNKS

Potatoes, swede (rutabaga), turnip, celeriac and parsnip are chopped into chunks and boiled before being mashed or served cooked as chunks. The size of the chunk determines how quickly the vegetable is cooked. If you are cooking different types of vegetable together in the same pan, some will cook more quickly than others, so boil first those that take longest to cook and add the other vegetables to the cooking water later.

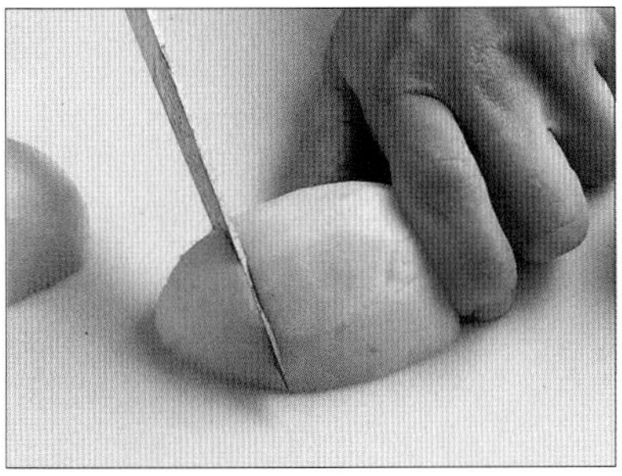

1 To chop chunks, cut the vegetable in half, then half again and again until it is cut up evenly, to the size required.

CHOPPING POTATO WEDGES

Potatoes and sweet potatoes can be cut into wedges to be roasted in oil.

1 Cut the potatoes in half lengthwise, then into long 1cm/½in wedges.

CUTTING CARROT RINGS

Cut carrots into thin rings to cook them quickly when steaming or boiling.

1 If the carrot is very long, cut the top, thicker end of it into slightly thinner slices than those cut from the root end.

DICING VEGETABLES

For casseroles, curries or quick cooking, root vegetables can be diced.

1 Cut into thick, even slices, then thick batons and finally into cubes.

CUTTING BATONS

Batons are thin strips of vegetable, which cook very quickly. Any root vegetable can be cut into batons.

1 Cut each vegetable lengthways into slices 6mm/¼in thick or less, guiding the side of the knife with your knuckles. Stack the slices and cut them lengthways into strips the same thickness.

MAKING HASSELBACK POTATOES

Hasselback potatoes look quite spiky when roasted to a crispy golden brown.

1 Peel, then slice two-thirds of the way through the potato. Use a skewer as a cutting guide. Brush with oil.

2 Roast in the oven, preheated to 190°C/375°F/Gas 5, for 40–50 minutes.

Cooking root vegetables

Root vegetables can be cooked in a wide variety of ways. Boiling and steaming vegetables are quick and easy methods. The plain cooked food can then be enhanced with a sprinkling of herbs and a knob (pat) of butter. Steaming is considered a healthier method than boiling, since vegetables cooked this way retain more nutrients. The boiled or steamed vegetables can then be mashed with other vegetables and butter or oil added to slacken the mixture.

Vegetables can be roasted in the oven. The fat used in the cooking tin (pan) adds flavour and the long cooking time helps to bring out the natural flavour of the vegetables. Potatoes can also be baked whole in their skins at a high temperature, then filled with any number of delicious ingredients.

BOILING TIMES FOR ROOT VEGETABLES

Potatoes	Minutes
Large chunks	about 20
Medium chunks	about 15
Small, salad or new	10–15
Dice	10–15
Carrots	
Large, whole	15–20
Large, halved or quartered	10–15
Small whole	5–10
Sliced	3–5
Parsnips	
Small to medium, whole	about 10
Halved or quartered	about 5
Swede (rutabaga) or celeriac	
Chunks	10–15
Turnips	
Small, whole	15–20
Jerusalem artichokes	
Whole, thoroughly scrubbed with skin on	15–20
Beetroot (beet)	
Whole small	30
Whole large	40–60

BOILING ROOT VEGETABLES

This is the simplest way of cooking root vegetables. Place similar size pieces of vegetables, with or without skins (sweet potatoes are best cooked in their skins to retain their bright colour) in a pan with sufficient water just to cover them. Small salad and new potatoes can be cooked whole.

1 Place the vegetables in a large pan. Sprinkle over 5–10ml/1–2 tsp salt or to taste, cover with a tight-fitting lid and bring slowly to the boil. Leave to gently boil until the centres of the vegetables are soft, or according to preference. To test, press the point of a sharp knife into the centre of the vegetable; if the knife can be inserted easily the vegetable is cooked. If vegetables are overcooked they have a soggy texture and fall apart.

2 Drain the vegetables in a colander in the sink and give them a shake to ensure all the water drains away.

3 Transfer to a warmed serving dish or plates. Add a knob of butter to the serving dish.

MASHING BOILED VEGETABLES

There are a few simple but vital tips for getting really good mashed or creamed vegetables. Potatoes, carrots, swede (rutabaga), parsnips and celeriac are all perfect contenders for mashing. Mix potato with any one or two of the others, or try carrot with swede, celeriac with carrot, or parsnips with carrot and/or swede. Vegetables to be mashed together can be boiled together, but if some take longer to cook than others, they need to be cut in smaller pieces (or cooked separately). For example, to cook potatoes and parsnips, cut the parsnips into large chunks and potatoes into small chunks; cut carrots and swede into smaller pieces than potato, so they cook evenly.

1 Drain the boiled vegetables well and return them to the pan. Dry them out for a few seconds over heat, then take off the heat and mash with a masher.

2 Add crushed white pepper with butter, or black pepper with olive oil and mash this in. Then stir in a little milk to soften the mixture to the required texture. Mash in all directions.

ROASTING TIMES FOR ROOT VEGETABLES

Parsnips Peel and cut into chunks. Blanch in boiling salted water for 10 minutes. Dry, then roast in butter or oil in the oven for 40 minutes at 400°F/200°C/Gas 6.
Swede (rutabaga) Peel and cut into chunks or sticks. Coat in oil. Roast in the oven for 45 minutes at 400°F/200°C/Gas 6.
Potatoes Peel and cut into chunks. Blanch in boiling salted water for 1–2 minutes. Dry, then roast in butter or oil in the oven for 1–1½ hours at 400°F/200°C/Gas 6.

STEAMING ROOT VEGETABLES

Some root vegetables steam well. Small potatoes, such as new potatoes, steamed in their skins, taste delicious.

1 Place the prepared vegetables in a steamer over a deep pan of boiling water. Cover tightly and steam for 5–7 minutes if sliced or cut small, increasing the time to 20 minutes or more if you are cooking large pieces of vegetables such as potatoes.

STEAMING TIMES FOR ROOT VEGETABLES

Baby carrots	10 minutes
Carrot rings	7 minutes
Turnip cubes	15 minutes
Swede (rutabaga)	9–12 minutes
Celeriac cubes	5–10 minutes

ROASTING ROOT VEGETABLES

Potatoes, sweet potatoes, carrots, beetroot (beet) and parsnips can all be roasted in fat in the oven.

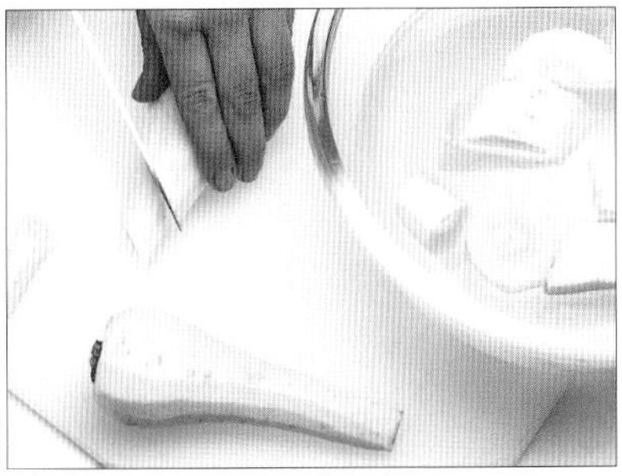

1 Prepare, chop and boil the vegetables for 10 minutes, until half cooked, then drain well and return to the pan to dry off on the heat.

2 Pour a shallow layer of fat into a roasting pan and place in the oven for 5–10 minutes, until very hot. The fat from roast meat, beef dripping, duck or goose fat makes delicious roast potatoes, or use sunflower oil. Toss the vegetables in the hot fat until coated and roast for about 1 hour, until crisp and brown.

3 To cook new or salad potatoes, or just small evenly sized old potatoes, place the potatoes in a roasting pan or ovenproof dish and drizzle with a little sunflower oil or olive oil or a mixture of both. Add rock salt, if you like. A sprig of rosemary or thyme adds flavour. Roll the potatoes to coat them evenly.

4 Put in the oven at 220°C/425°F/Gas 7 and cook for 45 minutes, turning once or twice, until crisp and golden.

DEEP- AND SHALLOW-FRYING VEGETABLES

Cooked or part-cooked, root vegetables all taste good shallow-fried. Deep-fried potato chips are a favourite with everyone.

1 To shallow-fry: heat 25g/1oz/2 tbsp butter and 30ml/2 tbsp oil until bubbling. Slice or grate the chosen vegetable such as potatoes, carrot and turnip. Cook for 4–5 minutes, until golden below, then turn and cook the other side.

2 To deep-fry: cut potatoes into sticks. Rinse and dry. Fry in oil heated to 375°F/190°C until beginning to colour: 3–8 minutes. Drain on kitchen paper, then fry again for 3 minutes until crisp.

SHALLOW-FRYING TIMES FOR ROOT VEGETABLES

Parsnips Peel and cut into chunks. Blanch in boiling salted water for 1–2 minutes. Fry in butter for 10–12 minutes.
Potatoes Peel and cut into chunks. Cook in boiling salted water for 7–8 minutes. Fry in butter until golden.

DEEP-FRYING TIMES FOR ROOT VEGETABLES

Potatoes Peel and cut into sticks (chips). Soak, drain and pat dry. Fry until golden in oil heated to 375°F/190°C for approximately 20 minutes, according to size.

Preparing and cooking greens

Green leafy vegetables should be used quickly, because the longer they are kept the more the nutritional value leaches away. Brassicas and leafy greens are used to accompany meat or fish, are added to stir-fries and soups, or are used to wrap other foods into parcels. Like root vegetables, they can be steamed and boiled. They can also be braised and added to stir-fries.

PEELING OUTER LEAVES AND REMOVING STALKS

A few basic preparation guidelines apply to the whole group.

1 Trim off damaged leaves, stem ends and tough stalks. Discard the root ends and separate leaves or hold them apart to wash out dirt. Handle tender leaves with care as they bruise easily, becoming limp and losing flavour. Remove the outer leaves and stalk.

SHREDDING LEAVES

This method is ideal for boiling, steaming, braising or stir-frying.

1 Shred cabbage and sturdy leaves so that they cook quickly and evenly.

USING SINGLE LEAVES

Use single leaves in the same way as shredded leaves.

1 Peel away single leaves.

PREPARING BROCCOLI AND CAULIFLOWER

Vegetables with large heads are cut into smaller florets to speed cooking time.

1 Remove any outer leaves and cut away the thick stalk from the base. Pull or cut the florets from the main head of the vegetable.

2 To prepare a cauliflower to cook it whole, slice off or scoop out some of the thick stalk with a small knife.

PREPARING BRUSSELS SPROUTS

Fiddly to prepare but worth the effort.

1 Trim off any damaged parts, then cut a cross in the bottom of each stalk so that the stalk end cooks quickly.

PREPARING ASPARAGUS

A late spring vegetable with minimal preparation requirements.

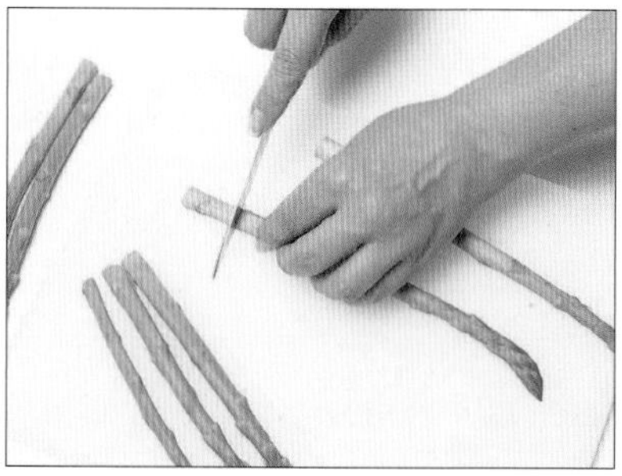

1 Trim off the wood ends from asparagus (use them to flavour stock) and peel the thicker end of the stem if it is tough outside.

2 Scrub edible stalks, which may harbour dirt. Trim off tough ribs or slightly bruised patches and rinse well.

STIR-FRYING VEGETABLES

Cabbage, broccoli or cauliflower, thinly sliced celery, fennel, or Brussels sprouts taste excellent stir-fried with spring onions (scallions).

1 Heat a little sunflower oil in a wok, large frying pan or sauté pan (with deep sides), then add the vegetables – start with sliced onion or leek and a crushed garlic clove, then add the shredded greens or other prepared vegetables.

2 Cook, stirring all the time, over medium to high heat. Keep the pan hot enough for the vegetables to sizzle constantly. Stir and turn to prevent the pieces from browning unevenly. When cooked, the vegetables should be tender but not soft and soggy.

STEAMING AND BOILING VEGETABLES

This is a quick, easy and healthy way to cook vegetables.

1 Place the vegetables in a steamer over a pan of boiling water. If you are boiling vegetables instead, place the prepared vegetables in a pan of boiling water with salt. Replace the lid. Bring to the boil and simmer gently.

BRAISING VEGETABLES

This is a good cooking method for all sorts of vegetables. It is a mixture of cooking in a little butter or oil to start with, then adding just a little liquid, which may be water, stock or wine, and simmering gently in the covered pan. The liquid provides some moisture without being deep enough to boil the vegetables. The liquid is also served as a sauce or dressing when cooked. The ingredients should be stirred once or twice during cooking so that they cook evenly. Onion and/or garlic may be cooked in the oil or butter and herbs, such as bay leaves, thyme, rosemary or sage, may be added.

1 Cut the prepared vegetables into short lengths or even slices.

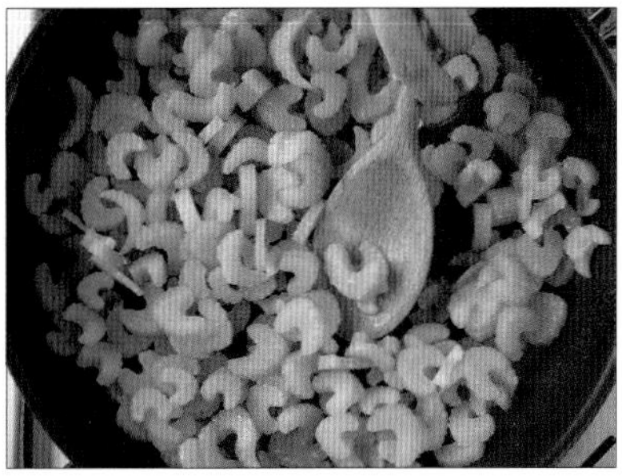

2 Cook the vegetables in a knob of butter for a minute, then add about 30ml/2 tbsp stock or wine. The butter and stock both add valuable flavour to the cooked vegetable.

3 Bring to the boil, reduce the heat and cover the pan. Cook very gently for 3–5 minutes for slices or 10–20 minutes for larger pieces. The vegetables should be soft and flavourful.

STEAMING TIMES FOR VEGETABLES

Leafy greens	2–3 minutes
Cauliflower	6–7 minutes
Broccoli	6–7 minutes
Asparagus	7–10 minutes
Brussels sprouts	5–10 minutes

PREPARING AND COOKING MUSHROOMS

Mushrooms are technically a fungi rather than a vegetable, but they are cooked and eaten as vegetables. They have a soft dense texture and quite a range of subtle flavours depending on the variety chosen. Button (white) mushrooms are the small closed type; closed cap are larger but still without any gap around the stalks; open cap have central stalks and wide caps; they have a dark or slightly paler section underneath.

1 Wipe mushrooms with a damp paper towel. Trim gritty stalks. Small ones can be left whole; larger ones are cut up.

2 Fry in a little butter and/or oil for about 4 minutes or until tender, stirring. The mushrooms will give up liquid: boil to evaporate this and concentrate the flavour.

3 To grill (broil) mushrooms, drizzle them with a little melted butter or oil. Grill stalk side first, turning and basting occasionally, for 5–8 minutes or until tender.

Preparing and cooking the onion family

Onions, leeks, spring onions (scallions), garlic and chives are all incredibly versatile. Finely chopped, cut into chunks, sliced or shredded, these foods can be fried in butter and oil, or roasted whole or in chunks in the oven.

PEELING AND CHOPPING ONIONS

Strong in flavour and aroma, onions add taste to food.

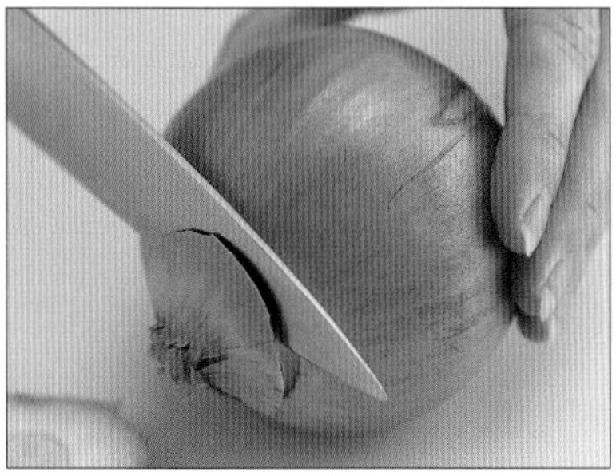

1 Cut off the top and bottom of the onion. Slit the skin and peel it off.

2 To cut onion rings, turn the onion on its side. Use a sharp knife to cut rings.

3 To finely chop an onion, chop in half, then cut in each direction.

TRIMMING, CLEANING AND SLICING LEEKS

Particles of soil can easily become trapped inbetween the leaf layers of a leek. Baby leeks and tight ready-trimmed leeks from the supermarket are unlikely to be very gritty. Leeks fresh from the garden or some markets always need to be washed thoroughly to remove the grit between the layers.

For chunky, long-cooked stews, cut thick slices. Medium slices are best for soups or casseroles.

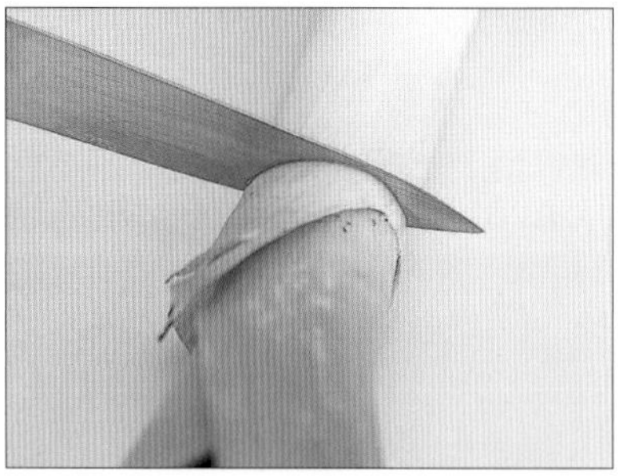

1 Trim off most of the loose green leaves or slice them up thinly width-ways. Discard any loose green leaves but unless the recipe specifies the white part of the leek only, do not waste the green part. Trim off the excess root.

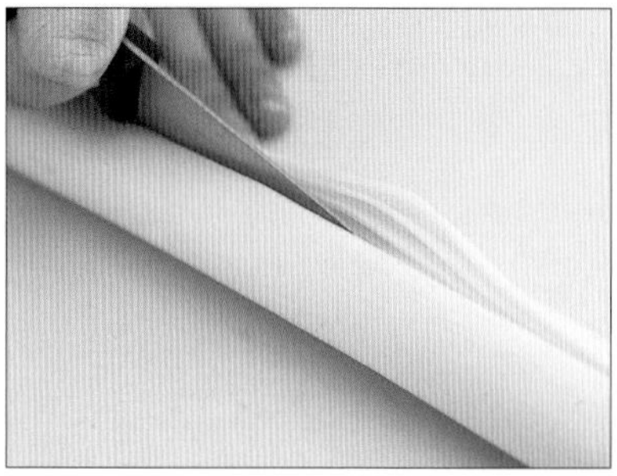

2 Alternatively, slit the leek, starting about 2.5cm/1in from the base, to the top, cutting through the centre. Wash the leek under cold running water, fanning out the layers with your fingers to make sure you wash away all the dirt. Hold the leek so that the water runs from the base to the top, so dirt will not be washed back into the leaves.

3 Cut the leek in half vertically, from top to root. Place cut side down.

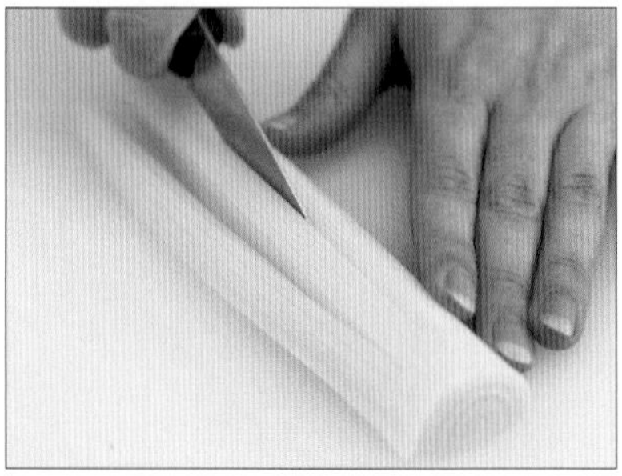

4 Make a series of cuts along the length of the leek from bottom to top leaving the root end intact. Cut across the leek and it will fall apart into pieces.

5 For stews or casseroles, cut across to the required thickness, straight or at an angle, using a very sharp knife. Slicing at an angle exposes a larger surface area of leek to the heat, ensuring that it cooks quickly. Thin or very fine slices can be separated into rings.

WATERY EYES

The stronger and juicier the onion, the more it will make you cry. Small onions are stronger than large mild ones. Shallots and garlic, though, contain less water, so produce less vapour and hence fewer tears. Leeks are very mild and hardly ever cause tears during preparation. There are many suggestions for how to avoid watery eyes but few work.

PEELING AND CUTTING GARLIC

The taste of garlic can vary depending on how it is prepared. Garlic can be overpowering, and the finer you chop or crush it, the stronger the flavour will be.

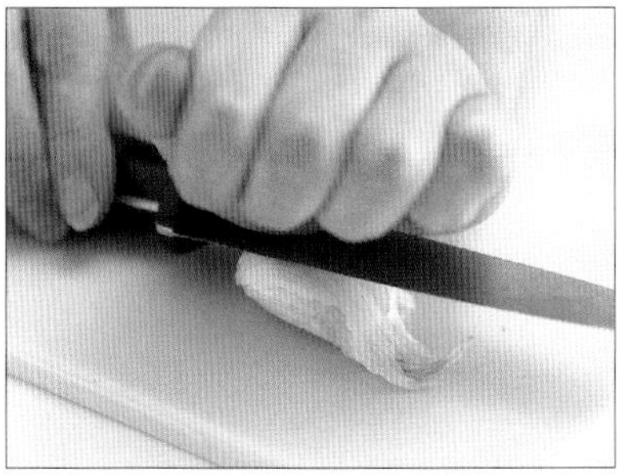

1 To skin garlic, place the blade of the knife flat on the clove or bulb and press down with the heel of your hand to break the garlic skin. The skin will peel off easily. This also bruises the garlic, which allows the flavour to come out. Remove any green shoots.

2 For a mild flavour, cut the garlic into thin slices across the clove.

3 For maximum garlic flavour, press the skinned clove through the garlic press or crusher.

TRIMMING SPRING ONIONS

Spring onions (scallions) can be sliced into rings and stir-fried, or eaten raw.

1 Trim off the top of the green leaves. Slice off the roots. Remove any damaged leaf wrappings.

FRYING ONIONS

Gentle frying in butter or oil softens onions. Use them as the base for soups, stews and casseroles.

1 Fry finely chopped onions in butter until soft. Stir frequently.

SWEATING LEEKS

This is a flavourful way of cooking leeks.

1 Fry leek rounds in butter, in a pan with a lid, for 6 minutes on each side.

ROASTING ONIONS

Onions are delicious roasted, either in their skins, which will produce a juicy centre, or they can be skinned and chopped into chunks, which produces a more caramelized taste. Red onions look appealing, but large, mild, ordinary onions become deliciously succulent.

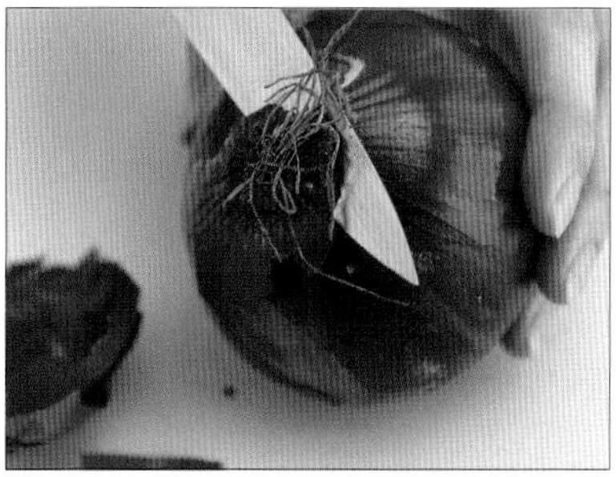

1 Remove any damaged skin and cut off excess root, leaving the base intact.

2 Brush with oil, if you like, then roast at 190°C/375°F/Gas 5 for about 1–1½ hours, until soft when gently squeezed.

3 To serve, cut a cross in the top and add butter or cheese. A flavoured butter, for example with herbs or chilli, is especially good.

Preparing and cooking vegetable fruits

There are many vegetables that are technically the 'fruit' of the plant, for example, aubergines (egglants), courgettes (zucchini) and avocados, or pods containing fruit, such as green beans or various types of peas. The range is broad, so these guidelines are general. The extent to which vegetables should be cooked is also a matter for personal taste.

PREPARING BEANS OR PEAS

Beans and peas taste best when they are fresh and in season.

1 Preparation is quite easy for all of these pods. Top and tail the pods of sugarsnap peas, mangetouts (snowpeas), and all small beans such as runner (green) beans, Mangetouts or sugarsnap peas sometimes have a string down the rib that needs to be pulled off. Slice larger beans such as runner beans into pieces about 2.5–5cm (1–2in) long.

2 Shell peas and broad (fava) beans. If the vegetable inside is ripe it will come away easily from the pod.

PREPARING THE SQUASH FAMILY

Minimal preparation is all that is required to prepare courgettes. Cut off the stalk ends and slice as specified in the recipe. Squashes need peeling and seeds removing.

1 Peel squashes but not aubergines and courgettes.

2 Halve squashes or pumpkins and scoop out the seeds and fibrous middle.

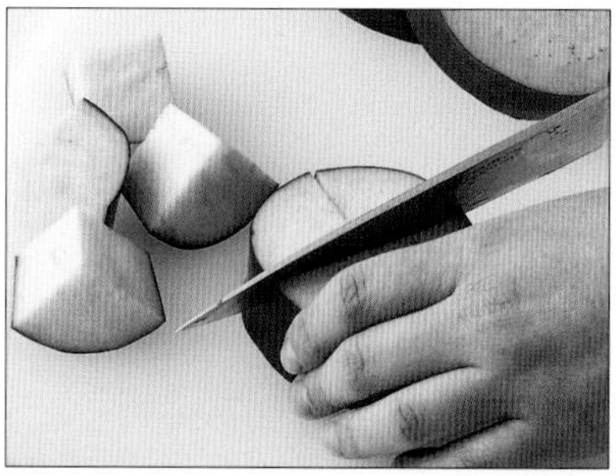

3 Aubergines and courgettes can be cut into large or small pieces; sometimes they may be cooked whole or cut in half, for example by baking. They do not need sprinkling with salt.

PREPARING CORN

Fresh or frozen corn on the cob is a meal in itself, brushed with salty butter or olive oil. Remove all the outer leaves. Bring a pan of salted water to the boil and add the corn. Bring the water back up to the boil and boil for 8–10 minutes for fresh corn, and according to the packet instructions for frozen corn.

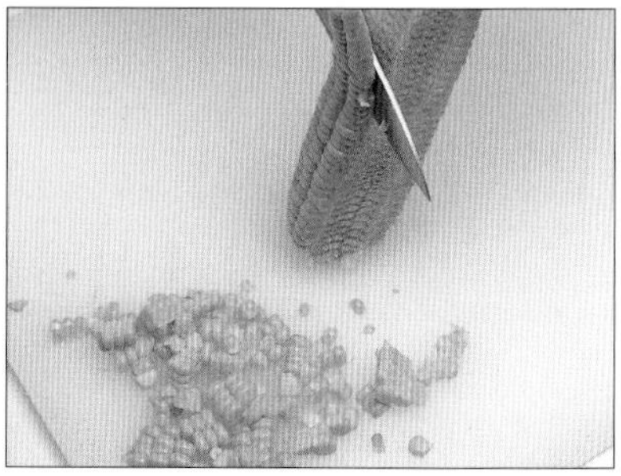

1 To remove the kernels from the cob, use a sharp knife and work with one end of the corn on the work surface. Scrape the kernels from the cob.

PEELING TOMATOES

Tomatoes are sometimes peeled to remove tough skin.

1 Slit a shallow cross in the base of each tomato. Place the tomatoes in a bowl and pour on boiling water to cover. Leave to stand for 45–60 seconds: ripe tomatoes need short soaking. Lift out the tomatoes using a slotted spoon and wait until cool enough to handle. If the tomatoes have soaked for long enough the skin will peel off easily.

FRYING VEGETABLE FRUITS

Shallow-frying in a little olive oil or butter is a good cooking method for fairly finely-cut vegetables, such as sliced or diced courgettes (zucchini) or aubergines (eggplants). It is not necessary to peel either vegetable as their peel contains a lot of their flavour. Turn or stir them frequently during cooking over medium to medium-high heat.

1 Large slices of aubergine have to be fried a few at a time so that they fit in the pan, and turned halfway through cooking to cook evenly. They absorb a lot of oil, so add more as necessary unless a dry-fried result is required, in which case use a good non-stick pan.

BOILING OR STEAMING BEANS OR PEAS

Trimmed whole, cut or sliced, beans, mangetouts (snow peas) or sugarsnap peas, fresh or frozen peas, and shelled broad (fava) beans all cook well by boiling or steaming.

1 Bring a pan of water to the boil, add the vegetables and bring the water back to the boil. Reduce the heat and part-cover the pan. Cook until tender.

GRILLING (BROILING) VEGETABLES

This is useful for courgettes, bell peppers, aubergines, tomatoes and mushrooms (start with the curved sides up, turning so the stalk sides are on top for the second half of the cooking time).

1 Cut the prepared vegetables into pieces that are evenly thick for grilling, slices, halves or wedges. The thickness is important because the pieces have to be thin enough to cook through without falling apart. If the slices are thick at one end and thin at the other, the thin areas will be further away from the heat than the thick ends, so the pieces will not cook evenly.

2 For a succulent but 'dry' result, arrange the vegetables on a rack and brush with oil, then place under the preheated grill (broiler). Cook under a medium heat until browned on one side, turn, brush with more oil and cook until browned on the second side. Vegetables can be cooked on a foil-lined grill pan to collect the cooking juices – this works well for thinly sliced mixed peppers, button (white) mushrooms or sliced courgettes. The cooking juices can be served spooned over the vegetables.

ROASTING MIXED VEGETABLES

Prepared peppers, courgettes, aubergines, onions and mushrooms can be roasted together successfully as the base for a delicious main dish. You could add cut up root vegetables, but part boil them first for a few minutes because they take longer to roast.

1 Simply toss your choice of vegetables with some olive oil, add a few sliced skinned garlic cloves and a couple of fresh bay leaves. Sprigs of thyme, marjoram or rosemary also go well. Sprinkle with fennel seeds or crushed coriander for a hint of spice.

2 Roast them at 220°C/425°F/ Gas 7, turning with a fish slice or metal spatula once or twice. They are ready when tender and well browned, or even beginning to char a touch along the edges – this takes about 30–40 minutes, depending on the temperature and size of vegetables.

GRILLING (BROILING) TIMES FOR VEGETABLE FRUITS

Each side	Minutes
Courgettes (zucchini)	10–15
Aubergines (eggplants)	10–15
Tomatoes (halved)	3–6

STEAMING TIMES FOR VEGETABLE FRUITS

Mangetouts (snowpeas)	2–3
Sugarsnap peas	2–3
Broad (fava) beans	6–7
Green beans, sliced	4–5

Carrot and coriander soup

Soups are easy to make and a good way to use up vegetables. The preparation time is spent chopping the vegetables. Carrot and coriander are a good flavour combination, and this is one of the most popular soup recipes – perfect for everyday eating. Serve with crusty bread.

Serves four

450g/1lb carrots, preferably young and tender
15ml/1 tbsp sunflower oil
40g/1½oz/3 tbsp butter
1 onion, chopped
1 stick celery, plus 2–3 pale leafy tops
2 small potatoes
900ml/1½ pints/3¾ cups vegetable or chicken stock
10ml/2 tsp ground coriander
15ml/1 tbsp chopped fresh coriander (cilantro)
150ml/¼ pint/⅔ cup milk
salt and ground black pepper

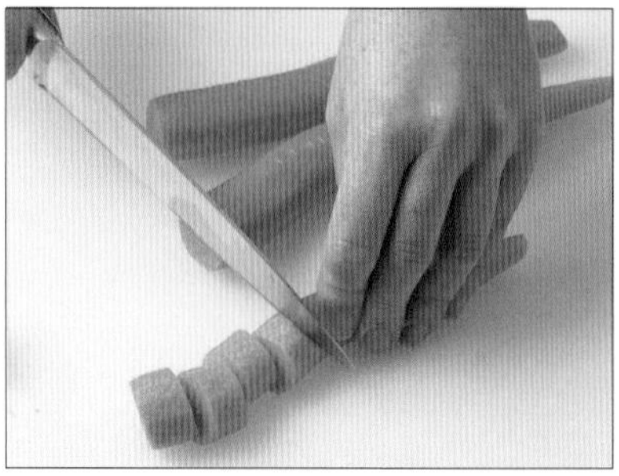

1 Trim and peel the carrots and cut into chunks. Heat the oil and two-thirds of the butter in a pan and fry the onion over medium heat for 3–4 minutes until slightly softened but not brown.

2 Slice the celery and chop the potatoes. Add the celery, potatoes and carrot to the onion and cook for a further 5 minutes, stirring occasionally.

3 Pour in the stock and bring to the boil. Reduce the heat, cover the pan and simmer the soup for about 30 minutes, or until the vegetables are soft.

4 Reserve 6–8 tiny celery leaves from the leafy tops for the garnish, then finely chop the remaining celery tops. Melt the remaining butter in a frying pan and add the ground coriander. Fry for about 1 minute, stirring constantly.

5 Reduce the heat under the pan and add the chopped celery tops and fresh coriander. Fry for about 30 seconds, then remove the pan from the heat.

6 Ladle the soup into a food processor or blender and process until smooth. Pour the soup back into the pan, add the celery tops and coriander. Stir in the milk and heat gently without boiling. Taste for seasoning and add salt and pepper, then serve garnished with the reserved celery leaves.

COOK'S TIP
The amount of salt and pepper to add depends on the type of stock used as well as personal taste.

Energy 168Kcal/697kJ; Protein 3g; Carbohydrate 11.9g, of which sugars 9.2g; Fat 12.4g, of which saturates 6g; Cholesterol 24mg; Calcium 94mg; Fibre 3.1g; Sodium 758mg.

Roasted root vegetable soup

This is a more complex soup involving another cooking stage, but well worth it because roasted vegetables gives a wonderful depth of flavour to soup. You can add other vegetables, such as pumpkin, or use chicken or ham stock in place of vegetable stock. Serve with brown bread.

Serves six

50ml/2fl oz/¼ cup olive oil
1 small butternut squash, seeded and cubed
2 carrots, cut into thick rounds
1 large parsnip, cubed
1 small swede (rutabaga), cubed
2 leeks, thickly sliced
1 onion, quartered
3 bay leaves
4 thyme sprigs, plus extra to garnish
3 rosemary sprigs
1.2 litres/2 pints/5 cups vegetable stock
salt and ground black pepper
soured cream, to serve

1 Preheat the oven to 200°C/400°F/Gas 6. Put the olive oil into a large bowl. Add the prepared vegetables and toss until coated in the oil.

2 Spread out the vegetables in a single layer on one large or two small baking sheets. Tuck the bay leaves, thyme and rosemary sprigs among the vegetables.

COOK'S TIP

This nutritious soup is good for cold days. The root vegetables contain filling carbohydrates that will help to make you feel full for longer. Make a batch and freeze any leftovers in portions, once it has gone cold. Label each with the soup name and date of freezing.

3 Roast the vegetables for about 50 minutes until tender, turning them occasionally to make sure they brown evenly. Remove from the oven, discard the herbs and transfer the vegetables to a large pan.

Variation

Dried herbs can be used in place of fresh; use 2.5ml/½ tsp of each type.

4 Pour the stock into the pan and bring to the boil. Reduce the heat, season to taste, and then simmer for 10 minutes. Transfer the soup to a food processor or blender (or use a hand blender) and process for a few minutes until thick and smooth.

5 Return the soup to the pan to heat through. Season and serve with a swirl of soured cream. Garnish each serving with a sprig of thyme.

Energy 134kcal/563kJ; Protein 3g; Carbohydrate 17.2g, of which sugars 11.3g; Fat 6.5g, of which saturates 0.9g; Cholesterol 0mg; Calcium 96mg; Fibre 5.2g; Sodium 160mg.

Garlicky roasties

Potatoes roasted in their skins retain a deep, earthy taste (and absorb less fat, too) while the garlic mellows on cooking to give a pungent but not overly-strong taste to serve alongside or squeezed over as a garnish. Serve with a traditional roast joint.

Serves four

1kg/2¼lb small floury potatoes
60–75ml/4–5 tbsp sunflower oil
10ml/2 tsp walnut oil
2 whole garlic bulbs, skins left on
salt

1 Preheat the oven to 220°C/425°F/ Gas 7. Place the potatoes in a pan of cold water and bring to the boil. Drain.

2 Combine the oils in a roasting pan and place in the oven to get really hot.

3 Add the potatoes and garlic and coat in oil. Roast for 45 minutes until golden.

Energy 312kcal/1310kJ; Protein 6.2g; Carbohydrate 44.3g, of which sugars 3.7g; Fat 13.4g, of which saturates 1.7g; Cholesterol 0mg; Calcium 20mg; Fibre 3.5g; Sodium 29mg.

Roast potatoes

Goose fat gives the best flavour to roast potatoes and is now widely available in supermarkets. However, if you can't find goose fat, or you want to make a vegetarian version, use a knob of butter or 15ml/1 tbsp olive oil instead. Serve as an accompaniment to a roast.

Serves four

675g/1½lb floury potatoes
30ml/2 tbsp goose fat
12 garlic cloves, skins left on
salt and ground black pepper

1 Preheat the oven to 190°C/375°F/ Gas 5.

2 Cut the potatoes into large chunks and cook in a pan of salted, boiling water for 5 minutes. Drain well and give the colander a good shake to fluff up the edges of the potatoes.

3 Return the potatoes to the pan and place it over a low heat for 1 minute to steam off any excess water. Shake the pan so the potatoes don't stick.

4 Spoon the goose fat into a roasting pan and place in the oven until hot, about 5 minutes.

5 Add the potatoes with the garlic and turn to coat in the fat. Season well and roast for 40–50 minutes, turning occasionally, until the potatoes are golden, crispy and tender inside.

Energy 114kcal/477kJ; Protein 3g; Carbohydrate 12.6g, of which sugars 3.1g; Fat 6.1g, of which saturates 0.8g; Cholesterol 0mg; Calcium 67mg; Fibre 4.3g; Sodium 114mg.

Bubble and squeak

Whether you have leftovers or cook this old-fashioned classic from fresh, be sure to give the potatoes and vegetables a really good 'squeak' in the pan so the mix turns a rich honey brown. Serve with grilled pork chops or fried eggs, or simply serve with warm bread for a quick supper.

Serves four

60ml/4 tbsp bacon fat or vegetable oil
1 onion, finely chopped
450g/1lb floury potatoes, cooked and mashed
225g/8oz cooked cabbage or Brussels sprouts, finely chopped

1 Heat 30ml/2 tbsp of the bacon fat or oil in a frying pan.

2 Add the onion and cook over a medium heat, stirring frequently, until softened but not browned. This will take about 5 minutes or longer – do not rush it if you want a mellow flavour.

3 In a large bowl, mix together the potatoes and cooked cabbage or sprouts and season to taste.

4 Add the potato mix to the onions, stir well, then press into a large, even cake. Cook over a medium heat for 15 minutes, until the cake is browned underneath.

5 Turn the cake out on to a plate. Return the pan to the heat and add the remaining bacon fat or oil. When hot, slide the cake back into the pan, browned side uppermost. Cook for 10 minutes, or until the underside is golden brown. Serve hot, in wedges.

Energy 306kcal/1273kJ; Protein 5.2g; Carbohydrate 45.5g, of which sugars 0.5g; Fat 11.2g, of which saturates 4g; Cholesterol 3mg; Calcium 17mg; Fibre 0.7g; Sodium 41mg.

Oven-roast wedges

This easy alternative to fried chips tastes as good and is much easier to cook. Cut the potatoes into relatively thin sticks or go for great big wedges and allow a little extra cooking time. To save washing up, lay non-stick baking parchment in the roasting pan, but don't preheat it.

Serves four to six

olive oil
4 medium to large baking potatoes
5ml/1 tsp mixed dried herbs (optional)
sea salt flakes
mayonnaise, to serve

1 Preheat the oven to the highest temperature, 240°C/475°F/Gas 9.

2 Lightly oil a large shallow roasting pan and place it in the oven to get really hot while you prepare the potatoes.

3 Cut the potatoes in half and then into long thin wedges. Rinse and dry the potatoes on a dish towel, then place in a bowl or plastic bag and toss in a little oil to coat them evenly.

4 When the oven is really hot, remove the pan carefully and scatter the potato wedges over it, spreading them out in a single layer over the hot oil.

5 Sprinkle with the herbs and salt and roast for about 20 minutes, until golden brown. Remove from the oven and serve with a dollop of mayonnaise.

Energy 377kcal/1589kJ; Protein 6.7g; Carbohydrate 58.9g, of which sugars 2.9g; Fat 14.4g, of which saturates 3.5g; Cholesterol 5mg; Calcium 24mg; Fibre 3.8g; Sodium 30mg.

Garlic mashed potatoes

These creamy mashed potatoes are delicious with all kinds of roast or sautéed meats as well as vegetarian main dishes and although it seems as if a lot of garlic is added, the flavour turns sweet and subtle when cooked in this way. The mash is fabulous with poached eggs.

Serves six to eight

3 whole garlic bulbs, separated into cloves, skins left on
115g/4oz/8 tbsp unsalted (sweet) butter
1.5kg/3lb baking potatoes, quartered
120–175ml/4–6fl oz/½–¾ cup milk
salt and ground white pepper

1 Preheat the oven to 200°C/400°F/ Gas 6.

2 Bring a small pan of water to the boil over a high heat. Add two-thirds of the garlic cloves and boil for 2 minutes. Drain and skin the garlic cloves. Place the remaining garlic cloves in a roasting tin (pan) and bake for 30–40 minutes.

COOK'S TIP

Instead of roasting the garlic, peel the cloves and cook them gently in a pan of melted butter until soft and golden.

3 In a heavy frying pan, melt half of the butter over a low heat. Add the blanched garlic cloves, then cover and cook gently for 20–25 minutes until very tender and just golden, shaking the pan and stirring occasionally. Do not allow the garlic to scorch or brown.

4 Remove from the heat and cool. Spoon the garlic and melted butter into a blender or a food processor fitted with a metal blade, and process until smooth. Tip into a bowl, press clear film (plastic wrap) on to the surface to prevent a skin forming and set aside.

5 Cook the potatoes in boiling, salted water until tender, then drain and press through a sieve (strainer) into the pan. Return the pan to a medium heat and, using a wooden spoon, stir the potatoes for 1–2 minutes to dry them out. Remove the pan from the heat.

6 Warm the milk over a medium-high heat until bubbles form around the edge. Gradually beat the milk and remaining butter and garlic purée into the potatoes. Season, and serve hot, with the roasted garlic cloves on the side or sprinkled on top.

Energy 261kcal/1093kJ; Protein 5g; Carbohydrate 33.3g, of which sugars 3.8g; Fat 12.8g, of which saturates 7.9g; Cholesterol 32mg; Calcium 43mg; Fibre 2.4g; Sodium 118mg.

Irish mashed potatoes

Simple but unbelievably tasty, this traditional Irish way with mashed potatoes makes an excellent companion for a hearty stew of lamb or beef. When it is not accompanying a hearty main dish, it is scrumptious topped with crumbled blue cheese, with a salad on the side.

Serves four

900g/2lb potatoes
1 small bunch spring onions (scallions), finely chopped
150ml/¼ pint/⅔ cup milk
50g/2oz/4 tbsp butter
salt and ground black pepper

1 Cut the potatoes up into chunks. Place in a large pan and cook in boiling water for 15–20 minutes or until tender.

2 Meanwhile, put the spring onions into a pan with the milk. Bring to the boil, then reduce the heat and simmer for about 5 minutes, stirring occasionally, until the spring onions are just tender.

3 Drain the potatoes well and leave to cool. When they are cool enough to handle, peel and return to the pan. Put the pan on the heat and, using a wooden spoon, stir for 1 minute until the moisture has evaporated. Remove the pan from the heat.

4 Mash the potatoes until they are smooth. Then pour in the milk and spring onions and mash until thoroughly combined. Taste and add seasoning, if liked. Serve hot, making a dent in each mound and adding a pool of melted butter to each portion.

COOK'S TIP
For speed and ease, peel the potatoes before step 1. Cut them into small chunks and reduce the cooking time to 10 minutes.

Energy 334kcal/1415kJ; Protein 13.2g; Carbohydrate 66.6g, of which sugars 10.5g; Fat 3.5g, of which saturates 1.7g; Cholesterol 9mg; Calcium 217mg; Fibre 5.2g; Sodium 92mg.

Baked potatoes and three fillings

Potatoes, baked in their skins until they are crisp on the outside and fluffy in the middle, make an excellent and nourishing meal when finished with a simple filling, such as chilli con carne, baked beans or tomatoes and cheese. Try one of these delicious fillings for a super supper.

Serves four

4 medium baking potatoes
olive oil
sea salt
filling of your choice (see below)

1 Preheat the oven to 200°C/400°F/ Gas 6. Score the potatoes with a cross and rub all over with the olive oil.

2 Place on a baking sheet and cook for at least 1 hour until a knife inserted into the centres indicates they are cooked.

COOK'S TIPS

- For even cooking choose potatoes that are similar sizes with undamaged skins and scrub them well, removing any black eyes.
- If the potatoes are cooked before you are ready, remove from the oven. Reheat later in the microwave.

3 Cut the potatoes open and push up the flesh. Season and fill.

STIR-FRIED VEGETABLES

A sweet and sharp-tasting filling.

45ml/3 tbsp groundnut (peanut) or sunflower oil
2 leeks, thinly sliced
2 carrots, cut into sticks
1 courgette (zucchini), thinly sliced
115g/4oz baby corn, halved
115g/4oz/1½ cup button (white) mushrooms, sliced
45ml/3 tbsp soy sauce
30ml/2 tbsp dry sherry or vermouth
sesame seeds, to garnish

1 Heat the oil in a frying pan. Add the leeks, carrots, courgette and baby corn and stir-fry for about 2 minutes. Add the mushrooms. Stir-fry for 1 minute.

2 Mix the liquids and pour over the vegetables. Heat until just bubbling and scatter over the sesame seeds.

RED BEAN CHILLIES

A filling combination of cheese and beans with additional spicy heat.

425g/15oz can red kidney beans, drained
200g/7oz/scant 1 cup cottage or cream cheese
30ml/2 tbsp mild chilli sauce
5ml/1 tsp ground cumin

1 Heat the beans in a pan and stir in the cheese, chilli sauce and cumin.

CHEESE AND CREAMY CORN

A mild and flavoursome topping that is filling, too.

425g/15oz can creamed corn
115g/4oz/1 cup Cheddar cheese, grated
5ml/1 tsp mixed dried herbs
fresh parsley sprigs, to garnish

1 Heat the corn gently until bubbling. Stir in the cheese and mixed herbs until thoroughly combined. Use to fill the potatoes and garnish with parsley.

Energy 223kcal/941kJ; Protein 7.3g; Carbohydrate 38.6g, of which sugars 8.3g; Fat 4.5g, of which saturates 0.8g; Cholesterol 0mg; Calcium 55mg; Fibre 5.4g; Sodium 1150mg.

Potato, onion and garlic bake

The cooking time for this dish depends on how thinly sliced the potatoes are, the depth of the dish (deeper takes longer) and the oven. Allow plenty of time because it is disappointing undercooked; if it is cooked too soon, reduce the heat. Serve with grilled chicken.

Serves four

40g/1½oz/3 tbsp butter
1 large onion, finely sliced
2–4 garlic cloves, finely chopped
2.5ml/½ tsp dried thyme
900g/2lb waxy potatoes, very finely sliced
450ml/¾ pint/scant 2 cups vegetable or chicken stock
salt and ground black pepper

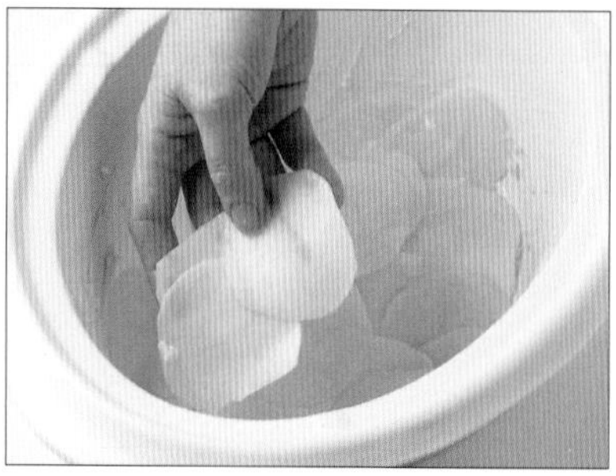

1 Preheat the oven to 200°C/400°F/Gas 6.

2 Grease an ovenproof dish with butter. Arrange a thin layer of onions in the dish, then sprinkle with a little of the garlic, thyme, salt and pepper.

3 Arrange an overlapping layer of potato slices on top of the onions. Continue to layer the ingredients until all the sliced onions, chopped garlic, herbs and finely sliced potatoes are used up, finishing with a layer of sliced potatoes on top.

4 Pour in the stock. Cover the dish with foil or a lid and bake for 30 minutes.

5 Reduce the oven temperature to 180°C/350°F/Gas 4. Remove the foil or lid and dot the remaining butter over the potatoes. Cook for a further 1 hour or until the potatoes are tender and juicy and browned on top.

Variations

- Fresh herbs taste far better than dried, so use them if available, picking the leaves off a few sprigs of thyme. To vary the flavour, try using chopped fresh rosemary, tarragon or sage.
- Using stock gives a light result that is great when serving the potatoes with a casserole, roast or grilled (broiled) meat or fish. Milk can be used instead of stock, or try single (light) cream for a rich dish.
- To make this dish more substantial, sprinkle 115g/4oz/1 cup of grated Gruyère cheese over the top of the cooked potatoes when removing the lid.
- Crumble 165g/5¼oz/scant 1 cup soft goat's cheese on the gratin 30 minutes before the end of cooking time.
- Flake a drained can of tuna and finely sliced red (bell) pepper in the layers and top with cheese.

Energy 260Kcal/1092kJ; Protein 5.1g; Carbohydrate 41.9g, of which sugars 6.4g; Fat 9.1g, of which saturates 5.4g; Cholesterol 21mg; Calcium 31mg; Fibre 3.3g; Sodium 171mg.

Cabbage with bacon

Though it may seem that there is a large quantity of cabbage here, particularly when shredded, it collapses quite quickly as it cooks. Bacon is delicious with all vegetables, and smoked bacon is particularly good with cabbage. Serve with jacket potatoes or plain grilled meat.

Serves four

30ml/2 tbsp oil
1 large onion, finely chopped
115g/4oz smoked bacon, rind removed and diced
500g/1¼lb cabbage (Savoy, red, or white) or Brussels sprouts (or a mixture of both)
salt and ground black pepper

1 Heat the oil in a frying pan over a medium heat. Add the onion and bacon and cook for 5–8 minutes, stirring occasionally with a wooden spoon. The onion should be soft and translucent but not browned and the bacon cooked but not too browned and crisp.

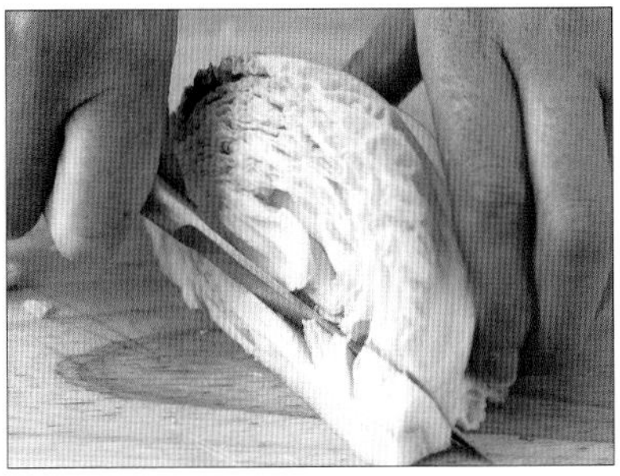

2 Remove any tough outer leaves and wash the cabbage or Brussels sprouts. Shred quite finely, discarding the core of the cabbage or the stalks of the Brussels sprouts. Add the cabbage to the pan and season with pepper. Stir for a few minutes until the cabbage begins to shrink in volume.

3 Continue to cook the cabbage, stirring frequently, for 8–10 minutes until it is tender but still crisp. Season.

Variations

- Try spring greens (collards) or curly kale instead of cabbage.
- For a main dish, add 225g/8oz sliced mushrooms and 2 crushed garlic cloves with the onion and bacon. Stir in two 425g/15oz cans chickpeas or borlotti beans about 5 minutes before the end of cooking.
- Add 10ml/2 tsp caraway seeds, lightly crushed, when adding the cabbage.

Energy 151kcal/623kJ; Protein 6.7g; Carbohydrate 7.4g, of which sugars 7g; Fat 10.5g, of which saturates 2.6g; Cholesterol 15mg; Calcium 67mg; Fibre 2.8g; Sodium 452mg.

Braised red cabbage

Lightly spiced with a sharp, sweet flavour, slow cooked braised red cabbage goes well with roast pork, duck and game dishes. It is also delicious with baked ham or crisp, well-browned sausages (garlicky sausages are great) or lamb kebabs.

Serves four to six

1kg/2¼lb red cabbage
2 cooking apples
2 onions, chopped
5ml/1 tsp freshly grated nutmeg
1.5ml/¼ tsp ground cloves
1.5ml/¼ tsp ground cinnamon
15ml/1 tbsp soft dark brown sugar
45ml/3 tbsp red wine vinegar
25g/1oz/2 tbsp butter, diced
salt and ground black pepper
chopped flat leaf parsley, to garnish

1 Preheat the oven to 160°C/325°F/ Gas 3.

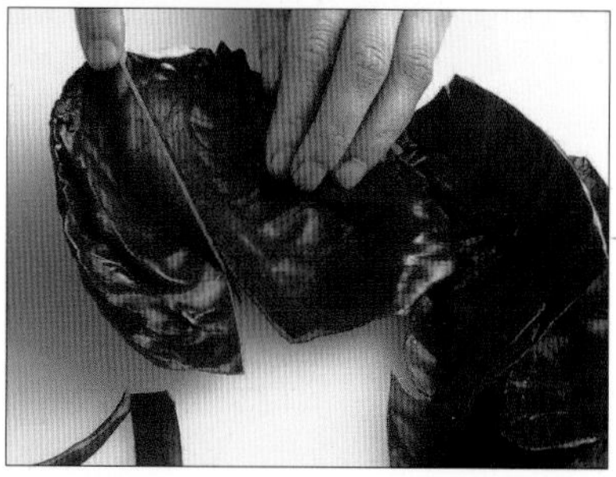

2 Cut away and discard the large white ribs from the outer cabbage leaves using a large, sharp knife, then finely shred the cabbage. Peel, core and coarsely grate the apples.

3 Layer the shredded cabbage in an ovenproof dish with the onions, apples, spices, sugar and seasoning. Pour over the vinegar and add the diced butter.

4 Cover with a lid and cook in the oven for 1½ hours, stirring a couple of times, until the cabbage is very tender. Serve immediately, garnished with the parsley.

COOK'S TIPS

- This dish can be cooked in advance and reheated on top of the stove, stirring frequently.
- The cabbage can be braised on top of the stove in a large heavy pan that will not burn. Cook the onions in a little oil first, allowing about 5 minutes so they are soft, but not browned. Add all the other ingredients plus 60ml/4 tbsp water. Bring to the boil, cover, reduce the heat to low and cook gently for 1 hour, stirring occasionally.

Energy 161kcal/669kJ; Protein 2.3g; Carbohydrate 5.8g, of which sugars 5.5g; Fat 14.6g, of which saturates 2.2g; Cholesterol 0mg; Calcium 37mg; Fibre 3.7g; Sodium 15mg.

Roast beetroot

The sweet flavour of beetroot is enhanced by slow roasting. Tangy horseradish and vinegar in cream contrast well with the sweet vegetable. Good with roast beef or venison, the beetroot is also excellent with grilled halloumi cheese or with crumbled feta and lots of crusty bread.

Serves four to six

10–12 small whole beetroot (beet)
30ml/2 tbsp oil
45ml/3 tbsp grated fresh horeseradish
15ml/1 tbsp white wine vinegar
10ml/2 tsp caster (superfine) sugar
150ml/½ pint/⅔ cup double (heavy) cream
salt

COOK'S TIPS

- If you are unable to find fresh horseradish root use preserved grated horseradish instead.
- For a sauce that is lighter in calories, replace the double (heavy) cream with Greek (US strained plain) yogurt.

1 Preheat the oven to 180°C/350°F/ Gas 4. Wash the beetroot without breaking their skins. Trim the stalks to 2.5cm/1in long.

2 Toss the beetroot in the oil and sprinkle with salt. Spread on a roasting pan and cover with foil. Cook for 1½ hours. Leave covered for 10 minutes.

3 To make the horseradish sauce, put the horseradish, vinegar and sugar into a bowl and mix well. Whisk the cream until stiff and fold in the horseradish mixture. Cover and chill until required.

4 When the beetroot are cool enough to handle, slip off the skins and serve with the sauce.

Energy 254kcal/1052kJ; Protein 2.1g; Carbohydrate 10g, of which sugars 9.1g; Fat 22.2g, of which saturates 3.2g; Cholesterol 1mg; Calcium 26mg; Fibre 2.3g; Sodium 143mg.

Roast Mediterranean vegetables

Aubergines, courgettes, peppers and tomatoes make a marvellous medley when roasted and served drizzled with fragrant olive oil. Shavings of sheep's milk Pecorino cheese add the perfect finishing touch. Offer lots of bread and a bowl of olives with the vegetables.

Serves four

1 aubergine (eggplant), sliced
2 courgettes (zucchini), sliced
2 bell peppers (red or yellow or one of each), cored and quartered
1 large onion, thickly sliced
2 large carrots, cut in sticks
4 firm plum tomatoes, halved
extra virgin olive oil
45ml/3 tbsp chopped fresh parsley
45ml/3 tbsp pine nuts, lightly toasted
125g/4oz piece of Pecorino cheese
salt and ground black pepper
crusty bread, to serve (optional)

1 Layer the aubergine slices in a colander, sprinkling each layer with a little salt. Leave to drain over a sink for about 20 minutes. Rinse thoroughly, drain well and pat dry. Preheat the oven to 220°C/425°F/Gas 7.

2 Spread out the vegetables in roasting pans. Brush the vegetables lightly with olive oil and roast them in the oven for about 20 minutes or until they are lightly browned and the skins on the peppers have begun to blister.

3 Transfer the vegetables to a large serving platter. Trickle over any vegetable juices from the pan and season with salt and pepper. As the vegetables cool, sprinkle them with more oil (preferably extra virgin olive oil). When they are at room temperature, mix in the parsley and pine nuts.

4 Using a vegetable peeler, shave the Pecorino and scatter the shavings over the vegetables. Serve with crusty bread.

Variation
Instead of Pecorino cheese, try Parmesan or Spanish manchego shavings, diced feta or Roquefort.

Energy 225kcal/936kJ; Protein 11.7g; Carbohydrate 13.2g, of which sugars 12g; Fat 14.3g, of which saturates 4.8g; Cholesterol 19mg; Calcium 288mg; Fibre 4.5g; Sodium 230mg.

Braised leeks with carrots

Sweet carrots and leeks go well together and are good finished with a little chopped mint, chervil or parsley. They complement roast or grilled meat, poultry or sausages and are delicious with boiled ham (home-made or bought) or simply tossed with flaked smoked mackerel.

Serves four

65g/2½oz/5 tbsp butter
675g/1½lb carrots, thickly sliced
2 fresh bay leaves
5ml/1 tsp caster (superfine) sugar
75ml/5 tbsp water
675g/1½lb leeks, cut into 5cm/2in lengths
120ml/4fl oz/½ cup white wine
30ml/2 tbsp chopped fresh mint, chervil or parsley
salt and ground black pepper

1 Melt 25g/1oz/2 tbsp of the butter in a pan and cook the carrots gently, without allowing them to brown, for 4–5 minutes.

2 Add the bay leaves, seasoning, sugar and water. Bring to the boil, cover and cook for about 5 minutes, until the carrots are tender. Uncover and then boil until the juices have evaporated, leaving the carrots moist and glazed.

3 Melt 25g/1oz/2 tbsp of the remaining butter in a wide pan or deep frying pan that will take the leeks in a single layer. Add the leeks and fry them in the butter over a low heat for 4–5 minutes, without allowing them to brown.

4 Add seasoning, a good pinch of sugar, the wine and half the chopped herb. Heat until simmering, then cover and cook gently for 5–8 minutes, until the leeks are tender, but not collapsed.

5 Uncover the leeks and turn them in the buttery juices. Increase the heat and then boil the liquid rapidly until reduced to a few tablespoons.

6 Add the carrots to the leeks and reheat them gently, then swirl in the remaining butter. Taste and adjust the seasoning, if necessary. Transfer to a warmed serving dish and serve sprinkled with the remaining chopped herbs.

Variations

- For a speedy alternative, use 2 bunches spring onions (scallions) instead of leeks. Slice and stir-fry them in a little butter or oil for about 2 minutes, then add them to the cooked carrots with the herbs.
- To make leeks in tarragon cream cook 900g/2lb leeks in 40g/1½oz/3 tbsp butter as above. Season, add a pinch of sugar, 45ml/3 tbsp tarragon vinegar, 6 fresh tarragon sprigs or 5ml/1 tsp dried tarragon and 60ml/4 tbsp white wine. Cover and cook as above. Add 150ml/¼ pint/⅔ cup double (heavy) cream and allow to bubble and thicken. Season and serve sprinkled with chopped fresh tarragon. A spoonful of tarragon-flavoured mustard is good stirred into the leeks.

Energy 163kcal/677kJ; Protein 3.8g; Carbohydrate 18.5g, of which sugars 16.4g; Fat 6.5g, of which saturates 3.6g; Cholesterol 13mg; Calcium 87mg; Fibre 7.8g; Sodium 85mg.

Peas with lettuce and onion

This is one of those classic dishes that sounds odd to the uninitiated but tastes excellent. Fresh peas vary enormously in the time they take to cook. The tastiest and sweetest are young and freshly picked. Frozen peas need less cooking time and are ready in minutes.

Serves four to six

15g/½oz/1 tbsp butter
1 small onion, finely chopped
1 small round (butterhead) lettuce
450g/1lb/3½ cups shelled fresh peas (from about 1.5kg/3½lb peas), or frozen peas
45ml/3 tbsp water
salt and ground black pepper

1 Melt the butter in a heavy pan until sizzling. Add the onion and cook over a medium-low heat, stirring once or twice, for about 3 minutes until just softened. Do not allow the onion to brown.

2 Cut the lettuce in half through the core, then place cut side down on a board and slice into thin strips. Place the lettuce strips on top of the onion and add the peas and water. Season lightly with salt and pepper.

3 Bring to the boil, then reduce the heat and cover the pan tightly. Cook over a low heat until the peas are tender – fresh peas will take 10–20 minutes, frozen peas about 5 minutes. Serve piping hot.

Energy 161kcal/670kJ; Protein 9g; Carbohydrate 15.9g, of which sugars 6.8g; Fat 7.4g, of which saturates 3.7g; Cholesterol 13mg; Calcium 73mg; Fibre 6.5g; Sodium 47mg.

Young vegetables with tarragon

This is almost a salad, but the vegetables here are just lightly cooked to bring out their different flavours. The tarragon adds a wonderful aniseed-like flavour to this bright, fresh dish. It goes well as a light accompaniment for fish and seafood dishes.

Serves four

5 spring onions (scallions)
50g/2oz/¼ cup butter
1 garlic clove, crushed
115g/4oz asparagus tips
115g/4oz mangetouts (snow peas), trimmed
115g/4oz shelled fresh or frozen broad (fava) beans
2 Little Gem (Bibb) lettuces
5ml/1 tsp finely chopped fresh tarragon
salt and ground black pepper

1 Cut the spring onions into quarters lengthways. Melt half the butter in a frying pan until gently foaming. Add the garlic and spring onions and fry gently over a medium-low heat for 1–2 minutes.

2 Add the asparagus tips, mangetouts and broad beans. Stir to coat all the pieces of vegetable with oil.

3 Add enough water just to cover the base of the pan. Season the mixture and heat until boiling, and then allow to simmer gently for 2–3 minutes.

4 Cut the lettuce lengthways into quarters and add these wedges to the pan, nestling them down among the other vegetables.

5 Simmer for 3 minutes then, off the heat, add the remaining butter and the tarragon, mix lightly and serve.

Energy 149kcal/619kJ; Protein 4.7g; Carbohydrate 6.1g, of which sugars 3g; Fat 12g, of which saturates 7.3g; Cholesterol 29mg; Calcium 55mg; Fibre 3.5g; Sodium 89mg.

Baked mushrooms

Large mushrooms, full of texture and flavour, taste terrific when topped with crunchy chopped hazelnuts, fresh parsley and lemony garlic in olive oil, then baked until succulent. Serve as a starter or a light lunch or supper dish with fresh crusty bread.

Serves four

2 garlic cloves, crushed
grated rind of 1 lemon
90ml/6 tbsp olive oil
8 large field (portabello) mushrooms
50g/2oz/½ cup hazelnuts, coarsely chopped
30ml/2 tbsp chopped fresh parsley
salt and ground black pepper

COOK'S TIP

A mixture of the crushed garlic, grated lemon rind and chopped parsley is known as gremolata. You could prepare a larger quantity of this mixture, without the oil, and store in the freezer ready to use to season meat.

1 Preheat the oven to 200ºC/400ºF/ Gas 6. Mix the garlic, lemon rind and olive oil. Leave to infuse if time allows.

2 Arrange the mushrooms, stalk side up, in a single layer in an ovenproof dish. Drizzle over about 60ml/4 tbsp of the oil mixture and bake for 10 minutes.

3 Remove the mushrooms from the oven and baste them with the remaining oil, then sprinkle the chopped hazelnuts evenly over the top. Bake for a further 10–15 minutes, or until the mushrooms are tender. Season and sprinkle with parsley. Serve immediately.

Variation

Almost any unsalted nuts can be used in place of the hazelnuts in this recipe – try pine nuts, cashew nuts, almonds or walnuts, whatever your preference. Nuts can go rancid quickly, so for the freshest flavour, buy them in small quantities from a shop with a high turnover and use them quickly.

Energy 255kcal/1052kJ; Protein 5.2g; Carbohydrate 1.7g, of which sugars 1g; Fat 25.4g, of which saturates 3.1g; Cholesterol 0mg; Calcium 43mg; Fibre 3.1g; Sodium 12mg.

Caramelized shallots

These shallots are good with grilled or braised poultry or meat, especially turkey, pork, veal and beef. They are also excellent mixed with other braised or roasted vegetables, such as carrots or chunks of butternut squash, as well as chestnuts.

Serves four to six

- 50g/2oz/¼ cup butter or 60ml/4 tbsp olive oil
- 500g/1¼lb shallots or small onions, skinned but with root ends intact
- 15ml/1 tbsp golden caster (superfine) sugar
- 30ml/2 tbsp red or white wine or port
- 150ml/¼ pint/⅔ cup chicken or beef stock or water
- 2–3 fresh bay leaves and/or 2–3 fresh thyme sprigs
- salt and ground black pepper
- chopped fresh parsley, to garnish (optional)

1 Heat the butter or oil in a large frying pan and add the shallots or onions. Fry gently, turning frequently and rolling the onions around in the pan, until they are evenly and lightly browned.

2 Sprinkle the sugar over the shallots and cook gently, turning the shallots in the juices, until the sugar begins to caramelize. Add the wine or port, then let the mixture bubble for 4–5 minutes until all the juices have evaporated.

3 Pour in the stock. Add seasoning and the herbs. Bring to the boil, stirring, and then reduce the heat so that the liquid simmers. Cover the pan and cook the shallots gently for a further 5 minutes until they are tender.

4 Remove the lid and bring to the boil, then cook until the liquid evaporates and the shallots are tender when pierced with a fork and glazed. Taste and adjust the seasoning, then sprinkle with the parsley, if liked.

Variation

To make shallots with chestnuts and pancetta cook the shallots in butter or bacon fat with 90g/3½oz pancetta, cut into thick strips. Use water or ham stock in place of the wine or port. Toss in 250–350g/9–12oz part-cooked chestnuts in step 3. Cook for 5–10 minutes, then serve sprinkled with chopped flat leaf parsley.

Energy 96kcal/399kJ; Protein 1.3g; Carbohydrate 5.4g, of which sugars 5.4g; Fat 7.5g, of which saturates 1.1g; Cholesterol 0mg; Calcium 22mg; Fibre 1.2g; Sodium 9mg.

Grilled vegetable pizza

Home-made pizza is far healthier than bought, with the topping of traditional Mediterranean vegetables, plum tomatoes and flavoursome basil and a non-traditional dough base.

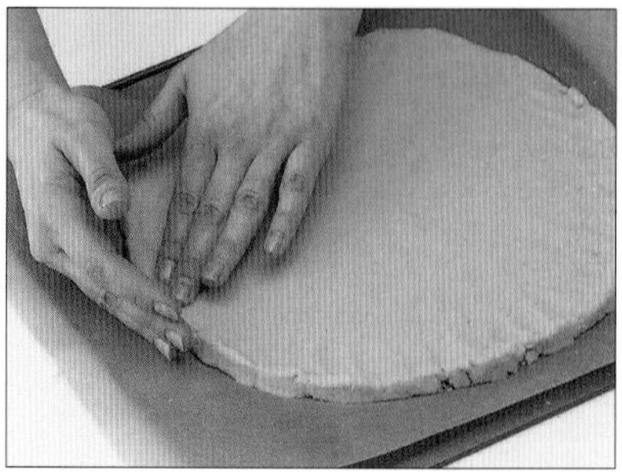

Serves six

- 1 courgette (zucchini), sliced
- 1 small aubergine (eggplant), sliced
- 30ml/2 tbsp olive oil
- 1 yellow (bell) pepper, seeded and sliced
- 115g/4oz/1 cup plain (all-purpose) flour
- 115g/4oz/1 cup wholemeal (whole-wheat) flour
- 5ml/1 tsp baking powder
- pinch of salt
- 50g/2oz/4 tbsp butter
- 105ml/7 tbsp milk
- 4 plum tomatoes, skinned and chopped
- 30ml/2 tbsp chopped fresh basil
- 115g/4oz mozzarella cheese, sliced
- salt and ground black pepper
- fresh basil sprigs, to garnish

1 Preheat the grill (broiler). Brush the courgette and aubergine slices with a little oil and place on a grill rack with the pepper slices. Cook under the grill until lightly browned, turning once.

2 Meanwhile, preheat the oven to 200°C/400°F/Gas 6. Place the plain and wholemeal flours, baking powder and salt in a mixing bowl and stir to mix.

3 Lightly rub in the butter until the mixture resembles coarse breadcrumbs. This can also be done in the food processor. Gradually stir in enough of the milk to make a soft, but not sticky, dough.

4 Place the dough on a sheet of baking parchment on a baking sheet and roll or press it out to form a 25cm/10in round, making the edges slightly thicker than the centre.

5 Brush the pizza dough with any remaining oil, then spread the chopped tomatoes over the dough.

6 Sprinkle chopped basil on top and season with salt and pepper. Arrange the grilled (broiled) vegetables over the herbs and top with the cheese.

7 Bake for 25–30 minutes until crisp and golden brown. Garnish with fresh basil and serve cut into slices.

COOK'S TIP

If it is more convenient, the vegetables can be prepared in advance. Slice and grill (broil) them and then store in a covered bowl, in the refrigerator, for up to 2 days.

Energy 400kcal/1666kJ; Protein 11.9g; Carbohydrate 34.6g, of which sugars 9.6g; Fat 23.9g, of which saturates 5.3g; Cholesterol 18mg; Calcium 166mg; Fibre 4.4g; Sodium 240mg.

Vegetable tortilla parcels

Seeded green chillies add just a flicker of fire to the spicy tomato filling in these tasty shallow-fried parcels, which are perfect as a main course with salad and potato wedges, or as a snack.

Serves four

675g/1½lb tomatoes
60ml/4 tbsp sunflower oil
1 large onion, finely sliced
1 garlic clove, crushed
10ml/2 tsp cumin seeds
2 fresh green chillies, seeded and chopped
30ml/2 tbsp tomato purée (paste)
1 vegetable stock (bouillon) cube
200g/7oz can corn, drained
15ml/1 tbsp chopped fresh coriander (cilantro)
115g/4oz/1 cup grated Cheddar cheese
8 wheat tortillas
fresh coriander (cilantro), shredded lettuce and soured cream, to serve

1 To skin the tomatoes, make a small cross with a sharp knife in the bottom of each. Place them in a heatproof bowl, add boiling water to cover and leave for 30 seconds. Lift out with a slotted spoon. Slip the skins off the tomatoes and chop the flesh.

2 Heat half the oil in a frying pan and fry the onion with the garlic and cumin seeds for 5 minutes, until the onion softens. Add the chillies and tomatoes, then stir in the tomato purée.

3 Crumble the stock cube over, stir, and cook gently for 5 minutes, until the chilli is soft but the tomato has not completely broken down. Stir in the corn and coriander and warm through. Keep warm.

COOK'S TIPS

- Mexican wheat tortillas (sometimes described as wheatflour tortillas or wraps) are available in supermarkets.
- Some packets are long-life and will keep for weeks (check the use-by date). They freeze well, are easy to separate and thaw quickly.

4 Sprinkle a little grated cheese in the middle of each tortilla. Spoon some tomato mixture evenly over the cheese. Fold over one edge of the tortilla, then fold over the sides and finally fold up the remaining edge, to enclose the filling completely.

5 Heat the remaining oil in a frying pan and fry the filled tortillas for 1–2 minutes on each side until golden and crisp. Lift them out carefully with tongs and drain on kitchen paper. Serve immediately, with coriander, shredded lettuce and soured cream.

Energy 484kcal/2030kJ; Protein 15.3g; Carbohydrate 58.3g, of which sugars 17.6g; Fat 22.4g, of which saturates 7.9g; Cholesterol 28mg; Calcium 313mg; Fibre 5.4g; Sodium 684mg.

Vegetable korma

Kormas are rich, creamy and subtly spiced one-pot dishes, and this is a delicious example. It is good with plain spiced grilled chicken or fish, or excellent as a meat-free main course.

Serves four

50g/2oz/¼ cup butter
2 onions, sliced
2 garlic cloves, crushed
2.5cm/1in piece fresh root ginger, grated
5ml/1 tsp ground cumin
15ml/1 tbsp ground coriander
6 green cardamom pods
5cm/2in piece of cinnamon stick
5ml/1 tsp ground turmeric
1 fresh red chilli, seeded and finely chopped
1 potato, peeled and cut into 2.5cm/1in cubes
1 small aubergine (eggplant), halved and sliced or cut into chunks
115g/4oz/1½ cups mushrooms, thickly sliced
175ml/6fl oz/¾ cup water
115g/4oz/1 cup green beans, cut into 2.5cm/1in lengths
60ml/4 tbsp natural (plain) yogurt
150ml/¼ pint/⅔ cup double (heavy) cream
5ml/1 tsp garam masala
salt and ground black pepper
fresh coriander (cilantro) sprigs, to garnish
boiled rice and poppadums, to serve

1 Melt the butter in a pan. Add the onions and cook for 5 minutes, stirring occasionally, until soft but not browned.

2 Add the garlic and ginger and cook for 2 minutes, then stir in the cumin, coriander, cardamom pods, cinnamon stick, turmeric and finely chopped chilli. Cook the spices, stirring constantly, for 30 seconds, until they are aromatic. Take care not to overcook or burn the spices as this makes them bitter.

3 Add the potato cubes, aubergine and mushrooms and the water. Cover the pan, bring to the boil, then lower the heat and simmer for 15 minutes. Add the beans and cook, uncovered, for 5 minutes. With a slotted spoon, remove the vegetables to a warmed serving dish and keep hot.

4 Increase the heat and allow the cooking liquid to bubble up until it has reduced a little. Season with salt and pepper, then stir in the yogurt, cream and garam masala. Pour the sauce over the vegetables and garnish with fresh coriander. Serve with boiled rice and crisp poppadums.

Energy 363kcal/1499kJ; Protein 4.8g; Carbohydrate 16.6g, of which sugars 8.2g; Fat 31.3g, of which saturates 19.2g; Cholesterol 78mg; Calcium 88mg; Fibre 3.7g; Sodium 104mg.

Stuffed peppers and tomatoes

Colourful peppers and tomatoes make perfect containers for stuffings. This version uses couscous with dried apricots and feta cheese. Serve with a dressed salad.

Serves four

3 ripe tomatoes
4 (bell) peppers
75g/3oz/½ cup instant couscous
75ml/2½fl oz/⅓ cup vegetable stock, boiling
15ml/1 tbsp olive oil
10ml/2 tsp white wine vinegar
50g/2oz dried apricots, finely chopped
75g/3oz feta cheese, cut into tiny cubes
45ml/3 tbsp pine nuts, toasted
30ml/2 tbsp chopped fresh parsley
salt and ground black pepper
flat leaf parsley, to garnish

1 Preheat the oven to 190°C/375°F/ Gas 5.

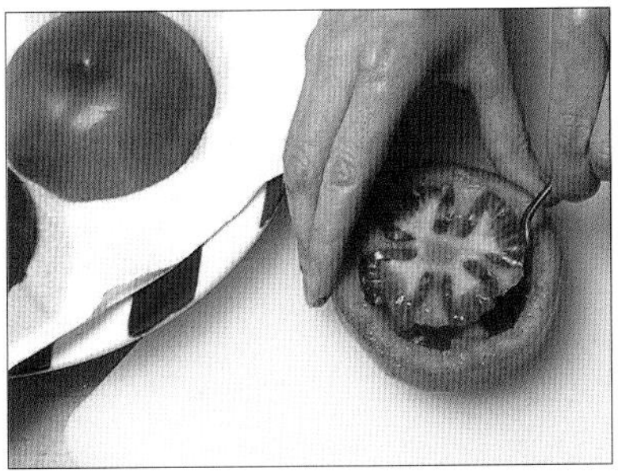

2 Cut the tomatoes in half and scoop out the pulp and seeds. Leave to drain on kitchen paper with cut sides down. Chop the tomato pulp and seeds.

Variation

Small aubergines (eggplants) or large courgettes (zucchini) make good vegetables for stuffing. Halve and scoop out the centres of the vegetables, then oil the vegetable cases and bake them for about 15 minutes. Chop the centres, fry for 2–3 minutes to soften and add to the stuffing mixture. Fill the cases with the stuffing and bake as for the peppers and tomatoes.

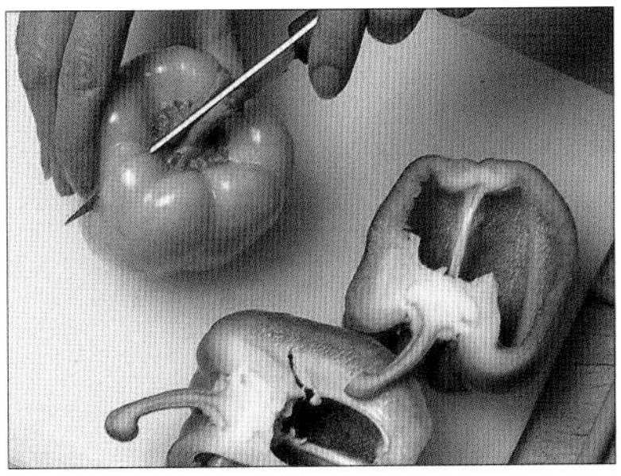

3 Halve the peppers, leaving the cores intact, and scoop out the seeds. Brush with 15ml/1 tbsp of the olive oil and bake on a baking tray for 15 minutes.

4 Place the pepper and tomato cases in a shallow ovenproof dish and season with salt and pepper.

5 Fry the onions in the remaining oil for 5 minutes. Add the garlic and chopped almonds and fry for 1 minute.

6 Remove the pan from the heat and stir in the rice, chopped tomatoes, mint, parsley and sultanas. Season well.

7 Spoon the mixture into the tomato and pepper cases. Pour 150ml/¼ pint/ ⅔ cup boiling water around the peppers and tomatoes and bake for 20 minutes.

8 Scatter with ground almonds, and spinkle with a little extra oil. Return to the oven and bake for 20 minutes.

Energy 303kcal/1266kJ; Protein 33.7g; Carbohydrate 33.6g, of which sugars 17g; Fat 15.8g, of which saturates 3.9g; Cholesterol 113mg; Calcium 105mg; Fibre 4.3g; Sodium 285mg.

Pasta

Pasta, in all its various shapes, sizes and flavours, is a popular food that can be presented in so many different ways. It is often the first ingredient that the beginner cook turns to for a quick, easy-to-prepare dish. Pasta is enjoyed in soups, salads and hearty dishes, such as lasagne, or it can be dressed in all kinds of sauces from the simplest tomato pesto to creamy wild mushroom sauce. There are pasta dishes in this section to suit every occasion from hearty dishes to light soups.

Pasta basics

A starchy food, pasta is full of complex carbohydrates that are used as a source of energy by the body. It is not digested quickly (wholewheat or wholegrain types are digested even more slowly) so it provides a steady supply of energy over a period of time. Wholegrain types also provide valuable dietary fibre. Depending on type, pasta also provides some protein, vitamins and minerals; on its own, plain pasta does not contain a lot of fat.

There are many types of dried pasta. Long, short and flat shapes are available, as well as stuffed types, and tiny shapes for soups. Among the more popular are fusilli spirals, farfalle butterflies, shell-shaped conchiglie, and quill-like penne, each perfect for specific types of sauce. Flat sheet pasta for lasagne and rod-like spaghetti make up the most well-known pastas.

BUYING AND STORING

There are almost as many types of pasta as there are cultures, from the internationally popular Italian varieties to little filled soup pasta from Poland, rice-size shapes used in Greek cooking and translucent rice-flour noodles of Chinese origin. They are all made commercially, sold ready to cook, with information on quantities and serving suggestions alongside cooking times on the packet. Buy a good-quality product, follow the instructions and enjoy one of the world's favourite foods.

WHAT DOES 'AL DENTE' MEAN?

The Italian term 'al dente' means 'to the tooth', in other words firm to bite, tender but not soft and soggy. Test pasta towards the end of the cooking time by lifting out and trying a piece. Drain the pasta as soon as it is 'al dente' – do not leave it sitting in the water as it will continue cooking.

Above: Noodles can be eaten in soup, or dressed like pasta.

Store dried pasta in a sealed container in a dark and dry cupboard. Fresh pasta can also be bought from supermarkets with a long sell-by date on it. Store in the refrigerator and use within one or two days once the packet is opened.

QUICK-COOK VERSIONS

Many types of noodles, such as Chinese-style egg noodles or rice noodles, cook very quickly. Some need no more than brief soaking in boiling water while others are brought to the boil and drained almost immediately.

COOKING TIMES

- Fresh pasta cooks in 2–4 minutes and stuffed fresh pasta in 5–7 minutes.
- The cooking time for dried pasta ranges from 8–15 minutes depending on the type and the manufacturer. Always check the time on the packet. Start timing the moment the water returns to the boil after adding the pasta.
- For spaghetti, or other long varieties, hold the pasta in the water until it softens, then press it down so that it curls around in the pan. Bring to the boil, stir and continue to cook.

PORTION SIZES

How much to serve depends on individual appetite and meal type, such as light supper or hearty meal; or the type of sauce or dressing, for example, a flavoured oil and some chopped herbs is far less substantial and filling than a sauce with lots of creamy mushrooms or ladlefuls of minced (ground) meat and vegetables. Make more if the dish is served as a main course, or if the sauce is rich and you only need a small helping of it. If it is a main dish, the accompaniments, if any, that will be served make a difference.

As a general rule, for a hearty main course, with a modest amount of sauce, Italian-style portions would be 115–175g/4–6oz per person. This can be halved for those with a less hearty appetite or when served with a more substantial sauce, or for a lighter meal.

The practical rule is to measure the amount when first experimenting with pasta, always thinking in terms of amount per portion. Using a familiar mug to measure the pasta helps.

Left: Italian pasta comes in all shapes and sizes, with each product designed to hold different weights of sauces.

HOW MUCH WATER?
The recommended amount for a 5-litre/8-pint pan is: for every 450g/1lb pasta add at least 3 litres/5 pints water. If there is not enough water, the pasta shapes will tend to stick together as they swell up and the pan will become overcrowded without room for the pasta to move. This will result in unpleasant, gummy-textured pasta.

COOKING PASTA

Whatever the type or brand of pasta, there are a few basic cooking tips that apply to the majority of standard pastas. Quantities and timing vary, but the basic method of boiling is standard and important to follow.

However, as usual, the rules are not as rigid in practice. Huge cooking pots are ideal for perfect pasta, but the largest pan that you've got will suffice. Flat pasta for lasagne and cannelloni pasta tubes don't usually need pre-cooking before they are layered or filled with other ingredients.

1 Pasta needs a large amount of water, so a big pan is essential. Special pasta cooking pots have drainers, otherwise use the largest pan you have and a large colander for draining the pasta.

2 Get the water boiling before adding the pasta; the water should be at a fast rolling boil. Boil water in the kettle, then pour it into the pan and bring back to the boil over a high heat. If the pan takes more than one kettleful of water, keep the pot covered and simmering.

3 Tip in the pasta all at once so that it will cook evenly and be ready at the same time. The quickest and easiest way is literally to shake it out of the packet or bowl, covering the surface of the water as much as possible.

4 Bring the water back to the boil as quickly as possible. Give the pasta a brisk stir with a long-handled fork or spoon to stop the pasta sticking together, and then cover the pan tightly with the lid – this will help to bring the water back to the boil quickly. Stay close or the water may boil over. Once the water is boiling remove the lid, turn down the heat slightly and let the water boil steadily without frothing over.

5 Stir the pasta occasionally during cooking (especially if the pan is slightly smaller than ideal to ensure the pasta is not sticking together).

6 Drain in a colander placed in the sink. If you have a pasta pot lift the draining pan and shake it vigorously, to remove all the excess water.

7 Dress plain pasta with olive oil and a grinding of salt and black pepper, and a few shavings of Parmesan.

DRESSING PASTA WITH SAUCE

Recipes vary in the way they combine sauce and pasta. The majority add the sauce to the pasta, but with some it is the other way around. There are no hard-and-fast rules. If you are going to add the sauce to the drained pasta, the most important thing is to have a warmed bowl ready. The larger the bowl the better, because it will allow room for the sauce and pasta to be tossed together easily so that every piece of pasta can be thoroughly coated in sauce.

1 After draining, immediately tip the pasta into the warmed bowl, then pour the sauce over the pasta and quickly toss the two together.

2 If the pasta is not moist enough, add a little of the pasta cooking water. Some recipes call for extra butter or oil to be added at this stage, others have grated Parmesan or Pecorino cheese tossed with the pasta and sauce.

3 Using two large spoons or forks, lift the pasta and swirl it around, making sure you have scooped it up from the bottom of the bowl. The idea is to coat every piece of pasta evenly in sauce.

Minestrone

The classic, wintry Italian minestrone soup is made by chopping and frying vegetables, then stirring in liquid. Any small pasta shapes can be used instead of the spaghettini, if you prefer.

Serves four to six

30ml/2 tbsp olive oil
2 onions, finely chopped
2 garlic cloves, finely chopped
2 carrots, very finely chopped
1 celery stick, very finely chopped
1.3 litres/2¼ pints/5⅔ cups boiling water
450g/1lb shelled fresh broad (fava) beans
225g/8oz mangetouts (snow peas), sliced
3 tomatoes, skinned and chopped
5ml/1 tsp tomato purée (paste)
50g/2oz spaghettini, broken into 4cm/1½in lengths
225g/8oz baby spinach
30ml/2 tbsp chopped fresh parsley
handful of fresh basil leaves
salt and ground black pepper
basil sprigs, to garnish
freshly grated Parmesan cheese, to serve

1 Heat the oil in a large pan and add the onions and garlic. Cook, stirring, for 4–5 minutes, until the onion is softened but not browned.

2 Add the carrots and celery, and cook for 2–3 minutes. Pour in the boiling water and bring to the boil. Reduce the heat and simmer for 15 minutes.

3 Cook the broad beans in boiling salted water for 4–5 minutes. Remove with a slotted spoon, refresh under cold water and set aside.

4 Bring the pan of water back to the boil, add the mangetouts and cook for 1 minute until just tender. Drain, then refresh under cold water and set aside.

5 Add the tomatoes and the tomato purée to the soup. Cook for 1 minute, then put two or three large ladlefuls of the soup and a quarter of the broad beans in a food processor or blender and purée until smooth. Set aside.

6 Add the spaghettini to the remaining soup and cook for 6–8 minutes, until tender. Stir in the purée and spinach and cook for 2–3 minutes. Add the rest of the broad beans, the mangetouts and parsley, and season well.

7 Stir in the basil leaves and immediately ladle the soup into deep cups or bowls. Garnish with sprigs of basil. Serve with grated Parmesan.

Variations

- Replace the fresh basil and Parmesan with a spoonful of pesto in each bowl of soup.
- Add bacon and borlotti beans instead of broad (fava) beans for a more hearty version.

Energy 324kcal/1356kJ; Protein 13.4g; Carbohydrate 32.3g, of which sugars 12.3g; Fat 16.6g, of which saturates 3.9g; Cholesterol 19mg; Calcium 111mg; Fibre 8.5g; Sodium 696mg.

Rigatoni with tomato sauce

Canned tomatoes combined with soffritto (the sautéed mixture of chopped onion, carrot, celery and garlic) and herbs make a sauce that is rich and full of flavour.

Serves six to eight

1 onion
1 carrot
1 celery stick
60ml/4 tbsp olive oil
1 garlic clove, thinly sliced
a few leaves each fresh basil, thyme and oregano or marjoram
2 x 400g/14oz cans chopped plum tomatoes
15ml/1 tbsp sun-dried tomato paste
5ml/1 tsp sugar
about 90ml/6 tbsp dry red or white wine (optional)
350g/12oz/3 cups dried rigatoni
salt and ground black pepper
coarsely shaved Parmesan cheese, to serve

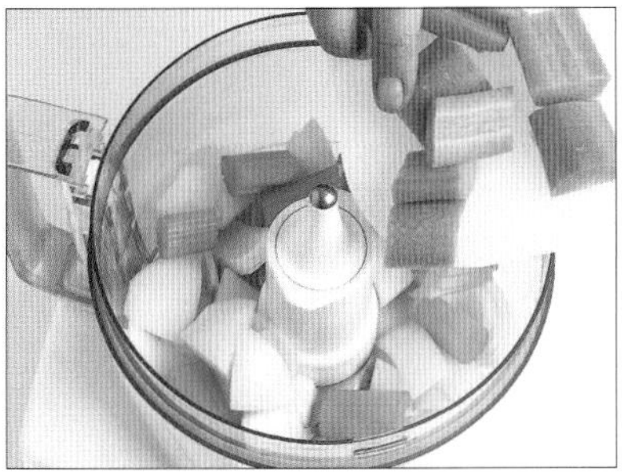

1 Chop the onion, carrot and celery finely, in a food processor or by hand.

2 Heat the olive oil in a pan, add the garlic and stir over a very low heat for 1–2 minutes. Add the chopped vegetables and herbs. Cook over a low heat, stirring frequently, for 5–7 minutes until the vegetables are soft and lightly coloured.

Variation
Add a seeded and chopped fresh green chilli with the garlic. Hard boil, shell and roughly chop 1 egg per person and sprinkle over each portion with lots of shredded basil.

3 Add the tomatoes, tomato paste and sugar, then stir in the wine, if using. Add salt and pepper to taste. Bring to the boil, stirring, then reduce the heat and simmer gently, uncovered, for about 45 minutes, stirring occasionally, until the sauce is well flavoured.

4 Cook the pasta according to the instructions on the packet. Drain and tip it into a warmed bowl. Taste the sauce for seasoning, pour the sauce over the pasta and toss well. Serve immediately, with shavings of Parmesan handed around separately. If you like, garnish with extra chopped herbs.

COOK'S TIP
Tomato sauce is a really versatile sauce to make in batches and store in the freezer. Use it as the base for a pizza topping, for serving with pasta, as the base for soup, or other vegetarian stew.

Energy 313kcal/1323kJ; Protein 8.8g; Carbohydrate 51g, of which sugars 8.8g; Fat 8.6g, of which saturates 1.2g; Cholesterol 0mg; Calcium 43mg; Fibre 3.3g; Sodium 62mg.

Spaghetti Bolognese

This dish was 'invented' by Italian emigrés in America in the sixties in response to popular demand for a spaghetti dish with meat sauce. There are many versions and this recipe is for a spicy version, spiked with cayenne pepper, Worcestershire sauce and tomato ketchup.

Serves four to six

30ml/2 tbsp olive oil
1 onion, finely chopped
1 garlic clove, crushed
5ml/1 tsp dried mixed herbs
pinch of cayenne pepper
450g/1lb minced (ground) beef
400g/14oz can chopped Italian plum tomatoes
45ml/3 tbsp tomato ketchup
15ml/1 tbsp sun-dried tomato paste
5ml/1 tsp Worcestershire sauce
5ml/1 tsp dried oregano
450ml/¾ pint/1¾ cups beef or vegetable stock
45ml/3 tbsp red wine
400–450g/14oz–1lb dried spaghetti
salt and ground black pepper
freshly grated Parmesan cheese, to serve

1 Heat the oil in a medium pan, add the onion and garlic and cook over a low heat, stirring frequently, for about 5 minutes until softened. Stir in the mixed herbs and cayenne and cook for 2–3 minutes more. Add the minced beef and cook gently for about 5 minutes, stirring frequently and breaking up any lumps in the meat with a wooden spoon.

2 Stir in the tomatoes, ketchup, tomato paste, Worcestershire sauce, oregano and pepper. Pour in the stock and wine. Bring to the boil, stirring, cover, lower the heat and simmer for 30 minutes, stirring occasionally.

3 Cook the pasta according to the packet instructions. Drain and divide among warmed bowls with the sauce. Hand around the Parmesan separately.

RICH BOLOGNESE
Add 115g/4oz diced bacon, 2 diced celery sticks, 2 garlic cloves and 2 diced carrots with the onion. Add 115g/4oz diced chicken livers with the beef. Omit the cayenne, ketchup, tomato paste and Worcestershire sauce. Add 250ml/8fl oz red wine and 2 cans of tomatoes. Simmer gently for 1¼ hours. Uncover and simmer for about 20 minutes. Season well.

Energy 639kcal/2692kj; Protein 30.9g; Carbohydrate 83.5g; of which sugars 11.5g; Fat 21.7g; of which saturates 7.1g; Cholesterol 53mg; Calcium 59mg; Fibre 4.2g; Sodium 312mg

Spaghetti with carbonara sauce

This is an all-time favourite combination of pasta coated in an egg, bacon and cream sauce. The pancetta or bacon gives depth and the cream adds a mellow flavour. Experiment with the quantities of each main ingredient until you have a combination you like.

Serves four

30ml/2 tbsp olive oil
1 small onion, finely chopped
8 rindless smoked streaky (fatty) bacon rashers (strips), cut into 1cm/½in strips
350g/12oz fresh or dried spaghetti
4 eggs
60ml/4 tbsp crème fraîche
60ml/4 tbsp freshly grated Parmesan cheese, plus extra to serve
salt and ground black pepper

1 Heat the oil in a large pan, add the onion and cook over a low heat, stirring frequently, for 5 minutes until softened but not coloured.

COOK'S TIP
Fresh pasta, if you can get it, tastes best with this dish.

2 Add the strips of pancetta or bacon to the onion in the pan and cook for about 10 minutes, stirring almost all the time. Meanwhile, cook the pasta in a pan of salted boiling water according to the instructions on the packet until al dente.

3 Put the eggs, crème fraîche and grated Parmesan in a bowl. Grind in plenty of pepper, then beat everything together well.

4 Drain the pasta, tip it into the pan with the pancetta or bacon and toss well to mix. Turn the heat off under the pan. Immediately add the egg mixture and toss vigorously so that it cooks lightly and coats the pasta.

5 Quickly taste for seasoning, then divide among four warmed bowls and sprinkle with black pepper. Serve immediately, with extra grated Parmesan handed separately.

Energy 708kcal/2966kj; Protein 30.7g; Carbohydrate 66.6g; of which sugars 4.2g; Fat 37.5g; of which saturates 15.5g; Cholesterol 261mg; Calcium 250mg; Fibre 2.8g; Sodium 824mg

Fusilli with wild mushrooms

A very rich dish with an earthy flavour and lots of garlic, this makes an ideal main course for vegetarians, especially when served with a mixed vegetable salad for colour and freshness.

Serves four

1½ x 275g/10oz jar wild mushrooms in olive oil
25g/1oz/2 tbsp butter
225g/8oz/2 cups fresh wild mushrooms, sliced if large
5ml/1 tsp finely chopped fresh thyme
5ml/1 tsp finely chopped fresh marjoram or oregano, plus extra herbs to serve
4 garlic cloves, crushed
350g/12oz/3 cups fresh or dried fusilli
200ml/7fl oz/scant 1 cup double (heavy) cream
salt and ground black pepper

1 Drain about 15ml/1 tbsp of the oil from the mushrooms into a pan. Slice or chop the bottled mushrooms into bitesize pieces, if they are large.

2 Add the butter to the oil in the pan and place over a low heat until sizzling. Add the bottled and the fresh mushrooms, the chopped herbs and the garlic, with salt and pepper to taste. Simmer over a medium heat, stirring frequently, for about 10 minutes or until the fresh mushrooms are tender.

3 Meanwhile, cook the pasta in plenty of salted, boiling water according to the instructions on the packet until tender but not soft.

4 When the mushrooms are cooked, increase the heat to high and stir and turn the mixture with a wooden spoon to evaporate any excess liquid.

5 Pour in the cream and bring to the boil, stirring, then remove from the heat at once. Taste and season if needed.

6 Drain the pasta and tip it into a warmed bowl. Pour the sauce over the pasta and toss well together. Serve immediately, sprinkled with herbs.

Energy 656kcal/2741kJ; Protein 13g; Carbohydrate 66.1g, of which sugars 4g; Fat 39.5g, of which saturates 21g; Cholesterol 82mg; Calcium 53mg; Fibre 3.6g; Sodium 56mg.

Pasta with green pesto

Rich and flavourful pesto is the perfect accompaniment to pasta. It has a sharp concentrated taste of basil and cheese. A little goes a long way, so use it sparingly.

Serves four

50g/2oz/1⅓ cups fresh basil leaves, plus a few fresh basil leave, to garnish
2–4 garlic cloves
60ml/4 tbsp pine nuts
120ml/4fl oz/½ cup extra virgin olive oil
115g/4oz/1⅓ cups freshly grated Parmesan cheese, plus extra to serve
25g/1oz/⅓ cup freshly grated Pecorino cheese
400g/14oz/3½ cups dried eliche
salt and ground black pepper

1 Put the basil leaves, garlic and pine nuts in a blender or food processor. Add 60ml/4 tbsp of the olive oil. Process until the ingredients are finely chopped, then stop the machine, remove the lid and scrape down the sides of the bowl.

2 Turn the machine on again and slowly pour the remaining oil in a thin, steady stream. Stop the machine and scrape down the sides of the bowl to make sure everything is evenly mixed.

3 Scrape the mixture into a large bowl and beat in the cheeses with a wooden spoon. Taste and season if necessary. Set aside while the pasta cooks, or decant into a smaller bowl to put in the refrigerator for use later (see cook's tip).

4 Cook the pasta according to the instructions on the packet. Drain it well, then add it to the bowl of pesto and toss well. Serve immediately, garnished with the fresh basil leaves and freshly grated Parmesan.

COOK'S TIP

Pesto can be made up to 2–3 days in advance. To store pesto, transfer it to a small bowl and pour a thin film of olive oil over the surface. Cover the bowl tightly with clear film (plastic wrap) and keep it in the refrigerator.

Energy 314kcal/1322kJ; Protein 15.4g; Carbohydrate 43.5g, of which sugars 3.6g; Fat 10.3g, of which saturates 3.4g; Cholesterol 14mg; Calcium 176mg; Fibre 2.7g; Sodium 216mg.

Conchiglie with roasted vegetables

Nothing could be simpler than tossing pasta with roasted vegetables. This is an easy meal to prepare and will smell heavenly while it is cooking. Serve with a dressed salad, if you like.

Serves four to six

- 1 red (bell) pepper, seeded and cut into 1cm/½in squares
- 1 yellow or orange (bell) pepper, seeded and cut into 1cm/½in squares
- 1 small aubergine (eggplant), roughly diced
- 2 courgettes (zucchini), roughly diced
- 75ml/5 tbsp extra virgin olive oil
- 15ml/1 tbsp chopped fresh flat leaf parsley
- 5ml/1 tsp dried oregano or marjoram
- 250g/9oz baby Italian plum tomatoes, hulled and halved lengthways
- 2 garlic cloves, roughly chopped
- 350–400g/12–14oz/3–3½ cups dried conchiglie
- salt and ground black pepper
- 4–6 fresh marjoram or oregano flowers, or chopped sprigs, to garnish

1 Preheat the oven to 190°C/375°F/Gas 5. Rinse the prepared peppers, aubergine and courgettes in a colander under cold running water, drain, then tip the vegetables into a large roasting pan.

2 Pour 45ml/3 tbsp of the olive oil over the vegetables and sprinkle with the fresh and dried herbs. Add a little salt and pepper and stir well. Roast for 30 minutes, stirring two or three times.

3 Stir the tomatoes and garlic into the vegetable mixture, then return to the oven and roast for another 20 minutes, stirring once or twice.

4 Meanwhile, cook the pasta in plenty of salted boiling water according to the instructions on the packet until al dente.

5 Drain the pasta in a colander and then tip it into a warmed bowl. Add the roasted vegetables and the remaining oil and toss well together.

6 Serve the pasta and vegetables hot, in warmed bowls. Sprinkle with a few herb flowers or chopped sprigs, to garnish.

COOK'S TIPS

- Try to match the sauce or ingredients to the pasta. For example, fairly large pieces of vegetable go with chunky pasta. Finely diced vegetables would go with small or thin pasta shapes.
- Pasta and roasted vegetables are very good served cold so, if you have any of this dish left over, cover it tightly with clear film (plastic wrap), chill in the refrigerator overnight and serve it the next day as a salad. It would also make a particularly good salad to take on a picnic with cubes of feta cheese.

Energy 281kcal/1188kJ; Protein 9.8g; Carbohydrate 50.8g, of which sugars 9.1g; Fat 5.7g, of which saturates 0.9g; Cholesterol 0mg; Calcium 63mg; Fibre 5.1g; Sodium 13mg.

Macaroni with four cheeses

Rich and creamy, this deluxe baked macaroni cheese is quick and easy to make. It goes well with either a tomato and basil salad or a leafy green salad.

Serves four

250g/9oz/2¼ cups short-cut macaroni
50g/2oz/¼ cup butter
50g/2oz/½ cup plain (all-purpose) flour
600ml/1 pint/2½ cups milk
100ml/3½ fl oz/scant ½ cup double (heavy) cream
100ml/3½ fl oz/scant ½ cup dry white wine
50g/2oz/½ cup Gruyère or Emmenthal cheese, grated
50g/2oz Fontina cheese, finely diced
50g/2oz Gorgonzola cheese, crumbled
75g/3oz/1 cup freshly grated Parmesan cheese
salt and ground black pepper

1 Preheat the oven to 180°C/350°F/Gas 4. Cook the pasta according to the instructions on the packet.

2 Gently melt the butter in a pan, add the flour and cook, stirring, for 1–2 minutes. Add the milk, a little at a time, whisking vigorously after each addition. Stir in the cream, followed by the dry white wine. Bring to the boil. Cook, stirring constantly, until the sauce thickens, and then remove the sauce from the heat.

Variation

Fontina has a slightly sweet, nutty flavour. If you can't get it, use Taleggio or simply double the quantity of Gruyère or Emmenthal.

3 Add the cheeses and about a third of the grated Parmesan to the sauce. Stir well to mix in the cheeses, then taste for seasoning and add salt and pepper if necessary.

COOK'S TIP

Cheese is often salty, especially strong or blue types, so always taste and season after it is added.

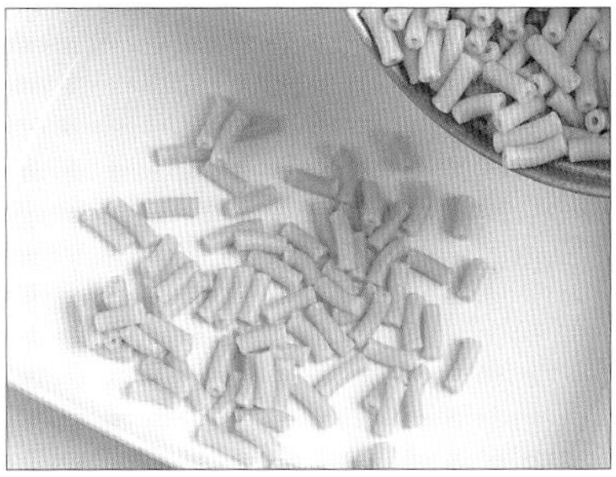

4 Drain the pasta well and tip it into an ovenproof dish. Spread the pieces out in an even layer.

5 Pour the sauce evenly over and mix lightly together with a fork, then sprinkle the remaining Parmesan over the top.

6 Bake the pasta in the oven for 25–30 minutes or until bubbling hot and golden brown. Allow to stand for 2–5 minutes before serving.

Energy 743kcal/3104kj; Protein 30.3g; Carbohydrate 52.1g; of which sugars 8.9g; Fat 37.5g; of which saturates 45.4g; Cholesterol 123mg; Calcium 673mg; Fibre 0.4g; Sodium 593mg

Lasagne

Every cook has to have their favourite recipe for home-made lasagne. This is a bit different from the traditional meat and white sauce combination – it is firm and cuts easily.

Serves six to eight

25g/1oz/2 tbsp butter
15ml/1 tbsp olive oil
225–250g/8–9oz/2–2¼ cups button (white) mushrooms, quartered lengthways
30ml/2 tbsp chopped fresh flat leaf parsley
1 quantity Bolognese Sauce (see page 98)
250–350ml/8–12fl oz/1–1½ cups hot beef stock
9–12 fresh lasagne sheets, pre-cooked if necessary
450g/1lb/2 cups ricotta cheese
1 large egg
3 x 130g/4½oz balls mozzarella cheese, drained and thinly sliced
115g/4oz/1⅓ cups fresh Parmesan cheese, grated
salt and ground black pepper

1 Preheat the oven to 190°C/375°F/Gas 5.

2 Melt the butter with the oil in a frying pan. Add the mushrooms, with salt and pepper to taste, and stir over a medium heat for 5–8 minutes until tender. Remove the pan from the heat and stir in the parsley.

3 Make the Bolognese sauce or, if it is cold, reheat it. Once it is hot, stir in enough hot beef stock to make the sauce quite runny.

4 Stir in the mushroom and parsley mixture, and then spread about a quarter of this sauce over the bottom of an ovenproof baking dish. Cover with three or four sheets of lasagne.

5 Beat together the ricotta and egg in a bowl, with seasoning to taste, then spread about a third of the mixture over the lasagne sheets. Cover with a third of the mozzarella slices, then sprinkle with a quarter of the grated Parmesan.

6 Repeat these layers twice, using half the remaining Bolognese sauce each time, and finishing with the remaining Parmesan.

7 Bake for 30–40 minutes or until the cheese is golden brown and bubbling. Allow to stand for 10 minutes, so that it settles into shape before serving.

Energy 533kcal/2226kJ; Protein 32.5g; Carbohydrate 29.7g, of which sugars 3.1g; Fat 32.4g, of which saturates 18.7g; Cholesterol 121mg; Calcium 370mg; Fibre 1.4g; Sodium 402mg.

Tuna cannelloni

There is something very appealing about cannelloni, and it is not difficult to make. The trick is to allow plenty of time because filling pasta tubes in a hurry is not a good idea.

Serves four to six

50g/2oz/¼ cup butter
50g/2oz/½ cup plain (all-purpose) flour
about 900ml/1½ pints/3¾ cups hot milk
2 x 200g/7oz cans tuna, drained
115g/4oz/1 cup Fontina cheese, grated
pinch of grated nutmeg
12 no-precook cannelloni tubes
50g/2oz/⅔ cup Parmesan cheese, grated
salt and ground black pepper
fresh herbs, to garnish

1 Melt the butter in a heavy pan, add the flour and stir over a low heat for 1–2 minutes. Remove the pan from the heat and gradually add 350ml/12fl oz/1½ cups of the milk, beating vigorously after each addition. Return the pan to the heat and whisk for 1–2 minutes until the sauce is very thick and smooth. Remove from the heat.

2 Mix the tuna with 120ml/4fl oz/½ cup of the white sauce in a bowl. Add salt and black pepper, to taste. Preheat the oven to 180°C/350°F/Gas 4.

3 Gradually whisk the remaining milk into the rest of the sauce, then return the pan to the heat and simmer the sauce, whisking constantly, until the sauce is smooth. Add the grated Fontina and nutmeg, with salt and pepper to taste. Simmer for a few more minutes, stirring frequently. Pour about one-third of the sauce into a baking dish and spread to the corners.

4 Fill the cannelloni tubes with tuna mixture, pushing it in with the handle of a teaspoon. Place the cannelloni in a single layer in the dish. Thin the remaining sauce with a little more milk if necessary, then pour it over the cannelloni. Sprinkle with Parmesan cheese and bake for 30 minutes or until golden. Serve hot, garnished with herbs.

Energy 502kcal/2110kJ; Protein 32.2g; Carbohydrate 44.3g, of which sugars 2.6g; Fat 22.7g, of which saturates 11.4g; Cholesterol 76mg; Calcium 293mg; Fibre 1.7g; Sodium 467mg.

Rice, grains peas and beans

Each of these staple groups of food can be served as an accompaniment or used to complement other ingredients in a dish. In many recipes, they may be the key ingredient for a main dish. They are classic store-cupboard items, incredibly versatile and valuable in a varied, balanced diet. All are available dried or in easy-cook versions, with canned legumes now more popular than their dried counterparts.

Rice and grain basics

Almost every culture has its own favourite rice dishes, ranging from creamy Italian risottos to spicy-sweet pilaff, or classic baked, sweet rice pudding. Grains are everyday foods too, used in breads and cereals, served as accompaniments to main courses, or forming the bulk carbohydrate to which other ingredients are added as part of a main course.

BUYING AND STORING RICE

Rice is a good food to keep to hand in the store cupboard. Kept in dark and dry, cool conditions, it has a long shelf-life. Economical to buy and use, rice has a distinct, if slightly bland, flavour. It takes on the flavour of other foods in the cooking process.

QUANTITIES

As a general rule, allow 50g/2oz/ scant ⅓ cup rice per portion when serving rice as an accompaniment. For main dishes, such as risotto, this can be increased to 75g/3oz/ generous ⅓ cup, or doubled.

BUYING AND STORING GRAINS

Like rice, other grains contain carbohydrate and protein. Some grains have more flavour than others. Each is identifiable by a distinct flavour, and all take on the flavour of other ingredients with stronger flavours. These grains should all be stored in a cool, dark place, in airtight containers. They quickly rot if they become damp. Oats, rye, corn and barley are easy to cook, inexpensive and versatile. Polenta is a thick, golden porridge, available as a quick-cook ingredient. All are delicious in or with soups, stews and bakes. Barley can also be used in a similar way to rice in risottos and pilaffs.

COOKING TIMES

Every grain has a different cooking time, which is determined by the amount of processing that the grain has undergone. Check the packet for manufacturer's instructions.

Below: When not in use, store rice in airtight containers away from the light.

RINSING GRAINS

All grains that have been stored and sold as dried ingredients must be rinsed under cold water before they are cooked. Rinsing removes excess starch and dust that has accumulated when the product was stored. Shake to remove all excess water before cooking. If the rice is to be fried at the beginning of the recipe, ensure it is properly dried out before cooking.

COOKING PERFECT RICE

Rice is available in so many varieties and each has a different cooking time requirement. It is important to ensure that sufficient water is added to the dry rice when it is put in the pan. As the rice cooks it absorbs the water, and will stick to the bottom of the pan if the water runs out. Suppliers usually state on the packet how much water to add to the rice when it cooks.

1 Rinse the rice thoroughly under cold running water. Bring a pan of water to the boil. Once it reaches boiling point, add the rice and replace the lid on the pan. Keep checking the water levels and stir the rice occasionally. Cook according to the packet instructions.

COOK'S TIP

Rice can be cooked in stock to add extra flavour to the dish. Use a stock cube that is appropriate to the meal, so for a chicken dish, use chicken stock.

MAKING RICE PUDDING

Pudding rice is a short grain rice specifically used to make this dish.

1 In a pan, bring 600ml/1 pint/ 2½ cups milk and a vanilla pod (bean) to simmering point, then leave to infuse for 1 hour.

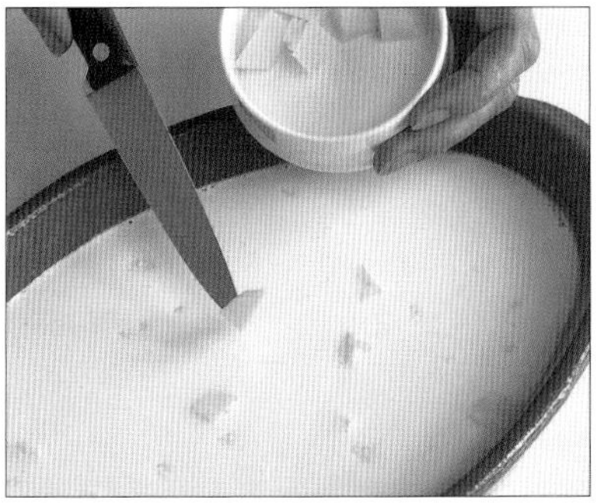

2 Preheat the oven to 150°C/300°F/ Gas 2. Put 50g/2oz/generous ¼ cup pudding rice in a heatproof dish with 45ml/3 tbsp sugar. Pour over the milk, and discard the vanilla pod. Mix. Dot the surface with 25g/1oz/2 tbsp butter.

3 Bake, uncovered, for 2 hours. Stir occasionally. Before serving, sprinkle grated nutmeg over the surface of the rice pudding.

MAKING PORRIDGE

Porridge makes a filling breakfast dish that can be sweetened to taste.

1 Put 1 litre/1¾ pints/4 cups water into a pan with 115g/4oz/1 cup pinhead oatmeal and a pinch of salt. Bring to the boil slowly over a medium heat, stirring constantly with a wooden spoon. When the porridge is smooth and beginning to thicken, reduce the heat to a simmer.

2 Cook gently for about 25 minutes, stirring occasionally, until the oatmeal is cooked and the consistency is smooth.

3 Serve hot with any of the following: cream, brown sugar, golden (light corn) syrup, honey, jam, raisins or fresh berries.

MAKING POLENTA

Polenta makes an excellent alternative to mashed potato.

1 Bring 1 litre/1¾ pints/4 cups water to the boil in a pan. Remove from the heat. Add 185g/6½oz/1½ cups instant polenta and whisk to avoid any lumps forming. Return to the heat and cook, stirring constantly with a wooden spoon, until it starts to come away from the sides of the pan. Season, then add a knob of butter and mix well. Remove from the heat.

2 To make polenta chips, add grated Parmesan cheese, stir well, then pour on to an oiled baking sheet to set. Cut into strips. Bake in a preheated oven for 40–50 minutes at 200ºC/400ºF/Gas 6.

Lentils, peas and beans basics

Beans, peas and lentils provide a diverse range of flavours and textures to meals. There is hardly a country that does not have its own favourite dish for these foods, from Indian dhal to bean casseroles and soups in Europe and the much-loved Texan chilli con carne. Low in fat and high in complex carbohydrates, vitamins and minerals, legumes, as they are known collectively, are also an important source of protein.

All beans are vital for well-balanced vegetarian meals. They are available dried and canned. There are plenty of varieties available, each with their own characteristics, from the well-known haricot (navy) beans used to make baked beans to the less common black-eyed beans with their distinctive black dot. Peas include dried peas, marrowfat peas and split peas. Red, yellow, brown and Puy lentils are all available, each with different cooking requirements and textures. They are good hot or cold for adding to warm salads and casseroles or serving instead of rice.

BUYING AND STORING LENTILS AND PEAS

Although these foods have a shelf-life that runs to years, the older they get, the tougher they become, which means they will need cooking for longer. Buy dried produce from shops with a fast turnover and store in airtight containers in a cool, dark place. Look for bright, unwrinkled produce that is not dusty. With no need to soak, lentils are quick and easy to cook.

Below: Red lentils disintegrate quickly when cooked, but add bulk to meals.

COOKING TIMES FOR LENTILS AND PEAS

This table should be used as a guide for soaked peas and lentils.

Dried peas	40 minutes
Red lentils	20 minutes
Yellow lentils	20 minutes
Green lentils	40–45 minutes
Brown lentils	40–45 minutes
Puy lentils	20–30 minutes
Marrowfat peas	40 minutes
Split peas	45 minutes

BUYING AND STORING BEANS

The edible seeds from plants belonging to the legume family, which include chickpeas and a vast range of beans, are packed with protein, vitamins, minerals and fibre, and are extremely low in fat. For the cook, the ability of beans to absorb the flavours of other foods means that they can be used as the base for an infinite number of dishes. Most dried beans require soaking overnight in cold water before use, so it is wise to plan ahead if using the dried type. Canned beans are ready cooked for instant use in cold dishes or for reheating. Store as for lentils.

Below: There are many types of dried beans, each with a distinct flavour and a good source of protein.

SOAKING DRIED BEANS

All dried beans need to be soaked for a lengthy period of time in water before they can be cooked. This means a bit of forward planning is required.

1 Rinse the beans under running water. Tip the beans into a large bowl and add three times the volume of water. Beans swell to twice their size once soaked. Leave overnight, then drain and refresh the soaking water until ready to use.

COOKING BEANS

Beans are boiled quickly for 10 minutes to kill the enzymes in the bean.

1 Put fresh water in a pan, add the beans and bring to the boil, and boil vigorously for 10 minutes. Turn down the heat and simmer gently for the required time.

NEVER ADD SALT

Salt causes beans to toughen. Avoid salted stock or the cooking liquid from salted meat. Once toughened, beans will not become tender.

MAKING LENTIL PURÉE

Red and yellow lentils cook and break down relatively quickly.

1 Place 250g/9oz/1 cup lentils in a sieve (strainer) and rinse well. Tip into a pan.

2 Cover with 600ml/1 pint/2½ cups water and bring to the boil. Reduce the heat, cover and simmer for 20–25 minutes, until the water is absorbed and the lentils mushy. Season to taste.

COOKING TIMES FOR BEANS

This is a general guide for soaked beans, after boiling for 10 minutes.

Aduki beans	30–45 minutes
Black beans	1 hour
Black-eyed beans	1–1¼ hours
Borlotti beans	1–1½ hours
Broad (fava) beans	1½ hours
Butter/lima beans	1–1¼ hours
Cannellini beans	1 hour
Chickpeas	1–1½–2 hours
Flageolet beans	1–1½ hours
Haricot (navy) beans	1–1½ hours
Kidney beans	1–1½ hours
Pinto beans	1–1¼ hours
Soya beans	2 hours

MAKING HUMMUS

This creamy purée is delicious as a dip with vegetable crudités and warm pitta bread cut into strips.

1 Drain and thoroughly rinse 2 cans of chickpeas. Place them in a blender or food processor and process to a coarse purée.

2 Add the juice of 2 lemons, 2 sliced garlic cloves, 30ml/2 tbsp olive oil, a pinch of cayenne pepper, and 150ml/5oz/¾ cup tahini paste and blend until smooth and creamy, scraping the mixture from the sides of the bowl.

3 Season the purée with salt and pepper and transfer to a serving dish.

4 Sprinkle with oil and cayenne pepper and serve with warmed pitta bread, if you like.

MAKING CANNELLINI BEAN DIP

Spread this dip on crackers.

1 In a sieve (strainer), drain and rinse a 400g/14oz can cannellini beans. Transfer to a bowl. Use a potato masher to purée the beans. Stir in 30ml/2 tbsp olive oil and the grated rind and juice of 1 lemon.

2 Stir in 1 crushed garlic clove and 30ml/2 tbsp chopped parsley. Add a dash of Tabasco sauce and season.

Provençal rice

Roast vegetables are especially delicious with brown rice that can be boiled and finished in the oven. Long grain brown rice is firm when cooked and is nutritionally superior to white rice.

Serves four

2 onions, 1 chopped and 1 cut into wedges
90ml/6 tbsp olive oil
175g/6oz/scant 1 cup long grain brown rice
10ml/2 tsp mustard seeds (optional)
475ml/16fl oz/2 cups vegetable stock
1 large or 2 small red (bell) peppers, seeded and cut into chunks
1 small aubergine (eggplant), cut into cubes
2–3 courgettes (zucchini), sliced
12 cherry tomatoes
5–6 fresh basil leaves, torn into pieces
2 garlic cloves, finely chopped
60ml/4 tbsp white wine
60ml/4 tbsp passata (bottled strained tomatoes) or tomato juice
2 hard-boiled eggs, cut into wedges
8 stuffed green olives, sliced
15ml/1 tbsp capers
3 drained sun-dried tomatoes in oil, sliced
salt and ground black pepper

1 Preheat the oven to 200°C/400°F/Gas 6. Heat 30ml/2 tbsp of the oil in a pan and fry the chopped onion gently for 5–6 minutes until soft.

2 Add the rice and mustard seeds (if using) and stir for 2 minutes.

3 Add the stock, bring to the boil, reduce the heat, cover and simmer gently for 35 minutes.

4 Put the onion wedges in a roasting pan with the peppers, aubergine, courgettes and tomatoes. Scatter over the basil and garlic. Pour over the remaining olive oil and season well.

5 Roast for 20–30 minutes, stirring halfway through cooking. Reduce the oven temperature to 180°C/350°F/Gas 4.

6 Spoon the rice into a casserole. Put the roasted vegetables on top, together with any juices from the roasting pan. Pour over the wine and passata.

7 Arrange the egg wedges on top of the vegetables, with the sliced olives, capers and sun-dried tomatoes. Cover and cook for 15–20 minutes until hot.

Variation

Fry the vegetables in oil in a large pan. Add the wine and juice. Boil, then add to the cooked rice with the other ingredients and serve.

Energy 359kcal/1511kJ; Protein 9.5g; Carbohydrate 59.2g, of which sugars 12.1g; Fat 10g, of which saturates 1.8g; Cholesterol 48mg; Calcium 74mg; Fibre 5.7g; Sodium 114mg.

Garlic rice with mushrooms

Rice is readily infused with the pungent aroma and flavour of garlic chives, creating a dish with an excellent flavour. Serve as a vegetarian supper dish or to accompany fish or chicken.

Serves four

350g/12oz/generous 1½ cups long grain rice
60ml/4 tbsp groundnut (peanut) oil
1 small onion, finely chopped
2 green chillies, seeded and finely chopped
25g/1oz garlic chives, chopped
15g/½oz fresh coriander (cilantro)
600ml/1 pint/2½ cups vegetable or mushroom stock
5ml/1 tsp salt
250g/9oz mixed mushrooms, thickly sliced
50g/2oz cashew nuts, fried in 15ml/ 1 tbsp oil until golden brown
ground black pepper

1 Wash and drain the rice. Heat half the oil in a pan and cook the onion and chillies over a gentle heat, stirring occasionally, for 10–12 minutes, until soft but not browned.

2 Set half the garlic chives aside. Cut the stalks off the coriander and set the leaves aside. Purée the remaining chives and the coriander stalks with the stock in a blender or food processor.

3 Add the rice to the onions and fry over a low heat, stirring frequently, for 4–5 minutes. Pour in the stock, then stir and season well. Bring to the boil, stir just once to make sure the rice does not stick to the pan and reduce the heat to very low. Cover tightly and cook for 15–20 minutes, until the rice has absorbed all the liquid.

4 Heat the remaining oil in a frying pan and cook the mushrooms for 5–6 minutes, until tender. Add the remaining chives and cook for 1–2 minutes.

5 When the rice is cooked, place a clean, folded dish towel over the pan under the lid and press on the lid to wedge it firmly in place.

6 Leave to stand for 10 minutes, allowing the towel to absorb the steam while the rice becomes completely tender.

7 Stir the mushrooms and chopped coriander leaves into the rice. Adjust the seasoning, transfer to a warmed serving dish and serve immediately, scattered with the cashew nuts.

Energy 535kcal/2227kJ; Protein 11g; Carbohydrate 74.7g, of which sugars 1.9g; Fat 21g, of which saturates 3g; Cholesterol 0mg; Calcium 37mg; Fibre 1.8g; Sodium 41mg.

Salmon risotto

The subtle flavour of cucumber is a familiar companion for salmon. In this simple risotto fresh tarragon adds its unmistakable, delicate aroma and flavour.

Serves four

25g/1oz/2 tbsp butter
small bunch of spring onions (scallions), white parts only, chopped
½ cucumber, peeled, seeded and chopped
350g/12oz/1¾ cups risotto rice
1.2 litres/2 pints/5 cups hot chicken or fish stock
150ml/¼ pint/⅔ cup dry white wine
450g/1lb salmon fillet, skinned and diced
45ml/3 tbsp chopped fresh tarragon
salt and ground black pepper

1 Heat the butter in a pan and add the spring onions and cucumber. Cook for 2–3 minutes, stirring occasionally. Do not let the spring onions brown.

2 Stir in the risotto rice, then pour in the stock and white wine. Bring to the boil, then lower the heat and allow to simmer, uncovered, for 10 minutes, stirring occasionally. The rice should absorb most of the liquid.

3 Stir in the salmon and then season to taste. Continue cooking for a further 5 minutes, stirring occasionally to avoid sticking, then remove from the heat. Cover the pan and leave the risotto to stand for 5 minutes.

4 Remove the lid, add the chopped fresh tarragon and mix lightly, preferably with a fork. Spoon the risotto into a warmed bowl and serve immediately.

COOK'S TIP

The classic method for making risotto is to add the liquid in stages. The standing time at the end of cooking is vital for succulent rice and fish.

Energy 597kcal/2492kJ; Protein 30.9g; Carbohydrate 67.1g, of which sugars 1.5g; Fat 19.1g, of which saturates 5.4g; Cholesterol 70mg; Calcium 59mg; Fibre 0.6g; Sodium 96mg.

Baked mushroom risotto

This risotto is easy to make because you don't have to stand over it stirring as it cooks. Porcini mushrooms have an intense flavour so only a small quantity is required.

Serves four

25g/1oz/½ cup dried porcini mushrooms
1 onion, finely chopped
225g/8oz/generous 1 cup risotto rice
30ml/2 tbsp olive oil
1 garlic clove, crushed
salt and ground black pepper.

1 Put the dried mushrooms in a heatproof bowl and pour over 750ml/1¼ pints/3 cups boiling water. Leave to soak for 30 minutes.

2 Drain the mushrooms, reserving the soaking liquid. Rinse the mushrooms under running water to remove any grit, and dry on kitchen paper.

3 Preheat the oven to 180°C/350°F/ Gas 4.

4 Heat the oil in a roasting pan on the hob and add the onion and garlic. Cook for 2–3 minutes, or until softened but not coloured.

5 Add the rice and stir for 1–2 minutes, then add the mushrooms. Pour in the mushroom liquid and mix well. Season, and cover with foil.

6 Bake in the centre of the oven for 30 minutes, stirring occasionally, until all the stock has been absorbed and the rice is tender.

7 Divide between warm serving bowls and serve immediately.

COOK'S TIP
Porcini mushrooms have a very short season, so most often are used dried. Check the packet and only buy whole mushrooms.

Energy 260kcal/1085kJ; Protein 4.8g; Carbohydrate 46.2g, of which sugars 0.9g; Fat 5.9g, of which saturates 0.8g; Cholesterol 0mg; Calcium 16mg; Fibre 0.5g; Sodium 2mg.

Special fried rice

More colourful and elaborate than other fried rice dishes, special fried rice is a meal in itself and is ideal for a midweek supper. It's ideal for using up leftover cooked meat.

Serves four

50g/2oz/⅓ cup peeled cooked prawns (shrimp), thawed if frozen
3 eggs
pinch of salt
2 spring onions (scallions), finely chopped
60ml/4 tbsp vegetable oil
115g/4oz lean cooked pork (or chicken), finely diced or shredded
15ml/1 tbsp light soy sauce
15ml/1 tbsp Chinese rice wine or dry sherry
450g/1lb/6 cups cooked rice
115g/4oz frozen peas

COOK'S TIP
Frozen peeled cooked prawns (shrimp) are a useful standby. They do not need cooking. Reheat them gently or they will be rubbery.

1 Pat the prawns dry with kitchen paper. Beat the eggs with a pinch of the salt and a little of the chopped spring onions.

2 Heat half the oil in a wok, add the pork and stir-fry until golden and thoroughly cooked. Add the prawns and cook for 1 minute, then add the soy sauce and rice wine or sherry. Decant the contents of the wok into a warmed bowl.

3 Heat the remaining oil in the wok. Pour in the eggs and cook, stirring constantly, to lightly scramble the eggs until creamy. Add the rice and stir with chopsticks to make sure that each grain of rice is separated.

4 Add the remaining salt and spring onions, the stir-fried prawns, pork and peas. Toss well together over the heat to combine and serve either hot or cold.

Energy 343kcal/1434kJ; Protein 20.2g; Carbohydrate 40.5g, of which sugars 4.2g; Fat 11.2g, of which saturates 1.6g; Cholesterol 124mg; Calcium 91mg; Fibre 2.4g; Sodium 632mg.

Kedgeree

The origins of this dish are to be found in 'khichiri', an Indian rice and lentil dish. Cooks adapted it to use smoked fish instead of the similar coloured Indian dhal and the result is delicious.

Serves two

250–350g/9–12oz smoked haddock
115g/4oz/generous ½ cup long grain rice
30ml/2 tbsp lemon juice
150ml/¼ pint/⅔ cup single (light) or soured cream (optional)
pinch of freshly grated nutmeg
pinch of cayenne pepper
2 eggs, hard-boiled, shelled and cut into wedges
25g/1oz/2 tbsp butter, cubed (optional)
about 30ml/2 tbsp chopped fresh parsley
salt and ground black pepper

1 Place the haddock in a pan and pour in 350ml/12fl oz water. Heat until simmering, then cook gently for 8–10 minutes, until the fish flakes easily.

2 Lift the fish from the cooking liquid using a slotted spoon, allowing it to drain well. Put on a plate and set aside.

3 Add the rice to the water in the pan and bring to the boil. Stir to make sure the grains do not stick, then reduce the heat to the lowest setting and cover. Cook gently for 15 minutes, until most of the liquid has been absorbed.

4 While the rice is cooking, use a knife and fork to remove any skin and bones from the fish. Separate the fish into large chunks or flakes.

5 Add the fish, lemon juice, cream (if using), nutmeg and cayenne to the pan of rice, leaving the ingredients on top of the rice. Quickly re-cover the pan without stirring anything into the rice and cook for a further 5 minutes. Remove from the heat.

6 Gently fork the ingredients into the rice, adding the egg wedges, butter (if using) and parsley. Taste for seasoning and serve at once.

Variation

This recipe is rich but barely spiced. You could add 5ml/1 tsp turmeric with the rice and 4–6 green cardamoms, if you like, and omit the nutmeg and cayenne for an alternative version. Add the grated rind of 1 lemon and 2 sliced spring onions (scallions) with the fish. Omit the cream and butter for everyday eating – serve with natural (plain) yogurt on the side instead.

Energy 339kcal/1414kJ; Protein 7.6g; Carbohydrate 52.4g, of which sugars 0.7g; Fat 10.9g, of which saturates 6.5g; Cholesterol 27mg; Calcium 44mg; Fibre 1.3g; Sodium 85mg.

Barley risotto

This is more like a pilaff, made with slightly chewy pearl barley, than a classic risotto. Sweet leeks and mellow roasted squash are superb with this nutty grain, which is very simple to cook. The result is a flavourful and filling supper.

Serves four to five

200g/7oz/1 cup pearl barley
1 butternut squash, peeled, seeded and cut into chunks
10ml/2 tsp chopped fresh thyme
60ml/4 tbsp olive oil
25g/1oz/2 tbsp butter
4 leeks, cut into fairly thick diagonal slices
2 garlic cloves, finely chopped
175g/6oz chestnut mushrooms, sliced
2 carrots, coarsely grated
about 120ml/4fl oz/½ cup vegetable stock
30ml/2 tbsp chopped fresh flat leaf parsley
50g/2oz Pecorino cheese, grated or shaved
45ml/3 tbsp pumpkin seeds, toasted, or chopped walnuts
salt and ground black pepper

1 Rinse the barley well under cold running wate. Drain and then cook it in simmering water, keeping the pan part-covered, for 35–45 minutes, or until tender. Drain.

2 Preheat the oven to 200°C/400°F/ Gas 6.

3 Place the squash in a roasting pan with half the thyme. Season with pepper and toss with half the oil. Roast for 30–35 minutes, stirring once.

4 Heat half the butter with the remaining oil in a large frying pan. Add the leeks and garlic and cook gently for 5 minutes. Add the mushrooms and remaining thyme, then cook until the liquid evaporates and the mushrooms begin to fry.

5 Stir in the carrots and cook for 2 minutes, then add the barley and most of the stock. Season well and part-cover the pan. Cook for a further 5 minutes. Pour in the remaining stock if the mixture seems dry.

6 Stir in the parsley, the remaining butter and half the Pecorino. Then stir in the squash. Add seasoning to taste and serve immediately, sprinkled with the toasted pumpkin seeds or walnuts and the remaining Pecorino.

Energy 498kcal/2089kJ; Protein 15.6g; Carbohydrate 55.6g, of which sugars 11.2g; Fat 25.2g, of which saturates 5.2g; Cholesterol 13mg; Calcium 287mg; Fibre 7.6g; Sodium 156mg.

Tabbouleh

This classic Middle Eastern dish is a wonderfully refreshing, tangy salad of bulgur wheat and masses of fresh mint and parsley. The deliciously nutty grains are simply soaked in water, rather than cooked. Increase the amount of fresh herbs for a greener salad.

Serves four to six

250g/9oz/1½ cups bulgur wheat
1 large bunch spring onions (scallions), thinly sliced
1 cucumber, finely chopped or diced
3 tomatoes, chopped
pinch of ground cumin
1 large bunch fresh flat leaf parsley, chopped
1 large bunch fresh mint, chopped
juice of 2 lemons, or to taste
60ml/4 tbsp extra virgin olive oil
cos or romaine lettuce leaves
olives, lemon wedges, tomato wedges, cucumber slices and mint sprigs, to garnish (optional)
natural (plain) yogurt, to serve (optional)

1 Pick over the bulgur wheat to remove any dirt. Place the grains in a large bowl, cover with cold water and leave to soak for 30 minutes. Tip the bulgur wheat into a sieve (strainer) and drain well, shaking it gently to remove any excess water, then return it to the bowl.

2 Add the spring onions to the bulgur wheat, then mix and squeeze together with your hands to combine. Add the cucumber, tomatoes, cumin, parsley, mint, lemon juice and oil to the bulgur wheat and toss well.

3 Heap the tabbouleh on to a bed of lettuce leaves and garnish with olives, lemon wedges, tomato, cucumber and mint sprigs. Serve with a bowl of natural yogurt, if you like.

Variation
Use fresh coriander (cilantro) instead of parsley.

Energy 232kcal/965kJ; Protein 5.2g; Carbohydrate 34.6g, of which sugars 2.7g; Fat 8.4g, of which saturates 1.1g; Cholesterol 0mg; Calcium 51mg; Fibre 1.4g; Sodium 12mg.

Spiced lentil soup

A subtle blend of spices and coconut alters the taste of this classic soup. Serve with crusty bread or warm naan bread to complement the smooth, luscious flavours. The fragrant spices give a warming quality without the harshness of chillies.

Serves six

2 onions, finely chopped
2 garlic cloves, crushed
4 tomatoes, roughly chopped
pinch of ground turmeric
5ml/1 tsp ground cumin
6 cardamom pods
½ cinnamon stick
225g/8oz/1 cup red lentils
400g/14oz can coconut milk
15ml/1 tbsp fresh lime juice
salt and ground black pepper
cumin seeds, to garnish

COOK'S TIP
If the fresh tomatoes are not really ripe and lack flavour or sweetness, you can stir in a little tomato purée (paste). Alternatively, use a small can of chopped tomatoes instead.

1 Put the onions, garlic, tomatoes, turmeric, cumin, cardamom pods, cinnamon and lentils into a pan with 900ml/1½ pints/3¾ cups water. Bring to the boil, lower the heat, cover and simmer gently for 20 minutes, or until the lentils are soft.

2 Remove the cardamom pods and cinnamon stick, then purée the mixture in a food processor. Sieve (strain) the soup, then return it to a clean pan.

3 Reserve a little of the coconut milk for the garnish and add the remainder to the pan with the lime juice. Stir well, then reheat the soup gently, stirring to prevent it from sticking to the pan, and without allowing it to boil. Taste the soup and season with salt and pepper, if needed.

4 Ladle the soup into bowls and swirl in the reserved coconut milk. Garnish with cumin seeds.

Energy 235kcal/991kJ; Protein 13g; Carbohydrate 28.4g, of which sugars 3.7g; Fat 8.8g, of which saturates 2.2g; Cholesterol 0mg; Calcium 66mg; Fibre 2.9g; Sodium 40mg.

Dhal

This spicy lentil mixture, cooked in the style of Indian dhal, makes a well-balanced meal when served with basmati rice or Indian breads. If you don't like hot chillies, leave out the dried red ones, but keep in the green for their flavour. Serve hot with rice or warm breads.

Serves four

45ml/3 tbsp groundnut (peanut) oil
4–5 shallots, sliced
2 garlic cloves, thinly sliced
1 onion, chopped
2 green chillies, seeded and chopped
15ml/1 tbsp chopped fresh root ginger
225g/8oz/1 cup yellow or red lentils
900ml/1½ pints/3¾ cups water
200g/7oz tomatoes, skinned and diced
a little lemon juice
45ml/3 tbsp puréed roasted garlic
5ml/1 tsp ground cumin
5ml/1 tsp ground coriander
salt and ground black pepper
5ml/1 tsp cumin seeds
5ml/1 tsp mustard seeds
3–4 small dried red chillies
8–10 fresh curry leaves
coriander (cilantro) sprigs, to garnish

1 Heat 30ml/2 tbsp of the oil in a large, heavy pan. Fry the shallots over medium heat until crispy, then add the garlic and stir until coloured. Remove with a slotted spoon and set aside.

2 Add the onion, chillies and ginger to the oil remaining in the pan and cook for 10 minutes, until golden.

3 Stir in the lentils and add the water, then bring to the boil, reduce the heat and part-cover the pan. Simmer, stirring occasionally, for 50–60 minutes, until it is the consistency of thick soup.

4 Stir the tomatoes into the dhal and then adjust the seasoning, adding a little lemon juice to taste, if necessary.

5 Add the roasted garlic purée, cumin and ground coriander, then season with salt and pepper to taste again.

6 Cook for 10–15 minutes, stirring to stop the mixture from sticking.

7 Heat the remaining oil in a frying pan. With the pan over low to medium heat, add the cumin and mustard seeds and fry for a few seconds until the mustard seeds pop. Remove from the heat immediately before the spices burn.

8 Stir the roasted seeds into the dhal with the chillies and curry leaves. Serve, garnished with coriander and shallots.

Energy 234kcal/979kJ; Protein 9.5g; Carbohydrate 23.8g, of which sugars 3.1g; Fat 11.8g, of which saturates 5.3g; Cholesterol 20mg; Calcium 28mg; Fibre 2.5g; Sodium 73mg.

Puy lentils with poached eggs

Small dark Puy lentils have a good nutty flavour and, combined with lemon juice and crème fraîche, they make a delicious, slightly tangy base for poached eggs. This makes an excellent vegetarian main meal – serve with lots of watercress and rocket as a side salad.

2 Heat the oil in a frying pan. Add the spring onions and garlic and fry over a medium heat for 1 minute or until softened.

3 Add the Dijon mustard, lemon rind and juice, and mix well. Stir in the tomatoes and seasoning, then cook gently for 1–2 minutes until the tomatoes are heated through but still retain their shape. Add a little water if the mixture becomes too dry.

Serves four

250g/9oz/generous 1 cup Puy lentils
1 bay leaf or bouquet garni
30ml/2 tbsp olive oil
4 spring onions (scallions), sliced
2 large garlic cloves, chopped
15ml/1 tbsp Dijon mustard
finely grated rind and juice of 1 large lemon
4 plum tomatoes, seeded and diced
4 eggs
60ml/4 tbsp crème fraîche
salt and ground black pepper
30ml/2 tbsp chopped fresh flat leaf parsley, to garnish

Variation
Fried eggs can be used instead of poached. Use a little oil and cover the pan to set the egg tops.

1 Put the lentils and bay leaf in a pan, cover with cold water and bring to the boil. Reduce the heat and simmer, partially covered, for 25 minutes. Stir occasionally. Drain.

Variation
Instead of poached eggs, top the lentils with grilled halloumi cheese.

4 Meanwhile, poach the eggs separately in a pan of barely simmering salted water. Keep warm under a kitchen foil tent.

5 Add the lentils and crème fraîche to the tomato mixture, remove the bay leaf, and heat for 1 minute.

6 Divide the lentil mixture into four portions and put each on a plate. Put a poached egg on top and sprinkle over a handful of chopped fresh parsley.

Energy 398kcal/1671kJ; Protein 22.4g; Carbohydrate 39g, of which sugars 5.2g; Fat 18.2g, of which saturates 6.6g; Cholesterol 207mg; Calcium 80mg; Fibre 4.2g; Sodium 106mg.

Spicy chickpea samosas

A blend of crushed chickpeas and coriander sauce makes an interesting nutty and aromatic filling in these little pastries. The samosas are delicious served with a simple dip made from Greek yogurt and chopped fresh mint leaves.

Makes eighteen

2 x 400g/14oz cans chickpeas, drained and rinsed
120ml/4fl oz/½ cup hara masala or coriander (cilantro) sauce
275g/10oz filo pastry
60ml/4 tbsp chilli and garlic oil

1 Preheat the oven to 220°C/425°F/ Gas 7.

2 Process half the chickpeas to a paste in a food processor.

3 Transfer the paste to a bowl and mix in the whole chickpeas, the hara masala or coriander sauce, and a little salt. Mix until well combined.

Variation
For a milder flavour use butter instead of oil when brushing the filo pastry.

4 Place a sheet of filo pastry on a work surface and cut into three strips. Brush the strips with a little of the oil. Place a dessertspoon of the filling at one end of a strip. Turn one corner diagonally over the filling to meet the long edge. Continue folding along the length of the strip, turning the filling and pastry and keeping the triangular shape.

5 Transfer to a baking sheet and repeat with the remaining filling and pastry.

6 Place the pastries on a baking sheet and brush with any remaining oil. Bake for 15 minutes, until the pastry is golden. Cool slightly before serving.

Energy 119kcal/499kJ; Protein 4.1g; Carbohydrate 13.7g, of which sugars 0.4g; Fat 5.7g, of which saturates 0.8g; Cholesterol 0mg; Calcium 36mg; Fibre 2.2g; Sodium 99mg.

Fish and shellfish

The variety of dishes in this chapter indicates how versatile and exciting fish and shellfish are as cooking ingredients. From indulgent crisp-coated fried fish or rich prawns in garlic butter to stylish poached salmon, there are all sorts of ways to treat fresh, frozen or canned seafood. This section shows you how to make the most of these quick-to-cook foods.

Fish and shellfish basics

There is a good range of fresh fish and seafood sold prepared and ready to cook, none of it requiring expert handling. As well as independent fishmongers, all supermarket fish counters provide a back-up service, cleaning whole fish, filleting, skinning and boning even the smallest piece. Remember to allow time for the staff to do this, especially in a busy store.

The fish that we buy is sourced from both freshwater suppliers and from the sea. Freshwater fish are those that live in rivers, streams and lakes. These environments have a low saline content, which the fish have adapted to live in. Of the fish that we eat, salmon and trout are most often associated with freshwater environments. Salmon begins life in freshwater, and from there makes its way out to sea, returning to the river environment to reproduce. Eel, on the other hand, begins life at sea and makes its way to estuaries to spend its life in freshwater. Fish caught at sea forms the bulk of the fish that we eat. A fish's habitat does not affect the way that it is cooked.

There are plenty of types of fish available, each with subtly different flavours and textures. Most fish can be divided into two types: round fish are those with thicker bodies. The flesh can be cut into steaks, fillets, or cutlets, all of which may contain small bones. Round fish include salmon, cod and haddock. Flat fish, on the other hand, have one thick central bone that runs the length of the body. A row of smaller bones at each side are attached to the larger bone. Such fish include sole, plaice and tuna.

Fish can also be divided into white fish and oily fish. Oily fish contains omega-3 oils that are good for us. The flesh of oily fish is usually pink in colour. Small fish, eaten whole, are available.

Shellfish include mussels, clams, cockles, oysters, prawns (shrimp), crabs, crayfish and lobster. Of these, mussels and crayfish may be found in fresh and salt waters.

BUYING FRESH FISH

When selecting fish, try to choose the freshest available. Smell is one simple indicator that may give a clue to quality. Fresh fish in clean surroundings does not give off a strong, nose-pinching odour. The whole display should look fresh and bright and be presented in refrigerated conditions. Modest amounts of good-looking fish that are likely to sell quickly are more appealing than mounds of fish that are days old.

Whole fresh fish should have shiny moist skin, clear, unsunken eyes and bright pink or rosy red gills, certainly not grey or dark green. The body should be plump, stiff and unyielding to touch.

Fish should look firm, not floppy. The flakes should look like flakes, not pulpy or 'fluffy' on top. White fish should look white, not beige or yellow.

Smoked fish that is bright yellow has been dyed and tastes of artificial smoke flavours. Look for naturally smoked fish, with a pale gold colour, for far better, subtle flavour.

As well as loose fish from the fish counter, there is usually a range of pre-packed fresh fish available in supermarkets. Select carefully, rejecting any fish that looks inferior.

Below: Plump, peeled cooked prawns are considered a luxury food.

BUYING SHELLFISH

Beginners are unlikely to be confident about tackling live lobster or crab, but mussels are relatively easy to handle (just a little time consuming). However, the rule is that live should be lively. Mussels, clams and cockles that may be sold live should be moist, bright and have closed shells. Open and damaged shells indicate dead shellfish that have to be discarded.

Raw prawns (shrimp) or squid should both look bright, moist and fresh and grey in colour. They should be firm, not watery. Check whether 'fresh' fish or shellfish and seafood have been frozen and thawed for the display. It is vital to know because you cannot then re-freeze the items raw (although they would be fine to re-freeze once cooked, for example in fishcakes or a fish pie). Cooked shellfish should be pink in colour.

BUYING FROZEN FISH

Plain frozen fish can be good quality, practical and an excellent standby item to keep in the freezer. Buy from a store that has a quick turnover. Check the quality carefully, looking for robust packaging that is sealed and stored in

Below: Succulent cod fillets have a robust flavour and a dense texture that can take strong spices.

freezers that are not over-filled and reserved for displaying frozen food (not ice-cream freezers, for example).

Inspect fish fillets for any signs of freezer burn or dry, very white-looking patches. This may occur as a result of poor packing and over-long storage and definitely won't add anything good to the flavour of the fish. When cooked the fish will be dry, stringy and tasteless. Avoid any fish fillets that look discoloured and packs in which the products are covered in lots of ice or stuck together. Freezers should be clean and not iced up. Check sell-by and use-by dates on packets – these should be extremely long, with months to go before the products need eating.

BUYING CANNED FISH

Anchovies are useful for all sorts of flavouring roles. Tuna is a basic store-cupboard item; salmon is also good for hot and cold dishes. Sardines, mackerel, smoked mackerel and other small fish are useful for pâtés, salads, pasta dressings, toast toppers and baked potato fillings. Packed in brine, or oil, they are extremely versatile.

Canned white or dressed crab is expensive but it is a good ingredient. Smoked oysters and lumpfish roe are also useful store-cupboard items for making stylish starters or main courses.

BUYING SMOKED FISH

Smoked salmon is available in a wide variety of qualities and different cuts. Whole or part sides, slices or trimmings have different uses. Sides are ideal for larger gatherings or special occasions, but a good large, sharp knife and confident cutting is necessary for slicing the fish thinly. Ready sliced smoked salmon makes an instant starter or light meal, with lemon and salad, and brown bread and butter. Off-cuts and trimmings are handy for salads, pasta dishes and a wide variety of other recipes, including pâté and mousses.

Smoked trout is finer in flavour than salmon and more of a treat now that smoked salmon is so widely available.

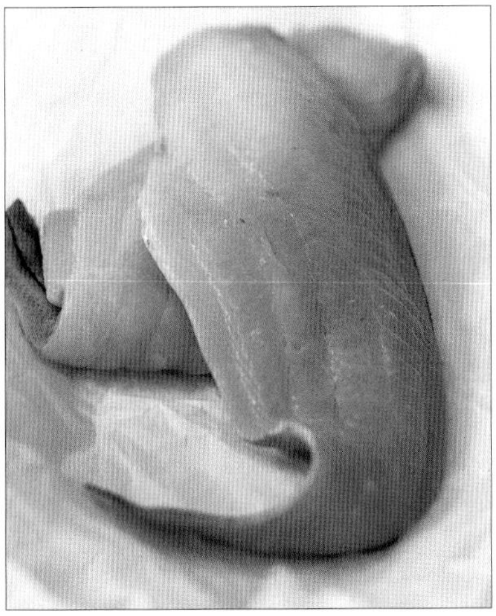

Above: Undyed smoked haddock is excellent in fish pies topped with mashed potato.

Smoked mackerel is hot smoked, which means it is cooked, so the fillets separate easily into chunks or flakes. This is useful for salads, pâtés and a wide variety of dishes. The fillets can be served as they are, with lemon and salad. The easiest way to flake the fish off the skin is by hand, removing any stray bones at the same time. Alternatively, place the fish on a plate and use two forks to pull them apart.

Below: Mussels are contained in tightly sealed shells that open when cooked to reveal their contents: any that remain shut should be discarded.

Above: King scallops are removed from their shell with the orange roe or 'coral'. They are considered a luxury food.

Hot smoked salmon is also available – it has a pale colour and cooked appearance with firm flakes.

STORING FRESH FISH

Unwrap loose-wrapped fish and seafood, transfer it to a large clean plate, dish or bowl, cover and chill it as soon as possible. Leave pre-packed items in their sealed packs. Use within 24 hours of purchase (or according to the date on the packet).

THAWING FROZEN FISH

Follow the packet instructions, usually by thawing the fish in a covered container in the refrigerator for several hours at least or preferably overnight.

The microwave is useful for thawing but do be aware that it is very easy to begin cooking fish fillets in places, or unevenly thaw prawns (shrimp) and small items, which can ruin the food. Follow the microwave manufacturer's instructions; if they are not available, the best emergency advice is to give the food a few seconds (10 seconds, for example) and check, turning and rearranging the items. It is best to thaw fish and seafood part-way, to get rid of the excess liquid, but leave the items icy in places, rather than completely thawed and part-cooked in places.

Preparing and cooking fish and shellfish

It should not be necessary to rinse filleted fish under cold water before cooking it, but if there are bits of black membrane around the fillet, they can be rubbed off easily with a piece of kitchen paper, then the fillet rinsed and dried. Gutted whole fish should be rinsed and dried. Prepared fillets, steaks and cutlets, cooked peeled or whole shellfish, and prepared squid should not need rinsing. If any products are taken out of packets, then it is best to give them a quick rinse under cold water and pat them dry.

Never soak or over-wash fish and seafood. The exceptions include mussels and similar shellfish that have to be thoroughly scrubbed.

Fish can be poached, steamed, baked, deep-fried, shallow-fried and grilled (broiled). It can be cut into chunks and added like shellfish, to stir-fries, tagines, pasta sauce and pies.

SKINNING FISH FILLETS

Round and flat fish fillets are skinned in the same way. A really sharp knife is essential for a clean cut and holding the knife at the right angle is vital to avoid cutting the skin. Fillets that are three-quarters frozen can be skinned. When enough tail skin is loosened, it can be pulled off the body without cutting.

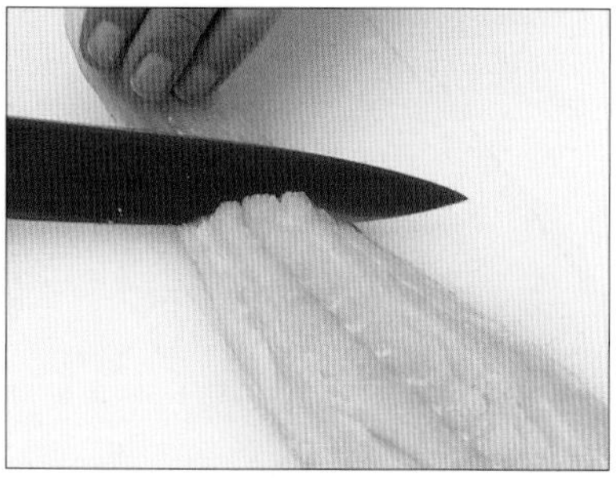

1 Place the fillet on a board with the skin side down and the tail towards you. Dip your fingers in a little salt to stop them slipping and grip the tail firmly. Hold the knife between skin and flesh at a 45 degree angle and cut from side to side using a sawing action.

2 Working from the tail to the head, cut along the length of the fillet, folding the flesh forwards as you go and making sure you keep the skin taut.

REMOVING SMALL BONES

Bones are easy to find and remove.

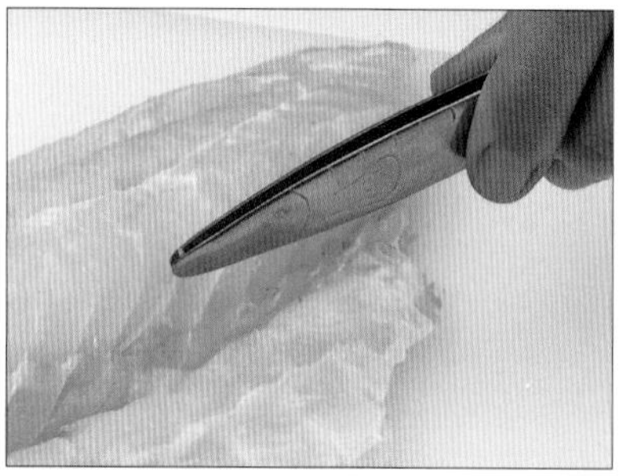

1 Run your finger lightly down the fillet to feel for any bones and pull them out as you come across them – tweezers are useful for doing this.

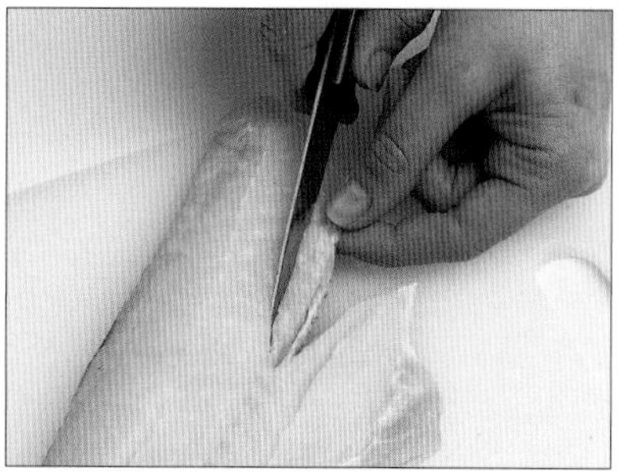

2 Some fillets have a group of tiny bones just behind the gill fins. Cut down each side of the line of bones with a sharp knife or scissors and remove the v-shaped piece of flesh holding the bones.

CLEANING AND COOKING FRESH MUSSELS

This plentiful shellfish is economic to buy, though slightly fiddly to cook from fresh. Mussels can be cooked on their own and enjoyed cold and plain as a snack, with or without vinegar, or more commonly, they are cooked with a sauce for a starter, or as a main course served with bread and chips.

1 Scrub the mussels to clean them using a brush or wire edged scrubbing pad and discard any that do not open when tapped. Those that will not open should not be cooked. Remove any beards by pulling them off with your fingers.

2 Put the mussels into a shallow heavy pan without any liquid. Cover tightly and cook over a high heat on the stove for a few minutes to steam the mussels inside. The steam causes the mussels to open. Discard any mussels that don't open at this stage.

3 Shell all the mussels and discard the shells unless you are going to make stock with them.

PEELING AND DEVEINING RAW PRAWNS (SHRIMP)

Raw prawns and large shrimp are often peeled before cooking. Raw prawns must have their intestinal tracts removed before cooking, a process that is known as 'deveining'. It is not necessary to devein shrimp.

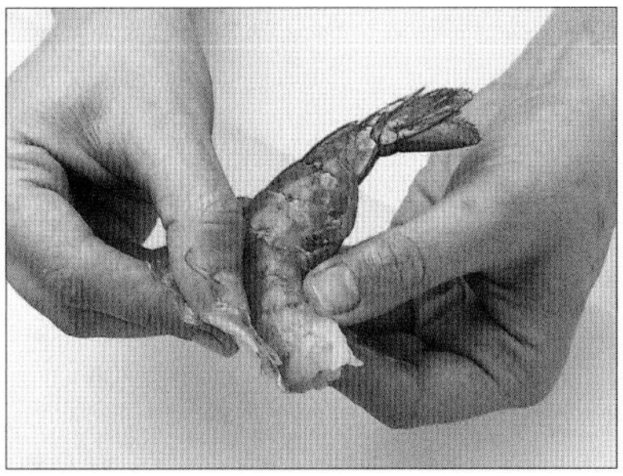

1 Pull off the head and legs from each prawn or shrimp, then carefully peel off the body shell with your fingers. Leave on the tail 'fan' if you wish.

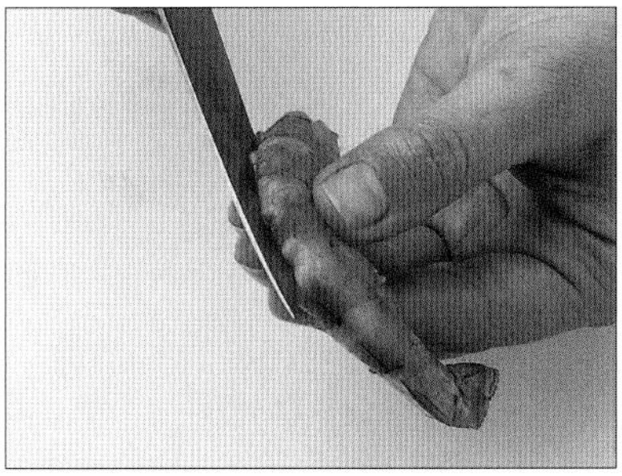

2 To remove the intestinal vein from prawns, make a shallow incision down the centre of the curved back of the prawn using a small sharp knife, cutting all the way from the tail to the head.

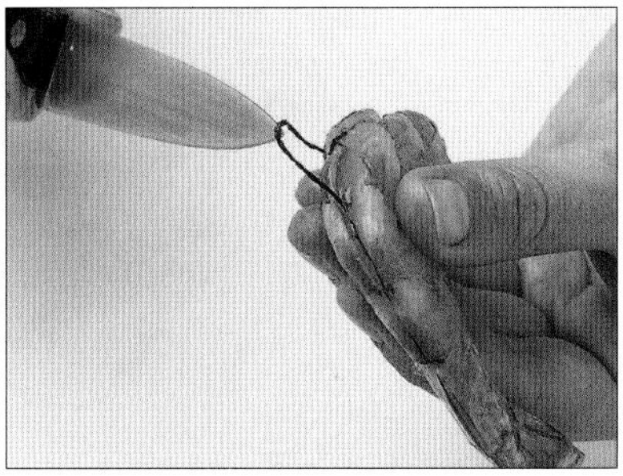

3 Pick out the thin black vein.

POACHING FISH

This is a good method for all fish and seafood. Large fish, such as a whole salmon, can be poached in a special fish kettle but thick chunks of fillet, steaks, cutlets and small whole fish (such as trout) can be cooked in a frying pan, casserole or pan.

The poaching liquid can be thickened with cornflour (cornstarch) or added to flour cooked in butter to make a sauce to serve with the fish.

Above: A fish kettle is the perfect container in which to poach whole fish suitable to serve to large gatherings of people.

1 Cook a little chopped onion and a bay leaf in butter or oil until softened. Diced celery and carrot can be added.

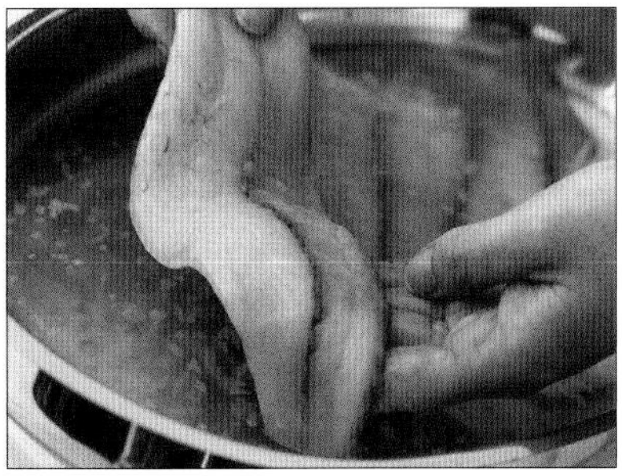

2 Add the fish and just enough milk, stock, water, or white wine to cover it. If the fish is thin (such as plaice) roll or fold the fillets in half so that they form a fairly even shape, otherwise very thin tail ends cook far more quickly (also, they will not fit in the pan, particularly if you are cooking several at a time.

3 Heat until just simmering, then cover and keep the heat low. If the liquid boils, the fish will fall apart. The fish will usually cook in about 5 minutes, but small whole fish, such as trout, take about 10 minutes or longer.

4 Remove the fish and then hold it over the pan to drain. Transfer to a serving dish or plates.

BAKING FISH

Whole fish, chunky fish steaks and fillets such as cod or halibut, or thinner rolled fillets are perfect for baking. As a rule about 180°C/350°F/ Gas 4 or one setting higher is perfect for baking fish.

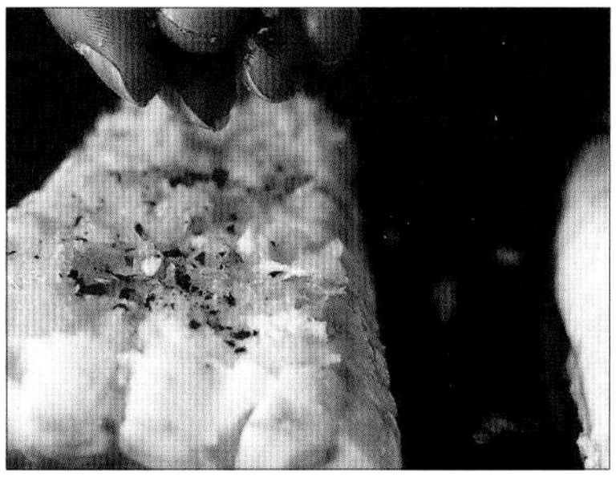

1 Season the fish, add herbs or citrus rind, dot with butter or drizzle with olive oil, and cover.

COOKING FROZEN FISH

In theory fish should be gently thawed but in practice time is often too short and having separate portions in the freezer means they can be cooked from frozen. Prawns and other frozen seafood should be thawed and drained as they tend to be covered in a thin layer of protective ice.

BRAISING FISH

This is an excellent moist cooking method for small or large fish or large fish portions.

1 Preheat the oven to 180°C/350°F/ Gas 4. Grease an ovenproof dish and add a layer of thinly sliced or shredded vegetables, such as carrots, onions, fennel and celery.

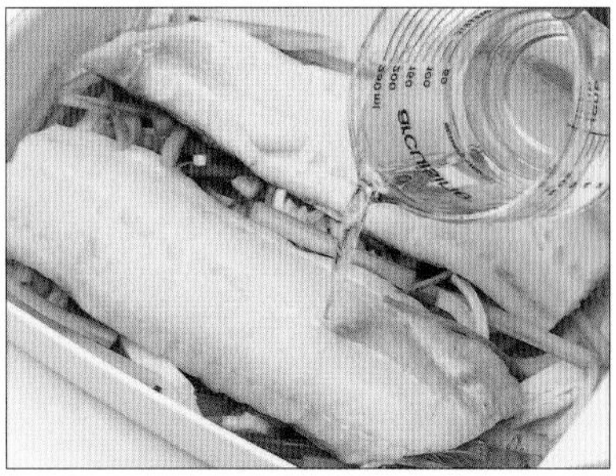

2 Place the fish on top and pour on enough white wine and/or stock to cover the vegetables and come a quarter to nearly halfway up the dish.

3 Dot with butter or drizzle with a little olive oil, and scatter over 15ml/1 tbsp of fresh chopped herbs . Cover with buttered baking parchment. Bake for 20–45 minutes.

GRILLING (BROILING) FISH

The intense dry heat of this method is ideal for fish, especially those types that contain a lot of natural oil, such as salmon, mackerel and tuna. Fish dries out quickly when overcooked, so it is important to stay 'hands on', watching the fish closely. Basting the fish frequently helps to keep it moist. Turning is best limited to once only to avoid breaking up fragile fish. Always preheat the grill (broiler). Line the pan with foil to catch juices.

1 Grilling is a useful technique for small whole fish, boned and butterflied fish, fillets, cutlets and steaks that are at least 1.5cm/½in thick, or cubes of fish for skewers. Rinse and pat dry.

2 Preheat the grill. Line the pan with foil and brush it well with oil. If the fish has skin on, arrange it skin side up first. Arrange the fish in the pan in one layer. Brush the fish with butter or oil.

COOK'S TIP

Grill (broil) the skin side of fish first. A fish slice or metal spatula slides easily between the grill pan and skin.

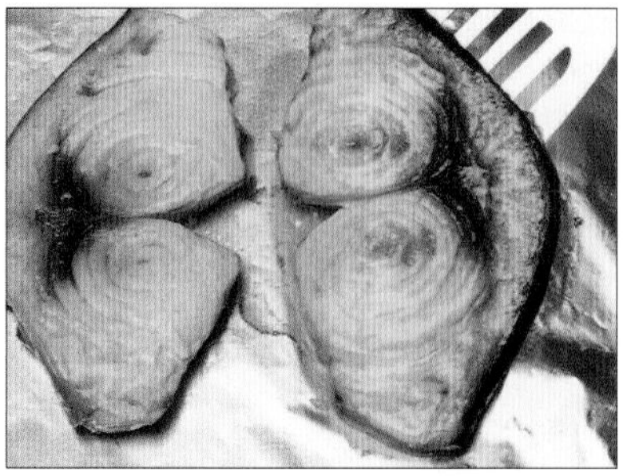

3 Grill (broil) until brown, turn and baste or dot with butter, and cook the second side until browned or just cooked.

MAKING FISH PARCELS

Baking *en papillote* (in a parcel) retains all the flavour of the fish. Non-stick baking parchment may be used, but foil is easier to handle. Small portions or rolls, single or several together, or whole fish (large or small) can be cooked this way.

1 Cut the foil or paper so it is large enough to enclose the fish completely.

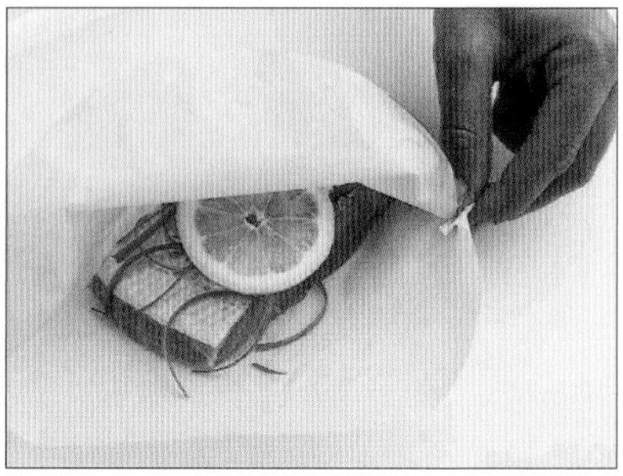

2 Centre the fish on the paper. Add diced onion, herbs, lemon, butter, olive oil and seasoning. Seal the paper around the fish and contents

3 Place on a baking tray or in a roasting pan and bake in the centre of the oven. Serve each individual packet on a separate hot dinner plate.

COOK'S TIP

Tail ends of fish don't contain any bones, so if you like boneless fish, try these, rather than fillets.

COATING FISH FOR FRYING

Fish to be fried is often coated with egg and breadcrumbs or batter. The coating makes a crisp crust.

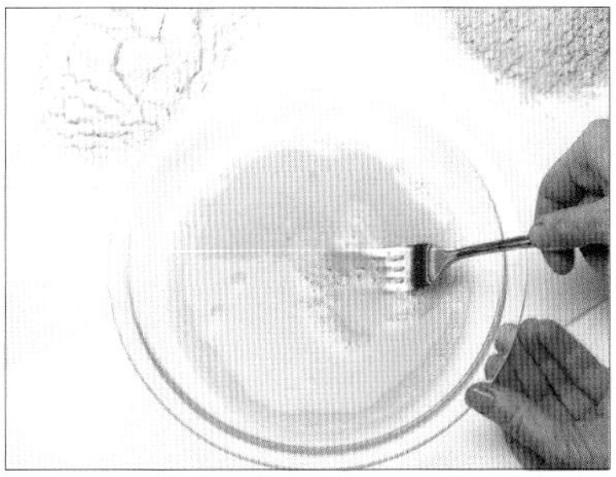

1 Lightly beat an egg in a shallow dish. Spread flour on a plate and season with salt and pepper. Spread fine white breadcrumbs on another plate.

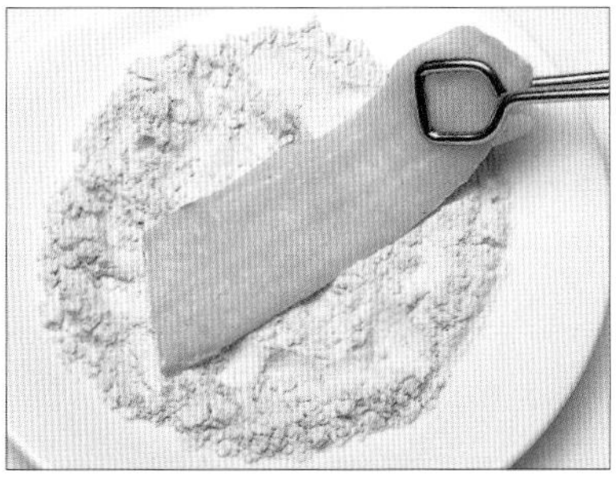

2 Dip the fish first in the seasoned flour, turning to coat both sides lightly and evenly. Shake or brush off excess flour.

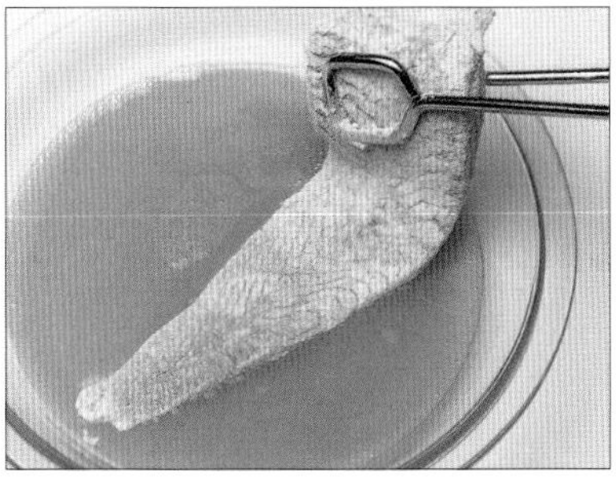

3 Dip the floured fish in the egg, turning to coat it thoroughly on both sides.

4 Dip the fish in the crumbs, turning to coat it evenly. Shake off any excess crumbs. Refrigerate for 20 minutes to set the coating.

SHALLOW-FRYING FISH

Fish that is fried needs constant vigilance. The finished product should be crispy and lightly browned. Getting the temperature right is the key to good results. Cut a cube of day-old bread and add it to the heated oil. If it makes the oil sizzle then the temperature is fine for cooking the fish.

1 Heat a little oil or mixture of oil and butter in a frying pan, adding enough fat to coat the bottom of the pan in a thin layer. When it is very hot, add the fish, in one layer. Fry until golden brown on both sides. Drain on kitchen paper.

DEEP-FRYING FISH

When fish is deep-fried, it means that it is completely submerged in the fat. The fish is coated with batter or bread-crumbs first and the fat penetrates this outer layer. The fish is steamed inside by this method.

1 Quarter to one-third fill a deep pan with oil and heat it to 375°F/190°C on a deep-frying thermometer. Gently lower the fish into the oil, adding one or two pieces at a time. Fry until golden brown, turning once or twice. Remove and drain on kitchen paper.

WHEN IS FISH COOKED?

When fish flakes separate easily and look opaque rather than translucent then the fish is cooked. Notice the term is 'separate' and not 'fall apart', so to check if the fish is cooked, gently insert the point of a knife between the flakes, selecting the thickest and/or central part.

Overcooking makes fish dry, and the flavour tends to become slightly too pronounced rather than subtle. Fresh tuna and swordfish both have a tendency to be quite dry, so it is important not to overcook them. Tuna should only just be opaque – many people prefer the fish to be dark in the middle, resembling rare meat.

Overcooking prawns (shrimp), mussels and squid makes them shrink and become tough and rubbery. Raw prawns (in their shells or peeled) are cooked when they become firm, opaque and turn pink. Peeled or shelled cooked seafood simply needs heating through, so should be added to cooked dishes at the last minute. Squid (the white rings or small whole body sacs) become firm when cooked: if they are fried or grilled (broiled) for too long, they become tough, but whole sacs, for example stuffed, and tentacles may be braised slowly until tender.

Below: When cooked the flesh separates into 'flakes'.

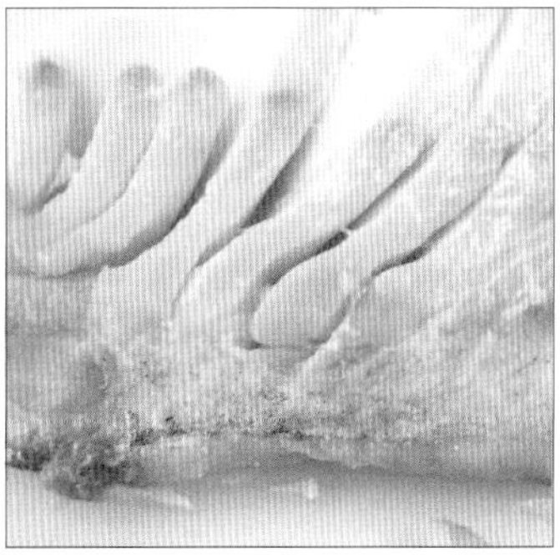

Seared tuna salad Niçoise

Freshly seared tuna steaks transform this classic salad from the south of France into a special dish that makes a great supper to share with friends. Be careful not to overcook the tuna.

Serves four

4 tuna steaks, each about 150/5oz
30ml/2 tbsp olive oil
225g/8oz fine French beans, trimmed
2 Little Gem (Bibb) lettuces
4 new potatoes, boiled
4 ripe tomatoes or 12 cherry tomatoes
2 red (bell) peppers, seeded and sliced
4 hard-boiled eggs, sliced
8 drained anchovy fillets in oil, halved lengthways
16 large black olives
salt and ground black pepper
12 fresh basil leaves, to garnish

For the dressing
15ml/1 tbsp red wine vinegar
90ml/6 tbsp olive oil
1 fat garlic clove, crushed

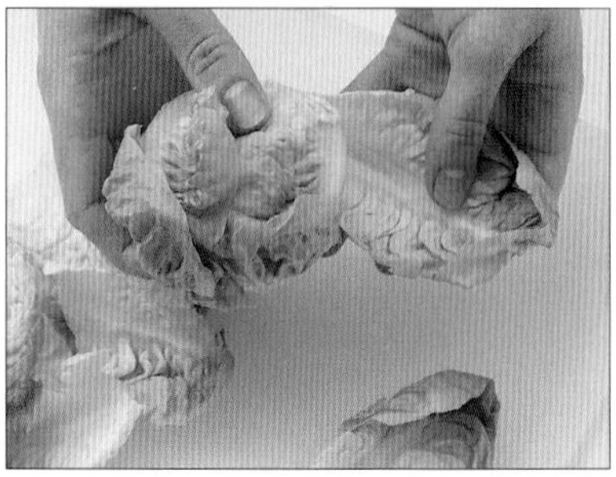

1 Brush the tuna on both sides with olive oil and season well. Heat the grill (broiler) until very hot, then grill (broil) the tuna for 1–2 minutes on each side; it should be pink and juicy in the centre.

2 Cook the beans in a pan of salted boiling water for 4–5 minutes. Drain, refresh with cold water and drain again.

3 Separate the lettuce leaves and wash and dry them. Arrange them on four plates. Slice the potatoes and tomatoes, and divide them among the plates. Arrange the fine French beans and red pepper strips over them.

4 Shell the hard-boiled eggs and cut them into thick slices. Divide the eggs among the four plates and drape over an anchovy fillet. Scatter four olives on each plate.

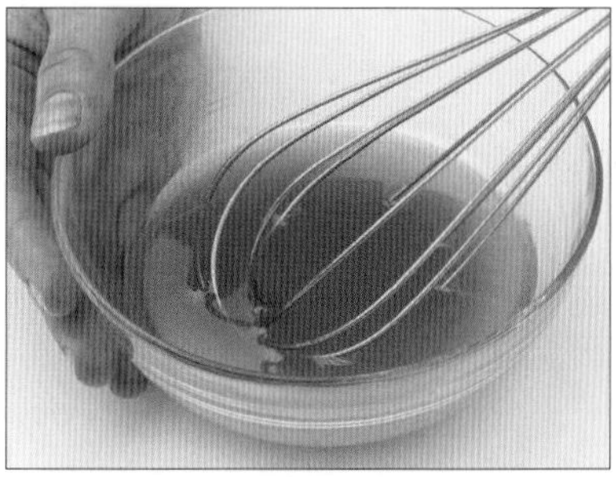

5 To make the dressing, whisk together the vinegar, olive oil and garlic and season to taste. Drizzle over the salads, arrange the tuna steaks on top, scatter over the basil leaves and serve.

COOK'S TIP
Tuna is often served pink in the middle, rare like beef. If you prefer it cooked through, reduce the heat and cook for an extra few minutes, but take care not to overcook.

Energy 578kcal/2408kJ; Protein 46.4g; Carbohydrate 15g, of which sugars 10.6g; Fat 37.5g, of which saturates 7.1g; Cholesterol 235mg; Calcium 127mg; Fibre 4.7g; Sodium 585mg.

Fish and chips

This classic dish of fish cooked in batter and served with chips is one of England's national dishes. A portion of peas goes well. Salt and vinegar are traditional accompaniments.

Serves four

115g/4oz/1 cup self-raising (self-rising) flour
150ml/¼ pint/⅔ cup water
675g/1½lb potatoes
oil, for deep frying
675g/1½lb skinned cod fillet, cut into four pieces
lemon wedges, to serve
salt and ground black pepper

1 Stir the flour and salt together in a bowl, then make a well in the centre. Gradually whisk in the water to make a smooth batter. Leave to rest for 30 minutes.

2 Cut the potatoes into strips about 1cm/½in wide and a similar length to each other so that they cook evenly. Put the potato chips in a colander and rinse them under cold running water. Dry well.

3 Heat the oil in a deep-fat fryer or large heavy pan to 150°C/300°F. Don't leave the pan unattended.

4 Using a wire basket, lower the potatoes in batches into the hot oil and cook for 5–6 minutes, shaking the basket occasionally until the chips are soft but not browned. Remove the chips from the oil and drain them thoroughly on kitchen paper.

5 Increase the heat of the oil in the fryer to 190°C/375°F. Season the pieces of fish with salt and pepper. Stir the batter, then dip the fish into it, one piece at a time, allowing the excess to drain off.

6 Working in two batches if necessary, lower the fish into the hot oil and fry for 6–8 minutes, until crisp and brown. Drain the fish on kitchen paper and keep warm.

7 Make sure the oil is hot again, then add a batch of chips, cooking for 2–3 minutes, until brown and crisp. Keep hot while cooking the other batches. Sprinkle with salt and vinegar to serve.

Energy 645kcal/2700kJ; Protein 32.6.4g; Carbohydrate 54.3g, of which sugars 0.7g; Fat 34.5g, of which saturates 3.5g; Cholesterol 38mg; Calcium 130mg; Fibre 3.4g; Sodium 294mg.

Salmon fishcakes

Home-made fishcakes are delicious and surprisingly easy to make. Fishcakes can be made ahead of time and chilled for up to a day until you are ready to cook them.

Serves four

450g/1lb salmon fillet
olive oil, for brushing
675g/1½lb potatoes, boiled and mashed
25g/1oz/2 tbsp butter, melted
10ml/2 tsp wholegrain mustard
15ml/1 tbsp each chopped fresh dill and chopped fresh flat leaf parsley
grated rind and juice of ½ lemon
15g/½oz/1 tbsp plain (all-purpose) flour
1 egg, lightly beaten
150g/5oz/generous 1 cup dried breadcrumbs
60ml/4 tbsp sunflower oil
salt and ground white pepper
rocket (arugula) leaves and fresh chives, to garnish
lemon wedges, to serve

1 Preheat the oven to 350°F/180°C/Gas 4. Place the salmon fillets on a baking sheet, brush with olive oil and bake for 20–25 minutes, or until cooked through. Allow to cool.

2 Flake the cooked salmon and discard any skin and bones.

3 Place the flaked salmon in a bowl with the mashed potato, melted butter and mustard. Mix well, then stir in the dill, parsley, lemon rind and juice. Season to taste.

4 Divide the mixture into eight portions and shape each into a ball, then flatten into a thick disc. Dip the fishcakes in flour, then in egg, then in breadcrumbs.

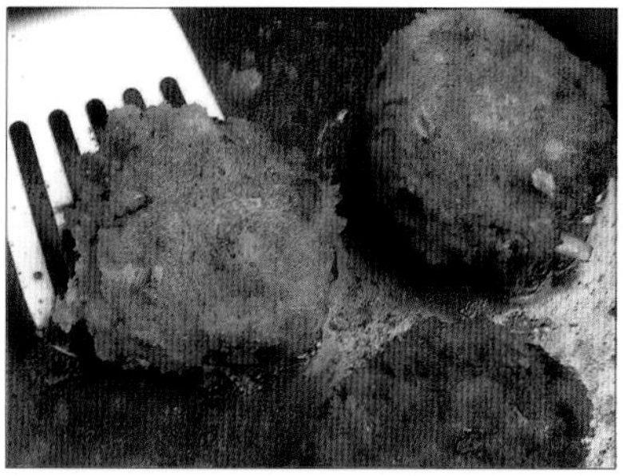

5 Heat the oil in a frying pan until very hot. Fry the fishcakes in batches until golden brown and crisp all over. Drain on kitchen paper and keep hot. Serve with rocket, chives and lemon wedges.

Variations

- Almost any white or smoked fish is suitable. Try smoked cod or haddock or a mixture of smoked and unsmoked fish.
- Try drained canned tuna or salmon (use the liquid from salmon in the mashed potato).
- Make prawn (shrimp) cakes with chopped peeled cooked prawns.
- To save coating, shape the cakes and dust with flour. Place on a greased ovenproof dish, dot with butter or drizzle with oil. Bake in a preheated oven at 200°C/400°F/Gas 6 for about 20 minutes, until lightly browned. Alternatively, grill (broil) on a greased baking tray, turning once.

Energy 586kcal/2453kJ; Protein 29.8g; Carbohydrate 49.9g, of which sugars 3.2g; Fat 31g, of which saturates 7.2g; Cholesterol 117mg; Calcium 79mg; Fibre 1.3g; Sodium 266mg.

Spiced salmon en papillote

Cooking fish in a paper parcel steams the fish and the aromatic ingredients, such as leeks and herbs that accompany it. The parcels may be prepared ahead of cooking and chilled.

Serves six

25ml/1½ tbsp groundnut (peanut) oil
2 large yellow bell peppers, seeded and thinly sliced
4cm/1½in fresh root ginger, peeled and finely shredded
1 large fennel bulb, finely sliced, feathery tops chopped and reserved
1 green chilli, seeded and finely shredded
2 large leeks, cut into 10cm/4in lengths and shredded lengthways
30ml/2 tbsp snipped chives
10ml/2 tsp light soy sauce
6 portions salmon fillet, each weighing 150–175g/5–6oz, skinned
10ml/2 tsp toasted sesame oil
salt and ground black pepper

1 Heat the oil in a large non-stick frying pan and cook the peppers, ginger and fennel for 5–6 minutes, until they are softened but not browned. Add the shredded chilli and leeks and cook for a further 2–3 minutes. Stir in half the chives and the soy sauce with seasoning to taste. Set the vegetable mixture aside to cool.

COOK'S TIP
Foil is simpler to manage than paper as it scrunches up and seals easily. Small cook bags also work well and they have ovenproof ties.

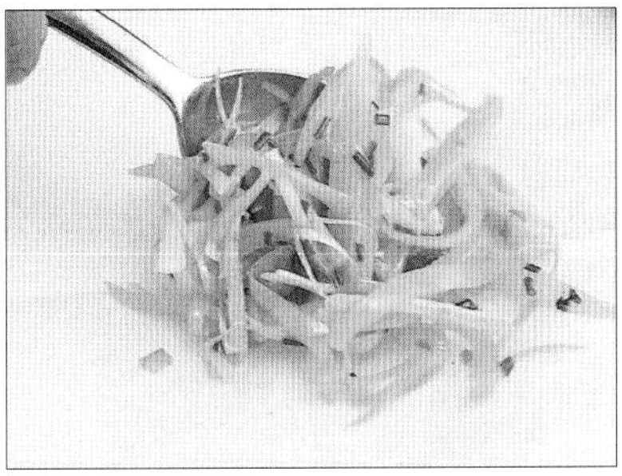

2 Preheat the oven to 190°C/375°F/Gas 5. Cut six circles of baking parchment or foil each 35cm/14in. Divide the vegetable mixture between the circles and place a portion of salmon on top. Drizzle with sesame oil and sprinkle with the remaining chives and the chopped fennel tops. Season with salt and pepper.

3 Fold the paper or foil over to enclose the fish, rolling and twisting the edges together to seal the parcels.

4 Place the parcels on a baking sheet and bake for 15–20 minutes, until the parcels are puffed up. Transfer the parcels to warmed individual plates and serve immediately.

Energy 394kcal/1640kJ; Protein 39.1g; Carbohydrate 6.5g, of which sugars 5.8g; Fat 23.6g, of which saturates 4g; Cholesterol 92mg; Calcium 70mg; Fibre 3.4g; Sodium 210mg.

Smoked haddock with spinach and egg

This is a really special light meal that is not difficult to cook and assemble. Use young spinach leaves and serve with crusty bread or lots of thinly sliced bread and butter.

Serves four

4 undyed smoked haddock fillets (each weighing 150–170g/5–6oz)
300ml/½ pint/1¼ cups milk
75ml/2½fl oz/⅓ cup double (heavy) cream
25g/1oz/2 tbsp butter
250g/9oz fresh spinach, tough stalks removed
15ml/1 tbsp white wine vinegar
4 eggs
salt and ground black pepper

COOK'S TIP
Use the freshest eggs for poaching, older eggs won't hold together when added to the boiling water.

1 Place the haddock in a frying pan and pour just enough milk into the pan to come halfway up the fish. Poach gently over a low heat for 5 minutes, shaking the pan carefully from time to time to keep the fish moist. When the flesh turns opaque and the 'flakes' begin to separate it is cooked.

2 When cooked, remove the fish with a spatula, transfer to a plate and keep warm. Increase the heat under the milk and allow to reduce by about half, stirring occasionally. Add the cream and allow to bubble up. Season to taste. The sauce will be thick but pourable.

3 Heat a frying pan, then add the butter. Add the spinach, stirring briskly for a few minutes. Season lightly, then set aside, keeping it warm.

4 Poach the eggs in two batches. Bring a pan of water to a simmer. Add a few drops of vinegar. Crack an egg into a saucer, then add it to the pan. Repeat with another egg. Cook for 3 minutes. Remove the eggs using a slotted spoon, resting the spoon on some kitchen paper to remove water. Cook the other eggs in the same way.

5 Spoon the spinach over the fillets and add a poached egg on top of each portion. Pour over the cream sauce and serve immediately.

Energy 350kcal/1455kJ; Protein 27.5g; Carbohydrate 1.5g, of which sugars 1.4g; Fat 26.3g, of which saturates 14g; Cholesterol 277mg; Calcium 170mg; Fibre 1.3g; Sodium 969mg.

Classic fish pie

Smoked and unsmoked fish make a great combination, especially with a hint of tomato and basil. Served with a green salad, it makes an ideal dish for lunch or a family supper.

Serves eight

1kg/2¼lb smoked cod
1kg/2¼lb white cod
900ml/1½ pints/3¾ cups milk
1.2 litres/2 pints/5 cups water
2 basil sprigs and 30ml/2 tbsp chopped fresh basil
1 lemon thyme sprig
150g/5oz/10 tbsp butter
1 onion, chopped
75g/3oz/⅔ cup plain (all-purpose) flour
4 firm plum tomatoes, skinned and chopped
12 medium potatoes
salt and ground black pepper
crushed black peppercorns, to garnish

1 Place both kinds of fish in a roasting pan with 600ml/1 pint/2½ cups of the milk, the water and the herb sprigs. Bring to a simmer and cook gently for 3–4 minutes. Leave the fish to cool in the liquid for about 20 minutes. Drain the fish, reserving the cooking liquid for use in the sauce. Flake the fish, removing any skin and bone.

2 Melt 75g/3oz/6 tbsp of the butter in a large pan, add the onion and cook for 5 minutes, or until softened but not browned. Sprinkle in the flour and add half the chopped basil. Gradually stir in the reserved cooking liquid, adding a little more milk if necessary to make a fairly thin sauce. Stir constantly and bring to the boil to make a smooth sauce. Taste, add salt and pepper and stir in the remaining basil.

3 Remove the pan from the heat, then add the fish and tomatoes and stir gently to combine. Pour into an ovenproof dish.

4 Preheat the oven to 180°C/350°F/Gas 4. Cook the potatoes in boiling water until tender. Drain, then add the remaining butter, milk and mash.

5 Season to taste with salt and pepper and spoon over the fish mixture, using a fork to create a pattern. (You can freeze the pie at this stage.) Bake in the oven for 30 minutes, or until the top is golden. Sprinkle with the crushed peppercorns and serve hot with salad leaves or some freshly cooked peas or green beans.

Energy 301kcal/1262kJ; Protein 26.5g; Carbohydrate 24.1g, of which sugars 2.6g; Fat 11.6g, of which saturates 6.2g; Cholesterol 132mg; Calcium 76mg; Fibre 1.6g; Sodium 173mg.

Grilled hake with lemon and chilli

Choose firm hake fillets, as thick as possible, or try other fish, either white fish or oily fish, such as mackerel fillets or tuna steaks. The lemon and chilli also taste good with rich salmon. Serve with creamy mashed potatoes, new potatoes or on a bed of couscous.

Serves four

4 hake fillets, each weighing 150g/5oz
30ml/2 tbsp olive oil
finely grated rind and juice of 1 unwaxed lemon
15ml/1 tbsp crushed chilli flakes
salt and ground black pepper

COOK'S TIPS

- Cook the fish fairly near to the heat source in step 2. The flesh should be opaque and almost cooked.
- When sprinkled with lemon and chilli, the fish will burn easily, so at step 3 cook it further from the heat.

1 Preheat the grill (broiler) to high. Brush the hake fillets all over with the olive oil and place them skin side up on a baking sheet.

2 Grill (broil) the fish for 4–5 minutes, until the skin is brown and crispy, then carefully turn each fillet over using a fish slice or metal spatula.

3 Sprinkle the fillets with the lemon rind and chilli flakes and season with salt and ground black pepper.

4 Grill for a further 2–3 minutes, or until the hake is cooked through. (Test using the point of a sharp knife; the flesh should flake.) Squeeze over the lemon juice just before serving.

Energy 188kcal/786kJ; Protein 27g; Carbohydrate 0.1g, of which sugars 0.1g; Fat 8.8g, of which saturates 1.2g; Cholesterol 35mg; Calcium 22mg; Fibre 0g; Sodium 150mg.

Roast cod wrapped in prosciutto

Wrapping chunky fillets of cod in wafer-thin slices of prosciutto keeps the fish succulent and moist, at the same time adding flavour and visual impact. Serve with baby new potatoes and a herb salad for a stylish supper or lunch dish.

Serves four

2 thick skinless cod fillets, each weighing about 375g/13oz
75ml/5 tbsp extra virgin olive oil
75g/3oz prosciutto, thinly sliced
400g/14oz tomatoes, on the vine
salt and ground black pepper

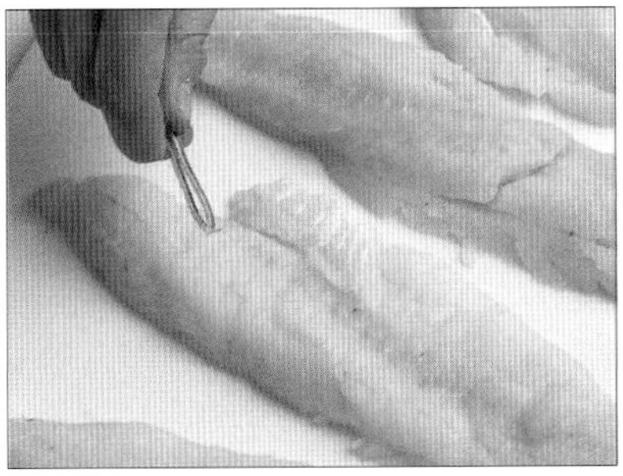

1 Preheat the oven to 220°C/425°F/ Gas 7. Pat the fish dry on kitchen paper and remove any stray bones.

2 Place one fillet in an ovenproof dish and drizzle 15ml/1 tbsp of the oil over it. Cover with the second fillet, laying a thick end on top of a thin end to create an even shape.

3 Arrange the ham over the fish, overlapping the slices to cover the fish in an even layer. Tuck the ends of the ham under the fish and tie it in place at intervals with fine string.

4 Using kitchen scissors, snip the tomato vines into four portions and add these to the dish. Drizzle the tomatoes and ham with the remaining oil and season lightly. Roast for about 35 minutes, until the tomatoes are tender and lightly coloured and the fish is cooked through. Test the fish by piercing one end of the parcel with the tip of a sharp knife to check that it flakes easily.

5 Slice the fish and transfer the portions to warm plates, adding the tomatoes. Spoon over the cooking juices from the dish and serve immediately.

Energy 281kcal/1172kJ; Protein 32.8g; Carbohydrate 3.1g, of which sugars 3.1g; Fat 15.3g, of which saturates 2.3g; Cholesterol 81mg; Calcium 23mg; Fibre 1g; Sodium 116mg.

Cod gratin

This rich version of an old favourite requires minimum effort and gives maximum flavour – forget about simmering sauces and try this rich cream and cheese topping for a special treat.

Serves four

4 portions of skinless cod fillet, weighing about 175g/6oz each
200g/7oz/1¾ cups mature (sharp) Cheddar cheese, finely grated
15ml/1 tbsp wholegrain mustard
75ml/5 tbsp double (heavy) cream
salt and ground black pepper

1 Preheat the oven to 200ºC/400ºF/Gas 6. Check the fish for any stray bones. Grease the base and sides of an ovenproof dish, then place the fish skinned side down in the dish. Season the fish lightly with salt and pepper.

2 Mix the grated cheese and mustard together with enough cream to form a thick but spreadable paste. Ensure that the ingredients are well mixed using the back of a spoon.

3 Divide the cheese mixture among the portions of fish, spreading it over thickly and evenly. Bake for 20 minutes until browned and bubbling. The fish should be flaky and tender. Serve immediately.

Variations

- Try 90ml/6 tbsp quark or low-fat soft cheese mixed with 45ml/2 tbsp grated Parmesan cheese and 15ml/1 tbsp Dijon mustard. Add a handful of chopped fresh dill or tarragon sprigs. Spread this over the fish instead of the Cheddar.
- Mash 100g/4oz feta cheese and mix in 2 chopped spring onions (scallions) and a few chopped black olives. Grated lemon rind and a crushed garlic clove go well. Use instead of the Cheddar mix.

Energy 445kcal/1852kJ; Protein 46g; Carbohydrate 0.4g, of which sugars 0.4g; Fat 27.7g, of which saturates 17.3g; Cholesterol 157mg; Calcium 395mg; Fibre 0g; Sodium 474mg.

Green prawn curry

A firm favourite, this prawn dish is quick and easy using just one cooking pot. This dish is mild and flavourful with a creamy taste; if you like more heat add more spice.

Serves four to six

30ml/2 tbsp vegetable oil
30ml/2 tbsp green curry paste
450g/1lb raw king prawns (jumbo shrimp), peeled and deveined
4 kaffir lime leaves, torn
1 lemon grass stalk, bruised and chopped
250ml/8fl oz/1 cup coconut milk
30ml/2 tbsp fish sauce
½ cucumber, seeded and cut into batons
10–15 basil leaves
4 fresh green chillies, sliced, to garnish

1 Heat the oil in a wok or large pan. Add the green curry paste and fry gently until bubbling and fragrant.

2 Add the prawns, kaffir lime leaves and chopped lemon grass. Fry for 2 minutes, until the prawns are pink.

3 Stir in the coconut milk and bring to a gentle boil. Simmer, stirring occasionally, for about 5 minutes or until the prawns are tender.

4 Stir in the fish sauce, cucumber batons and whole basil leaves, then top with the green chillies and serve from the pan.

Variation
Strips of chicken can be added in step 2 instead of prawns (shrimp).

Energy 115kcal/481kJ; Protein 14.1g; Carbohydrate 4g, of which sugars 2.6g; Fat 4.8g, of which saturates 0.6g; Cholesterol 146mg; Calcium 107mg; Fibre 1.3g; Sodium 567mg.

Scallops with garlic and coriander

Rather an expensive shellfish, the trick is to combine the scallops with ingredients that help to make them go further without overpowering them – courgettes do this perfectly here.

Serves four

20 scallops
2 courgettes (zucchini)
75g/3oz/6 tbsp butter
15ml/1 tbsp vegetable oil
4 garlic cloves, chopped
about 30ml/2 tbsp hot chilli sauce
juice of 1 lime
small bunch of fresh coriander (cilantro), finely chopped

1 To open the scallop shells, hold a shell in the palm of your hand, with the flat side uppermost. Insert the blade of a sharp knife close to the hinge that joins the two shells together and prise them apart. Run the knife blade across the inside of the flat shell to cut away the scallop.

2 Only the big white adductor muscle and the orange coral are eaten, so pull away and discard all other parts. Rinse the scallops under cold running water.

3 Cut the courgettes in half, then into four pieces. Melt the butter in the oil in a large frying pan. Add the courgettes and fry until soft. Remove from the pan.

4 Add the garlic and fry until golden. Stir in the hot chilli sauce.

5 Add the scallops to the sauce. Cook, stirring constantly, for 1–2 minutes only.

6 Stir in the lime juice, chopped coriander and the courgette pieces. Serve immediately on warm plates.

Energy 278kcal/1151kJ; Protein 13.7g; Carbohydrate 5.8g, of which sugars 3.9g; Fat 22.4g, of which saturates 12.4g; Cholesterol 71mg; Calcium 45mg; Fibre 1g; Sodium 350mg.

Mussels in white wine

This simple, delicious dish is perfect for informal entertaining. Serve with a big bowl of fries to share. To make a variation, cook the mussels in beer instead of wine, which tastes fantastic.

Serves two

25g/1oz/2 tbsp butter
300ml/½ pint/1¼ cups dry white wine
1kg/2¼lb mussels, cleaned
45ml/3 tbsp fresh parsley, chopped
salt and ground black pepper

1 Heat the butter in a large pan until foaming, then pour in the wine. Bring to the boil.

2 Discard any open mussels that do not close when sharply tapped.

Variation
You could add a couple of cloves of crushed garlic to this dish.

3 Add the mussels to the pan. Stir into the butter. Cover with a tight-fitting lid and cook over a medium heat for 4–5 minutes, shaking the pan every now and then.

4 By the end of cooking time, all the mussels should have opened. Discard any that are still closed.

5 Line a large sieve (strainer) with kitchen paper and strain the mussels and their liquid through it. Transfer the mussels to warmed serving bowls.

6 Pour the liquid into a pan and bring to the boil. Season well and stir in the parsley. Pour over the mussels and serve immediately.

Energy 189kcal/799kJ; Protein 26.4g; Carbohydrate 2.4g, of which sugars 1.9g; Fat 3.1g, of which saturates 0.5g; Cholesterol 60mg; Calcium 308mg; Fibre 0.4g; Sodium 319mg.

Seafood gumbo

Gumbo is a cross between a soup and stew, served over rice as a main course. Spicy sausage and seafood are key ingredients, and the combination is fabulous.

Serves four

450g/1lb fresh mussels
450g/1lb raw prawns (shrimp), in the shell
1 cooked crab, about 1kg/2¼lb
small bunch of parsley, leaves chopped and stalks reserved
150ml/¼ pint/⅔ cup vegetable oil
115g/4oz/1 cup plain (all-purpose) flour
1 green (bell) pepper, seeded and chopped
1 large onion, chopped
2 celery sticks, sliced
3 garlic cloves, finely chopped
75g/3oz smoked spiced sausage, skinned and sliced
275g/10oz/1½ cups white long grain rice
6 spring onions (scallions), shredded
cayenne pepper and salt, to taste
Tabasco sauce, to taste

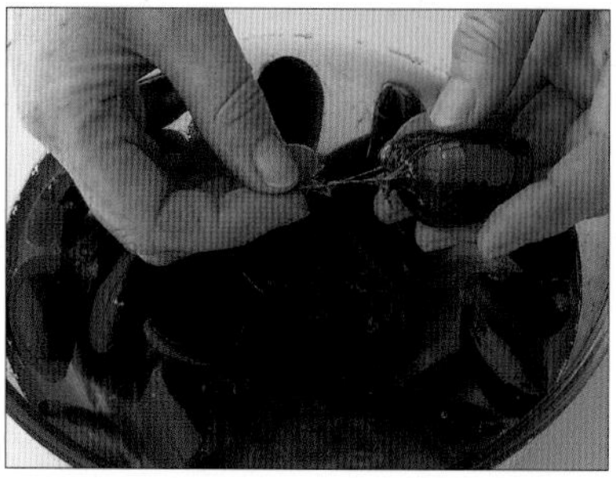

1 Wash the mussels in several changes of cold water, pulling away the black 'beards'. Discard any that are broken or do not close when you tap them firmly.

COOK'S TIPS

- It is vital to stir constantly to darken the roux without burning. Should black specks occur at any stage of cooking, discard the roux and start again.
- Have the onion, green (bell) pepper and celery ready to add to the roux the minute it reaches the correct golden-brown stage, as this arrests its darkening.

2 Bring 250ml/8fl oz/1 cup water to the boil in a deep pan. Add the mussels, cover the pan tightly and cook over a high heat, shaking frequently, for 3 minutes. As the mussels open, lift them out with tongs into a sieve (strainer) set over a bowl. Discard any that fail to open. Shell the mussels, discarding the shells. Return the liquid from the bowl to the pan and make the quantity up to 2 litres/3½ pints/8 cups with water.

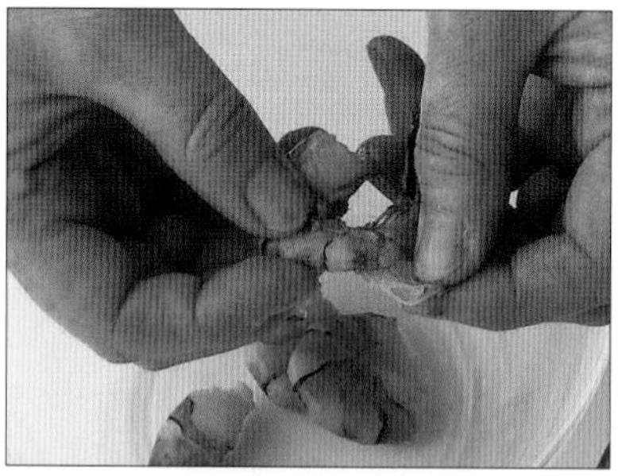

3 Peel the prawns and set them aside, reserving a few for the garnish. Put the shells and heads into the pan.

4 Remove all the meat from the crab, separating the brown and white meat. Add all the pieces of shell to the pan with 5ml/1 tsp salt.

5 Bring the stock to the boil, skimming it regularly. When there is no more froth, add the parsley stalks and simmer for 15 minutes. Cool, then strain it into a measuring jug (cup) and make up to 2 litres/3½ pints/8 cups with water.

6 Heat the oil in a heavy pan and stir in the flour. Stir constantly over a medium heat with a wooden spoon or whisk until the roux reaches a golden-brown colour. Immediately add the pepper, onion, celery and garlic. Continue cooking for about 3 minutes until the onion is soft. Stir in the sausage. Reheat the stock.

7 Stir the brown crab meat into the roux, then ladle in the hot stock a little at a time, stirring constantly until it has all been smoothly incorporated. Bring to a low boil, partially cover the pan, then simmer the gumbo for 30 minutes.

8 Cook the rice in plenty of lightly salted boiling water until the grains are tender.

9 Add the prawns, mussels, white crab meat and spring onions to the gumbo. Return to the boil and season with salt if necessary, cayenne and a dash or two of Tabasco sauce. Simmer for a further minute, then add the chopped parsley leaves. Serve with hot rice.

Energy 559kcal/2336kJ; Protein 31.1g; Carbohydrate 57.6g, of which sugars 3.7g; Fat 23g, of which saturates 3.4g; Cholesterol 183mg; Calcium 145mg; Fibre 1.9g; Sodium 474mg.

Poultry

Light poultry meat is popular worldwide. There are plenty of recipes for chicken dishes for everyday meals, as well as for special or festive dinners. Poultry is a versatile and economical food and it can be cooked in a wide variety of ways, from quick and easy ideas to more sophisticated dishes for a dinner party.

Poultry basics

Domestically reared birds, including turkey, chicken, duck, goose and guinea fowl are collectively known as poultry. Fresh or frozen, traditionally reared or organic, there is plenty of choice in supermarkets and butchers to suit every pocket. Free-range organic varieties are considered to be the most flavoursome birds. These poultry are fed an organic diet, that has not been adulterated with hormones, artificial additives and chemicals. They are free to roam and grow at a natural pace, which produces the correct quantity of meat and fat for the size of bird. The time taken for the poultry to mature adds flavour to the meat.

All poultry are excellent sources of protein. Chicken, turkey and guinea fowl breast meat are relatively low in fat, with the fat being concentrated in and under the skin. Duck and goose are fatty birds but again there is a high concentration of fat in and under the skin. Poultry also contributes B vitamins and minerals.

BUYING AND STORING POULTRY

Look for clear soft skin (there should be no blemishes or bruises). The bigger the bird, the better its value because its proportion of meat to bone will be higher. As well as whole birds, poultry is available in a choice of portions, such as quarters, legs, wings, thighs, breasts and drumsticks. The portions may be on the bone or boneless, with or without skin. Sliced, diced, stir-fry strips and minced (ground) poultry are available.

Place poultry that has been bought unpackaged in a deep dish and cover it closely. Check pre-packed poultry to make sure that the packs are sealed before placing them in the refrigerator. Use pre-packed poultry by the date suggested or poultry from the butcher within about two days of purchase.

CUTS OF POULTRY

A wide range of different portions are available, both on and off the bone. Chicken and turkey are commonly sold in portions, but you will also find some cuts of duck available at the butchers or pre-packed in the supermarket. **Quarters** Chicken and duck quarters include either the leg or the wing joint, the latter having a large portion of breast meat. The leg joint includes the thigh and drumstick sections. **Thighs** These are small neat joints from the upper leg. **Drumsticks** Chicken drumsticks are small but take a surprisingly long time to cook as the meat is quite compact. Turkey drumsticks are very large and tough – they need long slow braising. **Chicken wings** This cut has very little meat. **Breast portions** These are sold on or off the bone, skinned or unskinned. They include only the white meat, and are cut in slices or fillets from larger birds, such as turkey. **Supremes** These are breast portions with the wing bone included. **Part-boned breasts** This cut still has the short piece of bone connecting the wing and a fine strip of breastbone.

Above: Chicken tastes different according to the type of feed on which the bird has been reared and whether it is free range or intensively farmed.

Below: Portions of poultry, such as chicken and turkey, are ideal for freezing.

FREEZING POULTRY

Raw, fresh poultry can be frozen very successfully. Remove the giblets from a whole bird, if necessary. Wrap portions individually in clear film (plastic wrap). Pack the poultry or portions in a freezer bag and seal tightly.

The best way to thaw frozen poultry is in the refrigerator. Place in a suitable container, cover closely and leave overnight. Remove the giblets, if not already removed, from a whole bird as soon as possible.

FOOD SAFETY

Poultry is particularly susceptible to bacterial growth, which can cause food poisoning if it is allowed to contaminate uncooked foods that are eaten raw, such as salads, or if the poultry is eaten without being cooked through.

Thoroughly wash chopping boards (use plastic boards rather than wood), utensils, surfaces and hands after handling and cooking poultry. Also, remember to wash utensils used to lift or stir part-cooked poultry before using them with any cooked food.

Poultry preparation and cooking

Tender poultry can be marinated, poached, roasted, grilled (broiled) , barbecued, griddled, stir-fried, fried in a shallow pan or, once coated in breadcrumbs or batter, in deep oil. The same cuts of poultry can also be used in slow-cooked casseroles and stews.

SPATCHCOCKING A BIRD

To spatchcock means to split open and flatten out the carcass of the bird, so that the meat can be cooked at a quicker rate. Poultry that is spatchcocked is grilled or roasted and needs to be turned regularly to ensure that the awkward shape cooks evenly. This method is for smaller birds such as poussin or quail, where one whole bird would serve one person and where the whole bird is cooked as one piece of meat.

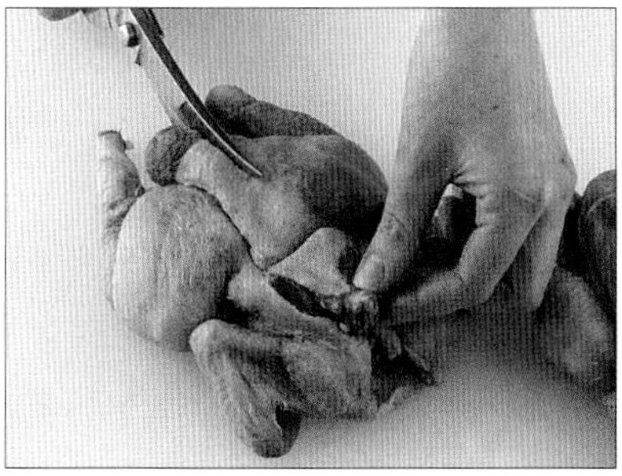

1 Using very strong scissors or a sharp knife, cut the bird in half down the back, then open it out flat. Press it firmly flat with the heel of your hand.

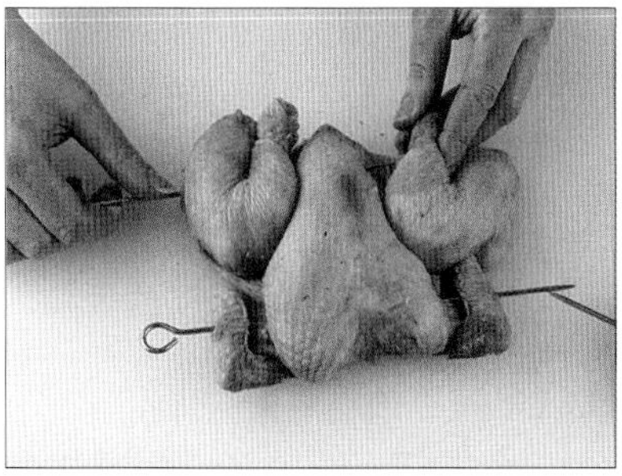

2 To keep the bird flat, thread two metal skewers through the wings and legs.

GRILLING (BROILING) POULTRY

Almost any cut of poultry is suitable for grilling, from whole poultry breasts to cubes or strips of meat threaded on skewers. Thick pieces of meat, or those containing large bones, have to be grilled (broiled) slowly and turned often to ensure they cook through.

Plain-grilled poultry is generally low in fat, so a good choice if you're counting calories. Without additional flavours, it needs flavourful accompaniments, so ensure that the sauces or seasonings to the dish are full of flavour.

1 Preheat the grill (broiler) on the hottest setting.

2 Thread the poultry on to skewers. Brush the bird or birds with oil and season well with salt and pepper.

3 Position the grill pan well below the heat source so the meat has time to cook through before the skin browns too much. Allow about 40 minutes cooking for a spatchcocked poussin, 20–25 minutes for a poultry breast, turning each frequently and brushing with oil to keep them moist.

FRYING POULTRY

Escalopes and boneless breasts cook quickly, so they are ideal for frying. Part-boned breasts are also suitable for shallow-frying, but they take longer to cook and should be turned frequently.

1 Heat a little olive oil in a large, non-stick frying pan. Add the poultry and cook until lightly browned underneath. For a more flavoursome dish, put 15ml/1 tbsp plain (all-purpose) flour in a saucer and season well. Press the poultry into it, then add to the pan.

2 Turn the pieces and cook until lightly browned on the second side. Reduce the heat to prevent the pieces from becoming too brown before they are cooked through.

3 Allow about 15 minutes for boneless breast meat. Part-boned portions require longer, up to 20 minutes (or more) on each side, until the thickest areas of meat are cooked through.

WHEN IS POULTRY COOKED?

Poultry should be cooked through, without any sign of raw flesh or bloody juices. (This ensures that all the bacteria are destroyed.) To check if poultry is cooked, pierce the thickest area of the meat with a thin metal skewer. If there is any sign of pink in either the flesh or the juices, then the meat is not cooked and it must be returned to the heat for further cooking.

STIR-FRYING POULTRY

Fine strips of poultry are lean and tender, and they cook quickly, so are ideal for stir-frying. Although thin strips are the classic cut for traditional stir-frying, diced meat or thin slices also work well. Minced (ground) chicken or turkey breast are also suitable for stir-frying but the darker minced turkey meat is better suited to slower cooking.

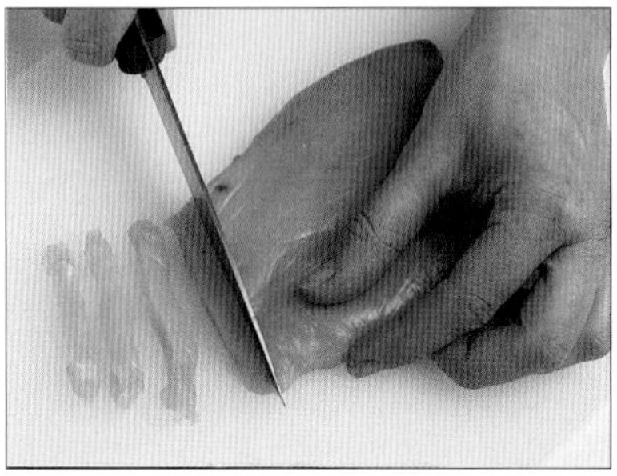

1 Cut skinless, boneless poultry breast crossways into thin, even pieces.

2 Heat the frying pan until hot before adding a little oil. Heat the oil until it is very hot – this will take a few seconds

3 Add the strips of poultry and stir-fry over a high heat for 3–5 minutes, until the pieces are cooked and browned.

CASSEROLING POULTRY

Moist cooking can enhance the flavour of poultry, enriching it with cooking liquid, herbs, spices and aromatics. Boneless portions, pieces on the bone and whole birds can be casseroled with delicious results.

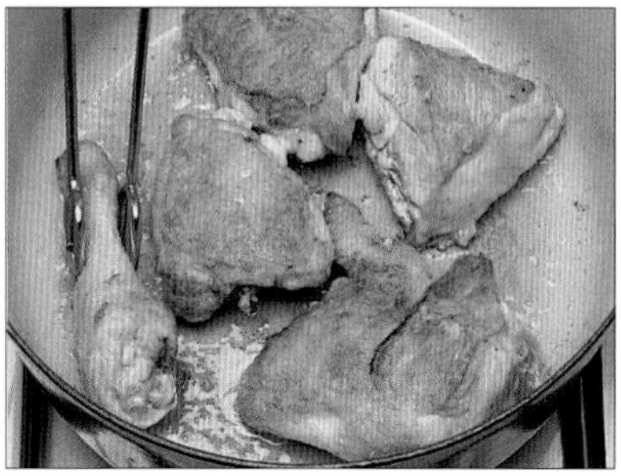

1 Heat a little oil or melt some butter in a flameproof casserole. Brown the poultry all over. Remove from the pan.

2 Add chopped onion, carrot, celery and herbs of your choice to the fat in the pan. Cook until slightly softened but not browned. Replace the poultry. Add stock, wine, canned tomatoes or water. Season well, then heat until just simmering. Cook in the oven at 180°C/350°F/Gas 4.

COOKING TIMES FOR CASSEROLES

Whole bird allow 20 minutes per 450g/1lb, plus 20 minutes.

Large portions 45–60 minutes.

Boneless breasts allow about 30 minutes.

Chunks 20–40 minutes, depending on size of pieces.

ROASTING POULTRY

Whole birds or large portions of birds, such as the crown, or the breast and leg, can be roasted. When cooking a larger bird, requiring longer cooking, you may need to cover the top of the breast loosely with foil when it becomes a light golden brown. The foil helps to conduct the heat and the tent shape keeps the meat moist as steam that rises runs back on to the meat. Remove the foil for the final 15 minutes of cooking time to complete the browning.

1 Rub the breast and the top of the bird generously with butter. Add any herbs or bacon at this stage.

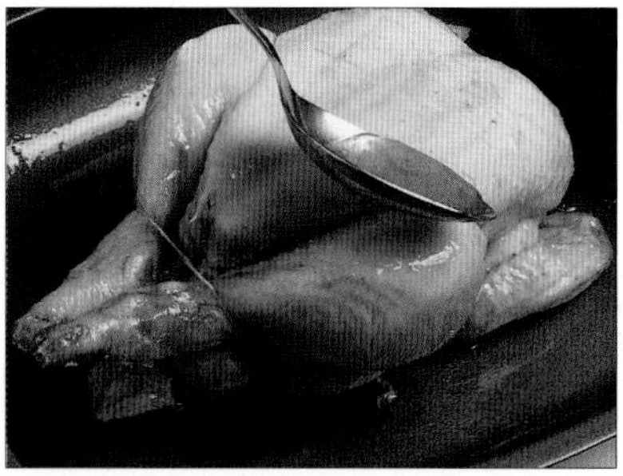

2 Place the bird breast-side down in the roasting pan for the first 30 minutes of the cooking time. Turn and baste the bird, then return it to the oven, basting every 15–20 minutes.

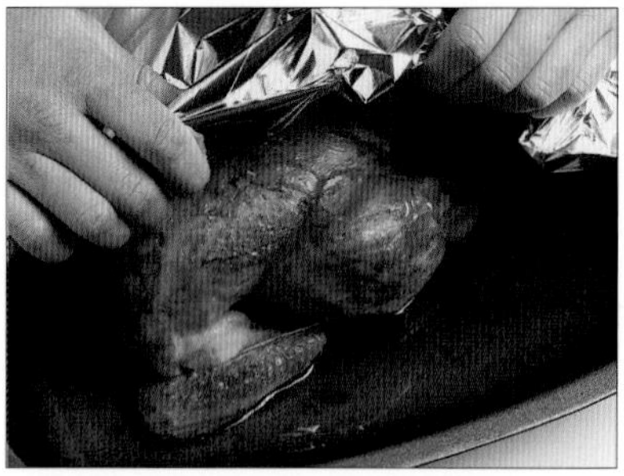

3 When it is cooked, remove from the oven and cover the bird tightly with foil Leave it to rest in a warm place for 10–15 minutes before carving and serving. Either do this in the roasting pan or, if you wish to make gravy or a sauce with the pan juices and fat, transfer the bird to a warmed serving platter.

POULTRY ROASTING TIMES
Calculate the cooking time based on the weight of the bird when it is ready to cook. Preheat the oven to 200ºC/400ºF/Gas 6.

Chicken	20 minutes per 450g/1lb, plus an extra 20 minutes.
Poussin	Allow 50–60 minutes total roasting time. Preheat the oven to 180ºC/350ºF/ Gas 4.
Turkey	15–20 minutes per 450g/1lb.
Duck	30 minutes per 450g/1lb. Preheat oven to 230ºC/ 450ºF/Gas 8.
Guinea fowl	Allow 15 minutes per 450g/1lb, plus 15 minutes.

STUFFINGS FOR POULTRY

Whole birds are delicious stuffed with a mixture of breadcrumbs, onions and other flavourings.

Sausagemeat and chestnut This is a favourite for turkey.

1 Peel 900g/2lb fresh chestnuts, slitting the peel and pulling it off. Remove the brown skin inside the shell. Cook the chestnuts in boiling water for 10–15 minutes. Drain well, then crumble the chestnuts into a large bowl.

2 Melt 25g/1oz butter in a frying pan and add 2 finely chopped onions and 1–2 crushed garlic cloves, if desired. Cook gently for 10 minutes, stirring occasionally, until soft but not browned.

3 Mix the onions into the chestnuts. Return the pan to the heat and add in 450g/1lb pork sausagemeat.

4 Cook the mixture over a low to medium heat, stirring frequently, until the sausagemeat is crumbly, evenly cooked and well browned.

5 Add the sausagement to the chestnut mixture with 115g/4oz fresh white breadcrumbs. Season and add chopped fresh herbs or citrus rind, if required. Beat 1 egg and mix it into the stuffing to bind the ingredients.

Sage and onion This classic stuffing is delicious with all types of poultry, pheasant and even pork.

1 Melt 25g/1oz butter in a frying pan. Add 4 finely chopped onions and cook for 10–15 minutes, until soft but not browned. Set aside to cool.

2 Add the onions to 115g/4oz fresh white breadcrumbs with 60ml/4 tbsp chopped fresh sage, seasoning and 1 beaten egg. Stir in a little stock or milk (up to about 125ml/4fl oz) to bind the stuffing without making it too wet. The amount depends on the breadcrumbs.

Duck ideas

- Whole duck or portions can be roasted or casseroled. Boneless breast fillets (with or without skin) are also suitable for grilling (broiling) or frying. The following are a few basic tips for dealing with duck.
- Skinless, boneless breast fillets can be cut across into medium-thick slices (producing medallions or 'medalions' the French term), into thin slices at an angle or into strips. All small pieces are suitable for pan frying or stir-frying.
- Skinless boneless duck breasts are also good diced and braised, casserole-style.
- For casseroling, first trim off any obvious pieces of excess fat and prick the skin all over. Brown the skin well in a frying pan over medium heat until the fat runs. Pour off the excess fat. During cooking, skim off any excess fat that rises to the surface of the liquid and skim off the fat at the end of cooking before serving.
- Roast duck is rich and excellent with a sharp sauce. Prick the skin of a duck all over before cooking and drain off the fat halfway through. Try glazing the skin with a little bitter orange marmalade towards the end of cooking.
- Duck breasts and quarters are excellent roasted with the skin on. Prick the skin all over and cook them, skin side uppermost, until well browned. For super-crisp skin on boneless breast portions, score the skin with a sharp knife in a criss-cross pattern, cutting through but not down as far as the meat. Heat a frying pan and press the skin on the pan until well browned. Transfer to the roasting pan or dish, skin up.
- Orange, lemon or lime wedges and quartered onions can be placed in the body cavity of whole duck before cooking. Sausagemeat or sage and onion stuffing should be cooked separately.

Cream of chicken soup

A rich and flavoursome creamy chicken soup makes a fabulous lunch served with crispy bread. Use decent chicken stock for this recipe to give the soup a full flavour – if you have the leftovers of a roast chicken, this is an ideal recipe for making the most of every last bit.

Serves six

50g/2oz/¼ cup butter
2 onions, chopped
2 medium potatoes, chopped
1 large carrot, diced
1 celery stick, diced
750ml/1¼ pints/3 cups chicken stock
150ml/¼ pint/⅔ cup milk
25g/1oz/¼ cup plain (all-purpose) flour
175g/6oz cooked chicken
300ml/½ pint/1¼ cups single (light) cream
salt and ground black pepper
parsley leaves, to garnish

1 Melt the butter in a large pan and cook the onions, potatoes, carrot and celery for 5 minutes, stirring often, until they are soft, but do not let the vegetables brown.

2 Add the stock and bring to the boil. Reduce the heat, cover the pan and simmer for 30 minutes.

3 Purée the soup. Return it to the pan. Blend the milk into the flour and stir into the soup. Bring to the boil, stirring.

4 Chop the chicken finely. Add to the soup and simmer for 5 minutes. Taste and add seasoning. Stir in half the cream and heat briefly without boiling.

5 Serve with a swirl of cream, black pepper and parsley leaves.

COOK'S TIPS
- To improve the flavour of home-made chicken soup use freshly made or defrosted frozen stock rather than that made with stock cubes.
- Use milk in place of single (light) cream, for a lower-fat dish.

Energy 295kcal/1231kJ; Protein 11g; Carbohydrate 23.6g, of which sugars 8.9g; Fat 18.2g, of which saturates 11.1g; Cholesterol 61mg; Calcium 111mg; Fibre 2.1g; Sodium 137mg.

Honey mustard chicken

This classic seasoning combination is excellent smeared on chicken portions or used to season whole chicken before roasting. Chicken thighs have a rich flavour but four chicken breast portions can be used instead. Serve with seasonal vegetables and new potatoes.

Serves four

8 chicken thighs
60ml/4 tbsp wholegrain mustard
60ml/4 tbsp clear honey
salt and ground black pepper

1 Preheat the oven to 190°C/375°F/ Gas 5. Put the chicken thighs in a single layer in a roasting pan.

2 Mix together the mustard and honey, season with a little salt and ground black pepper to taste. Do not add too much salt as some types of mustard are quite salty.

3 Brush the honey and mustard mixture over the chicken thighs. Roast for 25–30 minutes, basting with the pan juices occasionally, until well browned and cooked through.

Variations

Chicken with honey and mustard is brilliantly versatile as it can be served piping hot, warm or cold.

- Serve instead of a Sunday roast, with roast potatoes or boiled new or salad potatoes, buttery cabbage or broccoli and baby carrots.
- Serve hot, warm or cool on a bed of mixed salad leaves, with lots of halved cherry tomatoes and thinly sliced red onion.
- Serve instant couscous tossed with chopped chives and grated orange rind with the hot chicken. Make a salad of diced orange and diced cooked beetroot (beet) .
- Cool and chill, then pack in a container for a picnic. Take crusty bread, watercress and coleslaw.

Energy 287kcal/1205kJ; Protein 33.9g; Carbohydrate 12.1g, of which sugars 12.1g; Fat 11.8g, of which saturates 3g; Cholesterol 174mg; Calcium 30mg; Fibre 0.7g; Sodium 386mg.

Stuffed chicken wrapped with bacon

A simple cream cheese and chive filling flavours these chicken breasts and makes them deliciously moist when cooked in their bacon wrapping.

Serves four

4 skinless, boneless chicken breast portions, each weighing 175g/6oz
115g/4oz/½ cup cream cheese
15ml/1 tbsp chopped fresh chives
8 rindless unsmoked bacon rashers (strips)
15ml/1 tbsp olive oil
ground black pepper

1 Preheat the oven to 200°C/400°F/ Gas 6.

2 Using a sharp knife, make a horizontal slit into the side of each chicken portion without cutting all the way through (the filling is stuffed into each slit).

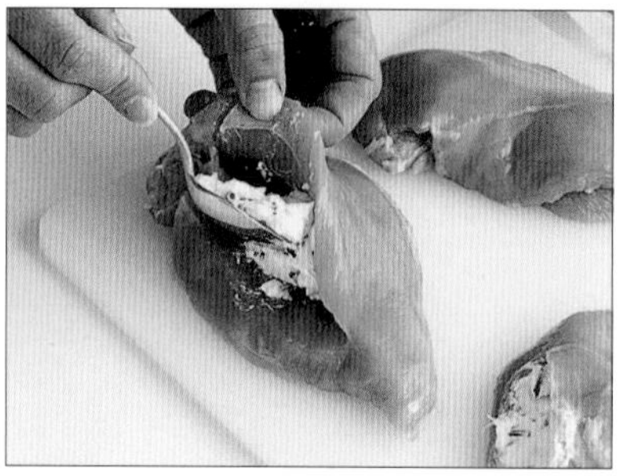

3 To make the filling, beat together the cream cheese and chives. Divide the filling into four portions and, using a teaspoon, fill each slit with a portion of the cream cheese. Press the filling in and push the sides of the slit together to keep it in place.

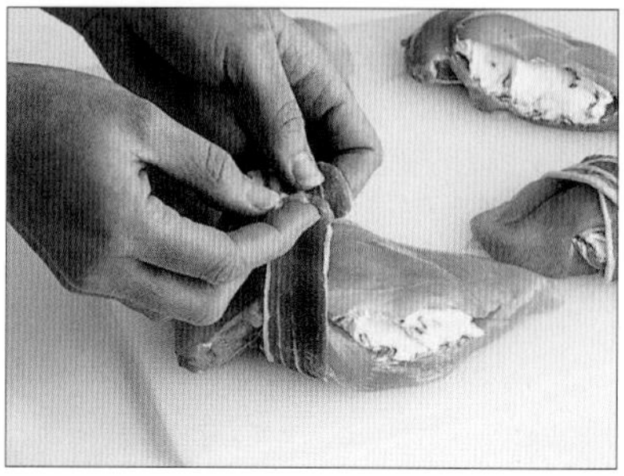

4 Wrap each stuffed breast in two rashers of bacon and place in an ovenproof dish. Drizzle the oil over the chicken and bake for 25–30 minutes, until lightly browned and cooked through. Season with black pepper and serve at once.

Energy 459kcal/1913kJ; Protein 52.3g; Carbohydrate 0g, of which sugars 0g; Fat 27.7g, of which saturates 13g; Cholesterol 0mg; Calcium 40mg; Fibre 0g; Sodium 1070mg.

Southern fried chicken

This simple version of fried chicken does not involve deep-frying, making it easier, less smelly and messy, and lower in fat. A good way of cooking the corn cakes is to place them in a grill pan, dot with butter and grill until golden, turning once, while frying the chicken.

Serves four

15ml/1 tbsp paprika
30ml/2 tbsp plain (all-purpose) flour
4 skinless, boneless chicken breast portions, each weighing 175g/6oz
30ml/2 tbsp sunflower oil
salt and ground black pepper

For the corn cakes
200g/7oz corn kernels
350g/12oz mashed potato, cooled
25g/1oz/2 tbsp butter

For the soured cream dip
150ml/¼ pint/⅔ cup soured cream
15ml/1 tbsp chopped fresh chives

1 Mix the paprika and flour together on a plate.

2 Coat each chicken portion in the seasoned flour. Heat the oil in a large frying pan and add the floured chicken. Cook over a high heat, turning once, until golden brown on both sides.

3 Reduce the heat and continue cooking for 20 minutes, turning once or twice, or until cooked through.

4 To make the corn cakes, stir the corn kernels into the cooled mashed potato and season to taste. Using lightly floured hands, shape the mixture into 12 even round cakes, each about 5cm/2in in diameter.

5 When the chicken is cooked, remove the pieces from the pan and keep hot. Melt the butter in the pan and cook the corn cakes for 3 minutes on each side, or until golden and heated through.

6 Meanwhile, mix together the soured cream with the chives in a bowl to make a dip. Transfer the corn cakes from the frying pan to serving plates and top with the chicken breast portions. Serve at once, offering the sour cream with chives on the side.

Energy 505kcal/2119kJ; Protein 47.8g; Carbohydrate 32.2g, of which sugars 3.3g; Fat 21.5g, of which saturates 9.3g; Cholesterol 158mg; Calcium 61mg; Fibre 2.5g; Sodium 172mg.

Escalopes of chicken with vegetables

This is a quick and light dish that is ideal when the weather starts to warm up and easy meals become the order of the day. Flattening the chicken breasts thins the meat and speeds up the cooking time. A frying pan can be used instead of a griddle.

Serves four

4 skinless, boneless chicken breast fillets, each weighing 175g/6oz
juice of 1 lime
120ml/4fl oz/½ cup olive oil
675g/1½lb mixed small new season potatoes, carrots, fennel (sliced if large), asparagus and peas
salt and ground black pepper
sprigs of fresh flat leaf parsley, to garnish

For the tomato mayonnaise
150ml/¼ pint/⅔ cup mayonnaise
15ml/1 tbsp sun-dried tomato purée (paste)

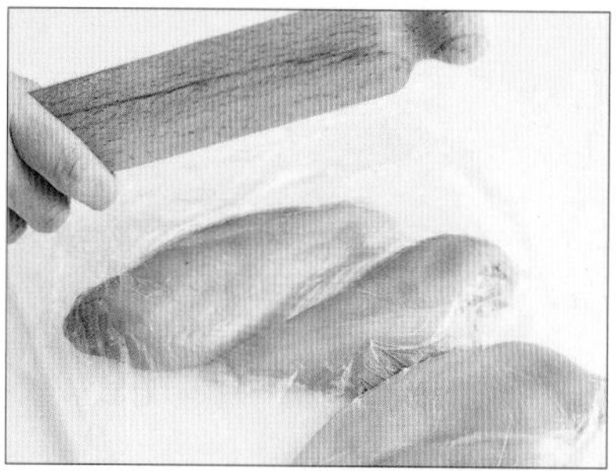

1 Place the chicken fillets between sheets of clear film (plastic wrap) or baking parchment and use a rolling pin to beat them until they are evenly thin. Season and sprinkle with the lime juice.

2 Heat 45ml/3 tbsp of the oil in a frying pan and fry the chicken for 20–24 minutes, turning frequently.

3 Put the potatoes and carrots in a pan with the remaining oil and season with salt. Cover. Cook over a medium heat for 10–15 minutes, stirring frequently.

4 Add the fennel and cook for a further 5 minutes, stirring frequently. Add the asparagus and peas and cook for 5 minutes more, or until all the vegetables are tender and cooked.

5 Mix together the mayonnaise and sun-dried tomato purée in a small bowl. Spoon the vegetables on to plates and put the chicken on top. Serve with the mayonnaise.

Variation
Any combination of baby vegetables can be used.

Energy 513kcal/2143kJ; Protein 44g; Carbohydrate 18.9g, of which sugars 9g; Fat 29.6g, of which saturates 4.7g; Cholesterol 141mg; Calcium 41mg; Fibre 3.2g; Sodium 251mg.

Crème fraîche and coriander chicken

The coriander leaves have a wonderfully fresh fragrant flavour, so don't be afraid to use them generously; flat leaf parsley could also be substituted. Boneless thighs are used in this recipe, but chicken breast fillets would work equally well.

Serves four

6 skinless chicken thigh fillets
15ml/1 tbsp sunflower oil
60ml/4 tbsp crème fraîche
1 small bunch of fresh coriander (cilantro), roughly chopped
salt and ground black pepper

COOK'S TIPS
• You could use any cut of chicken to make this recipe, although thigh meat is the most flavourful.
• Serve with a jacket potato and green herb salad.

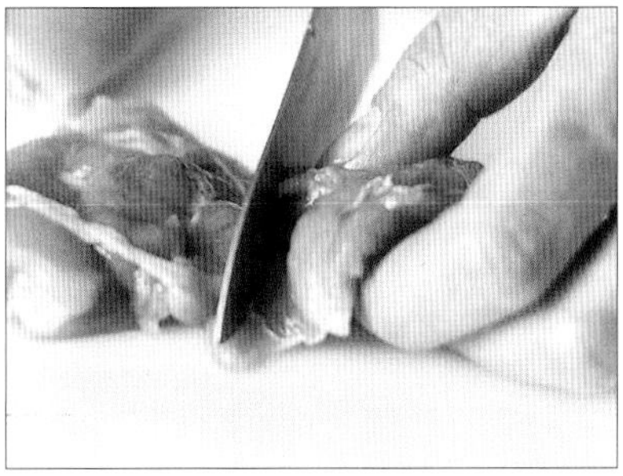

1 Cut each boneless chicken thigh into three or four pieces using a sharp knife. Heat the oil in a large frying pan, then add the chicken and cook for about 6 minutes, turning occasionally, until golden brown and cooked through.

2 Add the crème fraîche to the pan and stir until melted, then allow to bubble for 1–2 minutes.

3 Add the chopped coriander and stir to combine. Season to taste, and serve.

Energy 249kcal/1041kJ; Protein 32.1g; Carbohydrate 0.7g, of which sugars 0.6g; Fat 13.1g, of which saturates 5.6g; Cholesterol 174mg; Calcium 44mg; Fibre 0.6g; Sodium 143mg.

Chicken fajitas

Grilled marinated chicken and onions, served with soft tortillas, salsa, guacamole and sour cream makes a classic Tex-Mex meal that is a good choice for an informal supper.

Serves six

finely grated rind of 1 lime and the juice of 2 limes
120ml/4fl oz/½ cup olive oil
1 garlic clove, finely chopped
pinch of dried oregano
good pinch of dried red chilli flakes
5ml/1 tsp coriander seeds, crushed
6 boneless chicken breasts
3 onions, thickly sliced
2 large red or yellow (bell) peppers, sliced
30ml/2 tbsp chopped fresh coriander (cilantro)
salt and ground black pepper

To serve

12–18 soft flour tortillas
tomato salsa
guacamole
120ml/4fl oz/½ cup soured cream

1 In an ovenproof dish, combine the lime rind and juice, 75ml/5 tbsp of the oil, garlic, oregano, chilli flakes, coriander seeds and seasoning.

2 Slash the chicken skin several times and turn each in the mixture to coat. Cover and set aside to marinate for several hours in a cool place.

3 Preheat the oven to 200°C/400°F/ Gas 6.

4 Toss the onion slices and peppers with the remaining oil in a large roasting pan. Spread them out thinly and season lightly. Bake for 25–30 minutes, until softened and browned.

5 Meanwhile, uncover the chicken and make sure all the pieces are skin-side down. Bake for 10 minutes. Turn and bake for a further 15–20 minutes, until the skin is well browned and the chicken is cooked through.

6 Heat the tortillas following the instructions on the packet. Using a sharp knife, cut the chicken into strips and transfer it to a serving dish. Spoon the cooking juices over and sprinkle with the coriander. Transfer the onion and pepper mixture to a serving dish. Offer the salsa in another dish.

7 Serve each component in bowls for people to help themselves.

Energy 398kcal/1670kJ; Protein 23g; Carbohydrate 44.3g, of which sugars 11.8g; Fat 15.5g, of which saturates 4.4g; Cholesterol 60mg; Calcium 76mg; Fibre 2.9g; Sodium 51mg.

Citrus chicken salad

This salad is great for using leftover roast chicken. Hold the orange over a bowl to catch juices while cutting the orange flesh from the membranes – the only tricky technique in this salad.

Serves six

120ml/4fl oz/½ cup extra virgin olive oil
6 boneless chicken breasts, skinned
4 oranges
5ml/1 tsp Dijon mustard
15ml/1 tbsp clear honey
300g/11oz/2¾ cups white cabbage
300g/11oz carrots, finely sliced
2 spring onions (scallions), finely sliced
2 celery sticks, cut into matchstick strips
30ml/2 tbsp chopped fresh tarragon
2 limes
salt and ground black pepper

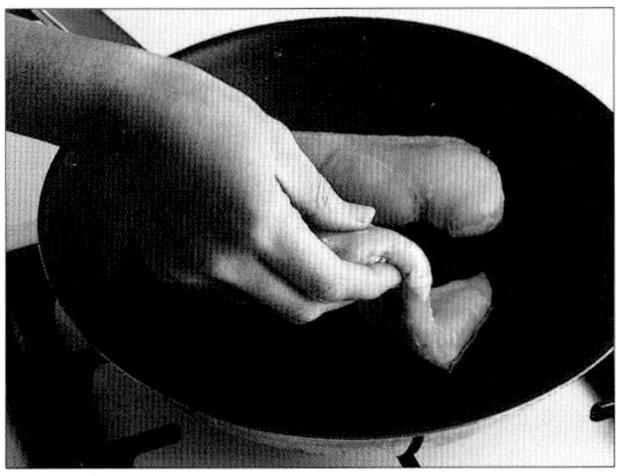

1 Heat 30ml/2 tbsp of the oil in a frying pan. Add the chicken and cook for 20–25 minutes, turning once. Remove from the pan and leave to cool.

2 Peel and cut the pith off two oranges. Cut out the segments from between the membranes and set aside. Grate the rind and squeeze the juice from one more orange into a bowl. Stir in the mustard, 5ml/1 tsp of the honey, 60ml/4 tbsp of the oil and seasoning to taste.

3 Mix in the cabbage, carrots, spring onions and celery, then leave to stand for 10 minutes.

4 To make the dressing, squeeze the juice from the remaining orange and mix it with the remaining honey, oil and tarragon.

5 Peel and segment the limes, and lightly mix into the dressing with the reserved orange segments and season.

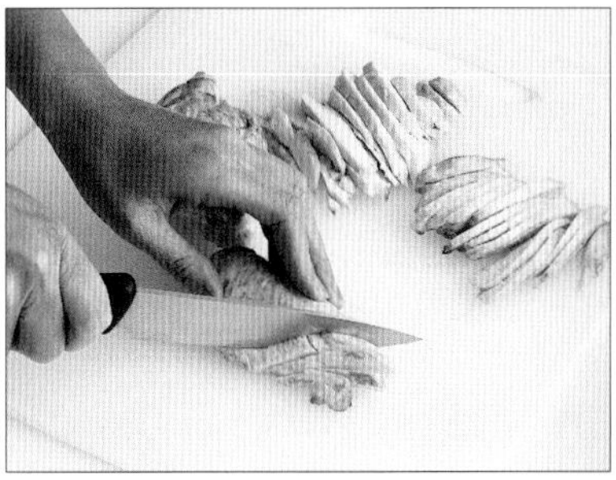

6 Slice the cooked chicken breasts and stir into the dressing. Spoon the vegetable salad on to plates and add the chicken mixture, then serve at once.

Energy 382kcal/1607kJ; Protein 42.5g; Carbohydrate 27.7g, of which sugars 24.6g; Fat 12g, of which saturates 2.5g; Cholesterol 110mg; Calcium 42mg; Fibre 2.6g; Sodium 279mg.

Coq au vin

This famous recipe from Burgundy, France, is a slow-cooked stew of chicken, wine, onions, bacon and mushrooms. The result is a rich and delicious dish with a depth of flavour that is perfect for Sunday lunch on a cold day. Serve with mashed potatoes and vegetables.

Serves four

1 bouquet garni
1 bottle full-bodied red wine
600ml/1 pint/2½ cups chicken stock
50g/2oz/4 tbsp butter
30ml/2 tbsp olive oil
24 small pickling onions
115g/4oz bacon, cut into small pieces
45ml/3 tbsp plain (all-purpose) flour
8 chicken portions
45ml/3 tbsp cognac
2 garlic cloves, chopped
15ml/1 tbsp tomato purée (paste)
250g/9oz button (white) mushrooms
30ml/2 tbsp chopped fresh parsley
salt and ground black pepper

1 Put the bouquet garnet in a large pan with the wine and stock and simmer, uncovered, for 15 minutes. Set aside to cool.

2 Melt 15g/½oz/1 tbsp of the butter with half the olive oil in a frying pan and brown 16 of the onions. Transfer the onions to a plate. Add the bacon and cook until browned, then set aside.

3 Season 30ml/2 tbsp of the flour with salt and pepper. Dust the chicken joints in the flour and fry them in the fat remaining in the pan over a medium heat, turning frequently, for 10 minutes.

4 Pour in the cognac and set it alight using a long match. Remove the chicken when the flames die down.

5 Chop the remaining onions and fry them in 15g/½oz/1 tbsp butter with the garlic until softened. Preheat the oven to 160°C/325°F/Gas 3.

6 Add the wine and stock with the bouquet garni and stir in the tomato purée. Lower the heat, then simmer for 20 minutes. Stir and season.

7 Put the chicken and bacon in a flameproof casserole. Pour over the sauce. Cover and put in the oven for 1½ hours. Add the browned onions and cook for a further 30 minutes.

8 Fry the mushrooms in another 15g/½oz/1 tbsp butter and the remaining oil. Set aside. Mix the remaining butter and flour to make a paste.

9 Using a slotted spoon, transfer the chicken and onions to a serving plate. Discard the bouquet garni. Heat the cooking juices on the stove until simmering. Add the butter and flour paste in small lumps, whisking to blend the paste into the sauce as it melts. Continue until the sauce is thickened.

10 Add the mushrooms and cook for a few minutes. Pour over the chicken.

Energy 630kcal/2618kJ; Protein 42.8g; Carbohydrate 19.3g, of which sugars 7.4g; Fat 41g, of which saturates 17.3g; Cholesterol 209mg; Calcium 67mg; Fibre 2.6g; Sodium 480mg.

Roast chicken with lemon and herbs

Make a Sunday roast with a hint of the Mediterranean. This dish is great for beginner cooks, with minimal ingredients and attention required. While the bird cooks there is plenty of time to cook roast potatoes and vegetables. Lemon and herbs impart a light scent to the meat.

Serves four

1.3kg/3lb chicken
1 unwaxed lemon, halved
small bunch thyme sprigs
1 bay leaf
15g/½oz/1 tbsp butter, softened
60–90ml/4–6 tbsp chicken stock
salt and ground black pepper

1 Preheat the oven to 200°C/400°F/ Gas 6. Season the chicken inside and out with salt and pepper.

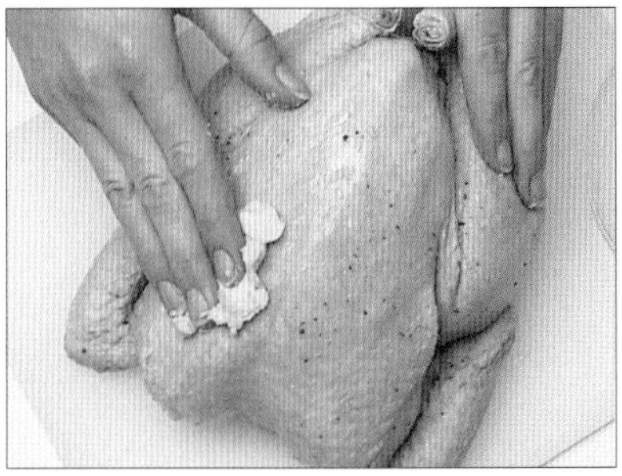

2 Squeeze the juice of one lemon half and then place the juice, the squeezed lemon half, the thyme and bay leaf in the chicken cavity. Rub the breast with butter.

3 Place the chicken in a roasting pan. Squeeze over the juice of the other lemon half. Roast the chicken for 1 hour, basting two or three times, until the juices run clear when the thickest part of the thigh is pierced with a knife.

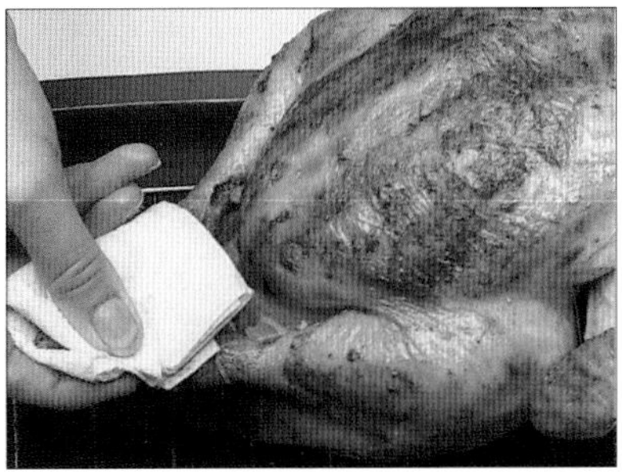

4 Pour the juices from the cavity into the roasting pan and transfer the chicken to a large plate or shallow dish (a board will not hold stray juices). Cover with foil, shiny side in, and leave to stand for 10–15 minutes.

5 Skim excess fat from the juices with a large spoon. Add the stock and boil over a medium heat, stirring and scraping the pan, until slightly reduced. Taste for seasoning. Strain, if required, and serve with the carved chicken.

Energy 444kcal/1848kJ; Protein 31.3g; Carbohydrate 22.8g, of which sugars 6.4g; Fat 25.8g, of which saturates 8g; Cholesterol 128mg; Calcium 94mg; Fibre 7g; Sodium 759mg.

Turkey patties

So much better than shop-bought burgers, these light patties are delicious served like hamburgers with relish, salad leaves and chunky fries in split and toasted buns. They can also be made using minced chicken, lamb, pork or beef.

Serves six

675g/1½lb minced (ground) turkey
1 small onion, finely chopped
small handful of fresh thyme leaves
30ml/2 tbsp olive oil
15ml/1 tbsp lime juice, freshly squeezed
salt and pepper, to taste

Variations

- As well as varying the minced (ground) meat, try chopped oregano, sage or tarragon and/or parsley, in place of the thyme.
- Sunflower oil can be used in place of the olive oil for cooking the patties.

1 Mix the turkey, onion, thyme, 15ml/1 tbsp of the oil, lime juice, salt and pepper until combined.

2 Divide the mixture into six portions. Roll a portion into a ball, then flatten into a patty. Rinse your hands to prevent the meat from sticking to them.

3 Preheat a frying pan. Brush the patties with half of the remaining olive oil, then place them on the pan and cook for 10–12 minutes. Turn the patties over, brush with more oil, and cook for another 10–12 minutes on the second side, or until cooked through. Serve at once, in split toasted buns.

Energy 141kcal/596kJ; Protein 24.8g; Carbohydrate 0.8g, of which sugars 0.6g; Fat 4.4g, of which saturates 1.1g; Cholesterol 69mg; Calcium 15mg; Fibre 0.2g; Sodium 62mg.

Turkey lasagne

This easy meal-in-one pasta bake is delicious with cooked turkey and broccoli in a rich, creamy Parmesan sauce. When shopping for cookware, do not be tempted by shallow lasagne dishes; a deep dish is essential for retaining bubbling hot layers without spills in the oven.

Serves four

30ml/2 tbsp light olive oil
1 onion, chopped
2 garlic cloves, chopped
450g/1lb cooked turkey meat, finely diced
225g/8oz/1 cup mascarpone
30ml/2 tbsp chopped fresh tarragon
300g/11oz broccoli, broken into florets
115g/4oz no pre-cook lasagne verdi

For the sauce
50g/2oz/¼ cup butter
30ml/2 tbsp plain (all purpose) flour
600ml/1 pint/2½ cups milk
75g/3oz/1 cup freshly grated Parmesan cheese
salt and ground black pepper

1 Preheat the oven to 180°C/350°F/Gas 4. Heat the oil in a pan and cook the onion and garlic until soft but not brown. Remove from the heat and stir in the turkey, mascarpone and tarragon, with seasoning to taste.

2 Bring a pan of salted boiling water to the boil. Add the broccoli for 1 minute to blanch, then drain and rinse under cold water to prevent the broccoli from overcooking. Drain well and set aside.

Variation
Use cauliflower florets in place of broccoli, if you prefer.

3 To make the sauce, melt the butter in a pan, stir in the flour and cook for 1 minute, still stirring. Remove from the heat and gradually stir in the milk. Return to the heat and bring to the boil, stirring constantly. Simmer for 1 minute, then add 50g/2oz/⅔ cup of the Parmesan and plenty of seasoning.

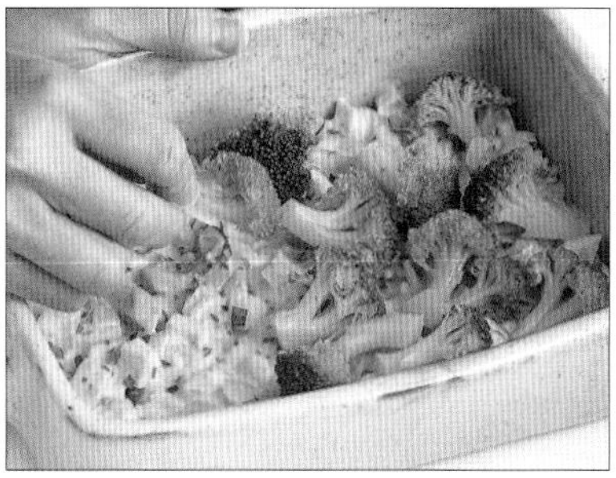

4 Spoon a layer of the turkey mixture into a large baking dish. Add a layer of broccoli and cover with sheets of lasagne. Coat with cheese sauce. Repeat these layers, finishing with a layer of cheese sauce on top. Sprinkle with the remaining Parmesan and bake for 35–40 minutes.

Energy 732kcal/3072kJ; Protein 61.6g; Carbohydrate 43g, of which sugars 13.1g; Fat 36.2g, of which saturates 19.4g; Cholesterol 138mg; Calcium 539mg; Fibre 3.6g; Sodium 475mg.

Duck with plum sauce

This is an up-to-date version of a classic dish. The sharpness of the plums cuts through the rich flavour of the duck meat. Use perfectly ripe plums that are soft and juicy; combined with redcurrant jelly the plums make a luscious-tasting sauce. Serve with seasonal vegetables.

Serves four

4 duck quarters
1 large red onion, finely chopped
500g/1¼lb ripe plums, stoned and quartered
30ml/2 tbsp redcurrant jelly
salt and ground black pepper

Variations

• White onions can be used in place of the red onions, but you will lose the pink flecks in the sauce and the taste will be slightly different.
• Fine-cut orange marmalade makes a tangy alternative to the redcurrant jelly. Cranberry sauce or jelly can easily be substituted instead, if you like.
• Try cherries in place of plums.

1 Prick the duck skin all over with a fork to release the fat during cooking and help give a crisp result, then place the portions in a heavy frying pan, with the skin sides down.

2 Cook the duck pieces for 10 minutes on each side, or until golden brown and cooked through. Remove from the frying pan using tongs, and keep warm.

3 Pour away all but 30ml/2 tbsp of the duck fat, then stir-fry the onion for 5 minutes, or until golden. Add the plums and cook for a further 5 minutes, stirring frequently. Add the redcurrant jelly and mix well.

4 Replace the duck and cook for 5 minutes, or until thoroughly reheated. Season to taste before serving.

Energy 608kcal/2515kJ; Protein 15.1g; Carbohydrate 17.4g, of which sugars 17g; Fat 53.5g, of which saturates 14.5g; Cholesterol 0mg; Calcium 35mg; Fibre 2.2g; Sodium 102mg.

Duck and sesame stir-fry

For a special-occasion stir-fried duck dish, breast fillets are ideal, and can be bought boned, with skin and fat removed. Any poultry or lean diced pork or lamb can be used instead of the duck to make a more economical everyday meal.

Serves four

250g/9oz skinless boneless duck breast
15ml/1 tbsp sesame oil
15ml/1 tbsp vegetable or sunflower oil
4 garlic cloves, finely sliced
2.5ml/½ tsp dried chilli flakes
15ml/1 tbsp Thai fish sauce
15ml/1 tbsp light soy sauce
about 225g/8oz broccoli, cut into small florets
coriander (cilantro) and 15ml/1 tbsp toasted sesame seeds, to garnish

Variation
Replace the Thai fish sauce with the same quantity of soy sauce.

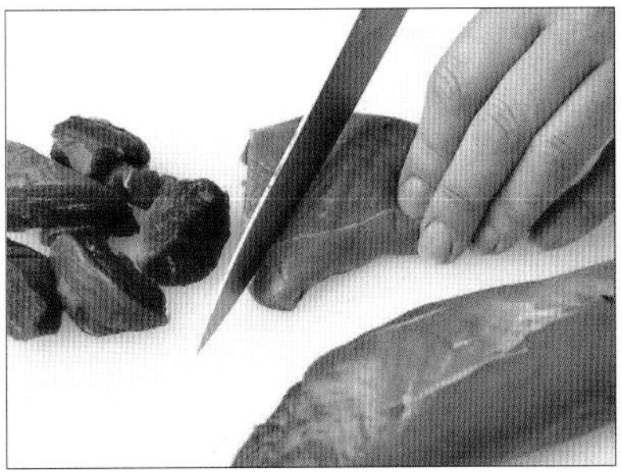

1 Cut the duck meat into bitesize pieces. Heat the oils in a wok and stir-fry the garlic over a medium heat until it is golden brown – do not let it burn. Add the duck to the pan and stir-fry for a further 2 minutes until the meat is just cooked and begins to brown.

2 Stir in the chilli flakes, fish sauce, soy sauce and 120ml/4fl oz/½ cup water. Add the broccoli and continue to stir-fry for about 2 minutes, until the duck is just cooked through. Serve on warmed plates, garnished with coriander and sesame seeds.

Energy 192kcal/798kJ; Protein 18.7g; Carbohydrate 2.7g, of which sugars 2.3g; Fat 12.9g, of which saturates 2.1g; Cholesterol 69mg; Calcium 104mg; Fibre 3.6g; Sodium 436mg.

Meat

Beef, lamb and pork are the basis for all sorts of different meals, from the most modest stewpot with little more than a meaty bone and humble vegetables, or a mouth-watering burger, to steaks and succulent roasts of banqueting proportions. Many people are fearful of cooking with meat, but there really is no need to be concerned; all the main techniques and tips for dealing with meat are fully explained in this chapter.

Meat basics

Methods of butchering, trimming and presenting meat to the customer vary, but there is absolutely no need to be an expert in order to buy and cook meat. In supermarkets, packed meat and open displays are labelled with cooking methods and suggested times. Independent butchers and meat counters in the better supermarkets or stores are well informed – not only will they be able to advise on the quantities you need to buy and choice of cuts for cooking methods, but they will suggest alternatives if the precise item suggested in a recipe is not available.

Meats provide protein, B group vitamins, minerals, especially iron, and fat. The visible fat outside meat can be trimmed off by anyone who specifically follows a low-fat diet for health purposes. Remember that fat gives flavour to a dish.

Many traditional diets include a high proportion of meat (or poultry) with a relatively modest quantity of vegetables, and focus on meat as a daily food for the main meal, so to balance it, it's a good idea to have several meat-free days a week, which means eating more vegetables. Also, traditional meat meals usually include a high proportion of starchy foods, which can be difficult for anyone who has a weight problem and would benefit from eating more vegetables, moderate starchy foods and some other protein.

Below: Raw meat and meat products should look fresh, firm and colourful.

BUYING AND STORING MEAT

Meat is best bought from a reputable butcher. Be sure to keep meat shopping cool and refrigerate it as soon as possible, leaving pre-packed products in their wrapping or transferring loose meat to suitable covered containers to avoid contaminating other refrigerated items. Purchase meat and other perishables last when shopping, so that they have the least amount of time out of refrigeration. Keep well away from dairy produce and from fish, and wash hands after touching any meat products.

CUTS OF MEAT

There is a wide choice of **beef**, **lamb** and **pork** available as traditional small cuts and large roasting joints, as well as boned, sliced, diced and trimmed raw meat products.

Among the most common cuts of beef is sirloin, a lean, tender cut from the back of the animal, used for roasting in joints or grilling (broiling) and frying when cut in steaks. Fillet steak is taken from the sirloin. It is lean and tender and can be roasted, cut into steaks, or thin strips for stir-frying. Rump is a quality cut for roasting, grilling, braising and frying. It can be stir-fried. Topside is quite lean, so good for pot-roasting, where it will be basted in fat. Shin or leg (shank) needs long slow cooking. It is a tough cut of meat made tender by the cooking method. Minced (ground) beef is used for some sauces, burgers and meatballs.

Like beef, lamb can be bought in specific cuts. Loin is a prime cut of lamb, which can be bought boned and is usually stuffed and rolled. Loin chops can be grilled or fried. Roasting joints of meat are taken from the saddle and may be called a double loin of lamb. The leg is a tender cut divided into fillet and shank. Rack of lamb is taken from the best end and is sold as chops or cutlets (US rib chops) or can be boned, stuffed and rolled. Minced or cubed lamb is used for pies and casseroles.

Pork loin is a lean cut of meat and the best for roasting. Tenderloin or fillet is fine-textured and good for grilling and frying. Leg makes a good roast and can be bought boned or on the bone. Belly pork is a fatty cut, which can be rolled and tied into a joint. It can be roasted, pot-roasted, grilled or stewed. Bacon and gammon are lean cuts of pork from the sides, back and belly of the animal. Sausages and sausagemeat are pork products.

SHOPPING TIPS

Avoid discoloured meat and any that shows the merest tinge of green, which indicates decay. The meat should be firm and moist, not dripping or wet. Avoid any meat sitting in stale juices, as well as dried-out meat. Fat should be firm and a good creamy colour. Any signs of yellowing, excess moisture or a slimy texture on fat indicates that the meat is beyond edible quality. The meat should have a fresh smell. Always use meat by the date on the packet. When buying loose meat, do so no more than two days before it is to be used.

Preparing and cooking meat

All cuts of meat are available ready to cook. There is always the option of buying pieces that need boning, slicing, cubing or trimming, if you like.

Meat does not need washing or rinsing before cooking. However, it is a good idea to check for fragments of bone. If meat is sitting in juices, then dry it on kitchen paper.

If there is any cutting to be done – slicing, cutting strips or cubes, or trimming off fat – it is essential to have a sharp knife, and one that is large enough to cut through the meat.

TRIMMING MEAT

Some cuts of meat have a fine or sinewy membrane or excess fat that needs removing before cooking.

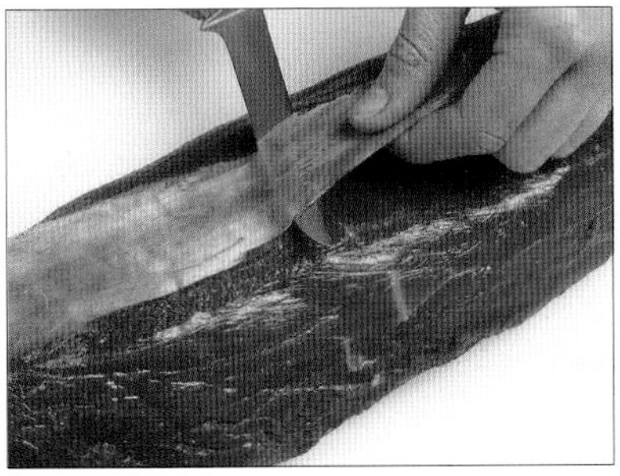

1 Trim off the outside excess of fat with a sharp knife. Cut off any membrane with a sharp knife.

BEATING OUT ESCALOPES

Pounding meat helps to give a tender result to the cooked dish.

1 Cover the steak with cling film (plastic wrap). Pound the meat evenly.

STEWING, BRAISING AND CASSEROLING MEAT

There are long, slow and moist methods of cooking meat either in the oven or on the stove. A large piece of meat or individual portions may be used; cubes of meat are most popular. Long cooking methods suit cheaper cuts of meat that would be tough to eat if cooked quickly. The slow cook method allows the flavour to develop and at the same time makes the meat melt-in-the-mouth tender.

1 Trim off any excess fat and cut the meat into 2.5cm/1in cubes.

2 For a traditional thickened casserole, toss the meat in seasoned flour, and shake off any excess. Do not season uncoated meat at this stage.

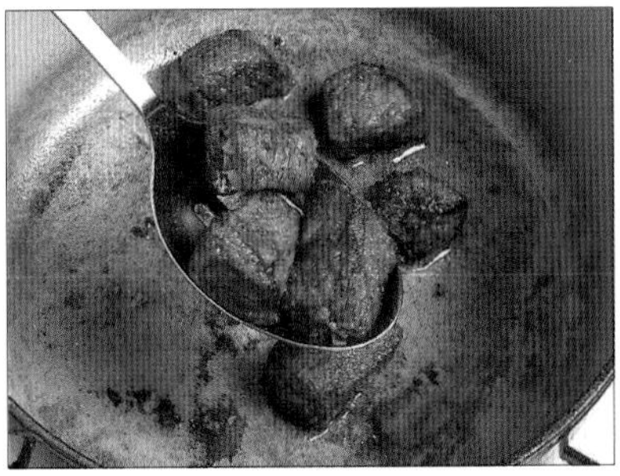

3 Heat about 30ml/2 tbsp oil in a flameproof casserole. Add the meat in batches and cook over a high heat until browned on all sides to caramelize the flavour. Let the meat brown underneath before stirring. Use a draining spoon to remove the meat before adding the next batch.

4 Add the flavouring vegetables, such as sliced or chopped onions, or wedges of onion. Cook, stirring occasionally, for about 5 minutes.

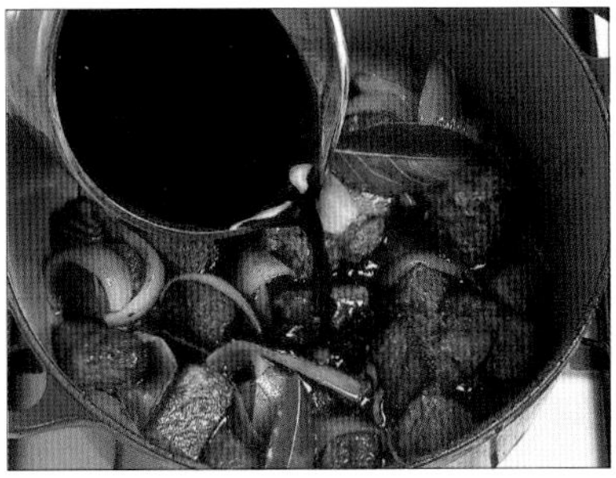

5 Replace the meat, add herbs or other flavouring ingredients, then pour in the cooking liquid. Stir to loosen all the residue from the base of the pan and heat until simmering. Cover and cook gently on the stove or in the oven until the meat is tender.

TENDERNESS TIP

Notice that 'stewing', the really long, gentle method that involves lots of liquid, is associated mainly with beef. Shin or leg of beef is tough but it has fabulous flavour. It needs long slow cooking with plenty of liquid to become completely succulent. Compared to stewing beef, most cuts of pork and lamb are relatively tender. The same cuts of pork used for braising or stewing can also be cooked successfully by dry methods such as roasting.

POT-ROASTING MEAT

This long, slow method of cooking is ideal for slightly tough joints such as brisket, beef or lamb shoulder. The meat is cooked in a covered pot on a bed of vegetables with a small amount of liquid.

1 Heat a little oil in a large, flameproof casserole until very hot. Add the meat and cook, turning, until browned on all sides. Remove the joint from the pan.

2 Add root vegetables, onions and leeks, then cook, stirring, for a few minutes. Replace the meat and pour in a little liquid, such as stock.

WHY BROWN MEAT?

Browning as the first stage creates a rich flavour. Browning does not seal the meat but it caramelizes the outside. It is important to brown meat in small batches in hot fat. If too much meat is added at once, the fat cools, juices seep out and the meat 'stews' rather than fries.

Adding salt also encourages juices to seep out and results in moist cooking rather than frying.

ROASTING TIMES FOR MEAT

Weigh the joint and calculate the cooking time as follows. (Remember to weigh the meat with any additional stuffing in place as this will increase the cooking time.)

BEEF ON THE BONE

For rare beef 20 minutes per 450g/1lb at 180°C/350°F/Gas 4 plus 20 minutes.

For a medium result 25 minutes per 450g/1lb, plus 25 minutes.

For well-done beef 30 minutes per 450g/1lb, plus 30 minutes.

BEEF OFF THE BONE

For rare beef 15 minutes per 450g/1lb at 180°C/350°F/Gas 4, plus 15 minutes.

For a medium result 20 minutes per 450g/1lb, plus 20 minutes.

For well-done beef 25 minutes per 450g/1lb, plus 25 minutes.

LAMB

For rare lamb Roast at 230°C/450°F/Gas 8 for 10 minutes. Reduce the temperature to 180°C/350°F/Gas 4 and cook for 18 minutes per 450g/1lb.

For a medium result Roast at 230°C/450°F/Gas 8 for 10 minutes, then at 180°C/350°F/Gas 4 for a further 25 minutes per 450g/1lb, plus 25 minutes.

For well-done lamb Roast at 230°C/450°F/Gas 8 for 10 minutes, then at 180°C/350°F/Gas 4 for a further 30 minutes per 450g/1lb, plus 30 minutes.

PORK

For well-cooked pork Roast at 230°C/450°F/Gas 8 for 10 minutes. Reduce the temperature to 180°C/350°F/Gas 4 and cook for a further 30 minutes per 450g/1lb plus an extra 30 minutes.

For joints on the bone Allow 35 minutes per 450g/1lb, plus an extra 35 minutes.

ROASTING MEAT

This is a dry cooking method using fat to baste the meat. Traditionally, the meat is not covered but sometimes, for a well-cooked result, the meat can be cooked uncovered for part of the time at first, then covered to prevent it from overcooking, and then uncovered at the end to crisp the surface. To be absolutely correct, the meat should be placed on a rack, so that the fat drains off, but meat is often placed straight in the roasting pan.

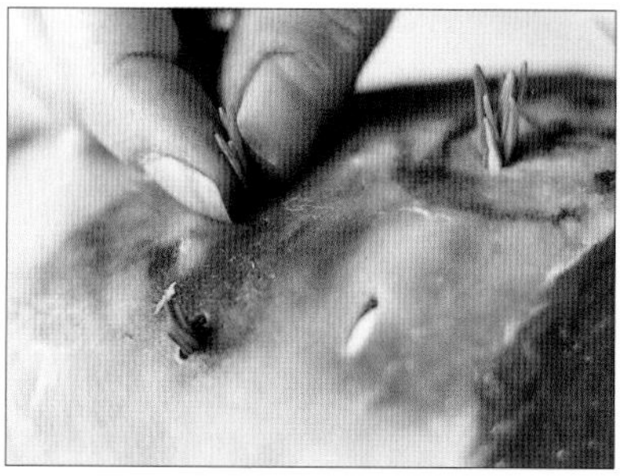

1 According to the recipe, rub the joint with oil or butter, or marinade, and season with salt and pepper. If you wish to add fresh herbs for extra flavour, add them now.

2 Put the meat on a rack or straight into the roasting pan. Add any vegetables or potatoes around the outside of the joint that you wish to cook in the meat's juices.

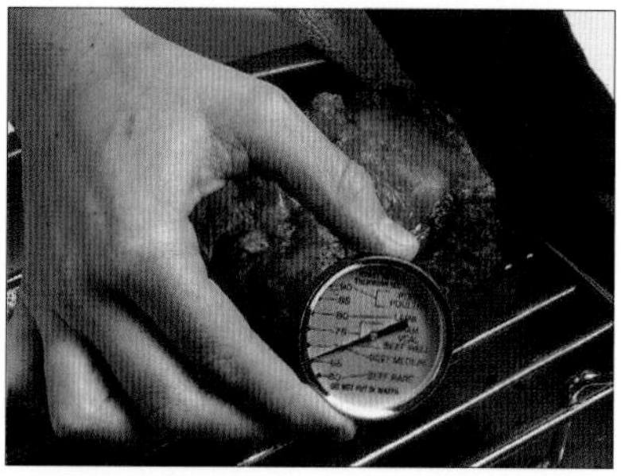

3 Insert a meat thermometer into the thickest part of the meat, not touching the bone. Roast for the suggested time, basting as necessary throughout the cooking time with fat that runs from the meat.

RARE, MEDIUM OR WELL DONE?

Cooking times are intended to be a guideline. The shape of a cut can affect how long it takes to cook, so testing is essential. We all have preferences for how we like our meat to be cooked. Meat that is rare when cooked should be pink on the inside and slightly bloody. Press the meat with the tip of a knife and the juices that run from it will be pink. A medium steak will be pink but not bloody. A well-done roast will be brown throughout and the juices will be brown.

Meat becomes stringy, dry and tasteless when it has been overcooked without any basting to keep it moist.

COOK'S ROASTING TIPS

- Weigh the meat with any stuffing or note the weight from the packet and use this to calculate the cooking time.
- Make sure the pan is big enough for the quantity of meat and deep enough for juices.
- Remember to allow room for roast potatoes around the meat, if necessary.
- If the meat has a covering of fat, rub this with salt.
- If the meat is lean outside, either cover it with thin rashers (strips) of streaky (fatty) bacon to keep it moist or rub butter, lard or meat dripping into it.
- Baste the meat with fat and juices occasionally during cooking.
- Turn a large piece of meat halfway through cooking for even cooking.
- Roasts should be cooked at a relatively high temperature. If they are cooked too long at too low a temperature, the meat simply dries out, without browning well on the outside, and becomes tasteless. Long, slow cooking is for moist methods, such as braising and casseroling, and should be done in covered dishes.

Above: Meat that is well done will be a uniform brown colour throughout. A medium-rare cut of meat (as above) will be brown on the outer edges and pink in the middle. A rare cut of meat will be pink throughout and will have pink juices that run from it.

MAKING GRAVY

Gravy made from the roasting juices is rich in flavour and colour.

1 Spoon off most of the fat from the roasting pan. Set the pan over moderately high heat until sizzling. Add 15ml/1 tbsp plain (all-purpose) flour and stir to combine well and thicken.

2 Cook, scraping the pan to mix in all the browned bits, until the mixture forms a smooth paste. Add a small amount of stock or other liquid and bring to the boil, stirring constantly. Simmer for 5–10 minutes.

FRYING STEAK

This is the traditional cooking method for steaks such as sirloin and fillet. Use a heavy pan, preferably non-stick. Cook steaks or chops in the minimum of fat, then add flavoured butter when serving, if you like. Butter burns easily, so heat the oil in the pan first and add the butter just before the meat.

1 Grease the frying pan with a little sunflower oil. Heat the pan until it is very hot before adding a knob of butter.

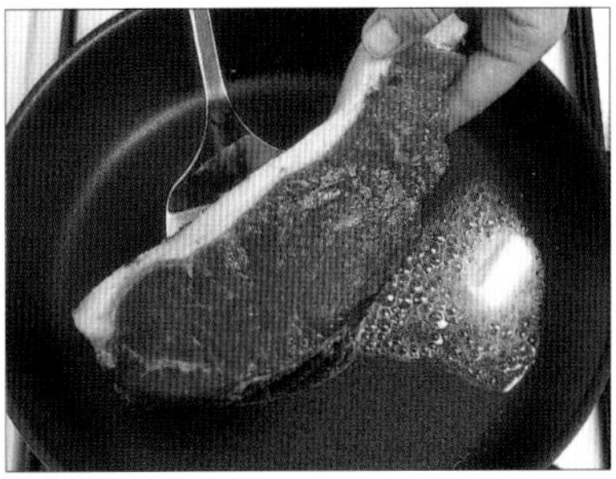

2 As soon as the butter melts, add the steak and cook for the required time.

FRYING TIMES FOR STEAK

For very rare fillet steak cut 2.5cm/1in thick, allow 1 minute on each side; for rump allow 2 minutes on each side.

For rare steak allow 2 minutes each side for fillet; 3 for rump.

For medium steak allow 2–3 minutes for fillet, and 2–4 minutes for rump.

For well-done steak allow 3 minutes, then reduce the heat and allow a further 5–10 minutes.

Spaghetti with meatballs

Meatballs simmered in a sweet and spicy tomato sauce are truly delicious with spaghetti or with other pasta. Children love them and to make the dish milder you can easily leave out the chillies. This is a filling, nutritious and economic dish to cook for a midweek supper.

Serves six to eight

350g/12oz minced (ground) beef
1 egg
60ml/4 tbsp flat leaf parsley, chopped
pinch of crushed dried red chillies
1 thick slice white bread, crusts removed
30ml/2 tbsp milk
about 30ml/2 tbsp olive oil
300ml/½ pint/1¼ cups passata (bottled strained tomatoes)
400ml/14fl oz/1¾ cups vegetable stock
5ml/1 tsp sugar
350–450g/12oz–1lb fresh or dried spaghetti
salt and ground black pepper
freshly grated Parmesan cheese, to serve

1 Put the minced beef in a large bowl. Add the egg, half the parsley and half the crushed chillies. Season well.

2 Tear the bread into small pieces and place in a bowl. Moisten with the milk. Leave to soak for a few minutes, then squeeze out the excess milk and crumble the bread over the meat.

3 Mix everything together with a wooden spoon, then use your hands to squeeze and knead the mixture so that it becomes smooth and quite sticky.

4 Rinse your hands under the cold tap, shake off the excess water, then pick up small pieces and roll the mixture between your palms to make 40–60 small balls. Place the meatballs on a tray and chill for about 30 minutes.

5 Heat the oil in a frying pan. Cook the meatballs until browned on all sides.

6 Pour the passata and stock into a large pan. Heat gently, then add the remaining chillies and the sugar. Season to taste. Add the meatballs, then bring to the boil. Lower the heat, cover and simmer for 20 minutes.

7 Cook the pasta according to the packet instructions. When it is al dente, drain and tip it into a warmed large bowl. Pour the sauce over the pasta and toss gently together. Sprinkle with the remaining parsley and serve with grated Parmesan handed around separately.

COOK'S TIP

Some recipes suggest dusting hands with flour to shape meat, but the flour gets messy and sticky. Instead, keep your hands wet, which means setting up near the sink and rinsing your hands frequently under cold running water. Works every time!

Energy 324kcal/1364kJ; Protein 17.1g; Carbohydrate 40.3g, of which sugars 7.7g; Fat 11.6g, of which saturates 3.8g; Cholesterol 50mg; Calcium 51mg; Fibre 2.7g; Sodium 156mg.

Cottage pie

This classic pie is so good that it is difficult to know when second or third helpings are enough. Serve with colourful vegetables. The meaty sauce can also be served with rice or pasta, rolled in wheat tortillas or pancakes and topped with grated cheese, or spooned into baked potatoes.

Serves four

30ml/2 tbsp sunflower oil
1 onion, finely chopped
1 carrot, finely chopped
115g/4oz mushrooms, chopped
500g/1¼lb minced (ground) beef
300ml/½ pint/1¼ cups beef stock or water
15ml/1 tbsp plain (all-purpose) flour
1 bay leaf
10–15ml/2–3 tsp Worcestershire sauce
15ml/1 tbsp tomato purée (paste)
675g/1½lb potatoes, peeled and cut in chunks
25g/1oz/2 tbsp butter
45ml/3 tbsp hot milk
15ml/1 tbsp chopped fresh tarragon
salt and ground black pepper

1 Heat the oil in a pan, add the onion, carrot and mushrooms and cook, stirring occasionally, until browned. Add the minced beef to the pan and cook, stirring to break up the lumps, until lightly browned.

2 Blend a few spoonfuls of the stock or water with the flour, then stir this into the pan. Stir in the remaining stock or water and bring to a simmer, stirring.

3 Add the bay leaf, Worcestershire sauce and tomato purée, then cover and cook very gently for 1 hour, stirring occasionally. Uncover the pan towards the end of cooking to allow any excess water to evaporate.

4 Preheat the oven to 190°C/375°F/ Gas 5. Place the potatoes in a pan with boiling water. Boil, reduce the heat a little and cover. Cook until soft (15 minutes). Drain. Return to the pan. Mash with butter, milk and seasoning.

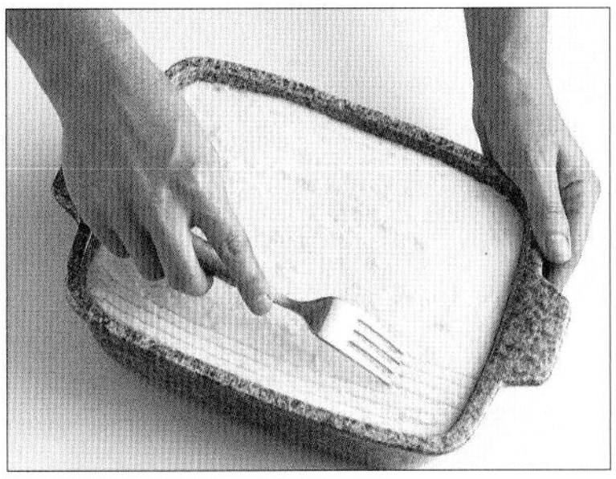

5 Add the tarragon and seasoning to the mince, then pour into a pie dish. Cover the mince with an even layer of potato and mark the top with the prongs of a fork. Bake for about 25 minutes, until golden brown.

Energy 426kcal/1788kJ; Protein 33.9g; Carbohydrate 39.2g, of which sugars 6.3g; Fat 15.9g, of which saturates 5.9g; Cholesterol 0mg; Calcium 66mg; Fibre 3.7g; Sodium 240mg.

Beef cooked in red wine

Shin of beef is a tough cut of meat that needs long, slow cooking to make it tender and bring out the flavour, but the result is worth the wait. Marinating the beef in red wine gives a tender, full-flavoured result. Sprinkle the stew with rosemary and serve with mashed potatoes.

Serves four

675g/1½lb boneless shin or leg (shank) of beef, cut into cubes
3 large garlic cloves, finely chopped
1 bottle fruity red wine
salt and ground black pepper
handful of rosemary sprigs, to garnish

COOK'S TIP

This beef stew freezes well for up to 2 months. Cool the mixture, then pour into a freezer container. Push all the cubes of meat down into the sauce to prevent them drying out, cover and freeze.

1 Put the beef in a casserole dish with the garlic and some ground black pepper, and pour over the red wine. Stir to combine thoroughly, then cover and chill for at least 12 hours. This will allow the wine to flavour and tenderize the meat as it slowly marinates.

2 Preheat the oven to 160°C/325°F/Gas 3. Cover the casserole with a tight-fitting lid and transfer to the oven. Cook for 3–3½ hours, or until the beef is tender. Season to taste, and serve, garnished with rosemary sprigs.

Variation

Add bacon and vegetables for a stew to serve six. Drain the meat (reserving the garlic and wine) and brown it. Add a chopped onion, 1 diced celery stick, 1 diced carrot with 2 diced bacon rashers (strips) with 2 bay leaves. Pour in the wine, then cook as in the main recipe.

Energy 287kcal/1196kJ; Protein 26.1g; Carbohydrate 1.1g, of which sugars 0.3g; Fat 10.5g, of which saturates 4.3g; Cholesterol 65mg; Calcium 15mg; Fibre 0.2g; Sodium 81mg.

Chilli con carne

Originally made with finely chopped beef, chillies and kidney beans by hungry labourers working on the Texan railroad, this famous Tex-Mex stew has become an international favourite. Serve with rice or baked potatoes to complete this hearty meal.

Serves eight

1.2kg/2½lb lean braising steak
30ml/2 tbsp sunflower oil
1 large onion, chopped
2 garlic cloves, finely chopped
15ml/1 tbsp plain (all-purpose) flour
300ml/½ pint/1¼ cups red wine
300ml/½ pint/1¼ cups beef stock
30ml/2 tbsp tomato purée (paste)
fresh coriander (cilantro) leaves, to garnish
salt and ground black pepper

For the beans
30ml/2 tbsp olive oil
1 onion, chopped
1 red chilli, seeded and chopped
2 x 400g/14oz cans red kidney beans, drained and rinsed
400g/14oz can chopped tomatoes

For the topping
6 tomatoes, peeled and chopped
1 green chilli, seeded and chopped
30ml/2 tbsp chopped fresh chives
30ml/2 tbsp chopped fresh coriander (cilantro)

1 Cut the meat into thick strips and then into small cubes.

2 Heat the oil in a flameproof casserole. Add the onion and garlic, and cook until softened but not coloured.

3 Meanwhile, heap the flour on a small plate, and season it well. Toss a batch of meat in it.

4 Use a slotted spoon to remove the onion from the pan, then add the floured beef and cook over a high heat until browned on all sides. Remove from the pan and set aside, then flour and brown another batch of meat.

5 When the last batch of meat is browned, return the first batches with the onion to the pan. Stir in the wine, stock and tomato purée. Bring to the boil, reduce the heat and simmer for 45 minutes, or until tender.

6 Meanwhile, for the beans, heat the olive oil in a frying pan and gently cook the onion and chilli until softened, about 10 minutes. Add the kidney beans and tomatoes and simmer gently for 20–25 minutes, or until thickened and reduced.

7 Mix the tomatoes, chilli, chives and coriander for the topping. Ladle the meat mixture on to warmed plates. Add a layer of bean mixture and tomato topping. Garnish with coriander.

Energy 469kcal/1963kJ; Protein 42g; Carbohydrate 28.3g, of which sugars 11.2g; Fat 18.8g, of which saturates 6.8g; Cholesterol 106mg; Calcium 127mg; Fibre 8.1g; Sodium 523mg.

All-in-one beef hot-pot

This heart-warming, rich pot-roast is ideal for a winter supper. Brisket of beef has the best flavour but this dish works equally well with rolled silverside or topside.

Serves eight

30ml/2 tbsp vegetable oil
900g/2lb rolled brisket of beef
275g/10oz onions, roughly chopped
2 celery sticks, thickly sliced
450g/1lb carrots, cut into large chunks
675g/1½lb potatoes, peeled and cut into large chunks
30ml/2 tbsp plain (all-purpose) flour
475ml/16fl oz/2 cups beef stock
300ml/½ pint/1¼ cups Guinness
1 bay leaf
45ml/3 tbsp chopped fresh thyme
5ml/1 tsp soft light brown sugar
30ml/2 tbsp wholegrain mustard
15ml/1 tbsp tomato purée (paste)
salt and ground black pepper

1 Preheat the oven to 180°C/350°F/Gas 4.

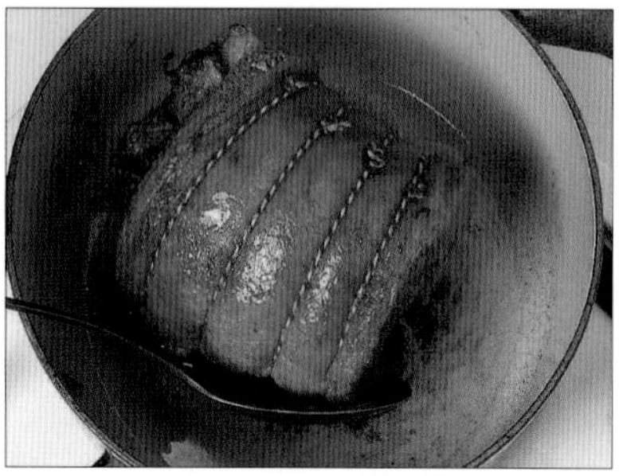

2 Heat the oil in a large, deep flameproof casserole and fry the meat until well browned on all sides. Use tongs to turn the meat.

3 Remove the meat from the pan and drain it on a double layer of kitchen paper. Add the chopped onions to the pan and cook for about 4 minutes, or until they are just beginning to soften and turn brown, stirring all the time.

4 Add the celery, carrots and potatoes to the casserole and cook over a medium heat for 2–3 minutes, or until they are just beginning to colour.

5 Stir in the flour and cook for a further 1 minute, stirring constantly. Pour in the beef stock and the Guinness and stir until well combined. Bring the sauce to the boil, stirring constantly with a wooden spoon.

6 Add the bay leaf, thyme, sugar, mustard, tomato purée and plenty of seasoning. Place the meat on top, cover tightly and transfer to the oven.

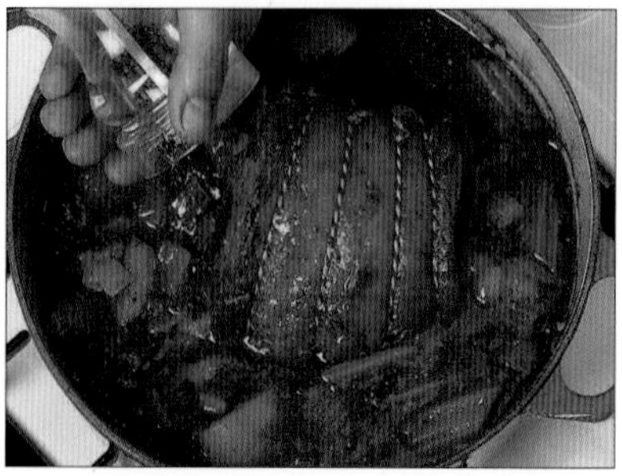

7 Cook for about 2½ hours, or until tender. Adjust the seasoning and add another pinch of sugar, if necessary.

Energy 402kcal/1691kJ; Protein 35.5g; Carbohydrate 33.8g, of which sugars 11.9g; Fat 13.6g, of which saturates 4.4g; Cholesterol 81mg; Calcium 58mg; Fibre 4g; Sodium 142mg.

Beef stroganoff

This classic recipe uses expensive fillet for a treat to share with friends. Try tender pork strips or lamb for an economical alternative. Serve with rice and a huge, leafy, herby salad on the side.

Serves eight

1.2kg/2½lb fillet of beef
30ml/2 tbsp plain (all-purpose) flour
large pinch each of cayene pepper and paprika
75ml/5 tbsp sunflower oil
1 large onion, chopped
3 garlic cloves, finely chopped
450g/1lb/6½ cups chestnut mushrooms, sliced
75ml/5 tbsp brandy
300ml/½ pint/1¼ cups beef stock
300ml/½ pint/1¼ cups soured cream
45ml/3 tbsp chopped flat leaf parsley
salt and ground black pepper

1 Thinly slice the fillet of beef across the grain, then cut it into fine strips. Season the flour with the cayenne pepper and paprika.

2 Heat half the oil in a large frying pan, add the onion and garlic and cook gently until the onion has softened.

3 Add the mushrooms and stir-fry over a high heat. Transfer the vegetables and their juices to a dish; set aside.

COOK'S TIP

If you do not have a very large pan, divide all the ingredients in half and use two pans. Alternatively, use a large flameproof casserole or even a heavy roasting pan.

4 Wipe the pan, then add and heat the remaining oil. Coat a batch of meat with flour, then stir-fry over a high heat until browned. Remove from the pan, then coat and stir-fry another batch. When the last batch of steak is cooked, replace the meat and vegetables. Add the brandy and simmer until it has almost evaporated.

5 Stir in the stock and seasoning and cook for 10–15 minutes, stirring frequently, or until the meat is tender and the sauce is thick and glossy. Add the soured cream, sprinkle with chopped parsley and remove from the heat immediately before the cream curdles. Serve at once with rice and a herby salad.

Energy 919kcal/3810kJ; Protein 32.5g; Carbohydrate 36g, of which sugars 11.7g; Fat 72.6g, of which saturates 34.6g; Cholesterol 194mg; Calcium 94mg; Fibre 3.4g; Sodium 177mg.

Rib of beef and Yorkshire puddings

This is the classic roast, with superb flavour from meat cooked on the bone, and crisp little puddings on the side. Think big to achieve the best results with roasts because small pieces of meat cook too quickly and dry out before their flavour develops.

Serves six to eight

rib of beef joint, weighing about 3kg/6½lb
sunflower oil for brushing
salt and ground black pepper
600ml/1 pint/2½ cups good beef stock, for the gravy

For the Yorkshire puddings
115g/4oz/1 cup plain (all-purpose) flour
pinch of salt
1 egg
200ml/7fl oz/scant 1 cup milk
oil or beef dripping, for greasing

For the horseradish cream
60–75ml/4–5 tbsp finely grated fresh horseradish
300ml/½ pint/1¼ cups soured cream
30ml/2 tbsp cider or white wine vinegar
10ml/2 tsp caster (superfine) sugar

1 Preheat the oven to 220°C/425°F/Gas 7. Weigh the joint and calculate the cooking time as follows: 10–15 minutes per 500g/1¼lb for rare beef, 15–20 minutes for medium, and 20–25 minutes for well done.

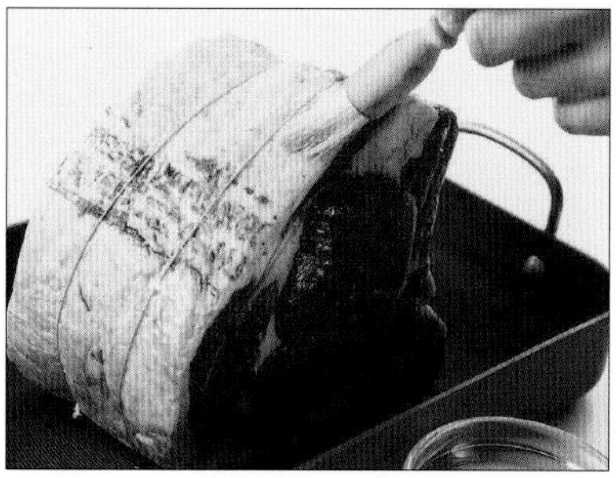

2 Put the joint into a large roasting pan. Brush with oil and season well. Put into the hot oven and cook for 30 minutes, until the beef is browned. Reduce the oven temperature to 160°C/325°F/Gas 3 and cook for the calculated time, spooning the juices over the meat occasionally during cooking.

3 To make the Yorkshire puddings, sift the flour and salt into a bowl. Make a well in the centre and break the egg into it. Add 100ml/3.5fl oz/1½ cups water to the milk and gradually whisk into the flour to make a smooth lump-free batter. Leave to stand while the beef cooks.

4 Generously grease eight Yorkshire pudding tins (muffin pans) measuring about 10cm/4in.

5 For the horseradish cream, put all the ingredients into a bowl and mix well. Cover and chill until required. Taste for seasoning.

6 At the end of its cooking time remove the beef from the oven, cover with foil and leave to stand for 30–40 minutes while you cook the Yorkshire puddings and make the gravy.

COOK'S TIP
To avoid the pungent smell of grated horseradish, use a jar of preserved grated horseradish.

7 Increase the oven temperature to 220°C/425°F/Gas 7 and put the prepared tins on the top shelf for 5 minutes until very hot.

8 Pour in the batter and cook for about 15 minutes until well risen, crisp and golden brown. Remove from the tins.

9 Transfer the beef to a warmed serving plate and cover it with foil (shiny side inwards).

10 To make the gravy, pour off the excess fat from the roasting pan, leaving the meat juices behind. Add the beef stock to the pan, bring to the boil and bubble until reduced by about half. Season to taste with salt and black pepper.

11 Carve the beef and serve hot with the gravy, Yorkshire puddings, roast potatoes and horseradish cream. Serve with seasonal vegetables of your choice.

Energy 1037kcal/4338kJ; Protein 129g; Carbohydrate 15.1g, of which sugars 4.1g; Fat 51.5g, of which saturates 24.3g; Cholesterol 352mg; Calcium 123mg; Fibre 0.5g; Sodium 249mg.

Three ways with fried steak

Melt-in-the-mouth fast-fried steak is often an occasional treat. Serve it with a choice of two rich sauces, or a coating of cracked peppercorns, fries and seasonal vegetables.

Serves two

2 rump, sirloin or fillet steaks,5cm/2in thick
25g/1oz butter

1 Trim any excess fat from the steaks, then season both sides.

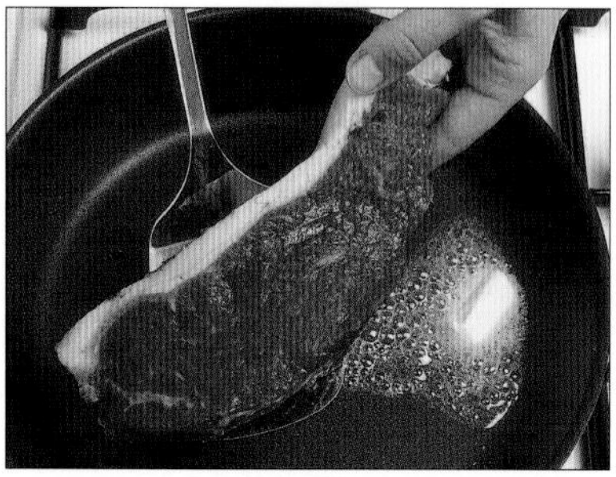

2 Melt the butter in a frying pan and cook the steaks for about 3 minutes on each side for medium rare. Cook for a little longer if you like your steak well cooked.

MUSHROOM SAUCE

A creamy sauce densely packed with sliced mushrooms makes a delightful addition to a well-cooked steak. Garlic adds piquant flavour notes.

115g/4oz mushrooms, cleaned and chopped
1 clove garlic
15ml/1 tbsp oil
15g/½oz oil
50g/2oz butter
30ml/2 tbsp plain (all-purpose) flour
600ml/1 pint/2½ cups milk

1 Fry the mushrooms and garlic in the oil over a medium heat until softened.

2 In another pan, melt the butter. Add the flour and cook for 1 minute, stirring constantly. Turn off the heat and add the milk. Return to the heat and bring to the boil. Simmer gently for 1 minute and season. Stir in the mushrooms and mix well to combine.

STEAK AU POIVRE

A coating of cracked peppercorns adds heat to a fried steak that is not for the faint-hearted.

30–45ml/2–3 tbsp black peppercorns

1 In a mortar and using a pestle, coarsely crush the black peppercorns.

2 Tip the crushed peppercorns on to a plate and press each side of the steak into them.

3 Cook the steak as in step 2 described in column 1.

BEARNAISE SAUCE

A tangy, but rich and creamy sauce.

90ml/6 tbsp white wine vinegar
12 black peppercorns
2 bay leaves
sprig of tarragon
2 shallots, finely chopped
4 egg yolks
salt and ground black pepper
225g/8oz/1 cup unsalted (sweet) butter

1 Put the first five ingredients in a small pan and simmer until reduced to 30ml/2 tbsp of liquid when strained through a sieve (strainer).

2 In a heatproof bowl set over a pan of gently simmering water, beat 4 egg yolks. Season. Beat in the strained vinegar liquid, then add 225g/8oz/ 1 cup unsalted butter, which has been cut into cubes, one cube at a time. Serve with the steak.

Fried steak with mushroom sauce Energy 826kcal/3434kJ; Protein 46.4g; Carbohydrate 23.4g, of which sugars 15.3g; Fat 61.8g, of which saturates 33.9g; Cholesterol 208mg; Calcium 392mg; Fibre 1.1g; Sodium 602mg. Au poivre Energy 263kcal/1095kJ; Protein 34.3g; Carbohydrate 0g, of which sugars 0g; Fat 14.1g, of which saturates 5.7g; Cholesterol 87mg; Calcium 19mg; Fibre 0g; Sodium 97mg. Bearnaise sauce Energy 1218kcal/5029kJ; Protein 40.6g; Carbohydrate 1g, of which sugars 0.7g; Fat 116.9g, of which saturates 69.6g; Cholesterol 749mg; Calcium 75mg; Fibre 0.2g; Sodium 958mg.

Chunky burgers

Burgers are easy to make and these taste terrific – far better than any you can buy. Use lean minced beef so that the burgers are not fatty. Serve in a bread bun with salad and fries.

Serves four

450g/1lb lean minced (ground) beef
1 shallot, chopped
30ml/2 tbsp chopped fresh flat leaf parsley
30ml/2 tbsp tomato ketchup
salt and ground black pepper
4 burger buns, to serve
1 Little Gem (Bibb) lettuce heart, separated into leaves, to serve

For the spicy relish
15ml/1 tbsp olive oil
1 shallot, chopped
1 garlic clove, crushed
1 small green chilli, seeded and finely chopped
400g/14oz can ratatouille

1 Mix the beef, shallot, parsley, ketchup and seasoning in a mixing bowl until thoroughly combined. Divide into four portions. Shape into balls, then flatten into patties. Press the meat firmly between the palms of your hands. To prevent meat from sticking, rinse your hands under cold running water.

2 To make the spicy relish, heat the olive oil in a frying pan and cook the shallot, garlic and chilli for a few minutes, stirring, until softened. Stir in the ratatouille and simmer for 5 minutes.

3 Preheat the grill (broiler) or a frying pan. Cook the burgers for 5 minutes on each side, or until cooked through.

4 Split the burger buns and toast them, if you like. Arrange a few lettuce leaves on the bun bases, then top with the burgers and add a little of the warm spicy relish. Add the bun tops and serve at once, offering the remaining relish and any extra lettuce leaves separately.

Variations

- For an Asian twist, add 5ml/1 tsp anchovy paste, 10ml/2 tsp ground coriander, 1 tsp ground cumin, 7.5ml/1½ tsp finely grated root ginger and two crushed garlic cloves. Serve with fresh coriander (cilantro) and mango chutney.
- Put a cube of mozzarella or blue cheese, such as Gorgonzola or Stilton in the centre for a delicious melting burger.
- Serve with chunky chips (French fries) and sour cream. A fresh green salad with spring onions (scallions) makes a good accompaniment.

Energy 484kcal/2021kJ; Protein 27.9g; Carbohydrate 30.2g, of which sugars 7.7g; Fat 28.8g, of which saturates 9.3g; Cholesterol 68mg; Calcium 120mg; Fibre 2.2g; Sodium 473mg.

Corned beef and egg hash

This is comfort food at its best! Whether you remember gran's version, or prefer this American-style hash, it turns corned beef into a supper fit for any guest.

Serves four

30ml/2 tbsp vegetable oil
25g/1oz/2 tbsp butter
1 onion, finely chopped
1 green (bell) pepper, seeded and diced
2 large potatoes, boiled and diced
350g/12oz can corned beef, cubed
pinch of grated nutmeg
pinch of paprika
4 eggs
salt and ground black pepper
parsley, to garnish (optional)
sweet chilli sauce or tomato sauce, to serve

COOK'S TIP
Put the can of corned beef into the refrigerator to chill for about half an hour before using – it will firm up and cut into cubes more easily. Buy good quality corned beef for the best flavour.

1 Heat the oil and butter together in a large frying pan. Add the onion and fry for 5–6 minutes until softened.

2 In a bowl, mix together the green pepper, potatoes, corned beef, nutmeg and paprika and season well. Add to the pan and toss gently to distribute the cooked onion. Press down lightly and fry without stirring on a medium heat for about 3–4 minutes until a golden brown crust has formed on the underside.

3 Stir the mixture through to distribute the crust, then repeat the frying twice, until the mixture is well browned.

4 Make four wells in the hash and carefully crack an egg into each. Cover and cook gently for about 4–5 minutes until the egg whites are set.

5 Sprinkle with parsley, if using, and cut into quarters. Serve the hash piping hot with sweet chilli sauce or a tomato sauce.

Energy 421kcal/1758kJ; Protein 30.9g; Carbohydrate 17g, of which sugars 5.4g; Fat 26.2g, of which saturates 10.6g; Cholesterol 277mg; Calcium 65mg; Fibre 1.7g; Sodium 871mg.

Braised lamb with barley

Lamb shoulder has a sweet flavour and moist texture that works well in this dish. It is also an economical dish to make. Ask a butcher to bone the shoulder for you. Serve with crusty bread.

Serves four

60ml/4 tbsp olive oil
1 large onion, chopped
2 garlic cloves, chopped
2 celery sticks, sliced
a little plain (all-purpose) flour
675g/1½lb boned shoulder of lamb, cut into cubes
900ml–1 litre/1½–1¾ pints/3¾–4 cups lamb stock
115g/4oz/⅔ cup pearl barley
225g/8oz baby carrots
225g/8oz baby turnips
salt and ground black pepper
30ml/2 tbsp chopped fresh marjoram, to garnish

COOK'S TIP
Serve with boiled or baked potatoes and a green vegetable for a hearty, warming meal, or eat on its own for a lighter meal.

1 Heat 45ml/3 tbsp of the oil in a flameproof casserole. Cook the onion and garlic until softened, add the celery, then cook until the vegetables brown.

2 Season the flour and toss the lamb in it. Use a slotted spoon to remove the vegetables from the casserole.

3 Add and heat the remaining oil with the juices in the casserole. Brown the lamb in batches until golden. When all the meat is browned, return it to the casserole with the onion mixture.

4 Add the pearl barley. Stir in 900ml/1½ pints/3¾ cups of the stock. Cover, then bring to the boil, reduce the heat and simmer for 1 hour, or until the pearl barley and lamb are tender.

5 Add the baby carrots and turnips to the casserole for the final 15 minutes of cooking. Stir the meat occasionally during cooking and add the remaining stock, if necessary. Stir in seasoning to taste, and serve piping hot, garnished with marjoram. Warm, crusty bread would make a good accompaniment.

Energy 565kcal/2364kJ; Protein 37.2g; Carbohydrate 37.2g, of which sugars 11g; Fat 30.9g, of which saturates 10.4g; Cholesterol 128mg; Calcium 85mg; Fibre 3.9g; Sodium 180mg.

Tagine of lamb with couscous

A North African tagine, named after the conical-shaped pottery dish in which it is traditionally cooked, is a stew of meat (or poultry) and vegetables, flavoured with mild, warm spices.

Serves six

1kg/2¼ lb lean boneless lamb, such as shoulder or neck fillet
25g/1oz/2 tbsp butter
15ml/1 tbsp sunflower oil
1 large onion, chopped
2 garlic cloves, chopped
2.5cm/1in piece fresh root ginger, peeled and finely chopped
1 red (bell) pepper, seeded and chopped
900ml/1½ pints/3¾ cups lamb stock
250g/9oz ready-to-eat prunes
juice of 1 lemon
15ml/1 tbsp clear honey
1.5ml/¼ tsp saffron strands
1 cinnamon stick, broken in half
50g/2oz/½ cup flaked (sliced) almonds, toasted
salt and ground black pepper

To serve
450g/1lb/2½ cups couscous
25g/1oz/2 tbsp butter
chopped fresh coriander (cilantro)

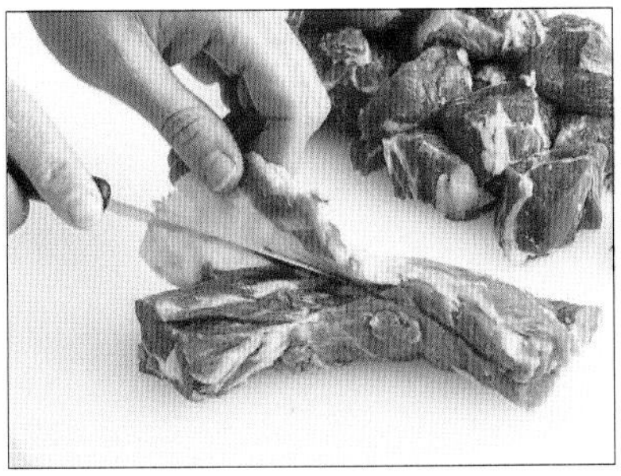

1 Trim the lamb and cut it into 2.5cm/1in cubes. Heat the butter and oil in a large flameproof casserole until foaming. Add the onion, garlic and ginger and cook, stirring occasionally, until softened but not coloured.

2 Add the lamb and red pepper and mix well. (It is not necessary to seal the meat in batches over high heat, as this is not the method for an authentic tagine.) Pour in the stock or water.

3 Add the prunes, lemon juice, honey, saffron and cinnamon. Season with salt and pepper and stir well. Bring to the boil, then reduce the heat and cover the casserole. Simmer for 1½–2 hours, stirring occasionally, or until the meat is melt-in-the-mouth tender.

4 Meanwhile, cook the couscous according to packet instructions, usually by placing in a large bowl and pouring in boiling water to cover the 'grains' by 2.5cm/1in. Stir well, then cover and leave to stand for 5–10 minutes. The couscous absorbs the water and swells to become tender and fluffy. Stir in the butter, chopped fresh coriander and seasoning to taste.

5 Taste the stew for seasoning and add more salt and pepper if necessary. Pile the couscous into a large, warmed serving dish or on to individual warmed bowls or plates. Ladle the stew on to the couscous and scatter the toasted flaked almonds over the top.

Energy 652kcal/2716kJ; Protein 35.2g; Carbohydrate 30.9g, of which sugars 26g; Fat 44.2g, of which saturates 16.4g; Cholesterol 141mg; Calcium 97mg; Fibre 5.4g; Sodium 223mg.

Lamb chops with a mint jelly crust

Mint and lamb are classic partners, and the breadcrumbs used here add extra texture. Serve the chops with sweet potatoes baked in their skins and some steamed green vegetables.

Serves four

8 lamb chops, about 115g/4oz each
50g/2oz/1 cup fresh white breadcrumbs
30ml/2 tbsp mint jelly
salt and ground black pepper

1 Preheat the oven to 190°C/375°F/ Gas 5.

2 Lightly grease a baking sheet to stop the meat from sticking, then place the lamb chops on the baking sheet and season with plenty of salt and ground black pepper.

3 Put the breadcrumbs and mint jelly in a bowl and mix together to combine. The mint jelly should be at room temperature to mix well. If it has been chilled, dip the teaspoon in a cup of boiling water and this will warm the jelly.

4 Spoon the breadcrumb mixture on top of the chops, pressing down firmly with the back of a spoon, making sure it sticks to the chops. Bake the chops for 20–30 minutes, or until they are just cooked through. Serve immediately.

Energy 551kcal/2309kJ; Protein 64.1g; Carbohydrate 11.3g, of which sugars 2g; Fat 27.9g, of which saturates 13.3g; Cholesterol 248mg; Calcium 46mg; Fibre 0.3g; Sodium 316mg.

Sweet-and-sour lamb chops

Buy lamb chops when the new season's lamb is in the shops, because these have the best flavour of all. This vinegar dressing brings out the flavour in the lamb.

Serves four

8 French-trimmed lamb loin chops
90ml/6 tbsp balsamic vinegar
30ml/2 tbsp caster (superfine) sugar
30ml/2 tbsp olive oil
salt and ground black pepper

COOK'S TIP
Be selective about balsamic vinegar because some of the very inexpensive products are inferior vinegar mixed with sugar. It is better to use red wine vinegar or cider vinegar than cheap balsamic dressing. Try fruit vinegar for a change, such as raspberry vinegar.

1 Put the lamb chops in a shallow, non-metallic dish and drizzle over the balsamic vinegar. Sprinkle with the sugar and season well. Turn the chops to coat them in the mixture, then cover with clear film (plastic wrap) and chill for at least 20 minutes or up to 12 hours before cooking.

2 Heat the olive oil in a frying pan and add the chops, reserving the marinade. Cook for 3–4 minutes on each side.

3 Pour the marinade into the pan and leave to bubble for about 2 minutes, or until reduced slightly. Remove from the pan and serve immediately.

Energy 258kcal/1077kJ; Protein 19.6g; Carbohydrate 7.9g, of which sugars 7.9g; Fat 16.7g, of which saturates 6g; Cholesterol 76mg; Calcium 12mg; Fibre 0g; Sodium 87mg.

Rosemary scented lamb

The marriage of rosemary and lamb is made in heaven. This simple dish is quick to cook and prepare. Ask your butcher to 'French trim' the lamb racks. Do allow plenty of time for marinating the lamb for a tender and juicy, mouthwatering result.

Serves four to eight

2 x 8-chop racks of lamb
8 large fresh rosemary sprigs
2 garlic cloves, thinly sliced
90ml/6 tbsp extra virgin olive oil
30ml/2 tbsp red wine
salt and ground black pepper

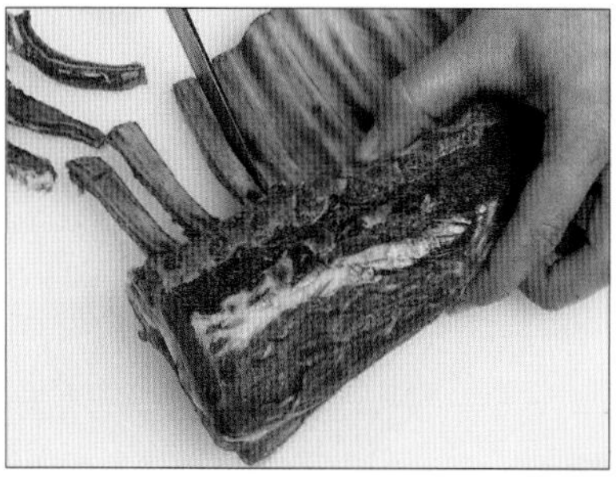

1 Cut the fat off the ribs down the top 5cm/2in from the bone ends. Turn over and score between the bones.

2 Cut and scrape away the meat and connective tissue between the bones. Cut the racks into eight portions, each consisting of two linked chops, and tie a rosemary sprig to each one.

3 Arrange the portions in a single layer in a bowl or wide dish. Mix the garlic, olive oil and wine together, and pour over the lamb. Cover and chill overnight if you can, turning them as often as possible.

4 Bring the marinating chops to room temperature 1 hour before cooking. Remove the lamb from the marinade, and discard the marinade. Season the meat 15 minutes before cooking.

5 Heat the grill (broiler) to high and grill (broil) on each side for 4 minutes, if you like rare meat, or 5 minutes each side if you prefer the lamb medium-cooked.

6 Remove the chops from the grill, transfer to serving plates, cover and rest for 5–10 minutes before serving.

COOK'S TIP
Allowing the hot chops to stand before serving gives the juices time to gather and create a light sauce in much the same way that a joint needs to rest before carving.

Energy 433Kcal/1788kJ; Protein 23.4g; Carbohydrate 0g, of which sugars 0g; Fat 37.6g, of which saturates 16.4g; Cholesterol 101mg; Calcium 17mg; Fibre 0g; Sodium 83mg.

Lamb's liver with bacon casserole

The trick when cooking liver is to seal it quickly in a hot pan, then simmer it briefly and gently. Prolonged and/or fierce cooking makes the liver hard and grainy, which needs to be avoided. Boiled new potatoes tossed in lots of butter go well with this simple casserole.

Serves four

30ml/2 tbsp extra virgin olive oil or sunflower oil
225g/8oz rindless unsmoked lean bacon rashers (strips), cut into pieces
2 onions, halved and sliced
175g/6oz/2 cups chestnut mushrooms, halved
450g/1lb lamb's liver, trimmed and sliced
25g/1oz/2 tbsp butter
15ml/1 tbsp soy sauce
30ml/2 tbsp plain (all-purpose) flour
150ml/¼ pint/⅔ cup hot, well-flavoured chicken stock
salt and ground black pepper

1 Heat the oil in a large frying pan. Add the bacon and fry until crisp, stirring occasionally. Add the sliced onions to the pan and cook for about 10 minutes, stirring frequently, or until softened.

2 Add the mushrooms and cook lightly for a further 1 minute, stirring well.

3 Use a slotted spoon to remove the bacon and vegetables from the pan and keep warm.

4 Add the liver to the fat remaining in the pan and cook over a high heat for 3–4 minutes, turning once to seal the slices on both sides. Remove the liver from the pan and keep warm.

5 Melt the butter in the pan, add the soy sauce and flour and blend together. Stir in the stock and bring to the boil, stirring until thickened.

6 Return the liver, vegetables and bacon to the pan and heat through for 1 minute. Season to taste, and serve with new potatoes and green beans.

Energy 418kcal/1739kJ; Protein 34.2g; Carbohydrate 9.3g, of which sugars 2.6g; Fat 27.3g, of which saturates 9.5g; Cholesterol 527mg; Calcium 34mg; Fibre 1.3g; Sodium 1257mg.

Pan-fried gammon with cider

Gammon and cider are a delicious combination with the sweet, tangy flavour of cider complementing the gammon perfectly. Serve with mashed potatoes for a traditional meal and have a crisp green salad to contrast with the creamy sauce.

Serves two

30ml/2 tbsp sunflower oil
2 gammon steaks (smoked or cured ham)
75ml/5 tbsp dry (hard) cider
30ml/2 tbsp double (heavy) cream
ground black pepper

Variation

Gammon (smoked or cured ham) tastes good fried in a mix of butter and oil. Serve with sliced fried new potatoes and a fried egg. You could also grill (broil) the gammon.

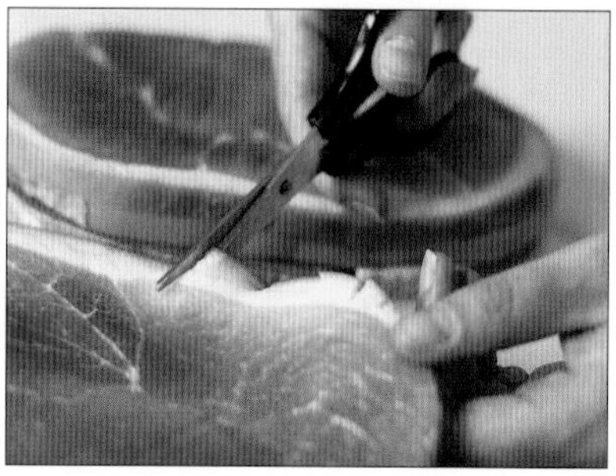

1 Heat the oil in a large frying pan until hot. Neatly snip the rind on the gammon steaks to stop them curling up during cooking. Cook the steaks for 3–4 minutes on each side.

2 Pour in the cider. Allow to boil for a couple of minutes, then stir in the cream and cook for 1–2 minutes, or until thickened. Season with pepper and serve immediately.

Energy 429kcal/1784kJ; Protein 39.6g; Carbohydrate 1.2g, of which sugars 1.2g; Fat 28.4g, of which saturates 10.1g; Cholesterol 67mg; Calcium 24mg; Fibre 0g; Sodium 1985mg.

Pork and potato hot-pot

Long, slow cooking makes the pork chops meltingly tender and allows the potato slices to soak up all the delicious juices from the meat. Serve with lightly cooked green vegetables for a family meal or casual supper with friends.

Serves four

25g/1oz/2 tbsp butter
15ml/1 tbsp oil
1 large onion, very thinly sliced
1 garlic clove, crushed
225g/8oz/generous 3 cups button (white) mushrooms, sliced
pinch of dried mixed herbs
900g/2lb potatoes, thinly sliced
4 thick pork chops, trimmed of excess fat
about 750ml/1¼ pints/3 cups vegetable or chicken stock
salt and ground black pepper

1 Preheat the oven to 160°C/325°F/Gas 3. Use 15g/½oz/1 tbsp of the butter to grease the base and halfway up the sides of a casserole with a lid.

2 Heat the oil in a frying pan, add the sliced onion and cook gently for about 5 minutes or until it is softened and translucent but not browned. Add the garlic and mushrooms and cook for a further 5 minutes. Remove from the heat and stir in the mixed herbs.

3 Spoon half the mushroom mixture into a casserole. Arrange half the potato slices on top and season well.

Variation
Use chopped fresh herbs instead of dried herbs.

4 Arrange the pork chops on top of the potatoes, in a single layer (overlap them if necessary). Repeat the layers of mushroom mixture and potatoes, finishing with a layer of potatoes.

5 Pour in enough stock just to cover the potatoes. Cover the casserole with the lid or tightly fitted foil, if your dish does not have a lid.

6 Place the hot-pot in the oven and cook for 2 hours, or until the potatoes and meat feel tender when pierced with a thin skewer.

7 Increase the oven temperature to 200°C/400°F/Gas 6. Uncover the casserole and dot the remaining butter over the potatoes. Cook uncovered for about 20 minutes, until golden brown on top.

Energy 511Kcal/2132kJ; Protein 17.9g; Carbohydrate 41.5g, of which sugars 6.5g; Fat 31.5g, of which saturates 12.1g; Cholesterol 67mg; Calcium 40mg; Fibre 3.7g; Sodium 529mg.

Sweet-and-sour pork

Originally created by the Chinese, sweet-and-sour cooking is now popular the world over. This version has a fresh, clean taste with pineapple for sweetness and Thai fish sauce for contrast. It makes an excellent meal served over rice or noodles.

Serves four

350g/12oz lean pork
30ml/2 tbsp vegetable oil
4 garlic cloves, thinly sliced
1 small red onion, sliced
30ml/2 tbsp Thai fish sauce (nam pla)
15ml/1 tbsp sugar
1 red (bell) pepper, seeded and diced
½ cucumber, seeded and sliced
2 plum tomatoes, cut into wedges
115g/4oz piece of fresh pineapple, cut into small chunks
2 spring onions (scallions), cut into short lengths
ground black pepper
coriander (cilantro) leaves, to garnish
spring onions (scallions), shredded, to garnish

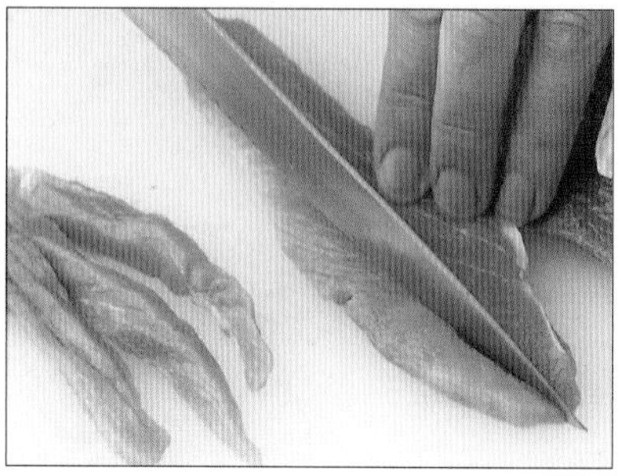

1 Place the pork in the freezer for 30–40 minutes, until firm. Using a sharp knife, cut it into thin strips.

2 Heat the oil in a wok or large frying pan. Add the garlic. Cook over a medium heat until golden, then add the pork and stir-fry for about 4–5 minutes. Add the red onion slices and toss to mix together.

3 Add the fish sauce, sugar and pepper to taste. Toss the mixture over the heat for 3–4 minutes more, until everything is thoroughly coated.

4 Stir in the red pepper, cucumber, tomatoes, pineapple and spring onions. Stir-fry for 3–4 minutes more, then spoon into a bowl. Garnish with the coriander and spring onions and serve.

Energy 727kcal/3035kJ; Protein 32.7g; Carbohydrate 76.5g, of which sugars 39.4g; Fat 32.8g, of which saturates 5.8g; Cholesterol 272mg; Calcium 85mg; Fibre 2.7g; Sodium 1048mg.

Pork with chickpeas

This is a basic meat and legume casserole that could equally well be made with lamb or poultry, using red kidney or flageolet beans. Diced celery, carrots and mushrooms can also be added. Serve with some warm crusty bread for a hearty meal.

Serves four

350g/12oz/1¾ cups dried chickpeas, soaked overnight in water to cover
75–90ml/5–6 tbsp extra virgin olive oil
675g/1½lb boneless leg of pork, cut into large cubes
1 large onion, sliced
2 garlic cloves, chopped
400g/14oz can chopped tomatoes
grated rind of 1 orange
1 small dried red chilli (optional)
salt and ground black pepper

1 Drain the chickpeas, rinse under cold water and drain again. Place them in a large pan. Pour in enough cold water to cover generously and bring to the boil. Boil the chickpeas for 10 minutes.

2 Skim any frothy scum off the water. Add more boiling water from a kettle to cover the chickpeas if necessary. Reduce the heat and cover the pan. Simmer the chickpeas for 1–1½ hours or until tender.

3 When the chickpeas are soft and tender, drain them, reserving the cooking liquid, and set them aside.

4 Heat the olive oil in the clean pan and brown the cubes of pork in small batches, so that the fat stays hot and fries the meat rather than stewing it. As each batch browns, lift the meat out with a slotted spoon and set aside.

5 When all the meat is browned, add the onion to the oil remaining in the pan and sauté the onion until light golden.

6 Stir in the garlic, then as soon as it becomes aromatic, add the tomatoes and orange rind. Crumble in the chilli, if using and stir well.

COOK'S TIPS

- Add canned chickpeas 30 minutes before the end of cooking.
- The longer the casserole is cooked, the better it tastes, but check it does not dry out.

7 Return the chickpeas and meat to the pan, with enough of the cooking liquid to cover. Add pepper, then cover and simmer for 1 hour, until tender. Stir occasionally and add more liquid if needed. Season before serving.

Energy 654kcal/2743kJ; Protein 56.4g; Carbohydrate 52.4g, of which sugars 9.6g; Fat 25.7g, of which saturates 4.9g; Cholesterol 106mg; Calcium 178mg; Fibre 11.4g; Sodium 164mg.

Pork sausages and mustard mash

Beat the winter blues with this simple meal. Long, slow cooking is the trick to remember for good onion gravy as this reduces and caramelizes the onions to create a wonderfully rich gravy with an underlying sweetness to its flavour.

Serves four

12 pork and leek sausages

For the onion gravy
30ml/2 tbsp olive oil
25g/1oz/2 tbsp butter
8 onions, sliced
5ml/1 tsp caster (superfine) sugar
15ml/1 tbsp plain (all-purpose) flour
300ml/½ pint/1¼ cups beef stock

For the mashed potato
1.5kg/3¼lb potatoes
50g/2oz/¼ cup butter
150ml/¼ pint/⅔ cup double (heavy) cream
15ml/1 tbsp wholegrain mustard

1 To make the onion gravy, heat the oil and butter in a large pan until foaming. Add the onion slices and mix well to thoroughly coat them in the fat. Cover and cook gently for about 30 minutes, stirring frequently. Add the sugar and cook for a further 5 minutes, or until the onions are softened, reduced and slightly caramelized.

2 Remove the pan from the heat and stir in the flour, then stir in the stock.

3 Return the pan to the heat. Bring to the boil, stirring, then simmer for 3 minutes, or until thickened. Season to taste with salt and pepper.

4 Meanwhile, cook the potatoes in a pan of boiling salted water for 20 minutes, or until tender.

5 While the potatoes are cooking, preheat the grill (broiler) to medium. Arrange the sausages in a single layer in the grill (broiling) pan and cook for 15–20 minutes, or until cooked, turning frequently so that they brown evenly.

6 Drain the potatoes well and mash them with the butter, cream and wholegrain mustard. Season with salt and pepper to taste. Serve the sausages with the creamy mashed potato and onion gravy.

Variation
Lots of butter and double (heavy) cream is a treat in mash, but a modest drizzle of olive oil and some milk is also good and healthier for everyday eating.

Energy 1425Kcal/5921kJ; Protein 31.4g; Carbohydrate 106.1g, of which sugars 22.3g; Fat 100.3g, of which saturates 45.1g; Cholesterol 176mg; Calcium 190mg; Fibre 10g; Sodium 1634mg.

Pork sausage stew

This hearty casserole, made with meaty sausages and haricot beans, is flavoured with fragrant fresh herbs and dry Italian wine. Serve with crusty bread for mopping up the delicious juices. Remember to leave time for the beans to soak before cooking.

Serves four

225g/8oz/1½ cups dried haricot (navy) beans
2 sprigs fresh thyme
30ml/2 tbsp olive oil
450g/1lb pork sausages
1 onion, finely chopped
2 sticks celery, finely diced
300ml/½ pint/1¼ cups dry red or white wine, preferably Italian
1 sprig of fresh rosemary
1 bay leaf
300ml/½ pint/1¼ cups boiling vegetable stock
200g/7oz can chopped tomatoes
¼ head dark green cabbage, such as cavolo nero or Savoy, finely shredded
salt and ground black pepper
chopped fresh thyme, to garnish

1 Put the haricot beans in a large bowl and cover with cold water. Leave to soak for at least 8 hours or overnight.

2 Drain the beans and place in a pan with the thyme and at least twice their volume of cold water. Bring to the boil and boil steadily for 10 minutes, then drain and place in a deep ovenproof casserole, discarding the thyme.

3 Preheat the oven to 160°C/325°F/Gas 3. Heat the oil in a frying pan and cook the sausages until browned all over. Transfer to the casserole and tip away any excess fat from the pan.

4 Fry the onion and celery gently for 5 minutes until softened but not coloured. Add the wine, rosemary and bay leaf and bring to the boil. Then pour the mixture into the casserole. Add the stock and season with pepper. Cover and place in the oven for 2 hours, until the beans are just tender.

Variations

- Try sausages flavoured with garlic (Toulouse-style) or with leeks and sage in this casserole.
- Alternatively, buy Polish boiling sausage (wiejska) from the deli counter and cut it into chunks.

5 Stir the tomatoes and the cabbage into the stew. Cover and cook for 30 minutes, or until the cabbage is tender but not overcooked. Divide among warmed plates or large bowls. Garnish with a little chopped fresh thyme and serve with crusty Italian bread.

Energy 620kcal/2593kJ; Protein 28.4g; Carbohydrate 47.4g, of which sugars 9.9g; Fat 30.9g, of which saturates 10.8g; Cholesterol 67.5mg; Calcium 205mg; Fibre 7.6g; Sodium 1139mg.

Pastry

Perfect pastry is a real treat to use and eat. It can be savoury or sweet and it is great for snacks, main meals and puddings. Make it or buy it ready-made, roll it or fold it, fill it and bake it. Some types of pastry are easy to make and some are best purchased ready-made. This chapter shows you how to make the most common varieties, as well as ways to add lightness, flakiness, sweetness and a crisp crunch to all your dishes.

Pastry basics

There are many types of pastry used to make pies, tarts, canapés and sweet and savoury snacks. Some are easy to make and others best left to the professionals. Pastry should be light, crumbly and crunchy in texture.

TYPES OF PASTRY

Shortcrust pastries Short pastries are crumbly, with a slightly crisp surface. Classic shortcrust pastry is made with half the weight of fat to flour, with water to bind the ingredients together. Increasing the proportion of butter makes the pastry richer, crumblier, and more flavourful. It can be used for savoury or sweet dishes. Egg yolk is used instead of water.

Suet (US chilled grated shortening) pastry This light, spongy pastry uses self-raising (self-rising) flour and suet (chilled grated shortening), a grated fat. Suet pastry is often steamed or boiled but it is also good baked. Vegetarian versions are available.

Puff and flaky pastries These are very light and crisp. Puff pastry is made with equal quantities of fat and flour. It has many fine layers. When baked, rolled and folded pastries rise as the trapped air and steam force the layers apart.

Below: Wholemeal flour can be used with white flour.

Rough puff pastry is quicker and easier to make than puff. It has a lower proportion of fat to flour and a rich buttery, flaky texture.

Flaky pastry is similar to puff, but it is easier to handle and not as rich.

Choux paste or pastry This is a paste of water, fat and flour with eggs beaten in. It is one of the easiest pastries to make and is used for profiteroles or savoury dishes such as gougère.

Filo pastry This paper-thin pastry is used for making large and small pastries. Filo can be cut, folded or scrunched into shape to make baskets, wrapped snacks and pies.

PASTRY INGREDIENTS

Flour, fat and liquid are the foundations for pastry doughs.

Flour Plain (all-purpose) flour is the basic ingredient. **Wholemeal (whole-wheat) flour** can be used, but it tends to be heavy when used without any white flour. This is really a matter for personal taste: traditional fine pastry relies on light white crumbs but using some wholemeal flour is perfectly acceptable.

Fat The combination of half butter and half lard or white vegetable fat

Below: Choux pastry puffs up and sets into a crisp, golden shell when baked.

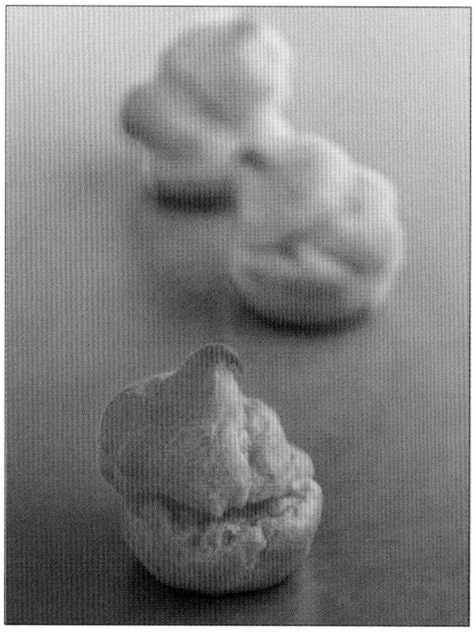

Above: Filo pastry is fine and used in layers, usually brushed with butter or oil.

(shortening) is the best for shortcrust. Butter gives flavour, and lard or white vegetable fat makes the pastry short or crumbly. Suet, either proper suet or vegetable fat, is used for suet pastry. Oil is used in some pastry recipes. If you are new to making pastry, stay with tried-and-tested recipes for success.

Liquid Cold water is the basic binding for all pastries. In short pastries, only a very small amount is used. The more water added, the tougher, closer, less short and heavier the result. Suet pastry is mixed with more water to a slightly softer consistency. This gives a light, spongy texture to the risen dough.

Egg yolk is used with a little water to enrich some pastry as well as bind it. Whole egg (beaten) is used in some recipes, but the white sets firm during cooking, making the pastry tougher.

STORING PASTRY

Use home-made pastry immediately, but remember to allow time for chilling if you are preparing food for a specific time. Bought chilled pastry usually has a long sell-by date on it. It contains preservative and should be kept in the refrigerator. Any unused pastry can be frozen. Wrap it first in freezer paper and then kitchen foil. Frozen pastry is available and should be defrosted at room temperature before being used. Do not refreeze any raw defrosted pastry.

Preparing and baking pastry

SHORTCRUST PASTRY

This is used for pies, pie tops, savoury tarts and canapé bases. It takes little effort to rub the fat into the flour. If you are short of time, use a food processor and pulse the power to mix the fat and flour for the first stage (over-working the mixture creates a stodge). Do not add too much water as this makes tough pastry and do not overchill the pastry or it becomes hard and difficult to handle. Do not use lard for vegetarians.

Makes enough to line a 25cm/10in flan tin (quiche pan)

225g/8oz/2 cups plain (all-purpose) flour
115g/4oz/½ cup chilled fat: half butter and half lard or white vegetable fat, diced
45–60ml/3–4tbsp chilled water

1 Put the flour in a bowl with the fat Use your fingertips or a mandolin to rub the fat into the flour.

2 When the mixture looks like fine breadcrumbs, sprinkle 45ml/3 tbsp of the water evenly over and mix lightly with a knife until the mixture begins to form moist clumps.

3 Using one hand, gather the mixture and press it gently into a dough. Incorporate any loose pieces of the mixture. Press gently together.

4 Wrap the dough in clear film (plastic wrap), and chill for 15 minutes.

Variations

Cheese pastry Add 50g/2oz/ ½ cup grated mature (sharp) Cheddar or 45ml/3 tbsp freshly grated Parmesan and a pinch of mustard powder.

Fresh herb pastry Add 45ml/ 3 tbsp chopped fresh herbs such as parsley, sage or chives or 15ml/1 tbsp stronger flavoured herbs such as rosemary or thyme.

FILO PASTRY

This is very thin and used several layers thick. It is readily available chilled or frozen and can be used for a variety of savoury and sweet recipes, from samosas to strudel. While there are recipes that explain how to mix and hand-stretch strudel dough, this requires large areas of work surface and plenty of practice. Frozen filo is very fragile and brittle, so avoid packets that have been thrown around in a freezer display, or are damaged. Similarly, buy only from a shop that has a high turnover as the chilled pastry can become mouldy.

RICH SHORTCRUST PASTRY

Use for sweet pies and tarts with a rich filling. For a very rich pastry add 1 egg yolk and 15–30ml/1–2 tbsp water.

Makes enough to line a 25cm/10in flan tin (quiche pan)

225g/8oz/2 cups plain (all-purpose) flour
50g/2oz sugar
175g/6oz/¾ cup chilled butter, diced
30–45ml/2–3 tbsp chilled water

1 For a sweet pastry, put the flour and sugar into the food processor. Process briefly to mix. Scatter the cubes of fat over the dry ingredients. Pulse for a few seconds until the mixture resembles fine breadcrumbs.

2 Sprinkle in the water or other liquid and pulse the mixture until it starts to hold together. Do not allow the pastry to clump together.

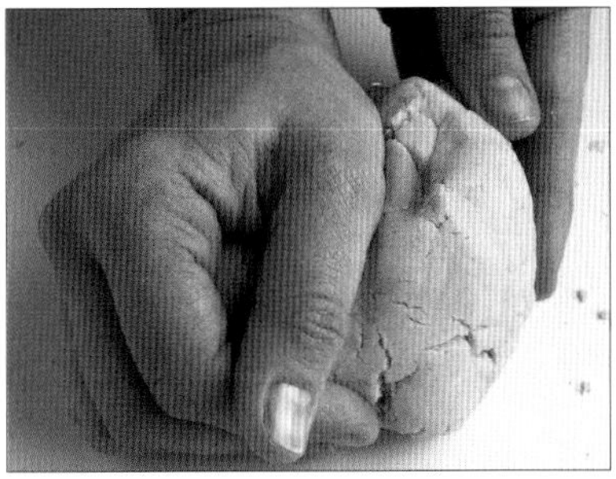

3 Remove the mixture and form into a ball. Lightly knead on a floured surface for just a few seconds until smooth, then wrap in clear film (plastic wrap) and chill for 15–30 minutes.

SUET (US CHILLED GRATED SHORTENING) PASTRY

This pastry can be used for both sweet and savoury steamed puddings and has a light, spongy texture. It is wonderfully easy to make. Because suet is a heavy fat, self-raising (self-rising) flour is always used. Lower-fat or vegetarian suet may also be used.

Makes enough to line a 1.75 litre/ 3 pint/7½ cup oven-proof bowl

275g/10oz/2½ cups self-raising (self-rising) flour
pinch of salt
150g/5oz/1 cup shredded suet (US chilled grated shortening)
175ml/6fl oz/¾ cup chilled water

1 Sift the flour and salt into a large bowl.

2 Stir in the shredded suet, followed by most of the chilled water (you may need a little less or more), and mix with a fork or spoon to form a soft dough.

3 Knead on a lightly floured surface for a few seconds until smooth. Roll out the suet pastry and use straightaway. Don't be tempted to roll the pastry too thinly. It needs to be 1cm/½in thick.

CHOUX PASTRY

Elegantly light and crisp, choux pastry puffs up during baking to at least double its original size, creating a hollow centre, perfect for both sweet and savoury fillings.

Makes about twenty-five choux buns

65g/2½oz/9 tbsp plain (all-purpose) flour
pinch of salt
50g/2oz/4 tbsp butter, diced
150ml/¼ pint/⅔ cup water
2 eggs, lightly beaten

1 Preheat the oven to 200°C/400°F/ Gas 6. Sift the flour and salt on to a small sheet of baking parchment.

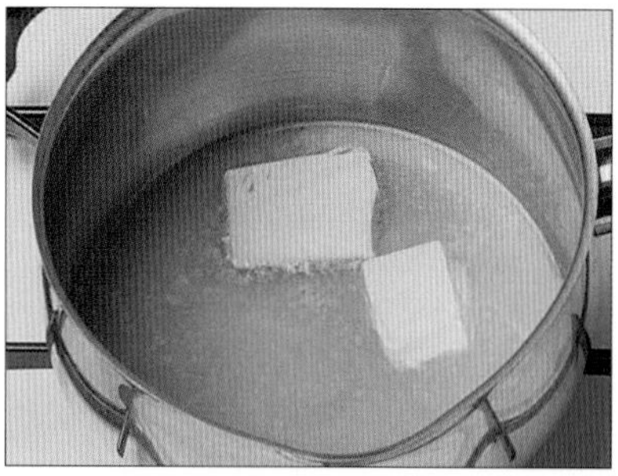

2 Put the butter and water in a pan and heat very gently until the butter has melted.

3 Increase the heat and bring to a rolling boil. Remove from the heat, tip in all the flour and beat vigorously until the flour is mixed into the liquid.

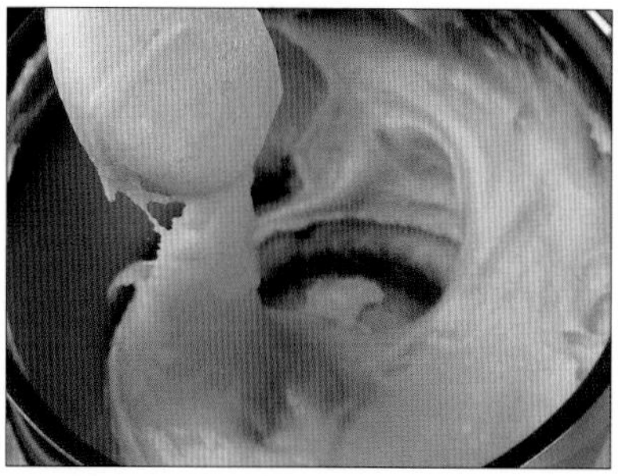

4 Return the pan to a low heat and beat the mixture until it begins to form a ball and leave the sides of the pan. This will take about 1 minute.

5 Remove the pan from the heat again and allow to cool for 2–3 minutes. Add the beaten eggs a little at a time, beating well between each addition, until you have a very smooth shiny paste, thick enough to hold its shape.

6 Spoon or pipe the pastry on to a baking sheet dampened or lined with baking parchment. Keep the spoonfuls to an even size so that the pastry bakes evenly.

7 Bake in the centre of the oven for 15–20 minutes, until risen and golden.

ROLLING OUT PASTRY

The more butter the pastry contains the more likely it is that cracks will appear around the edges of the pastry. Nip it back together with finger and thumb.

1 Dust the work surface and the rolling pin with flour. Never put flour on to the pastry.

2 Roll out the pastry lightly and evenly in one direction only, rolling from the centre to the far edge, but not actually over the edge. Always roll away from you and rotate the pastry after every roll. When rolling out a round, turn the pastry 45 degrees each time to keep an even shape and thickness. (If rolling out a pastry square, rotate the pastry by 90 degrees each time.)

3 Once or twice during rolling out, push in the edges of the dough with your cupped palms, to keep the shape and avoid ragged edges. Avoid pulling the pastry as you roll it, or it will shrink during cooking.

LINING A FLAN TIN (PAN) OR DISH

Picking up a large round of rolled pastry might seem daunting, but is actually quite easy to do.

1 On a lightly floured surface, roll out the pastry to a round about 5–7cm/2–3in larger than the flan tin (pan), depending on the depth of the tin.

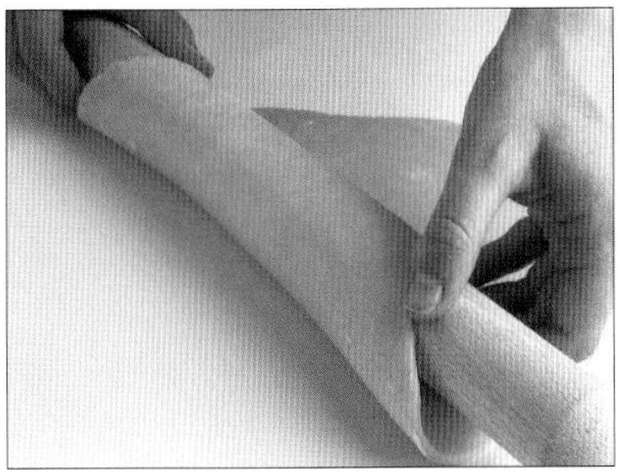

2 To transfer the pastry to the flan tin, fold the edge over the rolling pin, then roll the pastry loosely around the pin.

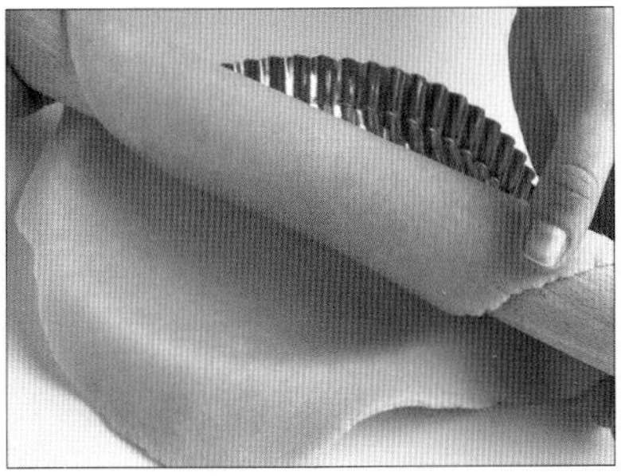

3 Unroll the pastry over the tin, letting it settle without being stretched. Lift the edge and gently ease the pastry into the base and sides so there are no gaps.

4 Roll the rolling pin over the top of the tin to cut off the excess dough. Prick the base all over with a fork, to stop it rising up during baking.

5 Cover with clear film (plastic wrap) and chill to rest the pastry.

HOLES AND TEARS
Use trimmings to patch up tears, dampening them with water.

MAKING A PIE TOP

A pastry top quickly transforms a meat or vegetable stew or casserole into a delicious pie, This is a good way to make a limited amount of filling go further. It also makes a healthier meal than having pastry sandwiching the filling at the top and bottom.

1 Line the pie dish/plate, fill it and then add the pie top. Roll out the pastry on a lightly floured surface until it is about 5cm/2in larger all round than the dish.

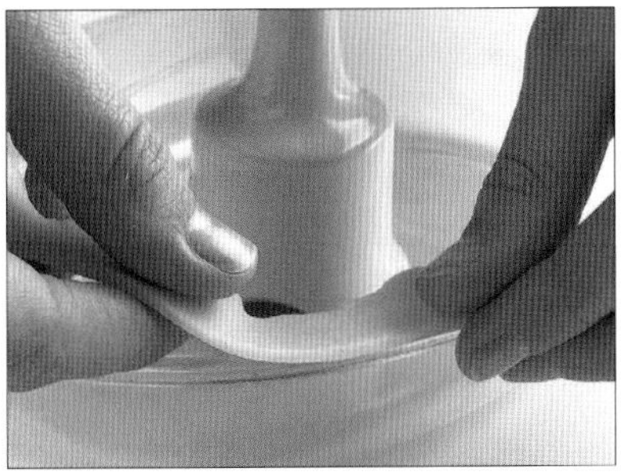

2 Place a pie funnel in the dish, if using. Cut a 2cm/¾in strip from the rolled out pastry. Brush the rim of the pie dish with water and place the pastry strip around the rim, pressing it down. Brush the pastry rim with water, then add the filling.

3 Using a rolling pin, place the pastry over the filling, using the pie funnel to support it. If you are not using a funnel, fill the dish so that the filling is dome-shaped, then cover with the pastry and press the edges together to seal them.

4 Trim the excess pastry with a knife, angling it slightly. Slit the pastry so the pie funnel is visible.

BAKING BLIND

Lining the pastry case with baking parchment and filling it with baking beans stops the pastry from rising up during cooking. Part-cooked pastry does not become soggy when filled and baked.

1 Cut out a round of baking parchment about 7.5cm/3in larger than the flan tin (quiche pan). Line the tin with pastry and prick the base all over with a fork.

2 Lay the paper in the pastry case and add baking beans, or dried beans or peas, spreading them out evenly.

3 Bake the case at 200°C/400°F/Gas 6 for 15 minutes, then remove the paper and beans and return to the oven. Bake for a further 5–10 minutes. Cool completely before filling.

PLANNING AHEAD
Fully baked pastry cases may be baked up to two days ahead if carefully chilled in airtight containers. Interleave them with baking parchment when they are completely cold.

Quiche lorraine

The classic quiche from France is perfect for any special meal and this recipe is an excellent guide to how quiche should be made, with thin shortcrust pastry and a creamy yet light filling. Baking the pastry blind first ensures the base is cooked thoroughly when served.

Serves six to eight

3 eggs, plus 2 yolks
6 smoked streaky (fatty) bacon rashers (strips), rinds removed
300ml/½ pint/1¼ cups double (heavy) cream
salt and ground black pepper

For the pastry

175g/6oz/1½ cups plain (all-purpose) flour, sifted
115g/4oz/½ cup butter, at room temperature, diced
1 egg yolk

1 To make the pastry, in a bowl rub the butter into the flour and then use a knife to mix in 1 egg yolk. Shape into a ball, cover and chill for 15 minutes only.

Variations

- For everyday quiche, omit the yolks in the filling and beat the eggs with milk rather than cream.
- Chop 1 onion and soften it in the fat from the bacon for 5 minutes. Add to the bacon. Sprinkle 50g/2oz grated Gruyère or Cheddar cheese over the bacon and onion.
- Dice 225g/8oz lean cooked ham. Thinly slice 1 large leek and fry it in a little butter until soft. Use the ham and leek instead of the bacon.
- Cook 115g/4oz sliced button (white) mushrooms with the bacon. Sprinkle 3 chopped spring onions (scallions) over the bacon mixture.

2 Lightly flour a 20cm/8in round, loose-bottomed flan tin (pan), and place it on a baking tray. Roll out the pastry and use to line the tin, trimming off any overhanging pieces. Press the pastry into the corners. Chill for 20 minutes. Preheat the oven to 200ºC/400ºF/Gas 6.

3 Prick the pastry base all over. Place a sheet of baking parchment in the pastry case and sprinkle with baking beans, then bake for 15 minutes. Reduce the heat to 180ºC/350ºF/Gas 4.

4 Cut the bacon into thin strips. Cook in a frying pan over medium heat until the fat runs. Use a slotted spoon to drain the bacon. Remove the paper and beans from the pastry and sprinkle in the bacon. Beat the eggs and remaining yolks with the cream and seasoning, and pour into the quiche.

5 Bake for about 40 minutes until set and golden. Leave to stand for about 5 minutes before serving.

Energy 976kcal/4043kJ; Protein 18.1g; Carbohydrate 35.5g, of which sugars 2.2g; Fat 85.8g, of which saturates 48.4g; Cholesterol 519mg; Calcium 149mg; Fibre 1.4g; Sodium 678mg.

Turkey and cranberry double crust pie

A pie with a filling entirely encased with a dense shortcrust pastry is a good choice when you have a large number of people to feed, since a little goes a long way. This delicious meat-filled pie uses relatively small quantities of meat to feed a large gathering of people.

Serves eight

450g/1lb pork sausage meat (bulk pork sausage)
450g/1lb lean minced (ground) pork
15ml/1 tbsp ground coriander
15ml/1 tbsp dried mixed herbs
finely grated rind of 2 large oranges
10ml/2 tsp grated fresh root ginger or 2.5ml/½ tsp ground ginger
large pinch of salt
450g/1lb turkey breast fillets
115g/4oz/1 cup fresh cranberries
ground black pepper
1 egg, beaten
300ml/½ pint/1¼ cups aspic jelly, made according to the instructions on the packet

For the pastry

450g/1lb/4 cups plain (all-purpose) flour
5ml/1 tsp salt
150g/5oz/ cup lard
150ml/¼ pint/⅔ cup mixed milk and water

1 Preheat the oven to 180°C/350°F/Gas 4. Place a baking sheet in the oven to preheat. In a bowl, mix together the sausagemeat, pork, coriander, herbs, orange rind and ginger. Season with salt and pepper.

2 To make the pastry, sift the flour and salt into a bowl. Heat the lard in a pan with the milk and water until just beginning to boil. Remove from the heat and allow to cool slightly.

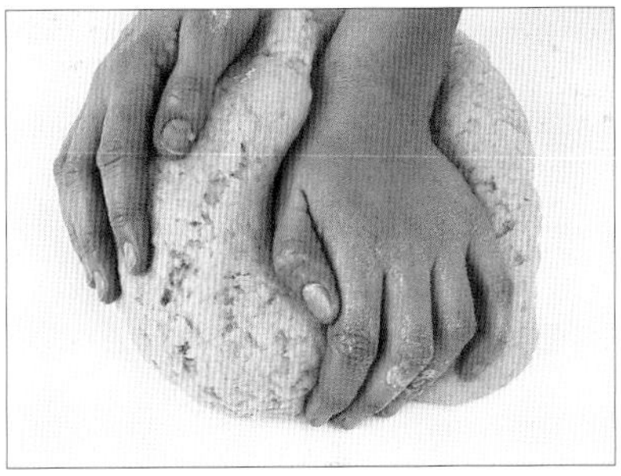

3 Quickly stir the liquid into the flour until a very stiff dough is formed. Place on a clean work surface and knead until smooth. Cut one-third off the dough for the lid, wrap in clear film (plastic wrap) and keep in a warm place.

4 Roll out the large piece of dough on a floured surface and use to line the base and sides of a greased 20cm/8in loose-based, cake tin (pan).

5 Thinly slice the turkey. Put between two pieces of clear film and flatten with a rolling pin to a thickness of 3mm/⅛in. Spoon half the pork mixture into the tin, pressing it well into the edges. Cover it with half the turkey slices and then the cranberries, followed by the remaining turkey and the rest of the pork mixture.

6 Roll out the remaining dough and use to cover the filling, trimming off any excess and sealing the edges with a little beaten egg. Make a steam hole in the centre of the lid and decorate the top with leaf shapes cut from pastry trimmings. Brush with beaten egg and bake for 2 hours. Cover with foil if the top gets too brown.

7 Allow to cool on a wire rack. When cold use a funnel to fill the pie with liquid aspic jelly. Leave to set overnight.

Energy 670kcal/2801kJ; Protein 38.1g; Carbohydrate 50.8g, of which sugars 4.1g; Fat 36.2g, of which saturates 13.9g; Cholesterol 119mg; Calcium 155mg; Fibre 2.5g; Sodium 558mg.

Spinach filo pie

Slightly creamy, full-flavoured feta is fabulous with a herby spinach mixture in crisp filo pastry. This pie is delicious hot or cool, especially with new potatoes and a stack of cherry tomatoes.

Serves six

1kg/2¼lb fresh spinach, thoroughly washed
4 spring onions (scallions), chopped
300g/11oz feta cheese, crumbled or coarsely grated
2 large eggs, beaten
30ml/2 tbsp chopped fresh flat leaf parsley
15ml/1 tbsp chopped fresh dill, plus a few sprigs to garnish
45ml/3 tbsp currants (optional)
about 8 sheets of filo pastry, each measuring 30 x 18cm/12 x 7in, thawed if frozen
extra virgin olive oil
ground black pepper

1 Ensure the spinach is cleaned thoroughly by rinsing in cold water and draining at least three times. Dry it thoroughly with kitchen paper.

2 Break off any thick stalks from the spinach, then blanch the leaves in a very small amount of boiling water for 1–2 minutes, or until just wilted.

3 Drain the spinach and refresh under cold water, then drain again, squeeze dry and chop it roughly. Place in a bowl together with the spring onions and the crumbled feta cheese.

4 Add the beaten eggs to the spinach and cheese and stir them in thoroughly. Mix in the fresh herbs and currants, if using. Season the mixture with pepper.

5 Preheat the oven to 190°C/375°F/Gas 5. Brush a sheet of filo pastry with oil and fit it into a 23cm/9in pie dish, allowing it to hang over the edges. Add three or four more sheets, placing them at different angles and brushing each very sparsely with olive oil.

6 Spoon the filling into the pastry case, then top with all but one of the remaining filo sheets, brushing each with olive oil. Fold the overhanging filo over the top to seal. Oil the reserved filo and scrunch it over the top of the pie.

7 Brush the pie with olive oil. Sprinkle with a little water to stop the edges from curling, then place on a baking sheet. Bake for about 40 minutes, or until the pastry is golden and crisp. Allow to cool for 15 minutes so that the filling firms up slightly before serving.

Energy 396kcal/1640kJ; Protein 16.8g; Carbohydrate 13.8g, of which sugars 4g; Fat 30.7g, of which saturates 10.1g; Cholesterol 111mg; Calcium 528mg; Fibre 4.8g; Sodium 988mg.

Steak, mushroom and ale pie

Crisp puffy pastry is delicious on an aromatic meaty filling. Serve with simply cooked vegetables, such as beans, cabbage or broccoli and carrots or cauliflower.

Serves four

25g/1oz/2 tbsp butter
1 large onion, finely chopped
115g/4oz/1½ cups chestnut or button (white) mushrooms, halved
900g/2lb lean beef in one piece, such as rump or braising steak
30ml/2 tbsp plain (all-purpose) flour
45ml/3 tbsp sunflower oil
300ml/½ pint/1¼ cups stout or brown ale
300ml/½ pint/1¼ cups beef stock or consommé
500g/1¼lb puff pastry, thawed if frozen
beaten egg to glaze
salt and ground black pepper

1 Melt the butter in a large, flameproof casserole, add the onion and cook gently, stirring occasionally, for about 5 minutes, or until it is softened. Add the mushrooms and cook for a further 5 minutes, stirring occasionally.

2 Trim the meat and cut it into 2.5cm/1in cubes. Season the flour and toss the meat in it.

3 Use a draining spoon to remove the onion mixture and set it aside. Add and heat the oil, then brown the meat in batches over high heat.

4 Replace the vegetables, stir in the stout or ale and stock or consommé. Bring to the boil, reduce the heat and cover. Simmer for 1 hour, until the meat is tender.

5 Preheat the oven to 230°C/450°F/Gas 8. Roll out the pastry slightly more than 5cm/2in larger than the top of a 1.5 litre/2½ pint/6¼ cup pie dish. Invert the dish on the pastry and cut out a piece slightly larger than the dish. Cut a 2.5cm/1in strip from the excess pastry.

6 Dampen the rim of the dish and press the strip on it. Fill with the meat mixture. Brush the pastry rim with beaten egg and press the pie lid in place. Trim.

7 Pinch and seal the edge of the pastry with your fingertips. Make a hole in the middle of the pie to allow steam to escape. Brush the top with beaten egg and chill for 10 minutes in the refrigerator to rest the pastry.

8 Bake the pie for 15 minutes, then reduce the oven temperature to 200°C/400°F/Gas 6 and bake for a further 15–20 minutes, or until the pastry is risen and golden.

Energy 1061kcal/4423kJ; Protein 58.8g; Carbohydrate 59.3g, of which sugars 7.6g; Fat 65.3g, of which saturates 24g; Cholesterol 164mg; Calcium 129mg; Fibre 3.2g; Sodium 622mg.

Deep double-crust apple pie

This pie is one of those 'like mother used to make' recipes, with melt-in-the-mouth shortcrust pastry. Sugar, spices and flour create a deliciously thick and syrupy sauce with the apple juices.

Serves six

115g/4oz/½ cup sugar
45ml/3 tbsp plain (all-purpose) flour
pinch of ground cinnamon
finely grated rind of 1 orange
900g/2lb tart cooking apples
1 egg white, lightly beaten
30ml/2 tbsp golden granulated sugar
whipped cream, to serve

For the pastry
350g/12oz/3 cups plain (all-purpose) flour
175g/6oz/¾ cup butter, diced
about 75ml/5 tbsp chilled water

1 To make the pastry, sift the flour into a bowl and rub the fat into the flour with your fingertips until the mixture resembles fine breadcrumbs. Sprinkle over the water and mix to a firm, soft dough. Wrap in clear film (plastic wrap) and chill for 30 minutes.

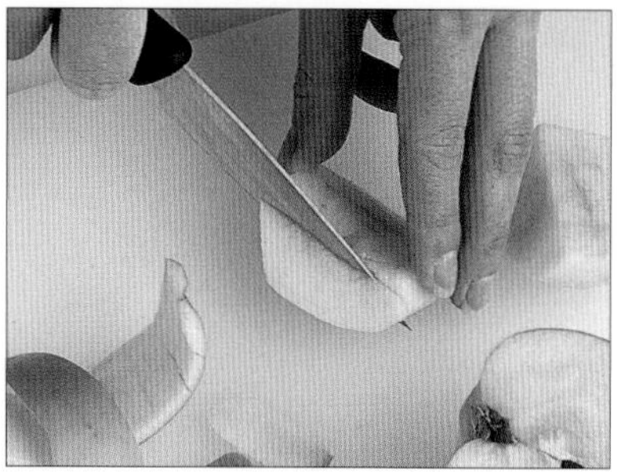

2 Mix the sugar, flour, cinnamon and orange rind in a bowl. Peel, core and thinly slice the apples. Add the apples to the sugar, then mix with a spoon and fork until they are evenly coated.

3 Preheat the oven to 200°C/400°F/ Gas 6. Roll out just over half the pastry and use to line a 23cm/9in pie dish that is 4cm/1½in deep, allowing the pastry to overhang the edges slightly. Spoon in the filling.

4 Roll out the remaining pastry to form the lid. Lightly brush the edges of the pastry case with a little water, then place the lid over the apple filling.

5 Trim the pastry with a sharp knife. Gently press the edges together to seal, then knock up the edge. Re-roll the pastry trimmings and stamp out apple and leaf shapes using a pastry cutter. Brush the pie with egg white.

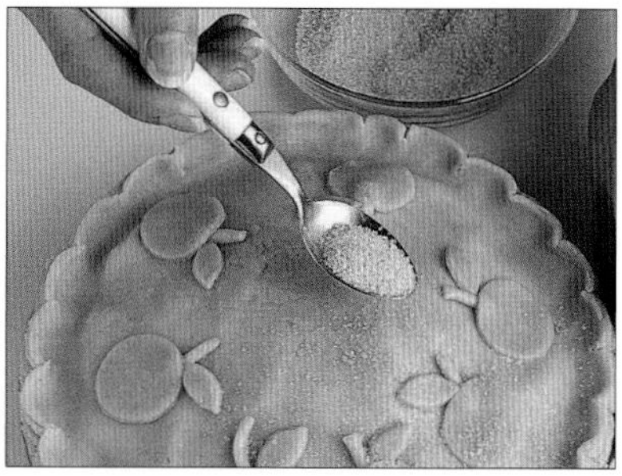

6 Arrange the shapes on top. Brush again with egg white, then sprinkle with sugar. Make two small slits in the top of the pie to allow steam to escape.

7 Bake for 30 minutes. Lower the oven temperature to 180°C/350°F/ Gas 4 and bake for a further 15 minutes, until the pastry is golden and the apples are soft. Check by inserting a small sharp knife through one of the slits in the pie.

COOK'S TIPS
- For a single crust pie, do not line the dish with pastry, but stick a pastry strip on the rim of the dish.
- For a plate tart, line a large ovenproof plate with about a third of the pastry, mound the filling on top and cover with pastry.
- For an open tart, line a plate or shallow dish with pastry and arrange ingredients on top.

Energy 600kcal/2524kJ; Protein 7.7g; Carbohydrate 91.9g, of which sugars 39.8g; Fat 25g, of which saturates 15.3g; Cholesterol 62mg; Calcium 120mg; Fibre 4.5g; Sodium 193mg.

Blueberry pie

Orange and lemon contribute sharpness to enhance the flavour of subtle blueberries. With warm and sweet shortcrust pastry, this pie is sure to be popular. Serve with cream.

Serves six

800g/1¾lb/7 cups blueberries
75g/3oz/6 tbsp caster (superfine) sugar, plus extra for sprinkling
45ml/3 tbsp cornflour (cornstarch)
grated rind and juice of ½ orange
grated rind of ½ lemon
pinch of ground cinnamon
15g/½oz/1 tbsp butter, diced
1 egg, beaten
whipped cream, to serve

For the pastry
275g/10oz/2½ cups plain (all-purpose) flour
pinch of salt
75g/3oz/6 tbsp butter, diced
50g/2oz/¼ cup white vegetable fat
60–75ml/4–5 tbsp chilled water

1 To make the pastry, sift the flour and salt into a mixing bowl. Rub in the fat until the mixture resembles breadcrumbs.

2 Sprinkle over most of the water and mix to a soft dough. Add more water if necessary. Knead lightly. Wrap in clear film (plastic wrap) and chill.

3 Preheat the oven to 200°C/400°F/Gas 6. Roll out half the pastry and use to line a 23cm/9in pie dish, allowing the excess pastry to overhang the edge.

4 In a bowl, mix the blueberries, caster sugar, cornflour, orange rind and juice, lemon rind and cinnamon. Spoon into the pastry case and dot with the butter.

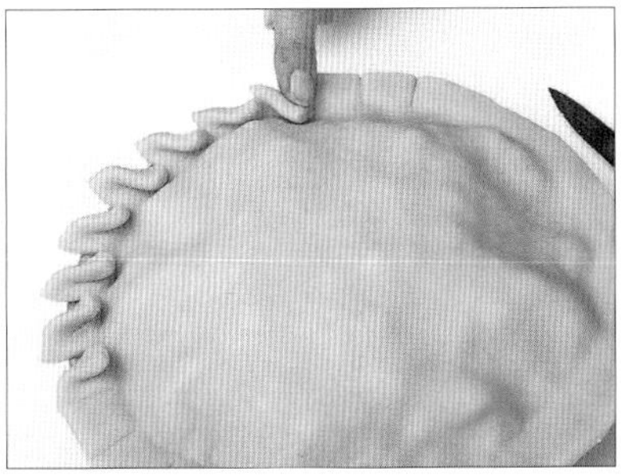

5 Roll out the remaining pastry and use to make a lid for the pie. Trim off the excess, leaving a rim all round. Cut the rim at 2.5cm/1in intervals, then fold each pastry section over on itself to form a triangle. Re-roll the trimmings and cut out decorations. Attach to the pastry lid with a little of the beaten egg.

Variations

Try combining different fruit to make the most of complementary types.
- Bananas go well with tangy rhubarb, plums or apple.
- Mix expensive raspberries, strawberries or redcurrants with apples or pears for fabulous flavour.
- Rhubarb is excellent with mango, peaches or papaya.
- Frozen mixed fruit, such as summer fruit, is brilliant with apple.

6 Glaze the pastry with the beaten egg and sprinkle with caster sugar. Bake for 30 minutes, or until golden. Serve warm or cold with whipped cream.

Energy 371kcal/1559kJ; Protein 4.4g; Carbohydrate 55.8g, of which sugars 25.7g; Fat 16g, of which saturates 4.9g; Cholesterol 8mg; Calcium 93mg; Fibre 3.2g; Sodium 228mg.

Blackcurrant tarts

These tarts are quick and easy to prepare using ready-made puff pastry. Serve with soft, whipped cream, Greek yogurt or scoops of good-quality bought ice cream.

Serves four

500g/1¼ lb/5 cups blackcurrants
115g/4oz/generous ½ cup caster (superfine) sugar
250g/9oz ready-made puff pastry, thawed if frozen
50g/2oz/½ cup icing (confectioners') sugar
whipped cream, to serve

1 Preheat the oven to 220°C/425°F/ Gas 7.

2 For speed, use a fork to slide the blackcurrants off their stalks into a bowl. Pick out any bits of stalk. Rinse and dry the fruit. Add the caster sugar and mix well.

3 Roll out the pastry to about 3mm/ ⅛in thick and cut out four discs roughly the size of a side plate or a large cereal bowl. Then, using a smaller plate or bowl, lightly mark with the point of a knife a circle about 2cm/¾in inside each disc.

4 Spread the blackcurrants over the discs, keeping them within the marked inner circle. Bake in the oven for 15 minutes. Dust generously with the icing sugar before serving. Serve hot with a large dollop of whipped cream, or serve cold as a tea-time snack.

Energy 426kcal/1798kJ; Protein 4.9g; Carbohydrate 73.2g, of which sugars 50.9g; Fat 15.3g, of which saturates 0g; Cholesterol 0mg; Calcium 133mg; Fibre 4.5g; Sodium 200mg.

Baked lemon cheesecake

As with all classic cheesecakes, this one is baked in a rich shortcrust pastry case. In this simple recipe the pastry is flavoured with lemon rind, enhancing the filling.

Serves eight to ten

675g/1½lb/3 cups quark or soft white cheese
4 eggs, separated
150g/5oz/⅔ cup caster (superfine) sugar
45ml/3 tbsp conflour (cornstarch)
150ml/¼ pint/⅔ cup sour cream
finely grated rind and juice of ½ lemon
5ml/1 tsp vanilla extract
red berry compôte, to serve
fresh mint sprigs, to decorate

For the pastry

225g/8oz/2 cups plain (all-purpose) flour
115g/4oz/½ cup butter, diced
15ml/1 tbsp caster (superfine) sugar
finely grated rind of ½ lemon
1 egg, beaten

1 To make the pastry, sift the flour into a mixing bowl. Rub in the butter until the mixture resembles breadcrumbs. Stir in the sugar and lemon rind, then add the beaten egg and mix to a dough. Wrap in clear film (plastic wrap) and chill for 30 minutes.

2 Roll out the pastry and use to line a 25cm/10in loose-based flan tin (quiche pan). Chill for 1 hour. Place the quark or soft cheese in a fine sieve (strainer) and drain over a bowl for 1 hour.

3 Preheat the oven to 200ºC/400ºF/Gas 6. Prick the base of the chilled pastry case all over with a fork and bake blind for 10–15 minutes. Remove the pastry case from the oven.

4 Lower the oven temperature to 180°C/350°F/Gas 4. Put the drained quark in a bowl with the egg yolks and sugar and mix. Blend the cornflour in a cup with a little of the sour cream, then add to the cheese mixture with the rest of the sour cream, the lemon rind and juice and vanilla extract. Mix well.

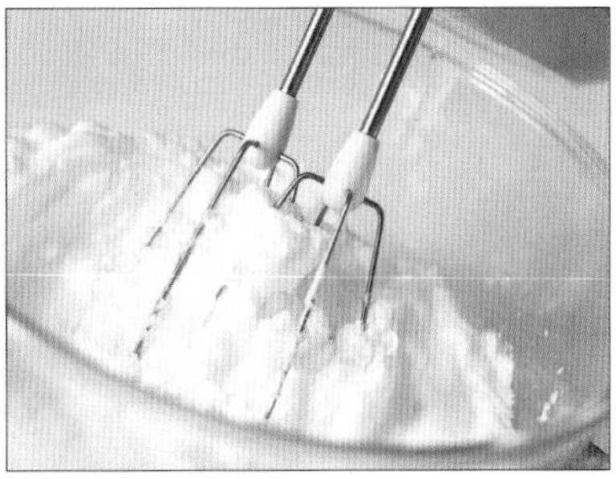

5 Whisk the egg whites in a grease-free bowl until stiff, then fold into the cheese mixture, one-third at a time. Pour the filling into the pastry case and bake for 1–1¼ hours, or until firm. Switch off the oven and leave ajar; let the cheesecake cool down in the oven, then chill for 2 hours. Serve with compôte and mint.

Energy 237kcal/1000kJ; Protein 10.9g; Carbohydrate 36.3g, of which sugars 33.9g; Fat 7.2g, of which saturates 3g; Cholesterol 14mg; Calcium 119mg; Fibre 0.1g; Sodium 299mg.

Mini millefeuilles

This pâtisserie classic is a delectable combination of tender puff pastry sandwiched with luscious pastry cream. As the pastry is difficult to cut, making individual servings is a good idea.

Serves eight

675g/1½lb raspberries
450g/1lb puff pastry, thawed if frozen
6 egg yolks
70g/2½oz/⅓ cup caster (superfine) sugar
45ml/3 tbsp plain (all-purpose) flour
350ml/12fl oz/1½ cups milk
30ml/2 tbsp Kirsch or cherry liqueur (optional)
icing (confectioners') sugar, to taste

1 Purée 225g/8oz of the raspberries in a blender or food processor and press the purée through a sieve (strainer) to remove the seeds. Sweeten with a little icing sugar to taste. Cover and chill. Lightly grease two large sheets and sprinkle them lightly with cold water.

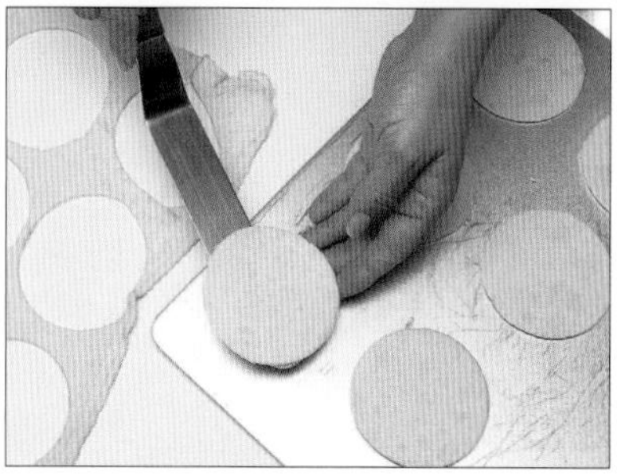

2 On a lightly floured surface, roll out the pastry to a 3mm/⅛in thickness. Using a 10cm/4in cutter, stamp out 12 rounds. Place the pastry circles on the baking sheets and prick each with a fork. Chill for 30 minutes. Preheat the oven to 200°C/400°F/Gas 6.

3 Bake the pastry rounds for about 15–20 minutes until golden, then transfer to wire racks to cool.

4 Whisk the egg yolks and sugar for 2 minutes until light and creamy, then whisk in the flour until just blended. Bring the milk to the boil over a medium heat and pour it over the egg mixture, whisking to blend. Return to the pan, bring to the boil and boil for 2 minutes, whisking constantly. Remove from the heat and whisk in the alcohol.

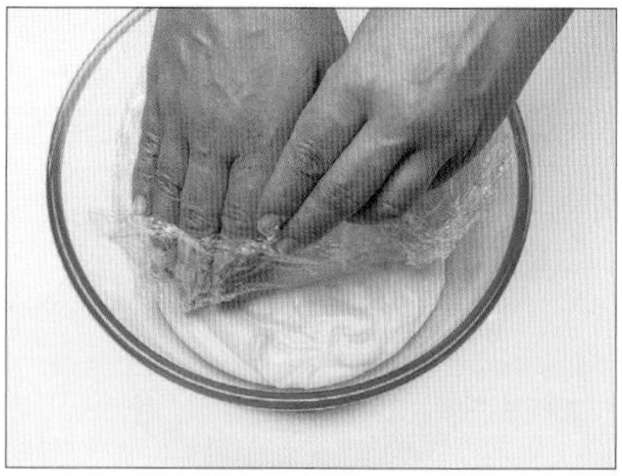

5 Pour into a bowl and press clear film (plastic wrap) on the surface to prevent a skin forming. Set aside to cool.

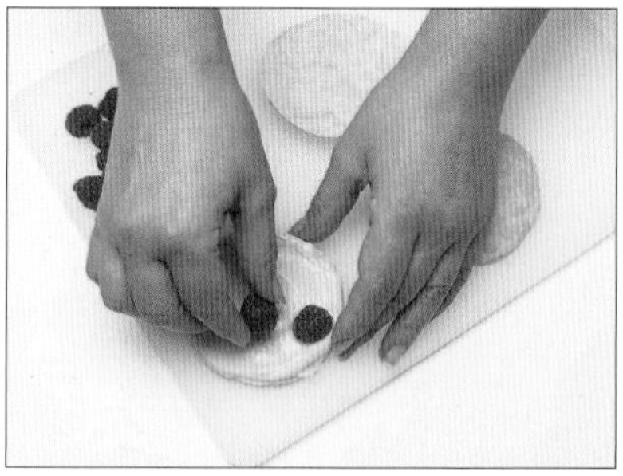

6 To assemble, split the pastry rounds in half. Spread one round at a time with custard. Arrange a layer of raspberries over the custard and top with a second pastry round. Spread with more custard and a few more raspberries. Top with a third pastry round flat side up. Dust with icing sugar and serve with the raspberry purée.

Energy 351kcal/1474kJ; Protein 8.2g; Carbohydrate 39.6g, of which sugars 15.2g; Fat 18.9g, of which saturates 1.7g; Cholesterol 154mg; Calcium 129mg; Fibre 1.6g; Sodium 203mg.

Baklava

Crisp layers of buttery filo pastry and nuts, soaked in syrup, make baklava a rich treat for dessert or as a snack with coffee. Whipped cream or thick Greek yogurt go well with baklava.

Serves twelve

175g/6oz/¾ cup unsalted (sweet) butter
100ml/3½fl oz/scant ½ cup sunflower oil
450g/1lb filo sheets, thawed if frozen
450g/1lb walnuts, or a mixture of walnuts, pistachios and almonds, finely chopped
5ml/1 tsp ground cinnamon

For the syrup
450g/1lb sugar
juice of 1 lemon, or 30ml/2 tbsp rose water

1 Preheat the oven to 160°C/325°F/Gas 3. Melt the butter and oil in a pan, then brush over the bottom and sides of a 30cm/12in square cake tin (pan). Place a sheet of filo in the bottom and brush with the butter and oil. Repeat with half the filo sheets. Ease into the corners and trim the edges.

2 Spread the nuts over the last buttered sheet and sprinkle with the cinnamon, then continue as before with the remaining filo sheets. Brush the top one as well.

3 Using a sharp knife, cut diagonal lines through the baklava to form diamonds. Bake for about 1 hour, until the top is golden brown – if it is still pale, increase the oven temperature for a few minutes at the end of the cooking time.

4 Make the syrup while the baklava is baking. Put the sugar into a heavy pan, pour in 250ml/8fl oz/1 cup water and bring to a rapid boil, stirring all the time.

5 When all the sugar has dissolved, lower the heat and stir in the lemon juice, or rose water if using, then simmer for about 15 minutes, until the syrup thickens. Leave to cool.

6 When the baklava is ready, remove it from the oven and slowly pour the cooled syrup over the piping hot pastry. Return to the oven for 2–3 minutes to soak up the syrup, then take it out and leave to cool.

Energy 973kcal/4059kJ; Protein 12.2g; Carbohydrate 89.9g, of which sugars 60.9g; Fat 65.2g, of which saturates 15.6g; Cholesterol 47mg; Calcium 139mg; Fibre 3.1g; Sodium 141mg.

Chocolate éclairs

These crisp choux pastry fingers are filled with fresh cream, slightly sweetened and flavoured with vanilla, and the éclairs are thickly coated in dark chocolate.

Makes twelve

300ml/½ pint/1¼ cups double (heavy) cream
10ml/2 tsp icing (confectioners') sugar, sifted
1.5ml/¼ tsp vanilla extract
115g/4oz plain (semisweet) chocolate
30ml/2 tbsp water
25g/1oz/2 tbsp butter

For the pastry
65g/2½oz/9 tbsp plain (all-purpose) flour
pinch of salt
50g/2oz/¼ cup butter, diced
150ml/¼ pint/⅔ cup water
2 eggs, lightly beaten

1 Preheat the oven to 200°C/400°F/ Gas 6. Grease a large baking sheet and line with baking parchment.

2 To make the pastry, sift the flour and salt on to a small sheet of baking parchment. Heat the butter and water in a pan very gently until the butter melts. Increase the heat and bring to a rolling boil. Tip in all the flour, stir and immediately remove the pan from the heat. Stir with a wooden spoon until the flour is mixed into the liquid.

COOK'S TIP
When melting the chocolate, ensure that the bowl does not touch the hot water and keep the heat low. If the chocolate gets too hot, it will become unworkable.

3 The mixture should leave the sides of the pan cleanly. Set the pan aside and allow to cool for 5 minutes. Stir briefly over low heat if the paste is sloppy.

4 Add the beaten eggs a little at a time, beating well after each addition, until you have a smooth, shiny paste, which is thick enough to hold its shape.

5 Spoon the choux pastry into a piping (pastry) bag fitted with a 2.5cm/1in plain nozzle. Pipe 10cm/4in lengths on to the prepared baking sheet. Use a wet knife to cut off the pastry at the nozzle.

6 Bake for 25–30 minutes, or until the pastries are well risen and golden. Remove from the oven and make a neat slit along the side of each to release steam. Lower the temperature to 180°C/350°F/Gas 4 and bake for a further 5 minutes. Slit the hot éclairs down one side and cool on a wire rack.

7 To make the filling, whip the cream with the icing sugar and vanilla extract until it just holds its shape. Spoon into a piping bag fitted with a 1cm/½in plain nozzle and use to fill the éclairs.

8 Place the chocolate and water in a small bowl set over a pan of hot water. Melt, stirring until smooth. Remove from the heat and gradually stir in the butter.

9 Dip the top of each éclair in the melted chocolate, then place on a wire rack. Leave in a cool place until the chocolate is set. The éclairs are best served within 2 hours of being made but can be chilled for 24 hours.

Energy 235kcal/1046kJ; Protein 2.7g; Carbohydrate 10.8g, of which sugars 6.5g; Fat 22.4g, of which saturates 13.5g; Cholesterol 86mg; Calcium 30mg; Fibre 0.4g; Sodium 58mg

Desserts and bakes

For the sweet-toothed, the dessert course is the most important part of a meal, rounding off dinner with a satisfying flourish. Desserts can be simple and inventive with minimal ingredients, such as a platter of fresh seasonal fruit or a bowl of high quality ice cream served with a flavourful compôte and shortcake biscuits. For those who love a moreish pudding or a squidgy cake, there are plenty of recipes included in this chapter. Delectable scones, biscuits and cakes feature, too.

Sweet course basics

Filling and comforting, sweet and moreish, lavish home-baked cakes and desserts round off a meal with a final flourish. Cookies and scones are perfect for occasional mid-week treats and are guaranteed to satisfy hunger pangs as well as sugar cravings.

Often the dessert is the easiest part of a meal to buy ready-made, but making your own is not difficult and is much more rewarding. There are plenty of simple ideas for delicious desserts that take just minutes to put together: a scoop of ice cream with fresh summer berries, or fruit purée, served with buttery biscuits; a fresh fruit salad made up of your favourite fruits, served with single (light) cream; a platter of artisan cheese with good-quality crackers and savoury biscuits; or a simple sorbet to follow a substantial main course.

EVERYDAY INGREDIENTS

Many easy cake and dessert recipes contain differing quantities of the same basic ingredients. Self-raising (self-rising) flour, sugar, eggs, butter and milk are all that you need to make a cake. Cut in half, fill with good-quality jam and

Above: Classic vanilla ice cream is a good accompaniment to many desserts, or can be served on its own.

serve dusted with icing (confectioners') sugar for a pretty cake that is suitable to serve at any time of day. Combining the basic ingredients with other flavourings such as unsweetened cocoa powder, instant coffee, almond extract, or lemon, and using them in different quantity combinations, will produce a whole array of different baked goods. Master the skills for baking and a wide range of delicious sweet treats will always be at your fingertips. The trick is to accurately weigh and measure all the ingredients before you begin.

STORING BAKES AND DESSERTS

Some cakes, such as dense fruit cakes, taste better when they have been left to mature and the flavours meld together. However, many cakes, including those in this chapter, are intended to be eaten fresh. Most will keep well wrapped for two or three days, but will quickly become stale and less appealing after that time. Store cakes, scones and cookies in airtight containers away from other strongly scented foods, or the cake will be contaminated by the flavour of whatever it is placed near. Leave all cakes and biscuits to go cold before packing them away in biscuit tins, or to put cakes in the freezer.

Desserts are meant to be made and eaten fresh. Hot desserts should be made and timed to be hot or warm when the main course is finished. So, if you put a dessert in the oven to cook when the main course has been removed, remember to note the time and check on it and remove it when appropriate.

Left: Cake mixes require accurate measuring of the ingredients to achieve perfect results.

COOK'S TIPS

- Use the correct tin (pan) size.
- Eggs and butter should be used at room temperature unless the recipe specifies otherwise.
- Bake cakes in the centre of the oven for even baking.
- Cakes without any icing can be frozen for up to six months. Interleave freezer paper between cakes and wrap in kitchen foil. Thaw at room temperature.

Making cakes

Making delicious cakes requires forward planning. Remove butter from the refrigerator ahead of time and have all the ingredients assembled ready to use on the work surface. Preheat the oven and ensure it is at the correct temperature before you put the goods to be baked into it. Many cakes and desserts are best cooked in the centre of the oven, so that the tins (pans) are not touching the side of the oven or other dishes that are also baking in the oven.

Metal conducts heat better than any other cooking container. Good quality tins will conduct the heat evenly, ensuring the goods bake consistently. Properly cared for, good cake tins will last a lifetime. Wash and dry thoroughly after every use before storing away.

LINING A CAKE TIN (PAN)

Cake batter or cookie dough will stick to the container in which it is baked unless the inside of the container is greased and lined first. Even non-stick containers are best lined.

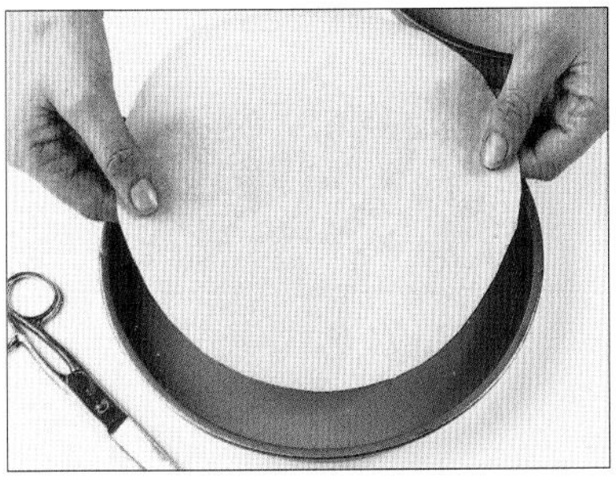

1 Place a cake tin (pan) on top of a sheet of baking parchment on the work surface. Draw around it with a pencil and cut out a circle inside the drawn line.

2 Cut one length of baking parchment long enough to fit the circumference of the tin and slightly deeper than the tin. Use scissors to clip along one long edge, effectively making a fringe that will stick to the bottom of the cake tin.

3 Melt a small quantity of butter over a gentle heat and using a pastry brush, coat the inside of the cake tin lightly. Stick the baking parchment to the sides and base of the tin. Add the baking parchment circle last. Alternatively, use a light vegetable oil.

MAKING CAKE BATTER

To have a light-as-air sponge cake, air needs to be beaten into the cake batter. Use an electric whisk, a food processor, or a wooden spoon and choose a large enough bowl. The basis of many cakes and cookies begins by beating together butter and sugar.

1 In a large mixing bowl, beat the butter until it is pale in colour and has a soft consistency. Add the sugar and continue to beat until the grainy texture disappears. The mixture will be light and fluffy.

2 Crack the eggs into a small bowl and beat lightly. Add the eggs to the butter and sugar in small quantities. The mixture may start to curdle if too much egg is added.

3 If the batter curdles add 15ml/1tbsp of the flour and combine it well before adding more egg, and then another 15ml/1 tbsp of the flour.

4 When adding flour, salt and baking powder, sift it first, preferably twice. Sifting adds air to the mixture. Add flour in two or three batches and stir well after each addition to incorporate it fully before adding any more. If the batter becomes stiff, add 10ml/2 tsp of milk and beat it in to slacken it.

5 Flavourings or additional ingredients are either added with the flour or once it has been incorporated.

6 Use a flexible spatula to scrape the batter from the bowl and into the cake tin. Aim to fill the centre of the tin and smooth the batter out to the edges. Level the batter as much as possible. Wipe away any drips from the sides of the tin because these will burn.

PROBLEM SOLVING

The cake sank: Cakes fail to rise if the oven door is opened and the heat let out when the cake is baking and rising. They may also sink or be leaden if the ingredients haven't been thoroughly beaten together. Beating helps to incorporate air into the batter, making the mix rise in the oven.

The cake burnt on top but wasn't cooked inside: This happens when the oven temperature is incorrect. Use a thermometer to check that the temperature of the oven matches the temperature gauge. In a conventional oven the cake may have been positioned too near the top of the oven; or the cake tin (pan) was an incorrect size.

The cake was higher on one side than the other: Check that the rails in the oven are level.

Dessert accompaniments

Creams and custards are used as a base for many sweet recipes and they are also traditional accompaniments for hot and cold desserts. You could also serve natural (plain) yogurt, Greek (US strained plain) yogurt, or crème fraîche with dense and sweet desserts to lighten the flavours or provide acidity to offset the sweetness of the dessert. Yogurt is lower in fat, so is good for anyone counting calories or following a low-fat diet. Ice cream is often popular with children, but choose good quality varieties. Frozen yogurt also works well.

SERVING WITH CREAM

There are three main types of cream.
Single (light) cream This is a thin pouring cream, for tarts, warm cakes or bakes. It can also be used in custards and many other mixtures.
Whipping cream As the name suggests, this can be whipped. It is richer than single cream, but not as rich as double (heavy) cream. It whips to a light, soft-peak consistency and can be used as a dessert topping or for folding into mixtures, such as mousses and ice creams. Although it is used in some gateaux, it is very light and not ideal for filling cakes as it collapses easily.
Double (heavy) cream This can be used as a slightly thicker pouring cream. It makes rich custards. It can be softly whipped for folding into mixtures or used as a soft topping. Whipped until it holds its shape, double cream can be used to fill cakes or pastries.

Cream should be chilled before whipping and the utensils cold, not freshly washed and warm, which results in the cream thickening quickly, becoming buttery rather than light and airy. A hand whisk is ideal but hard work. A hand-held electric whisk or beater is more practical. When whipping a small amount, use a hand whisk or single electric whisk or beater. Powerful free-standing electric mixers are likely to unevenly whip or over-whip the cream.

WHIPPING CREAM

The texture of whipped cream can vary. Adding a little fruit juice or liqueur to double (heavy) cream, or mixing two-thirds double cream with one-third single (light) or whipping cream, reduces the overall fat content and gives a softer texture.

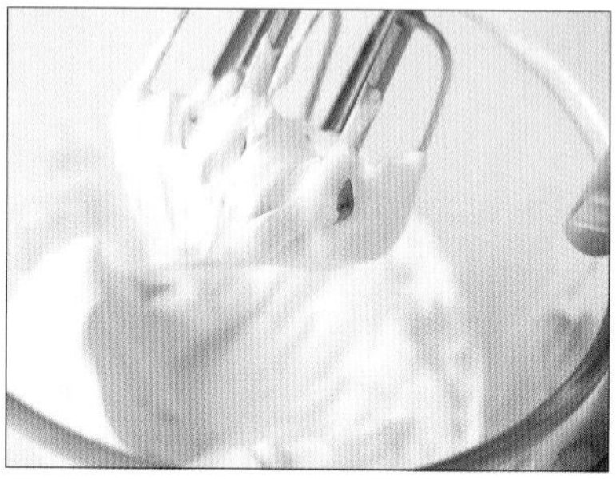

1 Use a hand or electric beater and whip the cream in a large, grease-free bowl. Whipping cream gradually becomes foamy, forming flopping peaks that are soft and light. Do not overwhip as the cream will separate and collapse.

2 Double cream lightens, increases in volume and forms soft peaks, then it gradually thickens slightly more to become light yet thick. Do not continue whipping after this point as the cream will become buttery and grainy.

Below: Classic custard is quick and easy to make but needs your full attention. It is less sweet than instant custard powder.

TRADITIONAL CUSTARD

Classic custard made with egg and milk requires patience to make. In taste it does not resemble custard made with powder mix, but is thinner with the consistency of pouring cream. Sweet and delicious, custard is comfort food at its best.

Makes about 400ml/14fl oz/1⅔ cup

300ml/½ pint/1¼ cups milk
1 vanilla pod (bean), split
3 egg yolks
15ml/1 tbsp caster (superfine) sugar

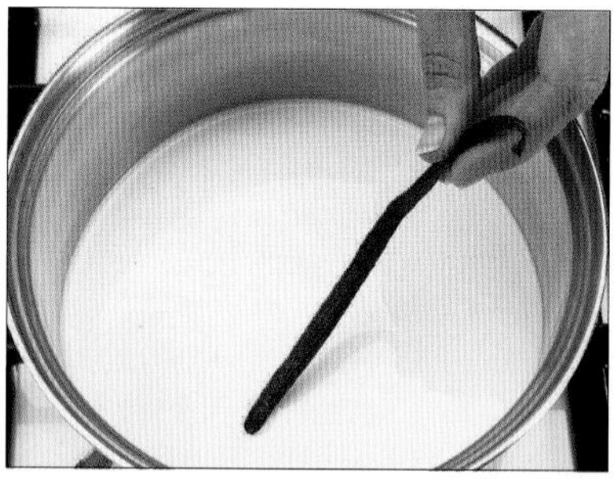

1 Heat the milk with the vanilla pod until it boils. Leave to stand off the heat for 15 minutes. Strain the milk.

2 Prepare a pan of barely simmering water. In a heatproof bowl that fits on top of the pan, beat the egg yolks and sugar. Stir in the milk. Place the bowl on the pan of water. Stir constantly until the custard is slightly thickened.

3 To keep custard warm, without a skin forming, cover the immediate surface with cling film (plastic wrap).

Preparing fruit

We all know that fruit is one of the foods that should feature in the daily diet. It is low in calories, high in natural sugar and contains vital food value that is good for us. Fruit is an instant food and is most often eaten raw as a snack or to follow a meal.

Most fruits are available all year round in good supermarkets, but often when they are naturally out of season, the varieties available will be lacking in flavour, so it's best to work with seasonal produce where possible.

A quick wash and wipe is enough preparation for many types of fruit eaten as the simplest dessert or snack. Often in soft fruits and orchard fruits, the skin contains nutritional value and is best eaten. Citrus and tropical fruits should be peeled. The following is a general guide and the simple rule is to prepare fruit as close as possible to serving or using.

For some dishes and desserts, basic preparation techniques require fruit to be peeled, trimmed, pitted and cut into bitesize pieces. Unless you're using very unfamiliar fruit, these are skills that you may already have mastered.

Below: Fruit and biscuits make a simple but special dessert, or you could add marshmallows and a chocolate fondue.

PEELING FRUIT

Use a potato peeler, if you want to skin orchard fruit. Citrus fruits can be peeled by pulling the skin off with your fingers.

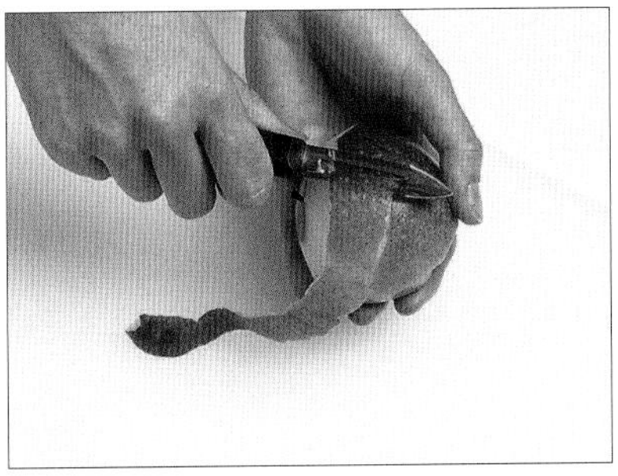

1 Wash the fruit and pat it dry using kitchen paper. Use a vegetable peeler to pare off the skin in long, thin strips. Pears are best peeled by removing strips vertically.

2 Peach, apricot and nectarine skin can be removed by cutting a cross in the base and blanching in boiling water.

PEELING PINEAPPLE

You need a sharp knife to peel pineapple.

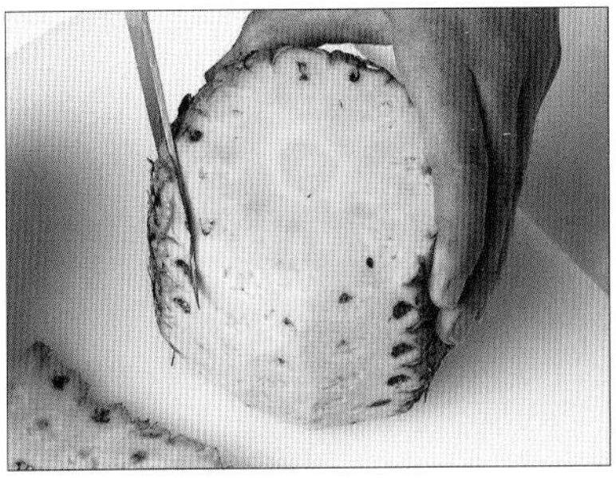

1 Cut off the leafy crown. Cut a slice from the base and set the pineapple upright. Cut off the peel lengthways, removing the brown 'eyes' with it.

PITTING STONE FRUIT

The stone (pit) in fruits is inedible.

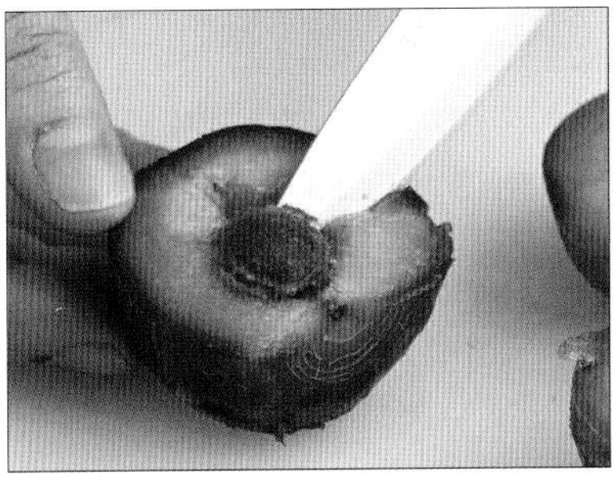

1 Most stones can be removed easily with a sharp knife.

REMOVING CITRUS MEMBRANES

This is a tricky technique, but worth it.

1 Slice between the membranes of the orange to remove all the pith.

Bread and butter pudding

This dessert is a traditional British favourite that is inexpensive and easy to make, and full of good ingredients. Essentially, it is custard mixture poured over bread and butter, sweetened and baked. There are many richer variations, but the basic recipe is still the best.

Serves four to six

50g/2oz/4 tbsp butter, softened
about 6 large slices of day-old white bread
50g/2oz dried fruit, such as raisins, sultanas (golden raisins) or chopped dried apricots
40g/1½oz/3 tbsp caster (superfine) sugar
2 large (US extra large) eggs
600ml/1 pint/2½ cups full cream (whole) milk

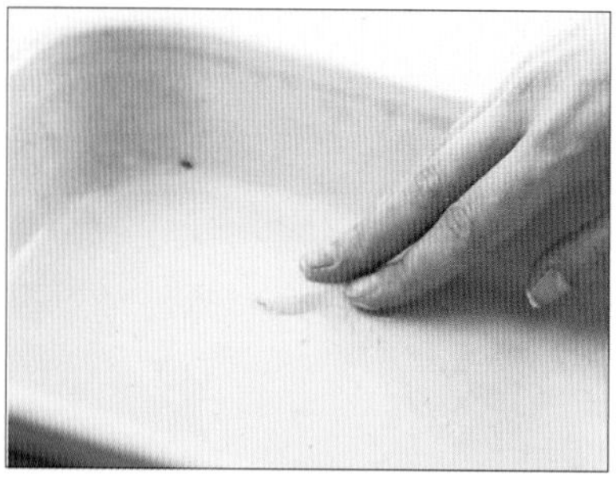

1 Preheat the oven to 160°C/325°F/ Gas 5. Lightly butter a 1.2-litre/2-pint/ 5-cup ovenproof dish.

2 Butter the slices of bread and cut them into small triangles or squares.

COOK'S TIPS
- Replace the bread with brioche and the milk with cream for a deluxe version.
- Use this recipe to use up bread that is past its best.

3 Arrange half the bread pieces, buttered side up, in the prepared dish and sprinkle the dried fruit and half of the sugar over the top.

4 Arrange the remaining bread slices, again buttered side up, evenly on top of the fruit, covering any gaps that might be visible. Sprinkle the remaining sugar evenly over the top.

5 To make the custard, beat the eggs lightly together, then stir in the milk. Do not worry about any stringy bits of egg white as these will be removed.

6 Strain the egg mixture and pour it over the bread in the dish. Push the top slices down into the liquid, if necessary, so that it is evenly absorbed.

7 Leave the pudding to stand for 30 minutes to allow the bread to soak up all the liquid.

8 Put the dish into the hot oven and bake for about 45 minutes or until the custard is set and the top is crisp and golden brown. Serve the pudding immediately with pouring cream.

Variations
- To make a special occasion chocolate bread and butter pudding, complete steps 1–4, omitting the dried fruit if you wish. Break 150g/5oz dark (bittersweet) chocolate into 500ml/17fl oz/ generous 2 cups milk and heat gently (on the stove or on low power in the microwave) until the milk is warm and the chocolate has melted. Stir frequently during heating and do not allow the milk to boil. Stir the warm chocolate milk into the beaten eggs in step 5, and then continue with the remaining steps.
- You could replace the dried fruit in either version of the pudding with slices of fresh banana.

Energy 622kcal/2597kJ; Protein 10.5g; Carbohydrate 55.6g, of which sugars 37.8g; Fat 39g, of which saturates 23g; Cholesterol 186mg; Calcium 203mg; Fibre 1.6g; Sodium 350mg.

Fruit crumble

Apple crumble is a time-honoured favourite, but you could add many orchard fruits to this dish and combine them with summer and autumn berries. Serve with custard or cream.

Serves six to eight

900g/2lb cooking apples
450g/1lb/4 cups blackberries
squeeze of lemon juice
175g/6oz/scan 1 cup sugar

For the crumble
115g/4oz/½ cup butter
115g/4oz/1 cup plain (all-purpose), or wholemeal (whole-wheat) flour
115g/4oz/1 cup soft light brown sugar

1 Preheat the oven to 200°C/400°F/Gas 6. To make the crumble topping, rub the butter into the flour, then add the sugar and continue to rub in until the mixture forms fine breadcrumbs.

2 Peel, core and slice the cooking apples into wedges.

Variation
Use plums, rhubarb spiced with ginger or summer fruits.

3 Put the apples, blackberries, lemon juice and 30ml/2 tbsp water and the sugar into a shallow ovenproof dish, about 2 litres/3½ pints/9 cups capacity. If the fruit is tart, heat it first in a pan with additional sugar, to taste, until soft.

4 Cover the fruit with the topping.

5 Bake in the oven for 15 minutes, then reduce the heat to 190°C/375°F/Gas 5 and cook for another 15–20 minutes until crunchy and brown on top. Serve hot with custard, cream or ice cream.

Energy 336kcal/1413kJ; Protein 4g; Carbohydrate 53.1g, of which sugars 30.8g; Fat 13.4g, of which saturates 6.8g; Cholesterol 27mg; Calcium 72mg; Fibre 3g; Sodium 81mg.

Poached pears

Unassuming pears are transformed when poached in red wine into the most fabulous treat. Make them a day ahead and chill them overnight for a hassle-free special occasion dessert.

Serves four

1 bottle of red wine
150g/5oz/¾ cup sugar
45ml/3 tbsp honey
juice of ½ lemon
1 cinnamon stick
1 vanilla pod (bean), split open lengthways
5cm/2in piece of orange peel
1 clove
1 black peppercorn
4 firm, ripe pears
whipped cream or soured cream, to serve

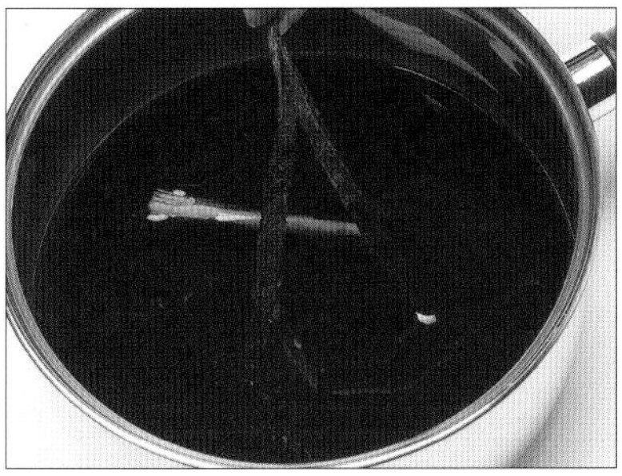

1 In a pan just large enough to hold the pears standing upright, combine all the ingredients except the pears and cream. Heat gently, stirring occasionally, until the sugar has dissolved. Remove from the heat.

2 Peel the pears, leaving the core and stem intact. Slice a small piece off the base of each pear so it will stand upright. Cut out the main piece of core from the bottom with the point of the knife. Add the pears to the wine.

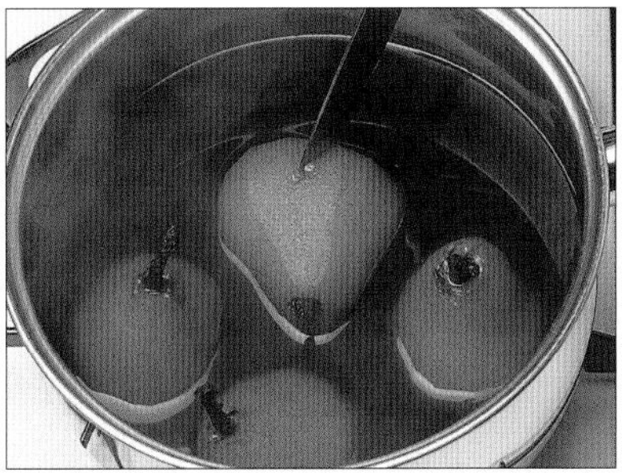

3 Bring just to the boil. Reduce the heat at once and simmer, uncovered, until the pears are tender, about 20–35 minutes. Do not overcook the pears.

4 With a slotted spoon, transfer the pears to a bowl. Boil the poaching liquid until reduced by half. Leave to cool. Strain the cooled liquid over the pears and chill for at least 3 hours. Serve with whipped or sour cream.

Variation

Use cider instead of wine. Omit the cinnamon, vanilla, orange peel, clove and peppercorn. Add 25g/1oz sliced fresh root ginger and grated rind and juice of a whole lemon.

Energy 378kcal/1595kJ; Protein 1g; Carbohydrate 65.7g, of which sugars 65.7g; Fat 0.2g, of which saturates 0g; Cholesterol 0mg; Calcium 53mg; Fibre 3.9g; Sodium 22mg.

Lemon surprise pudding

During cooking, this mixture separates to form a small amount of tangy lemon sauce that collects beneath the light sponge top. The result is superb. Serve with custard or cream.

Serves four

50g/2oz/¼ cup butter, plus extra for greasing
grated rind and juice of 2 lemons
115g/4oz/½ cup caster (superfine) sugar
2 eggs, separated
50g/2oz/½ cup self-raising (self-rising) flour
300ml/½ pint/1¼ cups milk

1 Preheat the oven to 190°C/375°F/ Gas 5. Lightly grease a 1.2-litre/2-pint/ 5-cup ovenproof dish.

Variation

Try oranges or limes in place of the lemons, if you like.

2 Beat the butter, lemon rind and caster sugar until pale and fluffy. Add the egg yolks and flour and beat well. Gradually whisk in the lemon juice and milk (the mixture may curdle horribly, but don't be alarmed). In a clean bowl, whisk the egg whites until they form stiff peaks.

3 Fold the egg whites lightly into the lemon mixture using a metal spoon, then pour into the prepared dish. Place the dish in a roasting pan. Pour in hot water to half fill the pan, then bake the pudding for 45 minutes, until set and golden on top. Serve immediately.

Energy 319kcal/1341kJ; Protein 7g; Carbohydrate 43.1g, of which sugars 33.8g; Fat 14.5g, of which saturates 8.1g; Cholesterol 126mg; Calcium 166mg; Fibre 0.4g; Sodium 190mg

Tiramisu

There are many versions of this popular Italian dessert, but all use minimal ingredients and are quick and easy to make. Make it the day before you will eat it so that it is well chilled and set.

Serves six to eight

3 eggs, separated
450g/1lb/2 cups mascarpone, at room temperature
10ml/2 tsp vanilla sugar
175ml/6fl oz/¾ cup cold, very strong, black coffee
120ml/4fl oz/½ cup coffee-flavoured liqueur
18 savoiardi (Italian sponge fingers)
sifted unsweetened cocoa powder and grated dark (bittersweet) chocolate, to finish

1 With an electric mixer, whisk the egg whites until they stand in stiff peaks.

2 Whisk the mascarpone, vanilla sugar and egg yolks in a separate large bowl until evenly combined. Fold in the egg whites. Spread a few spoonfuls of mixture evenly into a large bowl.

3 Mix the coffee and liqueur together in a shallow dish. Dip a sponge finger in the mixture, turn it quickly so that it becomes saturated but does not disintegrate, and place it on top of the mascarpone in the bowl. Add five more dipped sponge fingers, placing them side by side.

4 Spoon in about one-third of the remaining mixture and spread it out. Make more layers in the same way, ending with mascarpone. Level the surface, then sift cocoa powder all over. Cover and chill overnight. Before serving, sprinkle with cocoa and grated chocolate.

Variation
Use Madeira cake cut into slices in place of the savoiardi, if you like.

Energy 215kcal/894kJ; Protein 8.5g; Carbohydrate 12.4g, of which sugars 10.2g; Fat 13.3g, of which saturates 5.9g; Cholesterol 118mg; Calcium 22mg; Fibre 0.1g; Sodium 48mg.

Chocolate gooey cake

For perfect results it is essential to undercook this cake so that it is dense in the middle. Made with almonds instead of flour, the mixture does not rise and set into the usual cake-like texture.

Serves eight

115g/4oz dark (bittersweet) chocolate
5ml/1 tsp water
115g/4oz/½ cup unsalted (sweet) butter, diced
2 eggs, separated
175g/6oz/1½ cups ground almonds
5ml/1 tsp vanilla sugar

COOK'S TIP
Make vanilla sugar by decanting a quantity of caster (superfine) sugar into a jar. Add a vanilla pod (bean), seal and leave for the pod to infuse the sugar.

1 Preheat the oven to 180°C/350°F/Gas 4. Grease a 20cm/8in shallow round cake tin (pan).

2 Break the chocolate into a pan. Add the water and heat gently until the chocolate has melted. Add the butter to the chocolate and stir until melted.

3 Remove from the heat, then add the egg yolks, ground almonds and vanilla sugar. Whisk the egg whites until stiff, then fold them into the chocolate mixture.

4 Spread the mixture gently into the prepared tin and bake in the oven for 15–17 minutes until just set. The mixture should still be soft in the centre. Leave to cool in the tin. When cold, serve with a dollop of lightly whipped double cream, if you like.

Energy 311kcal/1288kJ; Protein 6.8g; Carbohydrate 10g, of which sugars 9.3g; Fat 27.4g, of which saturates 9.9g; Cholesterol 75mg; Calcium 66.2mg; Fibre 1.9g; Sodium 97mg.

Victoria sponge cake

Often referred to as Victoria sandwich, this cake is made with equal weights of fat, sugar, eggs and flour. The basic mixture makes this irresistible cake or it can be used for small cupcakes.

Serves six to eight

3 large (US extra large) eggs
few drops of vanilla extract (optional)
175g/6oz/¾ cup soft butter, softened
175g/6oz/¾ cup caster (superfine) sugar
175g/6oz/1½ cups self-raising (self-rising) flour
about 60ml/4 tbsp jam
icing (confectioners') sugar, to dust

1 Preheat the oven to 180°C/350°F/Gas 4. Grease two 20cm/8in sandwich tins (layer pans) and line the bases of each with baking parchment.

2 Beat the eggs with the vanilla extract, if using. In a large bowl, cream the butter and sugar until pale and fluffy.

3 Stir in the eggs, adding a spoonful of the flour to prevent the mixture from curdling. Fold in the remaining flour.

4 Divide the batter between the two sandwich tins. Bake for 20–25 minutes, until both sponges are golden and firm.

5 Leave to cool in the tins for a few minutes, then turn out on to a wire rack. Remove the paper and leave to go completely cold.

6 Sandwich the two halves together with plenty of jam. Sift a little icing sugar over the top.

Variations

- Add the grated rind of 1 lemon to the butter mixture. Omit the vanilla. Use lemon curd instead of jam.
- For cream cake, sandwich with jam and top with whipped double (heavy) cream or buttercream.
- For strawberry sponge, top the jam with sliced fresh strawberries before the whipped cream.
- For coffee cake, dissolve 15ml/1 tbsp instant coffee in 30ml/2 tbsp hot water. Beat this with the eggs. Sandwich the cakes with coffee buttercream, made by adding instant coffee dissolved in a little water to buttercream.

Energy 368kcal/1543kJ; Protein 4.6g; Carbohydrate 44.7g, of which sugars 28.5g; Fat 20.3g, of which saturates 12g; Cholesterol 118mg; Calcium 104mg; Fibre 0.7g; Sodium 241mg

Mini Madeira cakes

Madeira cake mixture has slightly more flour than a sponge cake, which makes it dome when it rises. Moistened with ground almonds and flavoured with Calvados, these little cakes taste good.

Makes twelve

225g/8oz/1 cup butter, softened
225g/8oz/1 cup caster (superfine) sugar
4 large (US extra large) eggs
225g/8oz/2 cups self-raising (self-rising) flour
115g/4oz/1 cup plain (all-purpose) flour
60ml/4 tbsp ground almonds
5ml/1 tsp vanilla extract
30ml/2 tbsp Calvados, brandy or milk

For the buttercream

175g/6oz/¾ cup unsalted (sweet) butter, softened
350g/12oz/3½ cups icing (confectioners') sugar, plus extra for dusting
25ml/1½ tbsp lemon juice
25ml/1½ tbsp warm water
60ml/4 tbsp raspberry jam

1 Preheat the oven to 180°C/350°F/Gas 4.

2 In a large bowl, cream the butter and sugar together until light and fluffy.

3 Beat in the first egg. Sprinkle 1 tbsp/15ml of the flour into the mixture and beat it in. Add the remaining eggs one at a time, beating in a tablespoon of flour after each addition until just combined. Sift the remaining flour into the mixture and fold it in lightly with the vanilla, Calvados, brandy or milk, if using.

4 Line a 12-cup muffin pan with paper cases and fill them almost full. Bake for 20–22 minutes until light golden and the tops spring back when touched.

5 Cool on a wire rack and store cold in an airtight container. Fill on the day they are served.

6 To make the buttercream, beat the butter in a large bowl with the icing sugar until smooth and fluffy. Stir in the lemon juice and water and beat until smooth. Slice the top off each cake. Using a large piping (pastry) bag fitted with a plain nozzle, pipe a circle of buttercream on each cake.

7 Add a spoonful of jam on top of the buttercream. Replace the cake tops. Sift a little icing sugar over, to serve.

Energy 574kcal/2406kJ; Protein 5.2g; Carbohydrate 75.5g, of which sugars 54g; Fat 29.5g, of which saturates 18.6g; Cholesterol 140mg; Calcium 81mg; Fibre 0.9g; Sodium 278mg.

Scones with jam and cream

Scones, often known as biscuits in the US, are thought to originate from Scotland where they are still a popular part of afternoon tea with jams and thick clotted cream.

Makes about twelve

450g/1lb/4 cups self-raising (self-rising) flour, or 450g/1lb/4 cups plain (all-purpose) flour and 10ml/2 tsp baking powder
large pinch of salt
50g/2oz/¼ cup butter, chilled and diced
15ml/1 tbsp lemon juice
about 400ml/14fl oz/1⅔ cups milk, plus extra to glaze
fruit jam, to serve
clotted cream or whipped double (heavy) cream, to serve

1 Preheat the oven to 230°C/450°F/Gas 8.

2 Sift the flour, baking powder, if using, and salt into a clean, dry mixing bowl. Add the diced butter and rub it into the flour with your fingertips until the mixture resembles fine, evenly textured breadcrumbs.

3 Whisk the lemon juice into the milk and leave for about 1 minute to thicken slightly, then pour into the flour mixture and mix quickly to form a soft but pliable dough. The wetter the mixture, the lighter the resulting scone will be, but if they are too wet they will spread during baking and lose their shape.

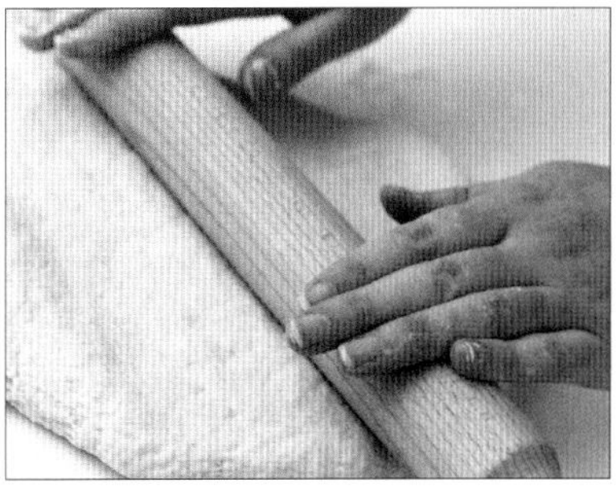

4 Knead the dough lightly to form a ball, then roll it out on a floured surface to a thickness of at least 2.5cm/1in. Using a 5cm/2in pastry (cookie) cutter, and dipping it into flour each time, stamp out 12 scones. Place them on a well-floured baking sheet. Re-roll any trimmings and cut out more scones.

5 Brush the tops of the scones lightly with a little milk, then bake in the preheated oven for about 20 minutes, or until risen and golden brown. Remove the baking sheet from the oven and wrap the scones in a clean dish towel to keep them warm and soft until ready to serve. Eat with fruit jam and a generous dollop of cream.

Energy 170kcal/720kJ; Protein 4.5g; Carbohydrate 29.9g, of which sugars 2.1g; Fat 4.4g, of which saturates 2.6g; Cholesterol 11mg; Calcium 172mg; Fibre 1.2g; Sodium 338mg.

Chocolate brownies

These brownies are packed with milk and dark chocolate, making them rich and intense rather than too sweet. Serve them in small squares, either cold or warm.

Makes sixteen

300g/12oz plain (semisweet) chocolate
300g/12oz milk chocolate
175g/6oz/¾ cup unsalted (sweet) butter
75g/3oz/⅔ cup self-raising (self-rising) flour
3 large (US extra large) eggs

COOK'S TIPS
• The brownies are fabulous for dessert with scoops of good ice cream or white chocolate sauce.
• Try them warm, drizzled with maple syrup.
• Melt 225g/8oz white chocolate in a heatproof bowl set over a small pan of simmering water. Stir in 225g/8oz mascarpone for a rich and dreamy topping.

1 Preheat the oven to 180°C/350°F/Gas 4. Line the base and sides of a 20cm/8in square cake tin (pan) with baking parchment.

2 Break the plain chocolate and 90g/3½oz of the milk chocolate into pieces and put in a heatproof bowl with the butter. Melt over a pan of barely simmering water, stirring frequently.

3 Chop the remaining milk chocolate. Stir the flour and eggs into the melted chocolate. Stir in half the chopped chocolate and turn the mixture into the tin, spreading it evenly. Sprinkle with the remaining chopped chocolate.

4 Bake for 30–35 minutes, until risen and firm. Cool in the tin, then cut into squares. Store in an airtight container.

Energy 297kcal/1239kJ; Protein 3.7g; Carbohydrate 30.2g, of which sugars 21.4g; Fat 18.8g, of which saturates 4.2g; Cholesterol 38mg; Calcium 37mg; Fibre 1.1g; Sodium 16mg.

Blueberry muffins

Light and fruity, these well-known American muffins are delicious at any time of day. Serve them warm for breakfast or brunch, as a tea-time treat or with scoops of ice cream for dessert.

Makes twelve

2 eggs
50g/2oz/4 tbsp butter, melted
175ml/6fl oz/¾ cup milk
5ml/1 tsp vanilla extract
5ml/1 tsp grated lemon rind
180g/6¼oz/generous 1¼ cups plain (all-purpose) flour
60g/2¼oz/generous ¼ cup sugar
10ml/2 tsp baking powder
pinch of salt
175g/6oz/1¼ cups fresh blueberries

1 Preheat the oven to 200°C/400°F/Gas 6. Arrange 12 paper cases in a muffin pan or grease the pan.

2 In a bowl, whisk the eggs until blended. Add the melted butter, milk, vanilla and lemon rind, and stir well to combine.

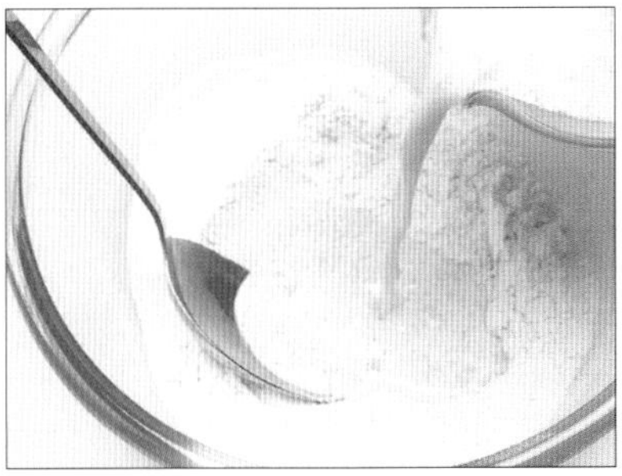

3 Sift the flour, sugar, baking powder and salt into a bowl. Make a well in the centre and pour in the egg mixture. Stir to combine with a metal spoon.

4 Add the blueberries to the muffin mixture and gently fold in.

5 Carefully spoon the batter into the muffin cases, leaving enough space at the top of each for the muffins to rise.

6 Bake for 20–25 minutes, until the risen tops spring back when pressed lightly with a fingertip. Leave the muffins in the pan, if using, for 5 minutes before turning out on to a wire rack to cool.

Variations

- Frozen fruit also works well in the muffins. Try frozen raspberries, blackberries or strawberries instead of blueberries.
- Rhubarb is good in muffins: use small young sticks and cut them into slices about 5mm/¼in thick.

COOK'S TIPS

- Take care not to over-mix the batter. This toughens the mixture and tends to break up the fruit, resulting in dense muffins.
- If you want to serve the muffins warm for breakfast, weigh out and prepare the dry ingredients the night before to save time.

Energy 127kcal/536kJ; Protein 3.3g; Carbohydrate 18.6g, of which sugars 7.1g; Fat 5g, of which saturates 2.7g; Cholesterol 48mg; Calcium 56mg; Fibre 1g; Sodium 96mg.

Oaty chocolate chip cookies

Rough-textured biscuits made with a soft mixture that rises and spreads into cookies are easy to make. There is no need for rolling and cutting, so they are quite chunky, but delicious.

Makes about twenty

115g/4oz/½ cup butter, plus extra for greasing
115g/4oz/½ cup soft dark brown sugar
2 eggs, lightly beaten
45–60ml/3–4 tbsp milk
5ml/1 tsp vanilla extract
150g/5oz/1¼ cups plain (all-purpose) flour
5ml/1 tsp baking powder
pinch of salt
115g/4oz/generous 1 cup rolled oats
175g/6oz plain (semisweet) chocolate chips
115g/4oz/1 cup pecan nuts, chopped

Variation
Use coconut instead of the rolled oats, if you like.

1 Cream the butter and sugar in a large bowl until pale and fluffy. Add the beaten eggs, milk and vanilla extract, and beat thoroughly.

2 Sift in the flour, baking powder and salt, and stir in until well mixed. Fold in the rolled oats, chocolate chips and chopped pecan nuts.

3 Chill the mixture for at least 1 hour. Preheat the oven to 180°C/350°F/Gas 4. Grease two large baking trays.

4 Using two teaspoons, place mounds well apart on the trays and flatten with the back of a spoon or fork. Bake for 10–12 minutes until the edges are just colouring, then cool on wire racks.

Energy 208kcal/871kJ; Protein 3.3g; Carbohydrate 22.1g, of which sugars 12g; Fat 12.5g, of which saturates 5g; Cholesterol 36mg; Calcium 30mg; Fibre 1.1g; Sodium 47mg.

Almond shortbread

This easy all-in-one recipe makes a very light, crisp shortbread with an excellent flavour, and it keeps well. Serve with tea or coffee, or to accompany light desserts.

Makes about twenty four

275g/10oz/2½ cups plain (all-purpose) flour
25g/1oz/¼ cup ground almonds
225g/8oz/1 cup butter, softened
75g/3oz/6 tbsp caster (superfine) sugar
grated rind of ½ lemon

1 Preheat the oven to 180°C/350°F/Gas 4. Grease a baking tin (pan) about 28 x 18cm/11 x 7in.

2 Put the flour, ground almonds, butter, sugar and lemon rind into a mixer or food processor and process or beat until the mixture comes together. Alternatively, beat the butter and sugar by hand or with a mixer until light and fluffy. Then stir in the flour, almonds and lemon rind.

3 Press the mixture into the tin and flatten the top with a palette knife.

Variation

For plain shortbread, omit the almonds and lemon. Try adding 115g/4oz chopped pistachio nuts.

4 Bake for about 20 minutes, or until pale golden brown. Remove from the oven and immediately mark the shortbread into fingers or squares while the mixture is soft. Allow to cool a little, and then transfer to a wire rack and leave until cold. If stored in an airtight container, the shortbread should keep for up to two weeks.

Energy 64kcal/266kJ; Protein 0.7g; Carbohydrate 6.1g, of which sugars 1.8g; Fat 4.2g, of which saturates 2.5g; Cholesterol 10mg; Calcium 11mg; Fibre 0.2g; Sodium 29mg.

Sauces and accompaniments

Savoury sauces include an incredible array of recipes, from humble milk mixtures to whisked liaisons of eggs and butter balanced carefully in equilibrium. This chapter concentrates on recipes that will enhance main course dishes of grilled and fried fish and meat. Sauces add the finishing touch and help to make a perfectly dressed dish.

Sauce basics

Sauces add flavour to cooked dishes, as well as supplying contrasting or complementary textures to the main ingredient. They can enliven the quality of a plain dish. When made well, sauces are the finishing touch to a meal, but because they are made last, often cause most anxiety, since the point at which they are made is when the other components of the meal are hot and ready to be served.

However, learning to make sauces is not difficult. It is a skill that will broaden your cooking repertoire as well as add new flavour interest to everyday dishes.

Many sauce-making ingredients such as flour, fat, milk and cheese are basics in every kitchen, but adding just a few other well-chosen ingredients will provide you with a store cupboard from which to make a whole range of flavourful accompaniments to meals. Herbs and spices are added to many sauces, each transforming the sauce by imparting its own defining aroma. Vegetables and even fruit play a part with their colourful flesh and flavour.

Many of these additional ingredients are used to make sauces that complement specific types of food. Many foods seem made to go together: apple sauce is good with pork or hot meats; cranberry sauce has a special affinity with turkey; and parsley sauce goes well with fried or grilled (broiled) white fish.

Above: Sauces are often presented in a sauceboat and handed around for diners to serve themselves.

EQUIPMENT

Sauce-making doesn't require any special equipment, and much of what you own, including pans, bowls, whisks, sieves (strainers), weighing scales and measuring jugs (cups) will suffice to make and serve many sauces. However, a blender or food processor will remove much of the anxiety of making sauces that are smooth. The trick is to blend each additional ingredient before adding the next.

Below: A hand-held blender will smooth a lumpy sauce, as well as process vegetables to a smooth pulp.

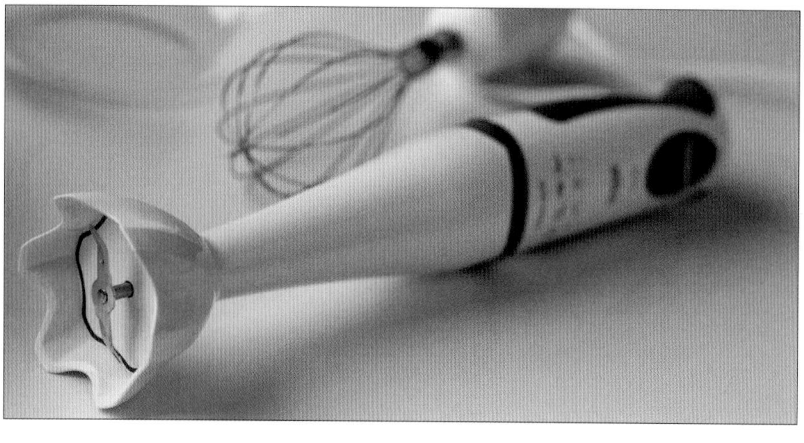

CORRECTING A LUMPY SAUCE

If flour-thickened sauce has gone lumpy, it can be corrected.

1 Try whisking the sauce hard with a light wire whisk in the pan to smooth out the lumps, then reheat gently, stirring.

2 If the sauce is still not smooth, rub it through a fine sieve (strainer), pressing firmly with a wooden spoon. Return to the pan and reheat gently, sitrring.

3 Alternatively, pour the sauce into a food processor and process until smooth, or use a hand-held blender and pulse. Return to the pan and reheat gently, stirring.

Stock

A good home-made stock is simple to make and adds rich flavour to all kinds of savoury sauces. Commercial stock cubes and bouillon powder are good, but home-made is better.

CHICKEN STOCK
The chicken carcass left after a roast dinner is the starting point for this stock.

Makes 1 litre/1¾ pints/4 cups

1 chicken carcass
chicken giblets
2 leeks, chopped
1 celery stick, chopped
bouquet garni
5ml/1 tsp white peppecorns
2.5ml/½ tsp sea salt
1.75 litres/3 pints/7½ cups water

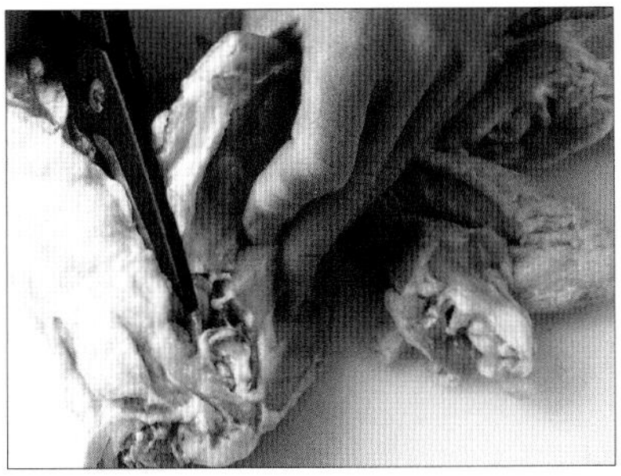

1 Break up the carcass, place in a large pan with the remaining ingredients. Bring to the boil.

2 Cover the pan and simmer very gently for 2½ hours, skimming occasionally to remove scum from the surface of the pan.

3 Strain the stock through a sieve (strainer) into a bowl. Allow to go cold. Discard all the additional ingredients.

BEEF STOCK
Use beef stock to make rich and flavourful gravy.

675g/1½lb shin of beef, diced
1 large onion, chopped
1 large carrot, chopped
1 celery stick, chopped
bouquet garni
6 black peppercorns
2.5ml/½ tsp salt
1.75 litre/3 pints/7½ cups water

1 Make as for chicken stock, and simmer for 4 hours.

VEGETABLE STOCK
Use vegetable stock for vegetarian dishes, soups and vegetarian gravy.

500g/1¼lb chopped mixed vegetables, for example, onions, carrots, celery, leeks
bouquet garni
6 black peppercorns
2.5ml/½ tsp salt
1litre/1¾ pints/4 cups water

1 Make as for chicken stock and simmer for 30 minutes.

Below: The vegetables and herbs in a stock impart essential flavour. They can be changed according to what's in season.

Above: Stock has an intense flavour.

FISH STOCK
Use fish stock for fish sauces, soups and stews.

1kg/2¼lb white fish bones and trimmings
1 large onion, chopped
1 large carrot, chopped
1 celery stick, chopped
bouquet garni
6 white peppercorns
2.5ml/½ tsp salt
150ml/¼ pint/⅔ cup dry white wine
1litre/1¾ pints/4 cups water

1 Make as for chicken stock and simmer for 20 minutes.

FREEZING STOCK
Stock can be frozen in small portions.

1 Fill an ice cube tray with stock and freeze on a flat shelf.

Basic white sauce

This is the classic method to make a basic white sauce, which is based on a fat and flour paste or 'roux'.

50g/2oz/4 tbsp butter
40g/1½oz/6 tbsp plain (all-purpose) flour
600ml/1 pint/2½ cups milk

1 Melt the butter in a pan, then add the flour. Cook, stirring on a low heat for 1–2 minutes.

2 Remove the pan from the heat and gradually stir in the milk. Return to the heat and stir constantly until boiling and thickened.

3 Reduce the heat and simmer, stirring for 2 minutes, until the sauce thickens.

TIPS FOR FLOUR-BASED SAUCES

The basic white sauce quantities make a versatile pouring sauce that is ideal for coating food, for example coating vegetables, hard-boiled eggs or fish, or as a base for onion, parsley or cheese sauces. It is also good as an accompaniment for hearty foods, such as grilled (broiled) sausages or fish (the sauce can be flavoured with a variety of ingredients).

- To make a thinner coating sauce, for example, to serve in small quantities with grilled plaice fillets, reduce the flour to 25g/1oz/4 tbsp. The butter can be reduced to 25g/1oz/2 tbsp or left as it is.
- For a thicker sauce, increase the flour to 50g/2oz/½ cup. This makes a thick coating sauce – a consistency that is useful when adding ingredients that give up juices that are likely to thin the sauce. For example, fish fillet and frozen peeled cooked prawns (shrimp) can be added. As the fish cooks and prawns thaw, the sauce thins. Grated cheese also thins the sauce as it melts.

AVOIDING LUMPS

Stir in the liquid very slowly at first, stirring all the paste off the bottom of the pan and making sure it is smooth, when about a quarter of the liquid has been added, before gradually adding the rest. With practice, there is no need to remove the pan from the heat.

- Once all the paste is smooth, use a hand whisk to stir the sauce vigorously when bringing to the boil. This reduces the chances of lumps forming.
- If the sauce looks too lumpy, press it through a sieve (strainer).

OTHER LIQUIDS

The basic quantities for the basic white sauce also work for stock or a mixture of stock and wine.

Stock and milk may be used together or wine can be combined with milk, but when a significant amount of wine is used (for example half and half with milk) the wine should be added first and brought to the boil to make a very thick sauce. Then the milk can be stirred in and the sauce reheated. If the milk is not stabilized by the flour first, the wine will make it curdle.

Using cream Use a quarter to half quantity of single (light) or double (heavy) cream with milk for a rich sauce.

Using wine and cream Use half dry white wine and half single cream. Heat the wine with 2 bay leaves and 2 onion slices, then set aside for 15 minutes before making the sauce.

Using sherry Use half single (light) cream and half milk. Add a little sherry at the end, when the sauce has boiled and before simmering. This is good with mushrooms.

ADDING CORNFLOUR

Cornflour (cornstarch) makes sauces with a different texture from wheat flour sauces. The cornflour has to be mixed with a little cold milk first until smooth (this is known as 'slaking'), then hot milk is added and the sauce brought to the boil. Cornflour sauce should be simmered for about 3 minutes.

For a plain white sauce, mix 45ml/3 tbsp cornflour with a little milk taken from the total quantity of 600ml/1 pint/2¼ cups. Bring the remaining milk to the boil, then pour it on to the cornflour mixture, stirring all the time. Return the sauce to the pan and bring to the boil, stirring. Simmer for 3 minutes. Season to taste with salt and pepper. Add flavouring ingredients, such as cheese or herbs.

Cornflour-thickened sauces do not rely on butter, so they can be used for lower-fat recipes.

Energy 581kcal/2439kJ; Protein 24.3g; Carbohydrate 50.7g, of which sugars 30.5g; Fat 33g, of which saturates 20.7g; Cholesterol 94mg; Calcium 806mg; Fibre 0.8g; Sodium 435mg.

WHITE SAUCE VARIATIONS

Be adventurous once you have mastered the basic white sauce recipe (see left). For example, frozen chopped, cooked spinach is good in the sauce – add a few chunks of the frozen vegetable and a little grated nutmeg – or try any of the following: flaked canned tuna, chopped spring onions (scallions) or chives, chopped fresh tarragon, pesto or finely shredded basil, or concentrated tomato purée (paste). The classic variations suggested here show how basic white sauce takes flavours. Remember to season with salt and ground white pepper at the end of cooking, tasting to check the flavour. Think about what the sauce is served with and adjust the seasoning. If it is to go with salty gammon or smoked haddock, then there may not be any need for salt or, at least, no more than a tiny amount.

MAKING ONION SAUCE

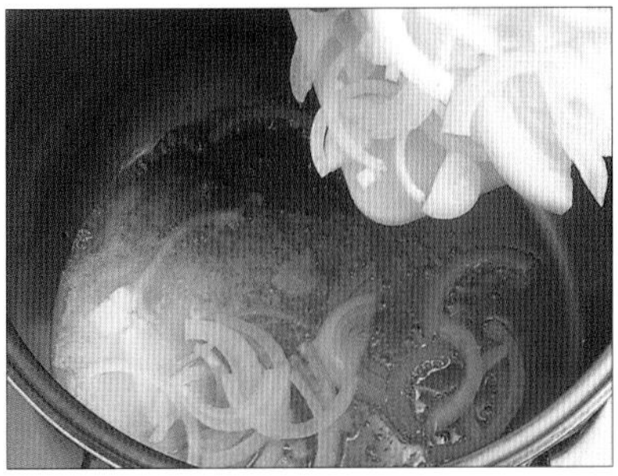

1 Finely chop 2 large onions and cook them in the butter over low to medium heat, stirring frequently, for 15–20 minutes. The onions should be soft but not browned. Stir in the flour and milk, then add seasoning to taste at the end of cooking. A bay leaf is good in onion sauce; cook it with the onions.

It is excellent with sausages, toad-in-the-hole or boiled ham.

MAKING CHEESE SAUCE

1 Add 115g/4oz/1 cup grated cheese to the sauce at the end of cooking and stir until it has melted. Try mature (shrap) Cheddar for a punchy flavour or a milder cheese for a slightly tangy, less-strong sauce. Stir in 5ml/1tsp mustard to taste.

For any fish, vegetables or eggs. Good for coating halved hard-boiled eggs on a bed of cooked spinach.

MAKING BÉCHAMEL SAUCE

1 Slowly heat the milk with 1–2 fresh bay leaves, a blade of mace, 3 cloves and a quartered onion. When boiling, remove from the heat, cover and leave to stand until cool. Strain the milk and use to make the sauce.

You can also use this sauce as the base for any of the variations or for savoury dishes such as lasagne or fish pie. It is good with fish, meat, vegetables or eggs.

MAKING BUTTER SAUCE

1 Stir 50g/2oz/4 tbsp butter into the cooked sauce. Remove from the heat, season and serve.

Eat with poached fish or vegetables.

MAKING MUSHROOM SAUCE

1 Thinly slice 225g/8oz button (white) or closed cap mushrooms (open dark mushrooms make the sauce grey) and cook them in the butter over low to medium heat for about 5 minutes, until they are reduced in volume. Add the flour and milk and finish cooking. Alternatively, instead of cooking the mushrooms first, make a thicker sauce and add the mushrooms at the end of cooking. Simmer for 3–4 minutes, during which time the mushrooms will thin the sauce.

Eat with fish, chicken, pork, eggs or for coating cooked and sliced salad potatoes (finish with a sprinkle of cheese and grill (broil) until brown).

MAKING PARSLEY SAUCE

1 Trim and finely chop a big bunch of parsley (a good couple of handfuls of leaves when trimmed before chopping), then stir this into the sauce with seasoning after cooking and immediately before serving.

- Delicious with grilled (broiled) or poached fish, gammon or ham.

MAKING EGG SAUCE

Hard boil, shell and chop 2 eggs. Add them to the sauce after cooking, immediately before serving, with seasoning to taste.

Eat with poached or grilled fish, spinach, baked or fried courgettes (zucchini) or baked red (bell) peppers.

Beurre blanc

This is one of the simplest sauces to make. White wine and vinegar are reduced in volume over a high heat to produce an intense flavour. Butter is whisked into the liquid to enrich and thicken it. It is delicious with poached or grilled fish or chicken.

Serves four

45ml/3 tbsp white wine vinegar
45ml/3 tbsp dry white wine
1 shallot, finely chopped
225g/8oz/1 cup unsalted (sweet) butter, cut into cubes
salt and ground black pepper

Variation
Add chopped parsley or chives and a squeeze of lemon juice.

1 Place the white wine vinegar and dry white wine in a small pan with the shallot. Bring to the boil and boil until reduced to about 15ml/1 tbsp.

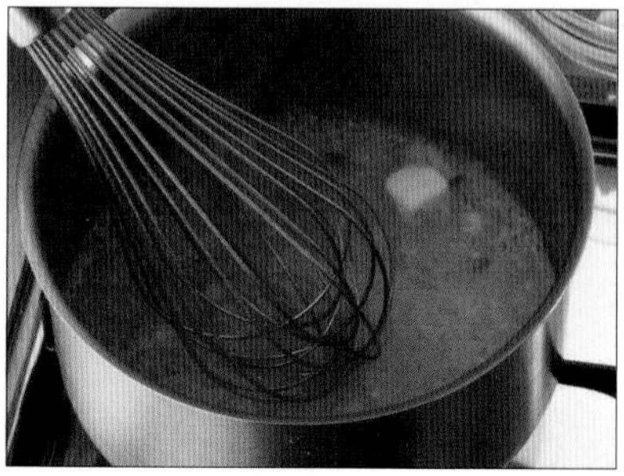

2 On a low heat, gradually whisk in the butter, cube by cube, allowing each piece to melt and be absorbed before adding the next. Season to taste.

Energy 235kcal/967kJ; Protein 0.6g; Carbohydrate 3.2g, of which sugars 2.35g; Fat 23.7g, of which saturates 15g; Cholesterol 61mg; Calcium 15.5mg; Fibre 0.5g; Sodium 176mg.

Quick hollandaise

Hollandaise is a rich butter sauce, rather like a hot mayonnaise. Using a blender or food processor to combine the ingredients until thick and smooth is fast and effective.

Serves four

60ml/4 tbsp white wine vinegar
6 peppercorns
1 bay leaf
3 egg yolks
175g/6oz/¾ cup clarified butter (ghee)
salt and ground black pepper

1 Place the white wine vinegar, peppercorns and bay leaf in a small pan and heat until boiling, then simmer to reduce the liquid to approximately 15ml/1 tbsp.

2 Remove from the heat and discard the flavourings.

3 Place the egg yolks in a blender or food processor and start the motor. Add the reduced white wine vinegar liquid through the feeder tube and blend for 10 seconds.

4 Heat the butter until hot, but not sizzling. With the motor running, pour the butter through the feeder tube in a thin, slow steady stream until the sauce is thick and smooth. Adjust the seasoning, and serve warm with poached fish, grilled (broiled) poultry or eggs.

COOK'S TIP
Do not overheat the butter: it should be hot but not sizzling.

Energy 364kcal/1498kJ; Protein 2.4g; Carbohydrate 0.25g, of which sugars 0.25g; Fat 39.3g, of which saturates 23.5g; Cholesterol 241mg; Calcium 25mg; Fibre 0g; Sodium 266mg.

Bread sauce

A classic sauce for roast game, chicken or turkey, In practice bread sauce is a versatile white sauce, with lots of flavour and excellent for all the same uses as a flour-based sauce.

Serves six to eight

475ml/16fl oz/2 cups milk
1 small onion, studded with 4 cloves
1 celery stick, chopped
1 fresh bay leaf, torn in half
6 allspice berries
1 blade of mace
90g/3½ oz/1¾ cups day-old breadcrumbs from a good-quality white loaf
freshly grated nutmeg
30ml/2 tbsp double (heavy) cream
15g/½oz/1 tbsp butter
salt and ground black pepper

1 Place the first six ingredients in a pan and bring to the boil. Take off the heat and half cover the pan. Set the milk aside to infuse for 30–60 minutes.

2 Strain the milk and place in a blender or food processor. Remove and discard the cloves from the onion and add the onion to the milk with the celery. Process until smooth, then strain the liquid back into the clean pan.

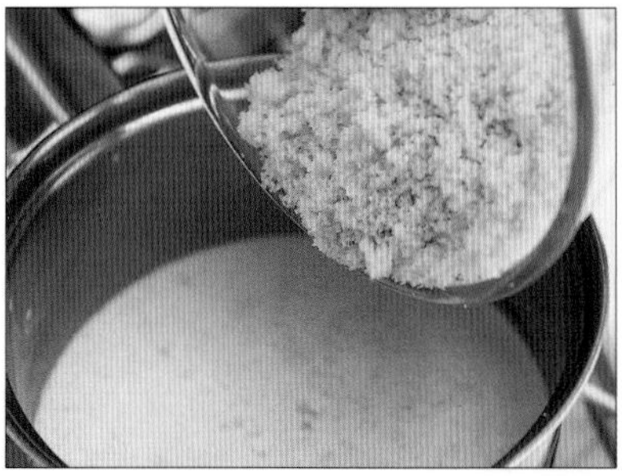

3 Bring back to the boil and stir in the breadcrumbs; simmer gently, whisking until the sauce thickens. Add extra milk if the sauce is too thick.

4 Season to taste with salt, pepper and freshly grated nutmeg. Just before serving, whisk in the cream and butter. Serve warm rather than piping hot.

Variations

The classic bread sauce is at its best for roast poultry; it is also good with grilled (broiled) sausages or pork chops. These subtle variations make versatile use of bread-thickened sauce.

- Add the grated rind of 1 lemon and a good squeeze of lemon juice with the cream and butter. Serve the sauce with poached chicken. Thin it slightly with a little extra milk and serve with baked fish.
- Sherried bread sauce is delicious served with grilled chicken, grilled mushrooms and bacon rolls. Add 45ml/3 tbsp dry sherry with the crumbs, simmer and finish as above.

Energy 100kcal/419kJ; Protein 3.4g; Carbohydrate 11.6g, of which sugars 3.2g; Fat 4.8g, of which saturates 2.9g; Cholesterol 13mg; Calcium 88mg; Fibre 0.3g; Sodium 123mg.

Vegetable sauces

Tomato and pesto sauce are classic sauces to serve with pasta. Tomato sauce can be used to top pizza before adding additional ingredients and cheese.

BASIC TOMATO SAUCE

Serves four

30ml/2 tbsp olive oil
1 onion, finely chopped
1 garlic clove, finely chopped
400g/14oz can chopped tomatoes
15ml/1 tbsp tomato purée (paste)
15ml/1 tbsp torn fresh basil leaves.

1 Heat the olive oil in a pan, add the onion and garlic and cook gently for about 5 minutes, stirring constantly, until softened and pale golden.

2 Stir in the tomatoes and tomato purée and simmer for 20–30 minutes, stirring occasionally. Season and stir in the basil.

Variation
Add a finely chopped carrot and stick of celery to the onions and garlic for a more subtle flavour.

PESTO SAUCE

Serves four

75g/3oz fresh basil leaves
2–3 garlic cloves
45ml/3 tbsp pine nuts
about 120ml/8 tbsp extra virgin olive oil
25g/1oz Parmesan cheese, grated
salt and ground black pepper

1 Put all the ingredients, except the cheese and seasoning, into a food processor and pulse until smooth, scraping the mixture down the bowl.

2 Pour the mixture into a bowl and stir in the grated Parmesan.

3 Taste and season. Use immediately or store in an airtight container in the refrigerator. The pesto will keep for 3–5 days in the refrigerator.

Variations
- Make a red pesto by adding drained canned or bottled red bell peppers and sun-dried tomatoes or sun-dried tomato paste to the basil and garlic. Omit the pine nuts.
- Fresh parsley or coriander (cilantro) are also good ground to a paste. Use a mixture of both instead of, or with, some basil.
- Make rocket pesto by blending 4 garlic cloves with 90ml/6tbsp pine nuts in a food processor with 150g/5oz rocket, stalks removed, 50g/2oz/⅔ cup grated Pecorino cheese and 90ml/6 tbsp olive oil.

Tomato Energy 94kcal/392kJ; Protein 1.2g; Carbohydrate 5.5g, of which sugars 5g; Fat 7.7g, of which saturates 3.2g; Cholesterol 11mg; Calcium 18mg; Fibre 1.6g; Sodium 53mg.
Pesto Energy 286kcal/1179kJ; Protein 5.8g; Carbohydrate 1.5g, of which sugars 0.7g; Fat 28.6g, of which saturates 5.2g; Cholesterol 10mg; Calcium 147mg; Fibre 1g; Sodium 114mg.

Cranberry sauce

This is the sauce for roast turkey, but don't just keep it for festive occasions. The vibrant colour and tart taste are a perfect partner to any meat, and it makes a great addition to sandwiches. It is also useful for sweet dishes, for example stirred into yogurt or with ice cream.

Serves six

1 orange
8oz/225g cranberries
1¼ cups sugar

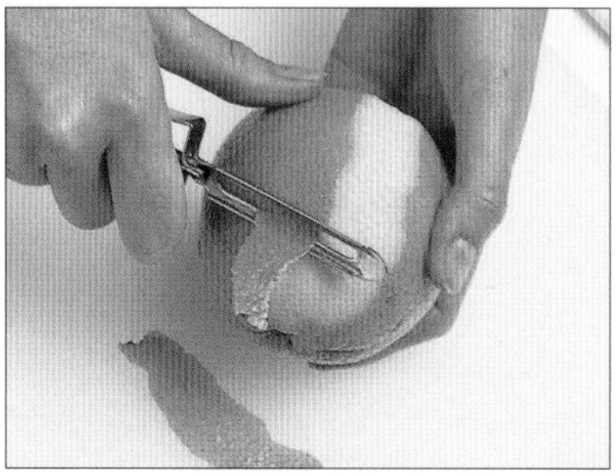

1 Pare the rind thinly from the orange. Remove any pith. Squeeze the juice.

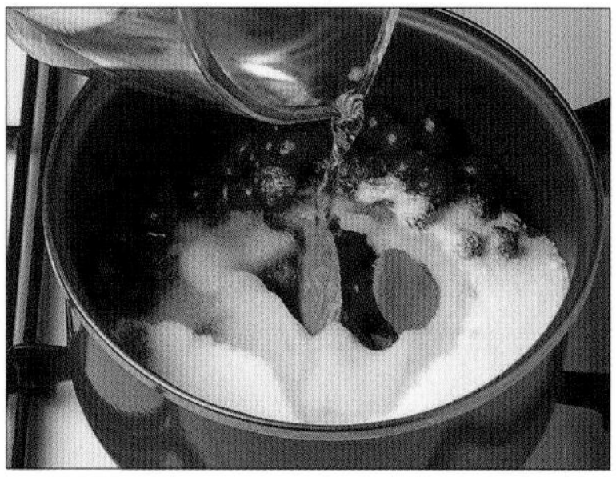

2 Place the orange juice and rind in a pan. Add the cranberries, sugar and 150ml/¼ pint/⅔ cup water.

3 Bring to the boil, stirring until the sugar dissolves. Simmer for 10–15 minutes.

4 Remove the rind and allow to cool before serving.

Energy 178kcal/759kJ; Protein 0.6g; Carbohydrate 46.8g, of which sugars 46.8g; Fat 0g, of which saturates 0g; Cholesterol 0mg; Calcium 46mg; Fibre 1.4g; Sodium 5mg.

Onion gravy

This delicious, dark onion sauce goes really well with all sorts of grilled, roast or fried meats, poultry or sausages. This sauce has a robust flavour and a thick texture. The choice of stock dictates the flavour and quality of the finished sauce.

Serves four

45ml/3 tbsp olive oil, butter or dripping
450g/1lb onions, halved and thinly sliced
45ml/3 tbsp plain (all-purpose) flour
400–500ml/14–17fl oz/1⅔–2 cups full-flavoured stock
1 fresh bouquet garni, for example, with thyme, sage, parsley and 1 bay leaf
salt and ground black pepper

1 Put the oil or fat in a small, heavy pan and heat gently. Add the sliced onions and fry, stirring occasionally, for 20 minutes, or longer, until the onions are soft and beginning to brown.

Variations

- The onions can be browned in the oven instead of on the stove. This is best done in sunflower or olive oil rather than butter, which would burn. Place the sliced onions in an ovenproof dish and toss with 45ml/3 tbsp oil. Cook in an oven preheated to 190°C/375°F/Gas 5 for 20 minutes, stirring once or twice, then increase the oven temperature to 220°C/425°F/Gas 7 and cook for 15–25 minutes.
- Part of the stock may be replaced with red wine or dark beer. You may need to add a little extra sugar to balance the acidity of the wine or beer.

2 Increase the heat slightly and cook for another 20–30 minutes, stirring occasionally, until the onions are a dark golden brown.

3 Stir in the flour, then cook for a few minutes, stirring all the time. Gradually stir in 400ml/14fl oz/1⅔ cups of the hot stock. Simmer, stirring, for a few minutes until thickened, adding a little more stock if the gravy is too thick.

4 Add the bouquet garni and then cover and simmer gently, stirring frequently, for 20 minutes.

5 Taste and add seasoning. Add a little more stock if the gravy is too thick, remove the herbs and serve.

FLAVOUR TIPS

The flavour of the fat and stock determine the flavour of gravy. For onion gravy, brown the onion slowly and thoroughly. If the flavour is poor, try adding a little sherry, brandy, soy sauce or tomato purée (paste) 5 minutes before the end of cooking.

Energy 294kcal/1225kJ; Protein 5g; Carbohydrate 35.1g, of which sugars 14.3g; Fat 15.9g, of which saturates 9.7g; Cholesterol 39mg; Calcium 88mg; Fibre 3.6g; Sodium 1107mg.

Apple sauce

Really more of a condiment than a sauce, this tart purée is usually served cold or warm, rather than hot. It is traditional with roast pork or duck, but it is also good with sausages, burgers, cold meats, pork pies, hot or cold meatloaf or cheese.

Serves six

225g/8oz cooking apples
30ml/2 tbsp water
thin strip of lemon rind
½ oz/1 tbsp butter
15–30ml/1–2 tbsp sugar

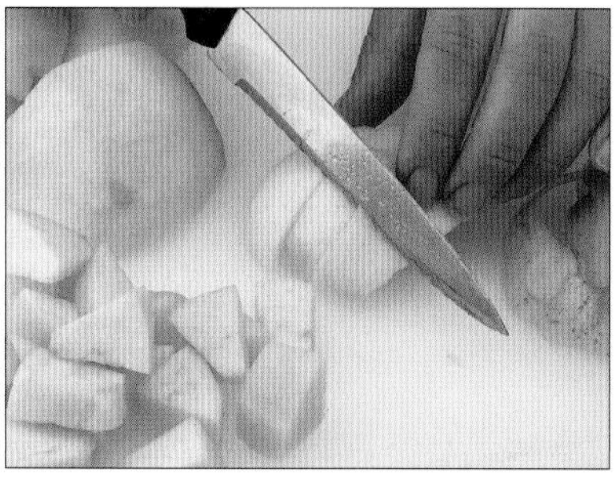

1 Peel the apples, cut into quarters and remove the cores. Dice or thinly slice the apple quarters.

2 Place the apples in a pan with the water and lemon rind. Cook, uncovered, over a low heat until very soft, stirring occasionally.

3 Remove the lemon rind from the pan and discard. Beat the apples to a pulp with a spoon.

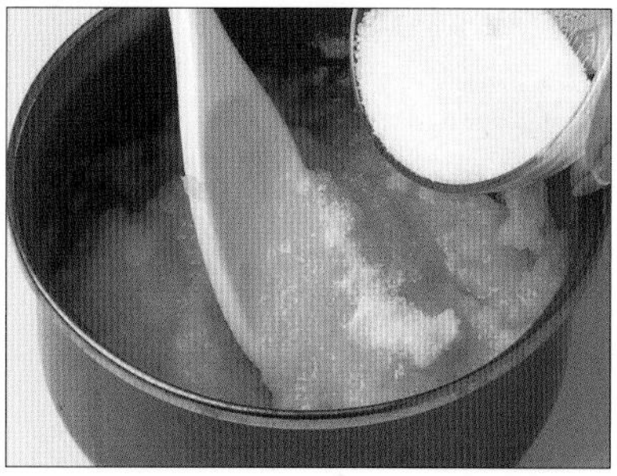

4 Stir in the butter, then add sugar to taste. Transfer to a serving dish, cover and leave to cool before serving.

Variations

- Stir in 15ml/1 tbsp Calvados with the butter and sugar at step 4 to make Normandy apple sauce.
- To make a creamy apple sauce, stir in 30ml/2 tbsp sour cream or crème fraîche at step 4.

Energy 60kcal/251kJ; Protein 0.2g; Carbohydrate 6g, of which sugars 6g; Fat 4.1g, of which saturates 2.7g; Cholesterol 11mg; Calcium 4mg; Fibre 0.6g; Sodium 35mg.

Herb butter

What could be simpler than creamed butter mixed with chopped fresh herbs. It is excellent with any grilled or roasted meat, adding flavour and moistness, as well as with poached or grilled fish; keep some in the freezer ready for use.

Makes about 115g/4oz

115g/4oz butter, preferably unsalted (sweet), at room temperature
2–4 tbsp chopped fresh herbs
squeeze of lemon juice
salt and ground white pepper

1 Put the butter in a mixing bowl and beat with a wooden spoon or an electric hand mixer until soft. Add the chopped fresh herbs of your choice (parsley, tarragon, mint or chives, for example, or a combination of two or three) and lemon juice. Season to taste with salt and pepper and blend well.

2 Chill slightly, then transfer the butter to a piece of baking parchment. Roll into a long sausage shape with the flats of your fingers, taking care not to handle for too long as the heat of your hands can melt it. Wrap and refrigerate until firm. Cut off into discs, or use a melon baller to scoop out mini servings and serve with your chosen dish.

SHAPED BUTTER PATS

Chill the herby butter lightly. Roll out between two sheets of baking parchment. Chill until firm, then remove the top sheet and stamp out shapes with cutter.

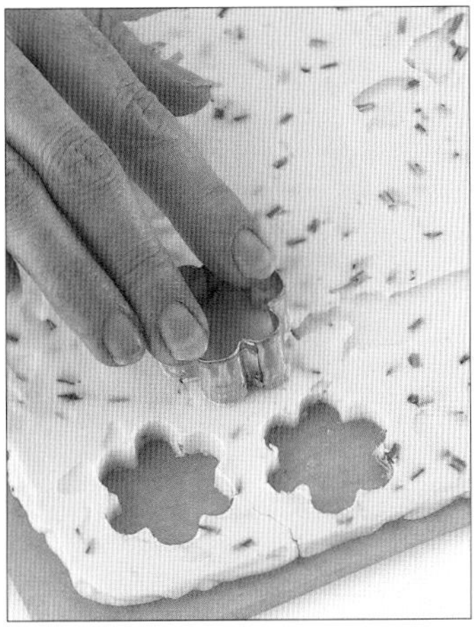

Variations

A traditional accompaniment to steak, flavoured butters can be rubbed on to meat before roasting or spread over chops and cutlets before grilling (broiling) and barbecuing. They can be spread on fish that is foil-wrapped and baked, or use as you would garlic butter to make delicious and flavourful breads.

- For a zingy citrus butter, use finely grated lemon, lime or orange zest and juice.
- Finely chopped gherkins or capers.
- Crushed, dried chillies or finely chopped fresh chillies.
- Ground coriander seeds, curry spices or paste.
- Finely chopped chives, parsley, dill, mint, thyme or rosemary.

Energy 853kcal/3507kJ; Protein 1g; Carbohydrate 0.4g, of which sugars 0.3g; Fat 94.1g, of which saturates 62.1g; Cholesterol 265mg; Calcium 47mg; Fibre 0.8g; Sodium 867mg.

Mayonnaise

A classic mayonnaise is endlessly versatile and a great standby recipe that uses only store-cupboard ingredients. This no-fail method is suitable for all beginner cooks.

Makes about 350ml/12fl oz/1½ cups

1 egg, plus 1 egg yolk
5ml/1 tsp Dijon mustard
juice of 1 large lemon
175ml/6fl oz/¾ cup olive oil
175ml/6fl oz/¾ cup grapeseed, sunflower or corn oil
salt and ground white pepper

COOK'S TIPS
- Have all the ingredients at room temperature before you begin.
- To make the mayonnaise more glossy, beat in about 15ml/1 tbsp boiling water at the end.

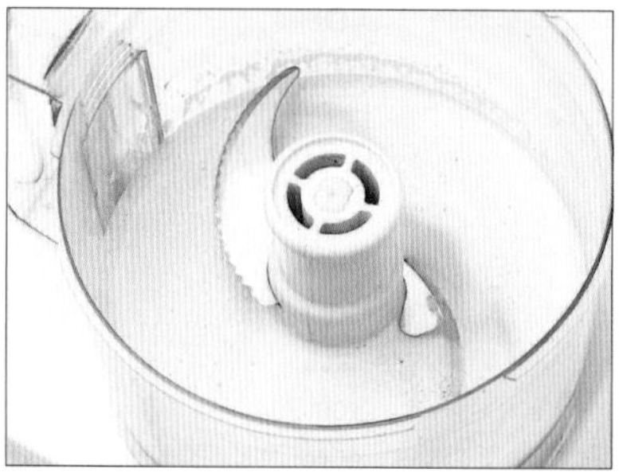

1 Put the whole egg and yolk in a food processor and process for 20 seconds. Add the mustard, half the lemon juice and a generous pinch of salt and pepper. Put on the lid, then process the mixture for about 30 seconds more, until thoroughly mixed.

2 With the motor running, pour in the oils through the feeder tube in a thin, steady stream. When the mayonnaise is pale and thick, taste and add more lemon juice and seasoning if necessary. Scrape the mayonnaise into a bowl using a spatula.

Variations

Mayonnaise can be flavoured with other ingredients to enhance the taste of specific foods.
- To make basil mayonnaise, use basil oil instead of sunflower oil.
- For garlic mayonnaise, crush 3–6 garlic cloves and add with the eggs in step 1.
- For green mayonnaise, combine 30g/1oz each of fresh parsley sprigs and watercress. Add 3–4 chopped spring onions (scallions) and 1 garlic clove. Blend with the mayonnaise at the end of step 2.
- For spicy mayonnaise, increase the mustard to 15ml/1 tbsp and add 5ml/1 tsp Worcestershire sauce and a dash of Tobasco sauce.
- For sun-dried tomato mayonnaise, mix 150ml/¼ pint/⅔ cup mayonnaise with 15ml/1 tbsp sun-dried tomato paste and serve with grilled (broiled) chicken.
- For basil and lemon mayonnaise, add 15ml/1 tbsp lemon juice and and a handful of shredded basil leaves at the end of step 2.

Energy 958kcal/3940kJ; Protein 3.3g; Carbohydrate 0.5g, of which sugars 0.4g; Fat 104.8g, of which saturates 13.1g; Cholesterol 202mg; Calcium 27mg; Fibre 0g; Sodium 157mg.

Salad dressings

A good vinaigrette is used to dress a salad. Most are made using a basic formula of three parts oil to one part acid (lemon juice or vinegar) beaten together to form an emulsion.

CLASSIC VINAIGRETTE

This is a light and flavourful dressing, perfect for any summer salad.

60–120ml/6–8 tbp extra virgin olive oil
juice of 1 lemon, or to taste
2 salted or preserved anchovies, rinsed and finely chopped
45ml/3 tbsp Greek (US strained plain) yogurt
45ml/3 tbsp finely chopped fresh dill
5ml/1 tsp French mustard

1 In a bowl, add the oil to the lemon juice, whisking to incorporate.

2 Add the anchovies. Whisk thoroughly until the dressing emulsifies and thickens. Whisk in the yogurt, dill and mustard, with salt and pepper to taste.

Below: Most dressing ingredients are everyday foods to be found in the store cupboard.

CAESAR SALAD DRESSING

Serve with grilled (broiled) chicken, green leaves and croûtons.

1 egg
10ml/2 tsp Dijon mustard
dash of Worcestershire sauce
30ml/2 tbsp lemon juice
30ml/2 tbsp extra virgin olive oil
salt and ground black pepper

1 Put all the ingredients in a sealed screw-topped jar and shake well to combine all the ingredients fully.

CREAMY ORANGE DRESSING

This is a tangy orange dressing to complement a green salad.

45ml/3 tbsp half-fat crème fraîche
15ml/1 tbsp white wine vinegar
finely grated rind and juice of 1 small orange
salt and ground black pepper

1 Put the ingredients into a screw-topped jar and seal. Shake well. Adjust the seasoning to taste.

BLUE CHEESE DRESSING

Quite a tangy dressing with a strong flavour, for mixed salad leaves.

4fl oz/125ml natural (plain) yogurt
7.5ml/1½ tsp white wine vinegar
2.5ml/½ tsp sugar
15ml/1 tbsp fresh lemon juice
1 garlic clove, crushed
30g/1oz blue cheese, crumbled

1 Combine the yogurt, wine vinegar, sugar, lemon juice and garlic in a small bowl and mix well. Fold in the cheese. The appearance is quite lumpy.

Below: Serve salad dressings separately so that guests can help themselves.

Vinaigrette Energy 652kcal/2686kJ; Protein 5.3g; Carbohydrate 4.7g, of which sugars 4.5g; Fat 68.2g, of which saturates 9.5g; Cholesterol 1mg; Calcium 204mg; Fibre 2.5g; Sodium 290mg.
Caesar salad Energy 286kcal/1183kJ; Protein 7g; Carbohydrate 1.3g, of which sugars 1.1g; Fat 28.4g, of which saturates 4.7g; Cholesterol 190mg; Calcium 39mg; Fibre 0g; Sodium 389mg.
Creamy orange Energy 91kcal/378kJ; Protein 1.5g; Carbohydrate 6.4g, of which sugars 5.8g; Fat 6.8g, of which saturates 4.6g; Cholesterol 0mg; Calcium 48mg; Fibre 0.1g; Sodium 21mg.
Blue cheese Energy 189kcal/789kJ; Protein 12.8g; Carbohydrate 12.8g, of which sugars 12.1g; Fat 10.2g, of which saturates 6.2g; Cholesterol 24mg; Calcium 390mg; Fibre 0.2g; Sodium 482mg.

Index